The World's Youth

The life stage of adolescence now occurs in most corners of the world, but it takes different forms in different regions. Peers, with such a central role in Western adolescence, play a comparatively minor role in the lives of Arabic and South Asian adolescents. Emotional turmoil and individuation from family occur in some societies but not others. Adolescent sexual revolutions are sweeping through Japan and Latin America. In this book, scholars from eight regions of the world describe the distinct nature of adolescence in their regions. They draw on research to address standard topics regarding this age – family and peer relationships, schooling, preparation for work, physical and mental health – and show how these have a different cast across societies. As a whole, the book depicts how rapid global change is dramatically altering the experience of the adolescent transition, creating new opportunities and challenges for adolescents, parents, teachers, and concerned others.

B. Bradford Brown is Professor of Human Development and former Chair of the Department of Educational Psychology at the University of Wisconsin–Madison. He received an A.B. in sociology from Princeton University and a Ph.D. in human development from the University of Chicago before joining the faculty of the University of Wisconsin in 1979.

Reed W. Larson is Professor of Human and Community Development in the Departments of Human and Community Development, Psychology, and Educational Psychology at the University of Illinois at Urbana-Champaign. He is author of *Divergent Realities: The Emotional Lives of Mothers, Fathers, and Adolescents* (with Maryse Richards) and of *Being Adolescent: Conflict and Growth in the Teenage Years* (with Mihaly Csikszentmihalyi).

T. S. Saraswathi is Professor Emeritus of Human Development, in the Department of Human Development and Family Studies at the Maharaja Sayajirao University of Baroda, India. She is a recipient of numerous professional awards and international fellowships for her contributions to the field of developmental psychology and has published several articles in reputed journals and edited books.

The World's Youth

Adolescence in Eight Regions of the Globe

Edited by

B. BRADFORD BROWN

University of Wisconsin–Madison

REED W. LARSON

University of Illinois at Urbana-Champaign

T. S. SARASWATHI

Maharaja Sayajirao University of Baroda

 **CAMBRIDGE**
UNIVERSITY PRESS

PUBLISHED BY THE PRESS SYNDICATE OF THE UNIVERSITY OF CAMBRIDGE
The Pitt Building, Trumpington Street, Cambridge, United Kingdom

CAMBRIDGE UNIVERSITY PRESS
The Edinburgh Building, Cambridge CB2 2RU, UK
40 West 20th Street, New York, NY 10011-4211, USA
477 Williamstown Road, Port Melbourne, VIC 3207, Australia
Ruiz de Alarcón 13, 28014 Madrid, Spain
Dock House, The Waterfront, Cape Town 8001, South Africa

http://www.cambridge.org

First published 2002

Printed in the United Kingdom at the University Press, Cambridge

Typeface Palatino 10/13 pt.   *System* LATEX 2$_\varepsilon$ [TB]

A catalog record for this book is available from the British Library.

Library of Congress Cataloging in Publication data available

ISBN 0 521 80910 X hardback
ISBN 0 521 00605 8 paperback

Contents

Contributors

Jeffrey Jensen Arnett, University of Maryland, College Park, MD, USA

Marilyn Booth, University of Illinois at Urbana-Champaign, USA

B. Bradford Brown, University of Wisconsin–Madison, USA

Elizabeth Fussell, Tulane University, New Orleans, LA, USA

Margaret E. Greene, Population Action International, Washington, DC, USA

Reed W. Larson, University of Illinois at Urbana-Champaign, USA

A. Bame Nsamenang, University of Yaounde and Human Development Resource Centre, Bamenda, Cameroon, Africa

Madelene Santa Maria, De La Salle University, Manilla, Philippines

T. S. Saraswathi, Maharaja Sayajirao University of Baroda, India

Anna Stetsenko, City University of New York, USA

Harold W. Stevenson, University of Michigan, Ann Arbor, MI, USA

Suman Verma, Government Home Science College, Chandigarh, India

Carlos Welti, Institute for Social Research, National Autonomous University, Mexico

Akane Zusho, University of Michigan, Ann Arbor, MI, USA

Preface

This volume is the result of a 3-year enterprise sponsored jointly by the Society for Research on Adolescence and the International Society for the Study of Behavioral Development. The Study Group on Adolescence in the 21st Century brought together an international set of scholars to consider possible life scenarios for adolescents over the next 30 to 50 years. With primary support from the W. T. Grant Foundation, the study group was chaired by Reed W. Larson, with Jeylan T. Mortimer and B. Bradford Brown playing a collaborative role in organizing the study group's activities.

To assist the study group in its work, 2 sets of papers were commissioned. For the set represented in this volume, each scholar was asked to describe current conditions and near-future possibilities for adolescents in a particular nation or region of the world. Mindful of the diversity of experiences among adolescents in their regions, the authors were asked to provide empirically based analyses of the transformation from childhood to adulthood with regard to a standard set of issues and social contexts that affect adolescents' lives. For the other set of commissioned papers, published as a separate volume (Mortimer and Larson 2002), the study group approached a set of experts knowledgeable about external institutions and changes that affect adolescents (e.g., education, health care, the criminal justice system). These authors were asked to forecast major trends in their domains of study and to sketch out various ways in which these trends might shape adolescent development and the transition to adulthood during the next 25 to 50 years. Based on both sets of papers and their own deliberations, study group members prepared a 3rd volume that deals with the influence of societal changes on adolescents' competence and well-being in 4 domains (Larson, Brown, and Mortimer 2002).

Generous additional support for the work represented in this volume was provided by the Johann Jacobs Foundation, the Kellogg Foundation, and the Carnegie Adolescent Forum. We also give special thanks to Suzanne Wilson, who played an invaluable role in coordinating the meetings of the study group and assisting with this volume. In addition, a number of scholars provided insightful reviews of initial drafts of the chapters in this volume; we are especially grateful to them for their comments. They include: Lourdes A. Carandang, Susan Davis, August Flammer, Giyoo Hatano, Tatyana Koshmanova, Eugene Matusov, Anne C. Petersen, Marcela Raffaelli, Robert Serpell, Neerja Sharma, and Keiko Takahashi. Students in two graduate seminars (one at the University of Illinois at Urbana-Champaign, the other at the University of Wisconsin–Madison) also provided feedback to authors on earlier drafts of their chapters: Jennifer Baumgartner, Tom Baskins, Patti Beth, Alyssa Clark, Jodi Dworkin, Kimberly Hamilton, Dave Hansen, Kate Hellenga, Koon Hwee Kan, Sarah Kiefer, Christa Klute, Vanessa Lall, Emily Mann, Ane Marinez Lora, Trent Maurer, Annette McDaniel, Ann Meier, Beth Mender, Melba Nicholson, Suh-Ruu Ou, Linda Pallock, Rogina Scott, Woochan Shim, Manuel Zamarripa, and Katalin Zaszlavik. Finally, we appreciate the contributions of 2 other graduate students, Jodi Dworkin and Wendy Theobald, who conducted library research for several authors.

Members of Study Group

Susan Nall Bales, Frameworks Institute, Washington, DC, USA
B. Bradford Brown, University of Wisconsin–Madison, WI, USA
Kathleen Thiede Call, University of Minnesota, Twin Cities, MN, USA
Marcelo Diversi, Utah State University, Logan, UT, USA
Jacquelynne Eccles, University of Michigan, Ann Arbor, MI, USA
Wendy Everett, Institute for the Future, Menlo Park, CA, USA
Frank Furstenberg, University of Pennsylvania, Philadelphia, PA, USA
Karen Hein, William T. Grant Foundation, New York, NY, USA
Michele Kipke, National Academy of Sciences, Washington, DC, USA
Helga Krueger, Universität Bremen, Bremen, Germany
Reed W. Larson, University of Illinois at Urbana-Champaign, IL, USA
Sharafuddin Malik, International Council on Alcohol & Addictions, Cairo, Egypt

Milbrey McLaughlin, Stanford University, Stanford, CA, USA
Vonnie McLloyd, University of Michigan, Ann Arbor, MI, USA
Jeylan T. Mortimer, University of Minnesota, Twin Cities, MN, USA
Anne Peterson, W. K. Kellogg Foundation, Battle Creek, MI, USA
Karen Pittman, The Forum for Youth Investment, Takoma Park, MD, USA
Michael Rutter, Institute of Psychiatry, London, UK
Madelene Santa Maria, De La Salle University, Manilla, Philippines
T. S. Saraswathi, Maharaja Sayajirao University of Baroda, India
Michael Shanahan, Pennsylvania State University, State College, PA, USA
Rainer Silbereisen, University of Jena, Jena, Germany
Lawrence Steinberg, Temple University, Philadelphia, PA, USA
Suman Verma, Government Home Science College, Chandigarh, India
James Youniss, Catholic University of America, Washington, DC, USA

Steering Committee

B. Bradford Brown, Jeylan T. Mortimer, Reed W. Larson (chair)

References

Larson, Reed W., B. Bradford Brown, & Jeylan T. Mortimer, eds. 2002. *Adolescents' preparation for the future: Perils and promise.* New York: Blackwell.
Mortimer, J. T., & R. W. Larson., eds. 2002. *The changing adolescent experience: Societal trends and the transition to adulthood.* New York: Cambridge University Press.

The Kaleidoscope of Adolescence

Experiences of the World's Youth at the Beginning of the 21st Century

B. Bradford Brown and Reed W. Larson

A century ago people were intrigued by a new invention, the forerunner of the modern kinescope. By inserting a strip of paper containing a series of pictures into a drum, then spinning the drum while peering through a set of slits around the drum's perimeter, one could watch the pictures on the paper slowly coalesce into a repetitive set of coordinated movements. From the drum's disparate pictures, a single, moving picture appeared before one's eyes.

In many respects, our understanding of adolescence at the outset of the 21st century mimics this instrument of entertainment from Victorian parlors. We spin together the related but distinctive features of life for youth around the world and discern a common image of their movement from childhood into adulthood. At a superficial level the pictures coalesce to give the impression that young people worldwide share the same challenges, interests, and concerns. We speak of the emergence of a "global youth culture" (Schlegel 2000), in which young people – at least in the middle class – wear the same clothing and hair styles, listen to some of the same music, and adopt similar slang expressions. We remark on how the world is "shrinking" by virtue of new technologies (e.g., the Internet) that bring people from far-flung corners of the globe into close contact with each other. We emphasize the commonality of experience among youth as opposing ideologies falter and economic systems begin to meld.

The provocative opening sentence to A. Bame Nsamenang's contribution to this volume (see Chapter 3), however, challenges any satisfaction we might take in this kinescopic image. "Adolescent psychology," he

contends, "is a Eurocentric enterprise." The truth is that a disproportionate number (if not most) of our images of what happens in adolescence are based on the American and European "teenager." In reality
there are markedly different "adolescences" in other parts of the world
that stand apart from Western accounts of what does or should happen
during this transitional period between childhood and adulthood. Consider that two-thirds of Indian adolescents dutifully – and willingly –
accept their parents' management in arranging a marital partner for
them (Chapter 4), or that many young women in the Philippines sacrifice
their own futures to go to cities to earn income to send home to their families (Peterson 1990). The negotiation of autonomy, which has been seen
to be central to Western adolescence, is not a central motif in these cultures. Consider, too, the thousands of street youth in Kenya, and in many
other parts of the world, who develop remarkable competence in surviving and carving a niche for themselves in urban environments (Aptekar
& Ciano-Federoff 1999). The developmental tasks – and achievements –
of these youth bear little resemblance to those one finds in textbooks on
adolescence. Millions of adolescent boys and girls in the Middle East are
permitted little contact with each other, even in school (Chapter 7). What
can be said of their development of gender roles and sexuality that has
any resemblance to what happens in other parts of the world? Even our
claim that the length of adolescence is expanding because of delayed
entry into marriage or work, while true in many parts of the world (e.g.,
see Chapter 10), is not evident in Russia; there, youth are actually marrying at *earlier* ages than in the past in order to legitimize sexual activity
(see Chapter 8). Likewise, Mexican women experience strong pressure
to marry and have children by their early 20s (see Chapter 9).

Scrutinizing the experiences of young people from this global perspective provides a very different image of adolescence than was common among 20th-century European and North American scholars. In
effect, as Verma and Saraswathi allude to in their portrayal of youth in
India (Chapter 4), we must replace the kinescope with a kaleidoscope –
with a more varied and colorful set of moving pictures. The forms that
adolescence takes within a given culture, let alone across cultures, are
remarkably diverse and distinctive. Certainly, there are some repeated
themes in the biological, cognitive, and psychological imperatives of
human development, and in common challenges brought on by the new
global world of the 21st century. But these issues are adapted to the needs
and exigencies of societies and are often transformed and given different
meaning within distinctive cultural systems.

As the world continues to get smaller, as peoples come into contact through increased communication and emigration, it is time to take a closer look at these kaleidoscopic variations. It is no longer sufficient to adopt the parochial view of adolescence in one culture and claim an understanding of this age period. Scholars who study adolescence, practitioners who work with youth, business leaders concerned with a new generation of employees, policy makers, and even parents must first divest themselves from Eurocentric, universalistic notions of adolescence. They must examine adolescence in historical and cultural context, be open to its variegated forms, and recognize its tentative or evanescent nature.

Objectives of This Volume

Our objectives in this volume are to ascertain the extent to which adolescence is a discernible stage of life in various regions of the world and to examine how this period is experienced in each region. We are concerned with how key societal institutions shape this phase of life, who the important people are in adolescents' lives, and how youth negotiate the opportunities available to them. We are also concerned with how the experiences of adolescents are changing, how the trajectories of their lives are being altered as the societies around them change and as adolescents look to the future.

To do this, we asked an international team of scholars with extensive background studying young people to comment on the nature of adolescence in 8 specific regions of the world. In some cases these regions were a single country, one we thought would provide some representation of a larger geographic area. In other cases, authors describe adolescence in 2 or more nations that share some cultural similarity. All authors are experts on their regions, and most are native to the locales they describe, so all could draw on personal experience, as well as findings from research studies, including sources in local languages that would be difficult to access from outside.

These scholars were given a formidable task, namely, to summarize and evaluate the character and conditions of adolescence within their regions of the world. Of course, even within a region or nation, there is enormous diversity on almost any criterion: family organization and routines, religious practices, norms and traditions, economic and human resources, leisure activities, and so on. Thus, authors were often forced to generalize features and trends and/or to focus on subgroups within a given region. To facilitate comparisons across nations and regions, authors agreed to organize their commentary around a standard set of topics: definitions of adolescence, family relations, peer relations, education, preparation for work, health issues, social services, civic engagement, and media use or influences. Chapters 3 through 10 each contain a section on each of these topics, except in cases where a topic is not really relevant to the lives of adolescents in that particular region of the world. Some chapters contain additional sections of specific relevance to adolescents in a region. To provide a general background for the regional reports, Chapter 2 describes current and projected demographic features of the world's youth. We end the book (Chapter 11) with a forward-looking commentary on the actions and policies that schools, governments, businesses, parents, and others should consider to improve the future life opportunities for youth.

Emerging from the chapters of this book is a more contemporary and comprehensive view of life circumstances of adolescents around the world. This first chapter highlights key features of this view by examining the way in which adolescence is defined in different cultures, the way that major social contexts nurture individual development during this stage of life, and recurrent themes that emerge from our contributors' assessments of the lives of youth in their sections of the globe.

Definitions of Adolescence

To begin with, one can learn a lot about the nature of adolescence in a given culture simply from the way it is defined. In some cases, there is simply no term to describe adolescence, a certain sign that the society does not regard it as a distinct and important stage of the life cycle. Until recently, this was the case in many East Asian societies, according to Stevenson and Zusho (see Chapter 5). Often, such societies were organized so that children take on major adult responsibilities at an early age; in their activities, young people are not commonly segregated from adults. Agrarian economies, in which children and young people work the fields or herds alongside adults are the most common examples of this arrangement, but it also persists in some more industrialized economies. There are also special historical circumstances that call for a redefinition of adolescence. In Chapter 9, for example, Welti describes how adolescence is suspended and childhood curtailed in several Latin

American countries in order to justify the recruitment of young people into the armed forces fighting civil wars or conflicts with neighboring nations.

In other societies (e.g., India and Japan), adolescence – at least until recently – has been subsumed under the larger label of "youth," which typically encompasses a broader age range than the 2nd decade of life. "Youth" may subsume all young people under age 20 (including young children). The implication is that there is nothing special about adolescence. In some instances, "youth" includes individuals from age 10 or so up to 30 or 35, an age categorization that suggests that one is not completely mature, responsible, and deserving of full respect as an adult until this much later age. This perspective may be encoded in laws, such as the Youth Policy Act in India, which is intended to provide services to people up to the age of 35 (see Chapter 4). Curiously, however, health and social service personnel who carry out the law's mandates have found it useful to formulate separate approaches for individuals under age 20 (children and adolescents) and those age 21 or older (who might be considered late adolescents or young adults).

Still other societies have no single term for adolescence, but a variety of words that are applied in specific circumstances or with reference to specific groups of young people. According to Booth (Chapter 7), the Arabic term for adolescence, *murahaqa*, is used in academic texts but not in common parlance. The term has sexual overtones and captures the layperson's perception of adolescence as fraught with sexual temptation, a period in which adults must closely supervise a young person's activities. Interestingly, G. S. Hall (1904) endowed the term with similar connotations. There are other Arabic terms that are used in daily conversation to refer to individuals in the adolescent stage: *fata/fatat* (masculine and feminine forms) or *shabb/shabba*, which connote marital status or level of responsibility for or obligation to others. These reveal important dimensions of the adolescent period in Arabian societies. China and Japan also have several terms that can be used to refer to individuals during the adolescent period, but no general term to designate this life stage as a whole (See Chapter 5). These terms refer to the stage of puberty, one's generational status within the family, or the legal rights and responsibilities a person has. Most often, however, people are likely to refer to a young person by her or his school status, as a middle school student or high school student. Because this is the central role for adolescents in Japanese or Chinese society, it is no surprise that it is the preferred reference point for understanding and organizing adolescence in these societies. The common term for adolescence in the United States, *teenager*, brings forth images of recklessness, rebellion, irresponsibility, and conflict – hardly a flattering portrait but one that captures the worried stance that most adults in that society take toward young people.

Beneath this kaleidoscope of nuance and innuendo, the common element we see is an interval of transition and preparation between childhood and adulthood. Whether it is short or long, whether it is unnamed, named, or understood through a variety of terms in different situations, nearly all societies have a period of transition when young people continue a process, begun in childhood, of equipping themselves to be full adult members of society.

Contexts of Development and Socialization

What preparation adolescents receive is shaped in large part by the fundamental contexts in which they spend time (Whiting 1980), and the chapters of this book provide penetrating descriptions of these contexts across societies. For our purposes here, we will examine these contexts as the domains in which adolescents gain (or fail to gain) valuable resources for their later lives. They provide reservoirs of experience. They offer models, guidance, teaching, social control, and material resources that prepare youth for adulthood.

Family: Diverging Forms and Altering Resources
Families are everywhere one of the most, if not the most, important contexts for adolescent development. But the nature of adolescents' family experience varies enormously. Some youth grow up in close-knit, hierarchically organized, extended families that provide a web of connections and reinforce a traditional way of life. Others come of age in nuclear or single-parent families, with whom they may spend little time – or have close, intimate relationships. In the Arab world, families continue to be quite authoritarian and patriarchal; adolescents are taught strict codes of conduct and family loyalty (Chapter 7). In the West, parent-child relationships are less hierarchical than in the past, and the diminished authority of parents may contribute to the relatively high rates of deviant behavior that characterize several European and North American societies (Chapter 10). Such variability occurs both between and within societies.

A trend noted by most of our authors is that the types of families adolescents experience are changing. Across nations, we see the expansion of family forms during the last half of the 20th century, including more divorced families, single-parent families, remarried families, multiresidence families, and, in some settings, more gay and lesbian families. Trends evident in most regions also include greater family mobility, migration to urban areas, family members working in distant cities or countries, smaller families, fewer extended-family households, and increases in mothers' employment (Larson et al. 2002).

These many changes alter the capacity of families to provide resources to adolescents and the types of resources they provide. When families live apart from extended relatives, it deprives adolescents of daily access to useful models and sources of advice. When youth leave impoverished rural areas to seek better employment opportunities in urban areas, they typically strain the family's capacity to provide emotional and instrumental support (Chapter 6). Maternal employment brings additional resources to the family, including money, new social capital, and – something particularly useful to female offspring – modeling of making one's way in the economic sphere. Smaller families have contributed undoubtedly to a trend in many parts of the world, including India, Southeast Asia, and the Arab nations, toward greater openness and communication between parents and children. This allows youth to benefit from a new level of attention, advice, and emotional support.

Thus, within this enormous diversity, a common theme is that families are facing new challenges and adapting in new ways. In some cases, adolescents are being deprived of resources that were of great value in the past – such as the ready advice and support of a grandmother and the stability and security of a rural village. But they also are gaining access to new family resources, like more-open relationships with parents and the indirect benefits that come with mothers' employment.

Schools: Expanding with Variable Effectiveness

Educational institutions make up another important context of many adolescents' lives, one that is specifically devoted to giving them resources to prepare them for adulthood. Several authors, but particularly Fussell and Greene (Chapter 2), regard improvements in education and vocational training as crucial to ameliorating current and future circumstances for young people. Indeed, expansion of educational opportunities for youth in Japan, Korea, and China helped to propel these nations into strong positions in the world economy in the latter portion of the

20th century (see Chapter 5). Educational participation and completion rates are high in these nations. Despite the stress that youth endure preparing for qualifying examinations, education has helped raise the standard of living for individuals and for these countries as a whole, lifting some of them out of the category of developing nation.

Generally speaking, developing countries are increasing the number of youth in school, with potential future benefits to their youth and their economies. However, many nations in Africa and South Asia, and some in Southeast Asia and Latin America, still have a long way to go before achieving even universal primary education. The authors also report that schools in these nations often fall far short of their mission. Welti (Chapter 9) laments a decline in recent years in the percentage of Latin American adolescents who have access to secondary education or who can afford to attend higher educational institutions. Verma and Saraswathi (Chapter 4) as well as Nsamenang (Chapter 3) depict the shortcomings of educational systems that nations carried over from colonial rule. Modeled on European systems, the schools were (and remain) remarkably insensitive to indigenous educational systems and the needs of adolescents in a particular region. Nsamenang comments that, "As it stands today, the school is not yet fully suited to the agrarian life paths of the bulk of the continent's peoples, as its quality has been declining and its relevance to the life journeys of Africans." The indigenous system, he explains, is peer oriented, features participatory learning, and is focused on socializing responsible participation in the family and community – objectives that are ignored in the formal educational system. The hierarchically organized formal system, with its didactic instructional techniques, forces adolescents to straddle two worlds in their quest for a meaningful identity and viable coping strategies. It is reminiscent of the "multiple worlds problem" that, according to Phelan, Davidson, and Yu (1998), ethnic minority adolescents face in the United States.

Even when they are culturally relevant, schools in many parts of the world are challenged to recruit quality staff and develop programming suited to the changing nature of adult work (Shanahan, Mortimer, & Kruger 2002). Santa Maria (Chapter 6) and Welti (Chapter 9) lament the disorganization and limited funding of schools, as well as the inadequate backgrounds of instructional staff in their regions. Likewise, Booth (Chapter 7) notes that despite their success in boosting literacy rates, many schools in the Arab states suffer from overcrowding and underpaid or unmotivated teachers. According to Santa Maria (Chapter 6), unemployment rates in the Philippines are highest among youth with the most advanced (postsecondary) degrees because their educational training is not tied to the labor needs of the society. Arnett (Chapter 10) points out that schools in the United States often fail to provide the background and training that students need to move easily into the labor market, a stark contrast to the apprenticeship system that operates effectively in several northern European nations.

The good news, then, is that more youth than ever before are in school. Two concerns, however, are that the schools are often poorly fitted to the culture of their students, and in many cases the curriculum fails to provide them with the skills that will be most useful to successful adult work.

Peers: Increasing Interactions with Mixed Results

By comparison to family and school, adults around the world often take a more ambivalent posture toward the role of peers in adolescents' preparation for adulthood. Peers do offer valuable resources: companionship, emotional support, and an arena in which to try out and learn important social skills. But peers are also implicated in promoting consumerism, negative attitudes toward school, and life-compromising behaviors such as drug use, violence, and other delinquent activity.

The societies described in this book display dramatic variability in their response to this ambivalence, from rigid restrictions to active promotion of interactions with peers. Rural India and the Arab states, in particular, exemplify a restrictive response. According to Booth (Chapter 7), opportunities for peer interaction (outside of kin relations) are severely limited in the Arab world, especially for girls. If girls attend school, it is usually in gender segregated institutions. In the same societies, opportunities for interaction with the other sex or the development of romantic and sexual relationships are constricted. The result is that peers make comparatively little contribution to adolescent development (indeed, there is little research on them). In other societies, however, peers figure prominently in adolescents' daily lives. Nsamenang (Chapter 3) comments that "[t]he peer group is a ubiquitous institution in sub-Saharan Africa." Similar circumstances are noticeable among youth throughout Europe and North America (see Chapter 10). In these contexts peers often subsume some responsibilities otherwise assumed by parents. In extreme cases, peers become surrogate families. Street youth in Latin America rely upon networks of peers to help negotiate survival in urban settings (see Chapter 9).

A common observation across this spectrum of societies is that the role of peers is expanding. In societies where peer interaction has been limited, the authors report that adolescents are having more peer interaction during school, going to and from school, and in shared leisure activities, with the clearest trends in the middle class (see Chapters 6 and 7). Adolescents are sharing interests with friends and relying more on friends for advice and support. A related change is that adolescents' involvement in romantic relationships and in premarital sexual activity are increasing, especially as age of marriage comes later. Rising rates of premarital intercourse appear to be more common among youth in higher social classes and urban areas, where parents wield less authority or cannot supervise youth as closely. Santa Maria (Chapter 6) links increased rates of sexual activity among South Asian youth to decreased parental supervision resulting from mothers' employment and young people's migration to the city for employment. Under these circumstances, peers emerge as a more powerful force in young people's lives as they are the preferred source of sexual information and the context for meeting sexual partners. Where societal norms discourage sexual activity, it remains a furtive activity, often engaged in without contraceptives. As a result, it is becoming a major source of the proliferation of sexually transmitted diseases, including HIV infection.

If there is a theme to the chapters' treatment of peer relations, then, it is that this expanding context of adolescents' lives is bringing both positives and negatives. In some cases, adolescents themselves seem ambivalent about the capacity of peers to meet their needs. Russian youth, for example, rate their peers as low in kindness and high in bullying, relative to their counterparts in European nations. Yet, Russian adolescents also value close friendships and seem to have no more difficulty maintaining good relations with friends than youth in other nations (see Chapter 8 for details). Greater interaction with peers is providing adolescents new resources – an arena for experimenting and learning new skills – but it is also, for some youth, a source of new problems.

Other Contexts of Preparation

Beyond family, school, and peers, there are other contexts that play a major role in adolescents' lives in different parts of the world. Like those we have already reviewed, these contexts can offer youth valuable resources as well as subject them to liabilities. Large numbers of youth from rural peasant and urban poor families in the developing world are not in school and spend much of their day in some form of labor. In some cases they work side by side with parents in the fields or in a family trade, which can provide a valuable means of education in indigenous skills (Chapter 3). Increasingly, however, these youth are employed in factories, household labor, or in the street. Such work contexts typically provide little remuneration, either in pay or in acquisition of useful resources for adulthood. In many cases the young people work in harsh, hazardous, or abusive conditions (Shanahan et al. 2002). The large number of American youth who work part-time are typically subject to more favorable conditions, and there is good evidence that they acquire skills and dispositions that benefit them later on (Mortimer, Harley, & Aronson 1999), but the evidence also suggests that when this employment exceeds 15 or 20 hours per week, it has a net negative effect on social and vocational development.

Participation in volunteer work and service organizations provides another context of socialization for youth in some parts of the world. In India, civic engagement is high, spurred by government- and religious-sponsored social programs. Volunteering is also reported to be common among youth in Southeast Asia, Europe, and the United States. Research is beginning to show that these activities can provide youth with valuable experiences that prepare them for civic participation as adults (Youniss et al. 2002).

A complete assessment of adolescents' contexts of preparation for adulthood would include other extracurricular and community activities, adolescents' experiences in religious activities, and the time that adolescents in some cultures spend alone, in their bedrooms or in natural settings. Details on these contexts are provided by some but not all of our authors, based largely on the amount of credible research on these topics in their area of the world.

Facing the Future

Through the course of their day or week, then, most young people encounter a variety of social contexts that aim to prepare them for adulthood. In some cases these contexts work well together and fit neatly with the cultural and economic demands that youth will encounter as adults. In others the fit is looser or the training for adulthood imperfect, like a kaleidoscope whose images are asymmetrical or unstable. The challenges that young people place on societal institutions and interpersonal contexts can be formidable. These challenges are reflected in 6 recurrent themes that emerge from our authors' depictions of adolescents. Like elements that add color and texture to the kaleidoscope's images, or that obscure and upset those images, these themes expose elements that help to differentiate adolescents' experiences in one historical moment or in a particular cultural or economic setting:

1. Susceptibility to Political and Historic Events

A conclusion one cannot miss in reading these chapters is that adolescents ride the waves of historical events. Major social changes or protracted political conflicts alter the course of adolescence for many young people. Events can suddenly close off opportunities or they can open them up. Adolescents are often drawn into the enmities of their elders in civil or international conflicts. From the British Isles and Latin America to the Arab world, portions of Africa, former Soviet states, and Southeast Asia, the authors comment on how adolescence is transformed or curtailed when youth are forced into the front lines of these armed conflicts. Adolescents and even preadolescents are drafted into the fighting forces in several warring states. Not only does this bring their adolescence (or childhood) to an abrupt end, but it also affects their sense of identity as they take on feelings of hatred toward the enemy they are compelled to fight. In the face of these conflicts young people may shy away from traditional family structures and turn to peers for emotional support and guidance (e.g., Barber 1999).

On the other hand, Stetsenko (Chapter 8) describes how the current generation of Russian youth benefit from the transformation of their society from a communist to democratic state. Although they suffer severe uncertainties about employment because of a faltering economy, they also enjoy new freedoms and opportunities that were unknown to previous generations. The collapse of communism in East Germany permitted young people on both sides of the Berlin Wall to forge a more unified sense of national identity than their parents or grandparents had been able to achieve (see Chapter 10). The transitional period of adolescence is anything but a fixed stage of life. When societies go through traumas or change, adolescents can be both the victims and beneficiaries.

2. Globalization Versus Fragmentation

One major current historical issue is the extent to which adolescents are being pulled together into a world community, as opposed to being thrust apart into religious, ethnic, socioeconomic, or other factions. This is a larger issue, about world society in general, that is a repeated theme of international writings (Clark 1997; Hoffman 1998), but adolescents are often at the center. In some respects, the authors in this volume depict a slow but steady convergence in the experience of adolescence across the globe. More and more youth are growing up in urban environments, preparing for jobs in capitalist labor markets, extending their education in age-graded schools that promote peer relationships outside the family, and consuming components of a youth culture that features standard elements of dress, grooming, and entertainment. Yet, as we have already intimated, these superficial similarities can easily be overstated. Booth (Chapter 7) points out that Arab youth adopt certain components of this global culture, but remain wary of Western social structures that promulgate them. Verma and Saraswathi (Chapter 4) note that Indian youth are devoted to their own society's film genre and television "soap operas," rather than concentrating on rock groups or movies popular in the Western world. In short, many societies engage in selective participation in global youth culture.

Similarly, the rapid urbanization of many societies creates a gulf between those who move to big cities and those who remain in rural areas. Authors emphasize the distinctions among urban and rural adolescents in their current social contexts and prospects for future economic success and social adjustment. A "digital divide," limiting computer and Internet access among poor youth, may have profound effects on their economic opportunities for the future (see Chapter 2). In the face of these cultural, economic, and educational divisions in young people's experiences, one might argue that adolescence is actually becoming a much more divergent phenomenon across the world, rather than a shared experience of youth.

As more young people are pulled into, or eagerly embrace, a global youth culture, similarities among the world's youth could become more pronounced. In the face of this, those who have little access to the trappings of this global culture, or who reject it in the face of religious or cultural mandates, may grow more estranged not only from adolescents in other nations but also from age mates in their own country. This could create social tensions as a fractured generation moves into adulthood and attempts to work together as social leaders; it also could enrich a society's diversity and increase sensitivity to social and cultural differences. Whether the kaleidoscope becomes fragmented or rich in complexity will be an interesting issue to observe as the world's youth mature into adulthood.

3. *Tensions Between Connection and Individualism*

Authors from diverse countries have reported signs of increasing adolescent self-centeredness and individualism (Omololu 1997; Santa Maria 2002; Stevenson & Zusho 2002). Yet, scholars have repeatedly concluded that Western individualism is not an inevitable result of the cluster of economic and social changes called "modernization" and that collectivist cultures are guided by different values (Kağitçibaşi 1997; Smith & Schwartz 1997). It should not be assumed that the world is converging toward Western individualism. In the Arab and South Asian worlds, people, including adolescents, do not experience themselves as separate and autonomous from the family (see Chapter 7). Strong, family centered traditions in China and Japan remain intact; at the same time some aspects of interdependency are dissipating (see Chapter 5). Japanese and Southeast Asian adolescents spend less time with their parents than was true of previous generations. Yet, family honor remains a crucial motivation to young people in their educational studies, career choices, and social pursuits. What seems to characterize the current generation of youth, then, is more of a tension between connection and individualism. In some societies this tension is manifest across different families, with some following a more traditional pattern of interdependence and others breaking away from this (e.g., Chapter 4). In other cases, the tension is more obvious within the family, as an adolescent struggles to assert autonomy while also maintaining traditions of interdependence (e.g., Chapters 5 and 8).

A similar struggle is manifest in adolescents' relationship with the larger society. Although memories of the 1989 student protests in Tienanmen Square remain fresh in many people's minds, the current generation of Chinese youth are markedly apolitical, according to Stevenson and Zusho (Chapter 5). No government organizations have replaced the youth groups that highlighted Mao's Cultural Revolution, and youth generally have not organized themselves into political action groups. Similarly, in Russia, youth are surprisingly nihilistic and apolitical, now that state-organized youth groups have disbanded in the wake of the collapse of communism (see Chapter 8). India, too, has witnessed a downturn in political activity among youth (see Chapter 4). According to Arnett (Chapter 10), "All across Europe as well as in the United States, young people's political participation is strikingly low by conventional measures."

This detachment from politics, however, is counterbalanced in many countries by an eagerness among youth to participate in volunteer service organizations. We have already referred to high rates of civic engagement among youth in India. In Western societies, rates of volunteer activities range from 20 percent of American high school seniors to over 50 percent of youth in eastern Europe. It would seem, then, as if young people are searching for new forms of connection to social and political institutions in their society, especially as there are major economic and political transformations in these societies. They live in the tension between a genuine lack of interest in or opportunities for civic engagement that characterized previous generations of adolescents and a discernible interest in serving the needs of at least some segments of their society.

In sum, what most characterizes the current generation of youth around the world is neither an obvious connection to nor a separation from others. This is so in youths' relationship to a specific social context (e.g., the degree of autonomy or interdependence they seek within the family) as well as their relationship to the society as a whole (e.g., involvement in versus alienation from broader political and social institutions). In some societies, or within certain subgroups or regions of a given society, young people tend to strive more toward connection than separation; in other societies or subgroups the tendency is toward connection. This is seen most obviously within the family, in how adolescents adhere to norms of striving for interdependence or autonomy. Other youth, however, simply live in tension between these two extremes, searching for new modes of connection that fit with emerging economic opportunities and social responsibilities.

4. Gendered Structures of Opportunity

A theme throughout the chapters is that the experiences and opportunities of adolescent girls and boys remain markedly different. With notable exceptions such as Japan, the Philippines, and Western nations, participation rates and completion rates in education at nearly all levels, but especially in institutions granting advanced training or degrees, are higher among males than females. Fussell and Greene (Chapter 2) lament this gender gap, pointing out that equity in educational achievement usually benefits men as well as women. The capacity to pursue particular careers, to engage in various leisure activities, even to exercise authority within family or peer relationships are often more restricted for girls than for boys. In India, Southeast Asia, Latin America, and the Arab world, double standards for sexual expression are quite obvious; sexual activity among boys is quietly tolerated or sometimes even encouraged. Even in cultures with more liberal attitudes toward sexual relationships prior to marriage, boys are generally given more license than girls. Although these gender gaps have diminished over time for adolescents in many nations, this is not always the case. Stetsenko (Chapter 8), for example, notes how the transformation in Russia from communism to capitalism in the past 2 decades has weakened women's authority and power and forced them into more traditional work and family roles.

In a curious exception to the typical pattern, young women in the Philippines are more likely to be the ones to seek employment in urban areas – although even educated women find that the job opportunities open to them are fewer (Chapter 6).

At the same time, most authors report evidence of increasing gender equality. This may be manifest in different ways among nations. Among upper-income families in India and Japan, fathers are assuming more responsibilities for child rearing (see Chapters 4 and 5). Rates of employment and specific career opportunities for women are expanding in many parts of the globe. Control over adolescent girls' social relationships, especially romantic and sexual relationships, is easing in some nations. As always, there are exceptions – for example, the move toward more-traditional gender roles for women in Russia following the collapse of communism (Chapter 8). Generally speaking, however, there is more differentiation among nations in the pace than in the direction of change in women's roles and opportunities.

5. Circumscribed Progress in Health and Well-Being

The chapters in this book confirm reports from other sources (Call et al. 2002; World Health Organization 1998; WHO) that advances across the world are more obvious in some domains of adolescent health than others. Infant mortality rates have diminished in many nations, prompting changes in fertility rates and population distributions (Chapter 2). The data suggest that fewer adolescents suffer mortality from infectious diseases and malnutrition than was the case in the past. Generally speaking, young people also benefit from better nutrition, one consequence of which has been an appreciable drop in the median age at which youth enter puberty across the world (this is more noticeable in some regions than others).

At the same time, many authors report an increase in the numbers of adolescents engaging in behaviors that compromise their physical health. Chief among these behaviors are illicit drug use and unprotected sexual contact. Several authors report a dramatic increase in rates of HIV infection or other sexually transmitted diseases. Some of this increase might be attributed to increased sensitivity to the diseases or better reporting procedures. But there is little doubt that adolescents are also engaging in more risky behavior than their predecessors in many parts of the world. Some authors attribute this trend to adolescents' limited access to health care or to health education. Others suggest it is a result of diminished supervision by adults and greater participation in peer social contexts. There are more-distal factors as well, such as shaky economies that frustrate adolescents in their failure to provide adequate employment.

Surprisingly little information is available about the mental health of adolescents, prompting several of our authors to not even mention the issue. Societies that struggle to meet the physical health needs of members often do not have the resources needed to address their mental health needs. Many regions depend upon nongovernmental organizations, especially organized efforts in the developed world to assist in health needs of the developing world, to address young people's mental health needs.

A compelling need in many parts of the globe, both among developed and developing nations, is for a focus on positive mental health and resiliency among youth. We need a better understanding of how youth cope successfully with environments that threaten their physical well-being or mental health. From this, more effective intervention programs properly suited to a given cultural context can be developed. In the meantime, there is reason for cautious optimism that health circumstances for most of the world's youth are improving.

6. Optimism for the Future
One of the most striking features of the regional chapters is the consistency with which authors report young people's optimism for the future. Whether adolescents are growing up in relatively stable or rapidly changing cultures, whether economic outlooks are promising or grim, whether educational training or health and social services are adequate or constrained, most young people face the future with anticipation and hope. Even in nations that face what appear to be daunting social or economic problems (e.g., India or Russia), youth express confidence in their future.

Understandably, there are exceptions to this rule. Welti (Chapter 9) perceives limited opportunities for many young people in Latin America and details the grim prospects for adolescents caught in armed conflict or forced to live "on the street" because of their country's struggling economies. These youth, he says, often express despair about their prospects for success and happiness. Yet, this does not appear to be endemic to the entire region. Youth in several Latin American nations seem quite sanguine about prospects for the future. In the minds of most Russian youth, freedoms and opportunities gained from the changing political structure seem to outweigh economic hardships, which they regard as temporary (Chapter 8). The situation is more complex in many nations; the worries of youth from economically deprived backgrounds contrast sharply with the optimism of their age mates from economically advantaged circumstances. The challenge in these societies is to recognize and attend to both outlooks among youth.

The optimism of youth should serve as strong motivation to adults to derive policies and programs that can meet their developmental needs. The final chapter of the book takes a social policy perspective and asks what adults can do to support adolescents. This chapter sees adolescents as the agents who will ultimately shape their own future, but it emphasizes the important role of researchers, practitioners, policy makers, business leaders, and others in opening opportunities that allow them to do this.

Appreciating the Kaleidoscope of Adolescence

Lined up on a toy shop shelf, a set of kaleidoscope tubes cast a deceptive image of similarity. No matter which one is selected, a customer might think, the images it produces will be the same. Adolescence around the world casts this same image at the beginning of the 21st century. Across nations, families and educational systems – and to an increasing extent, experiences with peers – play a central role in shaping an individual's experiences during this phase of life. There is even some evidence of convergence across the world in the experiences an adolescent has within each of these contexts. For example, gender equity in education is becoming more common; peers are routinely a force condoning if not urging more sexual involvement outside conventional institutions such as marriage.

Despite an uneven pace of change across the globe, common historical trajectories are discernible. Health and nutrition are improving; access to health care is expanding. Increasing numbers of young people are growing up in urban environments (or at least moving to such environments in the course of adolescence). More and more of them are exposed to peers with different cultural backgrounds, thereby allowing (if not forcing) them to adjust to cultural diversity. It is becoming more common for young people to grow up in the context of a democratic political and social system. In these respects, the world's youth appear to be gravitating toward a common set of experiences, a common destiny.

It is only upon closer inspection that one recognizes the differences among kaleidoscopes on the toy shop shelf. Indeed, the more they are turned to allow the image elements to converge, destabilize, and reform, the more distinctive each kaleidoscope becomes. Reading the chapters at this deeper level, one can appreciate the diversity in outlook and experiences among the world's youth. Marked variabilities in family forms, in the relevance of school systems to cultural norms and economic opportunities, in access to health care and leisure activities, in religious orientations and values – all of these can create deep fissures in the experiences of adolescents from one nation to the next or among different economic or social groups within a nation. This makes the task of policy makers, educational practitioners, and health and social service personnel who work with youth especially difficult. To meet the needs of youth one must forge a policy that aims at a certain level of convergence in opportunities for youth while maintaining their historical and cultural distinctiveness.

Thus, the major lesson to be learned from our authors is that one must look closely to recognize the challenges that any young person faces growing up in the 21st century. Although the same social forces may be at play in each of their lives, they "play out" in different ways. These differences can cascade to lead young people down increasingly different paths as they approach adulthood, or they may allow children from very different segments of a society to converge in adolescence toward a common destiny. Like a kaleidoscope, the opportunities and outcomes for adolescents are constantly changing and only partially predictable. In the final analysis, this is what makes the world's youth so intriguing.

References

Aptekar, L., & L. Ciano-Federoff. 1999. Street children in Nairobi: Gender differences in mental health. *Homeless and working youth around the world: Exploring developmental issues.* New directions in child development. 85:35–46. San Francisco: Jossey-Bass.

Barber, B. K. 1999. Youth experience in the Palestinian Intifada: A case study in intensity, complexity, paradox, and competence. In *Roots of civic identity: International perspectives on community service and activism in youth*, eds. M. Yates & J. Youniss, 178–204. New York: Cambridge University Press.

Call, K., A. Riedel, K. Hein, V. McLoyd, M. Kipke, & P. Petersen. 2002. Adolescent health and well-being in the 21st century: A global perspective. *Journal of Research on Adolescence*. In press.

Clark, I. 1997. *Globalization and fragmentation: International relations in the twentieth century*. Oxford: Oxford University Press.

Hall, G. S. 1904. *Adolescence*. New York: Appleton & Company.

Hoffman, S. 1998. *World disorders: Troubled peace in the post-Cold War era*. Lanham, MD: Rowman & Littlefield.

Kağitçibaşi, C. 1997. Individualism and collectivism. In *Handbook of cross-cultural psychology: Social behavior and applications*, eds. J. W. Berry, M. H. Segall, & C. Kağitçibaşi, 2:3:1–49. Boston: Allyn and Bacon.

Larson, R. W., S. Wilson, B. B. Brown, F. F. Furstenberg, & S. Verma. 2002. Changes in adolescents' interpersonal experiences: Are they being prepared for adult relationships in the 21st century? *Journal of Research on Adolescence*. In press.

Mortimer, J. T., C. Harley, & P. Aronson. 1999. How do prior experiences in the workplace set the stage for transitions to adulthood? In *Transitions to adulthood in a changing economy: No work, no family, no future?* eds. A. Booth, A. C. Crouter, & M. J. Shanahan, 131–159. Westport, CT: Praeger.

Omololu, O. O. 1997. Family formation. In *Status of adolescents and young adults in Nigeria*, eds. O. O. Dare, I. M. Isiugo-Abanihe, A. Jimoh, O. Omololu, & I. B. Udegbe, 58–69. Lagos, Nigeria: CHESTRAD.

Peterson, J. 1990. Sibling exchanges and complementarity in the Philippine highlands. *Journal of Marriage and the Family*, 52:441–451.

Phelen, P., A. L. Davidson, & H. C. Yu. 1998. *Adolescents' worlds: Negotiating family, peers, and school*. New York: Teachers College Press.

Schlegel, A. & H. Barry III. 1991. *Adolescence: An anthropological inquiry*. New York: Free Press.

Schlegel, A. 2000. The global spread of adolescent culture. In *Negotiating adolescence in times of social change*, eds. L. J. Crockett & R. K. Silbereisen, 71–88. London: Cambridge University Press.

Shanahan, M., J. Mortimer, & H. Kruger. 2002. Adolescence and adult work in the twenty-first century. *Journal of Research on Adolescence*, in press.

Smith, P. B. & S. H. Schwartz. 1997. Values. In *Handbook of cross-cultural psychology: Social behavior and applications*, eds. J. W. Berry, M. H. Segall & C. Kağitçibaşi, 2:3:77–118. Boston: Allyn and Bacon.

Whiting, B. B. 1980. Culture and social behavior. *Ethos*, 8:95–116.

World Health Organization. 1998. *The world health report 1998: Life in the 21st Century*. Geneva: Author.

Youniss, J., R. Silbereisen, V. Christmas-Best, M. Diversi, S. Bales & M. McLaughlin. 2002. Youth civic engagement in the 21st century. *Journal of Research on Adolescence*, 12:124–148.

2

Demographic Trends Affecting Youth Around the World

Elizabeth Fussell and Margaret E. Greene

Introduction

Every generation may believe its time is unprecedented. Yet the current generation of youth, the largest in history, is facing a combination of social and economic conditions and demographic trends certain to make their lives dramatically different from those of their parents and grandparents. In this chapter we ask how the absolute and relative numbers of young people and their nations' social and economic circumstances shape their futures. We do so to highlight how demographic conditions help or hinder governments' and families' investments in youth. In this way we complement the other chapters, which focus on the lived experience of adolescents in various world regions.

Who falls into the "youth" category, and what are the defining features of this group? The definition of youth is fluid and arbitrarily defined, both physically and socially, and varies across cultures and eras. The implications of defining this phase one way or another are significant for program development. For the purposes of this chapter, however, we can agree that in most cultures, the 2nd, and even 3rd, decade of life is an eventful time, a period in which young people experience changes in their roles and shifts in social expectations of them.

This chapter considers how differences in age distribution and in the culturally determined transitions that define youth together shape the experience of young people in various parts of the world. To illustrate the differences in the timing of events that mark transitions into adult status, we compare for each region the levels of school attainment and the ages at which young people enter into employment, marriage,

21

and childbearing. We also inquire into the resources youth have to draw on as they make transitions. Household consumption and inequality, access to health services and education, labor-market conditions and gender differences in these – all are indicators of the contexts in which youth make transitions into adulthood. We then examine the national resources invested in health and education and trends in the labor market by region to assess national preparedness for this large cohort of youth reaching adulthood early in the century. We conclude with a summary of demographic trends affecting youth in each global region.

Youth in the Age Structure

The United Nations estimates that in October 1999 the world's population reached 6 billion, with children under the age of 15 constituting one-third of the population in developing countries and nearly half in sub-Saharan Africa (Gelbard, Haub, & Kent 1999). Although the *number* of children and youth is large relative to previous cohorts in many countries, they constitute a variable *proportion* of national populations. The distribution of people across the age range is determined by its recent history of fertility, mortality, and migration.

Demographic transition theory presents a stylized model of how some countries have experienced and how other countries may experience a transition from high to low fertility and mortality. Before mortality declines, fertility and mortality rates are high, making the average age in the population quite young. As mortality declines, people of all ages live longer, but more importantly, more children survive to adulthood, making the already young population even younger. As survival to adulthood becomes more assured, people have fewer additional children for "insurance" purposes. This causes the population to age, as the relative number of older people increases and fewer children are born. Thus, fertility decline reduces the proportion of children and mortality decline increases the proportion of the surviving elderly, both of which cause the population to age.

Table 2.1 groups countries according to when their fertility began to decline, a system that serves to categorize their age structures as well (United Nations 1993). In Europe, North America, and several early initiation countries, the demographic transition is largely over. These countries are characterized by low growth rates and aging populations. In most of the late initiation countries of Latin America, East Asia, and some of the Middle East and South Asia, the decline of mortality

TABLE 2.1. *Countries Grouped by Timing of Fertility Transition*

Region	Early Initiation Countries	Late Initiation Countries	Preinitiation Countries
Sub-Saharan Africa		Mauritius, Réunion, South Africa	Angola, Benin, Botswana, Burkina Faso, Burundi, Cameroon, Cape Verde, Central African Republic, Chad, Comoros, Congo, Côte d'Ivoire, Djibouti, Equatorial Guinea, Ethiopia, Gabon, Gambia, Ghana, Guinea, Guinea-Bissau, Kenya, Lesotho, Liberia, Madagascar, Mali, Malawi, Mauritania, Mozambique, Namibia, Niger, Nigeria, Rwanda, Senegal, Sierra Leone, Sudan, Swaziland, Togo, Uganda, United Republic of Tanzania, Zaire, Zambia
The Middle East and North Africa	Cyprus, Israel	Bahrain, Egypt, Kuwait, Lebanon, Morocco, Tunisia, United Arab Emirates	Algeria, Libyan Arab Jamahiriya, Jordan, Oman, Qatar, Saudi Arabia, Sudan, Syrian Arab Republic, Yemen
East Asia, Southeast Asia and the Pacific	Australia, Japan New Zealand	China, Korea DPR, Rep. of Korea, Hong Kong, Cambodia, Fiji, Indonesia, Malaysia, Myanmar, Philippines, Singapore, Thailand, Viet Nam	East Timor, Lao PDR, Mongolia, Papua New Guinea

(continued)

23

TABLE 2.1. *(continued)*

Region	Early Initiation Countries	Late Initiation Countries	Preinitiation Countries
South Asia		India, Sri Lanka	Afghanistan, Bangladesh, Bhutan, Iran, Nepal, Pakistan
Western Europe	Austria, Belgium, Denmark, Finland, France, Germany, Iceland, Ireland, Italy, Luxembourg, Malta, Netherlands, Norway, Portugal, Spain, Sweden, Switzerland, United Kingdom	Albania	
Eastern Europe and the CIS	Bulgaria, Czechoslovakia, Hungary, Poland, Romania, Former USSR, Yugoslavia		
Latin America and the Caribbean	Argentina, Barbados, Cuba, Uruguay	Brazil, Chile, Colombia, Costa Rica, Dominican Republic, Ecuador, El Salvador, Guadeloupe, Guyana, Jamaica, Martinique, Mexico, Panama, Paraguay, Peru, Puerto Rico, Suriname, Trinidad and Tobago Venezuela	Bolivia, Guatemala, Haiti, Honduras, Nicaragua
North America	Canada, United States		

Source: United Nations 1993.

and fertility began more recently, and fertility still remains at a level that supports moderate population growth. In the preinitiation countries in most of sub-Saharan Africa, the rest of the Middle East and South Asia, and several countries in Latin America, mortality is not as low as it is in the countries that made earlier transitions. Here, fertility remains relatively high, and in combination with the higher mortality results in youthful populations and relatively rapid population growth.

These regional groupings contrast sharply with one another. People under age 15 make up almost half of the population in the preinitiation countries (with a median age of 17), one-third of the population of late-initiation countries (with a median age of 23), and less than a quarter of the population in the early-initiation countries (with a median age of 34) (United Nations 1993; United Nations 1990). In the coming years, these large groups of young people will be making the transition into adult roles, and the relative burden their numbers place on the economically active in their societies will have important implications for how they fare. When half the population is under age 17, as in the preinitiation countries, the demands on social institutions, particularly schools, are enormous.

Each of these different age structures poses challenges for governments trying to provide for their populations. The speed at which cohort size and demand for age-graded goods and services (e.g., school, health care, and family planning) fluctuate determines the extent to which these changes are defined as social problems. Populations and individual members of birth cohorts experience changes in the age structure very differently, of course. For example, although members of a large cohort may increase national productivity when they reach working age, a boon for the population or country as a whole, they may also experience the negative effects of being so numerous and having to compete for jobs as they enter the labor market together. We return to this point later in this chapter, with a discussion of how people and governments can respond to these demographic challenges.

Age Structures and Economic Growth

No simple model can fully explain the relationship between economic growth and demographic change, though the relationship is clearly important. Indeed, demography, economic geography, globalization, natural resource endowment, human capital supply, public policy, and the quality of social institutions all play critical roles in a nation's economic growth. Though the literature on economic growth often implies that economic development will necessarily follow from growth, economic growth, as measured by an increase in the gross domestic product (GDP) or gross national product (GNP), can occur in the absence of improvements in the standard of living. Thus, we see investments in youth as critical to economic development, especially when children and adolescents make up such a large portion of the population.

One rough summary measure of changes in age structure is the dependency ratio, which compares the relative size of the youngest and oldest segments of the population (age 0–14 and 60+) with the population most likely to be economically productive (age 15–59). A large youth dependency ratio emerges at the stage of the demographic transition when children are surviving infancy in greater numbers but fertility has not yet declined. After fertility declines, particularly if it falls sharply, a smaller youth dependency ratio becomes inevitable, emerging about 20 years later when the large birth cohort enters the labor market. Finally, when fertility and mortality are both low, the large cohorts born before the fertility decline age into economic dependency, relying on a working-age population made smaller by fertility decline. During the interval in which the overall dependency ratio is small, demographic forces contribute to economic growth, a window of opportunity for economic development if nations are prepared to take advantage of the situation.

The most impressive example of the positive role that age structure can play in economic growth is provided by the East Asian "miracle." The huge birth cohort resulting from the East Asian mortality decline in the 1940s and 1950s reached the labor market about 20 years later. Before 1970, per capita income growth in East Asia had been suppressed by the large youth dependency ratio. After 1970, the greater proportion of workers and the government's investments in education and job creation facilitated per capita income growth. By 2010, this low dependency ratio will have vanished as the workers of the economic miracle retire and are supported by subsequent smaller working-age cohorts (Williamson 1998). East Asia made the most of this transient opportunity, investing heavily in education and health services, and they have reaped the rewards of having done so.

Dependency ratios vary significantly between regions, reflecting different periods of demographic opportunity arriving at different times. North America, Oceania, and Europe are nearing the end of their period of low dependency, created by intense childbearing after World War II, and have begun to face the problems associated with growing elderly populations (United Nations 1995; United Nations 1998). In Figure 2.1 we see that the elderly dependency will exceed the youth dependency ratio in 2000 on average for countries in Europe, North America, and Oceania, an unprecedented demographic situation that demands serious attention to the budgeting of resources across the population age structure (Fussell 2002). Though immigration to these countries may slow population aging by adding to the youthful population, it is generally not sufficient to reverse the trend. Asia and Latin America and the Caribbean are currently experiencing low elderly dependency ratios and high but declining youth dependency ratios. Both regions have prepared for it by investing in children and youth, but Latin America's economic crises have diminished economic opportunities for youth (Welti this volume). Africa, whose huge youth population will soon become workers, can prepare to take advantage of this demographic period potentially favorable to economic development by investing in youth with Afrocentric education and improved living conditions (Nsamenang this volume). Unless governments prepare well for this "demographic opportunity," circumstances could just as likely result in a demographic disaster as large cohorts of youth enter adulthood without sufficient preparation.

For low dependency ratios to translate into economic growth and development, governments must commit to creating equal opportunities for youth to learn and grow. Thus investments in health and universal education are critical to the productive employment of the burgeoning labor force. In addition, the development of financial markets that make savings and investment possible for a majority of the population are critical for translating growth into development (Bloom and Canning 1999, 4).

When these favorable conditions do not exist, individuals often take matters into their own hands in ways that affect both local age structures and economic growth. Youth and young adults contribute substantially to the flow of migrants from rural to urban areas as well as to international migration. Rural-to-urban migration, which fuels urbanization, is one way in which young adults attempt to access better education, employment, and housing and in other ways try to improve their life chances. However, this migration flow also leads to urban underemployment and unemployment as urban population growth exceeds labor demand. Thus rapid urbanization in developing countries often

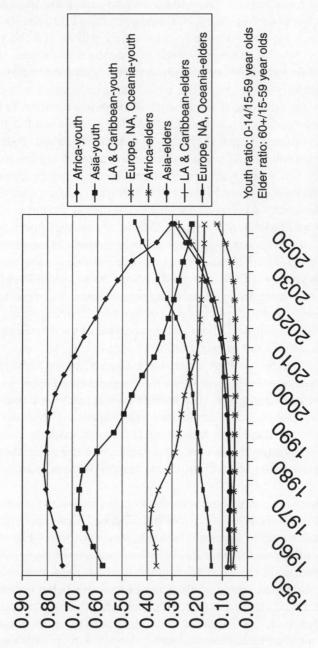

FIGURE 2.1. Youth and elder dependency ratios in Africa, Asia, Latin America and the Caribbean, and Europe, North American, and Oceania. *Source:* United Nations 1998.

Legend:
- Africa-youth
- Asia-youth
- LA & Caribbean-youth
- Europe, NA, Oceania-youth
- Africa-elders
- Asia-elders
- LA & Caribbean-elders
- Europe, NA, Oceania-elders

Youth ratio: 0-14/15-59 year olds
Elder ratio: 60+/15-59 year olds

leads to a breakdown of community safety nets – an effect seen most acutely in the numbers of street children in such cities and more subtly in the mixing of indigenous and imported cultures (Nsamenang this volume). In industrialized countries with high median ages, one solution to the inevitable shrinking of the population is to incorporate international migrants, a trend already occurring in much of western Europe and North America (Massey et al. 1999; Sinding 2000). This international movement creates social networks that channel monetary remittances, trained labor, and new ideas back into developing countries (Massey et al. 1999). Internal and international migration are strategies undertaken to improve the economic lives of individuals, but they carry substantial costs in terms of loss of community and culture for the migrants.

In sum, population processes – births, deaths, and migration – are some of the few predictable factors shaping a country's future. The young people coming of age in the beginning of the 21st century do so at a time of rapid demographic change. Youth in developed countries are in relatively small cohorts in aging populations. Youth in developing countries are in large cohorts likely to be followed by similarly large cohorts. This rapid change presents opportunities for improving the conditions of youth if the process and implications of change are well understood.

Investments in Youth

Parents and communities invest in children and youth by providing for their health, education, and preparation – physical, vocational, and cultural – for a productive adulthood. In the previous discussion, we showed how important the relative size of youth cohorts is, highlighting the fact that when young people come of age in a context of low dependency ratios they potentially contribute to economic growth and development. Here we argue that the demographic and economic context in which youth cohorts come of age is critical in predicting the amount of parental and social "investment" in young people.

The experiences of Europe and North America and the industrialized countries of East Asia suggest that people in large birth cohorts benefit in times of economic expansion because parents and governments are able to invest generously in youth. Furthermore, markets in healthy economies expand to accommodate large cohorts, creating economies of scale. For example, schools grow in size and number, health and recreation services expand, and entrepreneurs compete for youth markets. In the context of economic stagnation (and a lack of commitment to equity), large youth cohorts may be short-changed with regard to social investments, as the example of Latin America shows. In this case, the growth potential offered by low dependency ratios will be weakened by a lack of social investment in youth. In this section on investments in youth we consider the interplay between economic context and investments in youth by examining education and health measures and reflecting on regional trends affecting national economies.

Increased global trade has already radically changed the economies of industrialized countries in the past 30 years and those developing countries that participate in manufacturing production for global markets. However, more developing countries are left out of the global economy than drawn in, as there are relatively few countries that export high-priced manufactured goods and many more that export low-priced primary commodities (United Nations Development Program 1999; UNDP). While youth in countries participating heavily in global trade benefit from the economic growth that may follow, youth in countries that have little to sell on global markets have fewer market-based opportunities for improving their economic condition. While participation in global markets is not the only way to improve one's circumstances, being excluded from global trade certainly limits a country's access to basic resources, such as clean water, health care, and adequate nutrition, that promote youth well-being and potential. In the following sections we examine trends in education and health in different global regions as indicators of investments in youth.

Education

Given the widely acknowledged need to improve standards of living and reduce population growth around the world, education serves multiple purposes. It prepares youth by equipping them with literacy, numeracy, and knowledge to solve problems and improve their lives and conditions in ways consistent with cultural values and national goals. This period of individual growth can also be an alternative to early childbearing. In light of this reasoning we examine the variation in years of schooling and early transitions into adult roles, including marriage, childbearing, and labor force participation as a means of assessing the degree of competition between schooling, the need for additional household income, and norms governing family formation.

As economies move from agricultural to industrial production or from industrial production to services and commerce, formal training and skills in all sectors and levels of the labor force become more critical. As a result, the purpose of education has expanded to include teaching people how to learn new skills and adopt new technologies. Widespread education also plays a fundamental role in reducing inequality by raising baseline productivity and reducing education-based earning differentials. The restructuring of labor markets has made universal basic education as well as technical training a top policy priority of international lending agencies (World Bank 1995).

The commitment – at least on paper – to education, is often expressed in the years of compulsory schooling national governments require. While Africa, Asia, and Latin America tend to require fewer years of schooling, North America, Oceania, and Europe require more (United Nations 1997; United Nations Education, Scientific, and Cultural Organization 1995; UNESCO, Table 3.1). Beyond establishing national guidelines for school attendance, states and communities must struggle to provide quality education and enforce educational norms. In fact, in many developing countries, low school attendance and failure to complete school levels are now seen as the most critical threat to universal primary and secondary education, particularly when children face competing demands as earners (UNESCO 1998). Cross-national educational statistics do not adequately measure these shortcomings of educational systems.

Enrollment ratios at the primary, secondary, and tertiary school levels provide a rough indicator of educational participation and capacity, although it is difficult to compare differing national education systems. Gross enrollment ratios (the ratio of total enrollment, regardless of age, to the population of the age group that officially corresponds to a given level of education) may exceed 100 as younger or older children who start a grade early or repeat a grade are included with children of the normative age-grade group in the numerator, although the denominator is the number of children of the normative age for that class.

Developed countries register enrollment ratios of 100 students per 100 children of appropriate school age at both the primary and secondary levels and high tertiary gross enrollment ratios as well (Figure 2.2).[1] In fact, in developed countries the aging of the population is shifting demand toward tertiary education as smaller cohorts of children enter primary and secondary schools and more adults return to school for additional training (Organization for Economic Cooperation and development 1998; OECD). Widespread enrollments in secondary and tertiary levels reflect the long period of familial and social investment

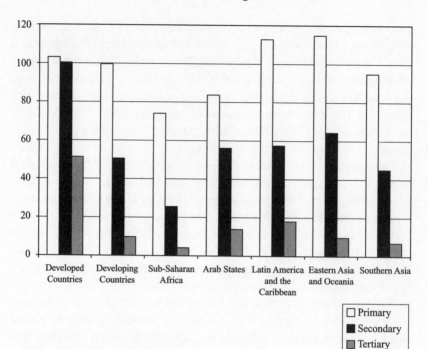

FIGURE 2.2. Gross enrollment ratios by region and educational level, 1996. (No. students at level of schooling/No. people of appropriate age for that level of schooling). *Source:* UNESCO 1998.

in youth. This investment has come to be seen as necessary in order for youth to position themselves advantageously in the labor market, but it has also delayed the average timing of entry into family roles prompting concern about population aging in these countries (Fussell 2002).

Most developing countries have made small advances in increasing primary enrollment ratios over the past 2 decades, although in many cases the enrollment rates were already quite high (Figure 2.3). Only sub-Saharan Africa and the Arab states have significantly lower enrollments at the primary level. Sub-Saharan Africa is the only region that experienced a *decline* in gross enrollment ratios at the primary school level between 1980 and 1996. Debt crises and the subsequent austerity policies, in combination with a high youth dependency ratio means that few resources are available for schooling, a reality that undoubtedly underlies the stagnation of primary education enrollments in sub-Saharan Africa (Woodhall 1994; Nanda 2000).

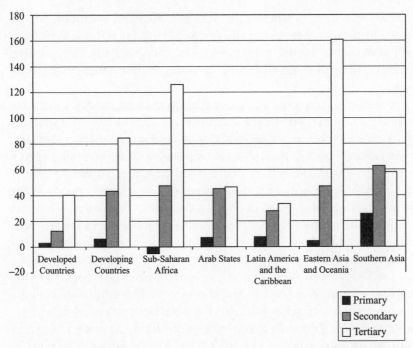

FIGURE 2.3. Percentage change in gross enrollment ratios between 1980 and 1996. *Source:* UNESCO 1998.

Secondary enrollment ratios have increased to at least 50 students per 100 children of appropriate age in all regions except sub-Saharan Africa and Southern Asia, though both regions made substantial gains between 1980 and 1996. In general, regions with the lowest gross primary and secondary enrollment ratios (sub-Saharan Africa, South Asia, and the Middle East and North Africa) are also facing a growing school-aged population and, hence, increasing demand for primary and secondary education. This fact calls attention to the need for more investments in primary and secondary schooling in these regions.

In Latin America and the Caribbean and Eastern Asia and Oceania, overall enrollment rates were quite high in 1980. However, during the 1980s many Latin American and Caribbean countries experienced economic crises and government austerity in social spending, resulting in only small gains in education at all levels. In contrast, Eastern Asia and Oceania and Southern Asia made significant gains in primary and secondary education enrollments, building toward more universal basic education. Eastern Asia and Oceania made very large gains in tertiary enrollments. These gains resulted from and contributed to industrial growth throughout the region. The tight reciprocal relationship between economic growth and education suggests that countries cannot afford to forgo education spending during times of economic crisis.

Prioritizing more costly higher education over universal basic education, as some developing countries are now doing, often reflects nations' short-term economic realities but bears consequences for future generations. During the 1980s, an increasing share of public spending went toward secondary and tertiary education at the expense of primary education in both developing and developed regions of the world, with the exception of South Asia (World Bank 1995). This shift in spending makes sense where universal primary education has been achieved, but where it has not, for example, the Arab states, Latin America and the Caribbean, and sub-Saharan Africa, it represents increased inequity in public education expenditures. These patterns reflect a greater emphasis on higher education, even when universal basic education has not been achieved, a short-sighted tactic given the large youth cohort coming of age in a time when education has never been more important.

Indeed, throughout the developing regions of the world public spending per student in higher education is between 7 and 44 times greater than spending per student in primary school, in contrast with a ratio of 2.5:1 in the OECD countries (World Bank 1995). Since the rates of return to investments in primary and secondary education are greater in developing regions than investment in tertiary education, this represents significant inequity in public spending. This is not to say that tertiary education is not important; in fact, people's technical and professional skills are increasingly necessary for their nations to take advantage of technological advances. Rather, we argue that public spending on higher education could easily be subsidized by payments from students, since most of these students come from higher income households. A more efficient way of paying for tertiary education would be to distribute need-based scholarships for people from financially disadvantaged households.

Equity in Education

Equitable education also requires the elimination of gender, race, ethnic, religious, class, and urban/rural differences in access to schooling. While there is certainly educational discrimination in most countries

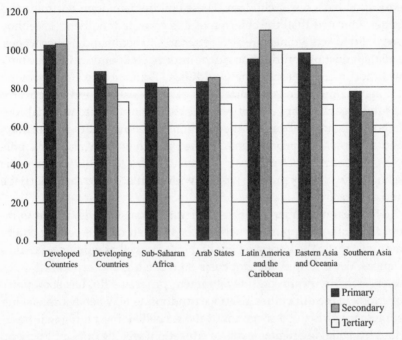

FIGURE 2.4. Ratio of female to male enrollment ratios by region, 1996. Girls: Boys (No. students at that level of schooling/No. people of appropriate age for that level of schooling). *Source:* UNESCO 1998. Regions defined in Appendix A.

along these dimensions, gender is the best documented of these differentials (UNESCO 1995). In many regions men's education is valued more highly than women's, as evidenced by sex differentials in enrollment ratios (Figure 2.4). The deficit of girls in school is greatest in the Arab states, sub-Saharan Africa, and Southern Asia, where fewer than 85 girls are enrolled for every 100 boys at the primary and secondary levels, and where it is likely that girls have even lower relative attendance rates. These differences in enrollment ratios are reflected in years of schooling achieved. Boys attain between 1 and 3 more years of schooling than girls do in sub-Saharan Africa, the Arab states, and South Asia. In contrast, in East Asia and the Pacific the difference is 1 year and it is less than a quarter year in Latin America and the Caribbean. In European and North American countries that are members of the OECD, girls attain almost a half a year more schooling than boys (World Bank 1995).

Achieving gender equity in education promotes national goals as well as women's individual well-being. Women with higher levels of education have fewer children. These children are often healthier and better educated than the children of less educated mothers (Jejeebhoy 1995). Educated women are also better able to command higher wages, and their unsung contributions to the informal economy are increasingly well documented around the world (e.g., Tzannatos 1998). Improving the status of women is a central goal of many nations and nongovernmental organizations, a priority made clear at recent international conferences organized by the United Nations.[2] Gender equity in education and employment, in addition to being basic to women's human rights (Sen, Germain, & Chen 1994), also contributes to fertility decline, as schooling and work provide women with alternatives to early marriage and childbearing.

The ideal of gender equity is difficult to translate into action without the explicit support of men and boys, even though gender equity may also mean the improvement of men's, as well as women's, circumstances. For example, the emphasis on changing and expanding girls' roles, as many health and development programs do, has sometimes overlooked the difficulties girls face in adopting new behaviors. Asking adolescent girls to be social innovators, challenging patriarchal traditions by achieving higher levels of education, seeking out employment, often in male-dominated arenas, and delaying entry into marriage lays a great responsibility on their shoulders.

Girls who have the opportunity to attend secondary school are often punished sharply for their nonconformity. In sub-Saharan Africa, where traditional age at marriage is quite young, numerous studies have documented the irrevocable changes in the lives of schoolgirls who become pregnant. A survey of the students and heads of 13 secondary schools in Tanzania showed for the early 1980s a pregnancy rate of 42 per 1,000 female students per year (Kaijage 1990). About 6 percent of pregnant students died from suicide or abortion, while an additional 2 percent had unsuccessfully attempted suicide. School policy resulted in the dismissal of the remaining pregnant teens. A review of abortion studies from 27 developing countries found that adolescent girls accounted for 60 percent of hospital admissions for abortion-related complications, from which they inferred that a substantial number of adolescent girls die of abortion complications (Hirsch & Barker 1992). Both boys and girls need the guidance and support of adult men and women in their communities to negotiate the challenges of their changing bodies and changing lives and to navigate their schooling and work decisions, which will influence the rest of their lives.

Health

In general, youth are the healthiest members of any population, having survived early childhood with its concentration of often-fatal diseases. Their higher rates of violent death are still much smaller than the health risks of older and younger members of the population. The variation in life expectancy at birth and infant mortality rates across regions offers some example of the varying health contexts in which youth come into adulthood (Figure 2.5). Gains in life expectancy in developing countries between 1970 and 1997 largely result from declines in infant mortality rates. Better hygiene, safer water supplies, low-cost interventions such as oral rehydration salts for the treatment of diarrhea, programs to combat early childhood diseases and immunize children, improved nutrition and maternal and child health programs have all improved infants' and children's chances of survival (Gelbard et al. 1999). Nevertheless, large proportions of the population in developing countries are not expected to survive to the age of 60. Much of this premature death is still accounted for by high infant mortality.

The work still to be done in achieving health for all is shown by the gap of over 13 years in life expectancy at birth between industrialized countries and developing countries, down by only 3.6 years since 1970. While youth may not face as many direct health risks as children and the elderly, by this age they have learned the health practices that will carry them through the rest of their lives. Thus practices ranging from hygiene and diet to use of medical services and healthful sexual practices are important for further reducing the gap in life expectancy between developing and developed countries.

The major causes of death for youth are accidents, homicide, and suicide, though HIV/AIDS threatens to dominate in some areas. The relative weight of problems such as youth suicide, homicide, and substance abuse is exacerbated in the developed world due to anomie and risk-taking behavior, including drug taking and accidents. An additional factor, particularly in the lives of poor youth in developing countries, is work-related disability and mortality. In Brazil and other settings where children begin doing agricultural work at an early age, they are often exposed to mechanical and chemical dangers that affect them more severely than they affect adults (Raymundo 2000). Adolescent mortality is not only generally low, but its causes are largely preventable and reflect the stresses young people experience during this stage of life.

The HIV/AIDS epidemic threatens to reverse gains in life expectancy by killing people in the prime of adulthood and, increasingly, in youth,

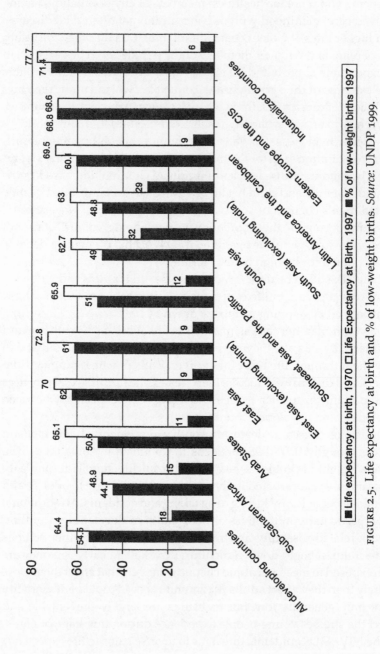

FIGURE 2.5. Life expectancy at birth and % of low-weight births. *Source:* UNDP 1999.

Life expectancy at birth, 1970 ☐ Life Expectancy at Birth, 1997 ■ % of low-weight births 1997

although it is a preventable disease (United Nations Development Program [UNDP] 1999; Csillag 1999). In 12 countries, all of them in sub-Saharan Africa, the HIV infection rate among adults exceeds 10 percent (Brown & Halweil 1999). Zimbabwe, Botswana, South Africa, and Namibia all have adult HIV infection rates over 20 percent. In other regions, HIV infection has not reached such high levels, but lack of awareness of the disease and a lack of supplies for detecting HIV infection may mask prevalence levels in developing countries. In contrast to HIV/AIDS, tuberculosis is well documented and easily treated, making it a good indicator of the availability or unavailability of health care. The regions with few doctors and nurses tend to be the same regions in which the incidence of tuberculosis is higher: sub-Saharan Africa, Southeast Asia and the Pacific, and South Asia (UNDP 1999). This suggests that lack of health care systems is a structural problem underlying much of the health problems in developing regions.

The sexual activity, contraceptive use, and fertility of adolescent girls, and to a lesser extent, boys, is the one area of adolescent health that has received international research attention due to concern about early childbearing and its contribution to population growth (e.g., Mensch, Bruce, & Greene 1998). Using data from Demographic and Health Surveys conducted over the past decade, Mensch and her colleagues show that adolescent girls are frequently sexually active but have little knowledge of reproduction or contraception and even less access to reproductive health services. They find that in sub-Saharan Africa and Latin America and the Caribbean, fewer than half of sexually active never-married girls aged 15–19 are using modern contraception, placing many young girls at risk of premarital pregnancy and its consequences for their schooling, marriage prospects, and work lives. The risk of premarital births increases as girls' schooling has become more widespread and they delay marriage. This results in more unwanted or unplanned pregnancy, particularly in sub-Saharan Africa (Worthman & Whiting 1987; Kulin 1988; Bledsoe & Cohen 1993).

Teenagers in some industrialized countries have successfully achieved low rates of unwanted pregnancy by finding sufficient motivation to use effective contraception and abortion (Jones et al. 1989). In western European countries, there is a strong emphasis on providing young people with the skills and information to negotiate their own sexual relationships safely and responsibly – and even with enjoyment (Berne & Huberman 1999). Regardless of the context, teenagers need resources and incentives to delay early childbearing and learn healthy sexual practices.

The payoffs to investments in health are perhaps not as appealing or profitable as investments in education, but they are a prerequisite to youth achievement. Spending on health remains at a low 2 percent of GDP in developing countries compared with over 6 percent in industrialized countries (United Nations 1997a). When children are not healthy, it is difficult to imagine that they can achieve their potential and contribute to building their societies as young adults.

Transitions into Adulthood

As youth stay in school longer, they frequently delay entering into employment, marriage, or parenthood. The timing of transitions at the aggregate level offers some initial insight into the normative ages at which transitions are made and what this implies about the termination of the period of social investments in youth. We focus on these transitions because comparative data are available, and we leave the more culturally specific aspects of the transition to adulthood to the authors of the other chapters in this volume.

Labor Force Participation

Adolescent and young adult labor force participation vary widely, both within and between nations, but in the aggregate provide some sense of how much education nations and families can afford. National data on economically active men aged 15–19 during the 1980s and 1990s show that they are less likely to work in countries with higher levels of compulsory education (U.S. Census Bureau 1999).[3] The developed country exceptions to this generalization are the Scandinavian and some western European countries, as well as the United States, Canada, Australia, and New Zealand, which have a tradition of combining education and employment (OECD 1998). China, Mali, and some South American countries also have high levels of adolescent employment among men in spite of compulsory education of at least 9 years. Young men's economic activity in most developing countries is quite high, registering employment rates above 40 percent, suggesting that at this age few young men are attending school full-time.

Clearly education in developing countries is not the normative route for men aged 15–19, in contrast to developed countries, where work is much less likely to displace education as the primary activity of young men. By entering the labor market at relatively early ages, most young men in developing countries forgo additional education and consequently the possibility of more-skilled employment. Considering that future cohorts of youth entering the labor market in developing countries will be larger than previous cohorts, there will be greater competition among young men, and increasingly women, to find formal employment. Where formal employment is not available, these youth are likely to turn to low-wage informal work that usually provides a poor income for themselves and their young families.

In contrast to teenage boys, teenage girls have low employment rates regardless of the years of compulsory education, particularly in developing countries. This is not surprising because girls' employment is discouraged in many cultures and women face the competing possibility of becoming wives and mothers at this age. Objections to girls' schooling include a reluctance to allow them freedom of mobility, concern with the lack of supervision, and a sense that it is inappropriate for women to earn money. Furthermore, women's productive work is often undercounted because much of it is income-generating activity in the informal economy or family-related businesses.

Countries with higher female teenage employment rates (30 to 60 percent or more) are either the economically developed countries, where it is common to combine education and employment, or some sub-Saharan African or Asian countries where women work in traditional female occupations. Although less than 29 percent of women aged 15–19 are employed in the Middle East and North Africa, some countries in Asia, and Latin America and the Caribbean, some high-profile export-oriented industries in these countries seek out female labor because of their willingness to accept low wages (Standing 1999). While this type of employment has the potential to change young women's life courses by delaying their entry into marriage and childbearing and possibly offering them some measure of economic independence within marriage (e.g., Wolf 1992), the low rates of overall female employment in these countries show that these trends are exceptional.

Marriage and Parenthood
As was suggested by the preceding discussion of male and female youth employment, adult roles for young men and women often follow quite distinct trajectories. While men enter into employment after they finish school, women are more likely to enter into family roles. From Lesotho to Luxembourg, over 90 percent of men aged 15–19 remain single. Far

greater regional variation exists in the percentage of women aged 15–19 remaining single. In sub-Saharan African countries and the Middle East and West Asia it is common for women to marry in their teens. In other regions there are some differences between countries. For example, among Asian nations, more than 80 percent of East and Southeast Asian women remain single throughout their teens, while fewer than 79 percent of women in Bangladesh, Nepal, Pakistan, and Iran remain single (we have no data for India, where the median age at marriage can be as low as 15 or 16 in some states). There is similar variation in Latin America and the Caribbean: more than 90 percent of women in the Caribbean nations remain single at this age, whereas only 70 to 89 percent of women in Central and South America do so.

Young women's early marriage and childbearing is a cause of concern because of the well-documented relationship between women's early entry into family roles, lower autonomy, social status, education, and higher fertility and poor child outcomes (Jejeebhoy 1995). In the regions where women are more likely to marry in their teens, they are also more likely to begin bearing children while young. Adolescent fertility rates are highest among women in sub-Saharan Africa, ranging from 50 to over 150 births per 1,000 women aged 15–19. In other developing regions young women are embarking on their childbearing careers at young ages, though the rates are not as high and are declining in many regions. The lowest teen birth rates (0–24 per 1,000 women aged 15–19) occur in Western Europe and East Asia, as well as Canada and Australia. In these more industrialized countries young women generally attend school or begin working in their teens, and it is unusual to begin having children so young. Among industrialized countries, the United States' exceptionally high teen birth rate is attributed, not to greater sexual activity, but to less information, sex education, and contraceptive use resulting from the moral ambivalence of parents, community leaders, and policy makers (Jones et al. 1989). Early childbearing is significant because it transforms young men and women from people whom society cares for and invests in, to caretakers and investors in the next generation of youth. Early marriage and childbearing shortens the period of time in which society invests in youth, particularly for women who begin childbearing earlier than men.

In reviewing data describing the timing of transitions into adult roles we see that many of these transitions are quite delayed in the industrialized countries of Europe, North America, and East Asia. In contrast, the process of entry into employment for men and marriage and parenthood for women in many developing countries is well underway in the late teens. Putting this together with the duration of education suggests that as education increases to secondary and tertiary levels it competes with entry into these adult roles, but education participation in the late teens is not widespread enough in many developing regions to have this effect.

Education does not only delay entry into marriage and parenthood by occupying youth in some other way, it also operates through the process of ideational change. Literacy and access to information allow young adults to consider a broader range of life choices. Indeed, globalization, in terms of the spread of ideas and values as well as increased industrial production and trade, powerfully transmits the notion that youth is a particular time in the life course when one should be free of adult responsibilities and develop individual talents and interests. Likewise, the rapid urbanization of many developing country populations erodes the rural-based traditions that encourage early entry into adult roles and more communal values. For example in rural societies where families practice dowry or bride-wealth, economic and cultural incentives encourage parents to arrange their child's marriage relatively early. Often these incentives are diminished in an urban context. For better or for worse, we expect that transitions into adult economic and family roles will be increasingly delayed in areas of the developing world where urbanization is expected to include more than half the population by 2015 (Arab states, East Asia (excluding China), Latin America and the Caribbean). However, change in the life context of youth is unlikely to be altered in regions with majority rural populations (sub-Saharan Africa, China, Southeast Asia and the Pacific, and South Asia).

Household Structure and Income Inequality

In previous sections we have focused on regional differences in societal investments in youth. Here, we turn to measures of variation within countries in the ability of households to invest in youth. The success and smoothness of young people's transitions into adult roles depends on the resources available to them in their parental households. The longer a young adult can remain economically dependent upon a parent, the more education and training he or she can potentially acquire in order to achieve greater socioeconomic security in the future. Without substantial national economic growth and government programs to redistribute resources to children with fewer parental resources, inequality in the parents' generation will be transmitted to their children.

Inequality in income or consumption is thus an important indicator of social inequities that shape the transition to adulthood. The standard measure of income inequality, the Gini Index, measures the extent to which the distribution of income or consumption among individuals within a population deviates from a perfectly equal distribution. Thus a Gini Index of 0 represents perfect equality, while an index of 100 indicates perfect inequality, i.e., some have all, while most have nothing. Table 2.2 shows the distribution of Gini indices by region. These figures have been adjusted for household size to provide a more consistent measure of per capita income or consumption. The greatest income or consumption inequality occurs in sub-Saharan Africa and Latin America and the Caribbean, where the Gini Index is typically greater than 40. In contrast, the lowest measures of inequality register in Europe, particularly eastern Europe and Scandinavia, where socialist income redistribution policies have mitigated inequality in the past. This difference illustrates the extent to which government social support programs attenuate household inequality, and the greater inequality that exists in countries without these programs.

The characteristics of households themselves also contribute to inequality. The presumption that children are raised in a household with two biological parents whose efforts are entirely devoted to the rearing of their children cannot be taken for granted. Other family structures, such as children living with 1 or 2 nonbiological parents (step-parents, foster parents, or other relatives) or children living in single parent homes exist alongside the biological two-parent family. Though these different family structures are sometimes associated with poor health, education, and adjustment outcomes for children, of particular concern are those families with numerous dependents per worker. This often lessens per capita household income by causing resources to be distributed among more people. Several factors contribute to greater within-household dependency ratios. Cross-national studies suggest that children in larger families are disadvantaged in terms of health and nutrition (Desai 1995). Children in single-parent households (most often headed by women) resulting from divorce, separation, widowhood, and nonmarital childbearing are also at greater risk of living in poverty (Lloyd & Desai 1992). These scant quantitative studies are supported by qualitative research.

Though we don't wish to problematize female headship per se, we are obliged to rely on data that distinguish households in this way

TABLE 2.2. *Income or Consumption Inequality – Gini Coefficients*

Region	19–29	30–39	40–49	50–63
Sub-Saharan Africa (a,b)	Rwanda	Ghana, Côte d'Ivoire, Tanzania, Mauritania, Uganda	Ethiopia, Guinea, Kenya, Nigeria, Madajascar, The Gambia, Burkina Faso, Zambia	Mali, Niger, Senegal, Lesotho, Guinea-Bissau, Zimbabwe, South Africa, Sierra Leone
The Middle East and West Asia (a,b)		Egypt, Algeria, Morocco, Israel, Republic of Yemen	Tunisia, Jordan	
East, Southeast Asia and the Pacific (a,b)		Lao PDR, Indonesia (c,d), Vietnam	China (c,d), Philippines, Thailand, Malaysia (c,d)	
South Asia (a,b)	Bangladesh, India	Sri Lanka, Pakistan, Kazakhstan (c,d), Mongolia, Kyrgyz Republic (c,d), Turkmenistan (c,d), Nepal		
Western Europe (c,d)	Austria, Denmark, Sweden, Belgium, Norway, Finland, Luxembourg, Germany	Italy, Netherlands, Spain, United Kingdom, France, Ireland, Switzerland		

(continued)

TABLE 2.2. (*continued*)

Region	19–29	30–39	40–49	50–63
Eastern Europe and the Commonwealth of Independent States (c,d)	Slovak Republic, Czech Republic, Poland (a,b), Hungary, Romania, Latvia, Belarus, Slovenia	Bulgaria, Lithuania, Moldova, Estonia	Ukraine, Russian Federation (a,b)	
Latin America and the Caribbean (c,d)			Guyana (a,b), Jamaica (a,b), Bolivia, Peru, Ecuador (a,b), Venezuela, Costa Rica, El Salvador	Nicaragua (a,b), Dominican Republic, Honduras, Mexico, Chile, Panama, Colombia, Paraguay, Guatemala, Brazil
North America (c,d)		Canada	United States	
Oceania (a,b)		Australia		Papua New Guinea

All of the data shown here are from the 1990s, except for Côte d'Ivoire, Lesotho, Sierra Leone, Malaysia, United Kingdom, France, Ireland, Switzerland, Dominican Republic, Guatemala, and Australia, whose data are from the 1980s. Each region's data follow the criteria marked next to the region name, and exceptions appear marked next to each country name: a. refers to expenditure shares by percentiles of population; b. ranked by per capita expenditure; c. refers to income shares by percentiles of population; d. ranked by per capita income.

Source: The World Bank 1999.

and acknowledge the factors correlated with single-female household headship. The reduction of adult household earners and caregivers from 2 to 1 significantly reduces the income of the household and the children in it, as well as diminishing the time the mother can devote to the care of her children. A review of research on men's family roles indicates a de-linking of marriage and parenthood around the world, with the result that fathers are often absent from their children's households (Greene & Biddlecom 2000). In Ghana, Kenya, and Malawi, for example, two-fifths of school-age children live in households without their biological fathers, while about one-third of children live in similarly fatherless households in Tanzania, Cameroon, and Zambia (Lloyd & Gage-Brandon 1994; Lloyd & Blanc 1996). Female-headed households with dependent children are also common in Latin America, the United States, and Western European countries (De Vos & Richter 1988; De Vos 1995; Farley 1996; Lestaeghe 1995). There is also evidence that children living in households without one or both of their biological parents fare poorer than those who live with both (Case, Li & McLanahan 1999). Consequently, female headship is one of the strongest predictors of child poverty (McLanahan & Sandefur 1994; Lloyd & Desai 1992; Ono-Osaki 1991).

The HIV/AIDS epidemic has left ever increasing numbers of children parentless. The Joint United Nations Programme on HIV/AIDS (1998) estimates that by mid-1996, 9 million children under age 15, over 90 percent of whom live in sub-Saharan Africa, had lost their mothers to AIDS. In Zambia, for example, a recent study showed that at least one orphan is cared for in over 35 percent of households (Baggaley et al. 1999). In other settings where the incidence of AIDS is high or increasing, many children have been orphaned or have HIV-positive mothers. General measures of child health and well-being are eroded by the loss of a child's mother or by fostering (e.g., Bledsoe 1980). Extended families have traditionally taken in orphans, but under the barrage of the current epidemic, the numbers of orphans are overwhelming the working-age adults available to support them. As a result, children – with and without AIDS – are increasingly being abandoned (Akukwe 1999). Very young children in sub-Saharan Africa have been called upon to be caregivers and to support their younger siblings and dying parents (Preble 1990). The burden on children does not bode well for young people's future, as it occurs during a period in which they would ideally receive care, rather than be caring for others.

The poverty of parental households often drives young people and their parents to great lengths to earn money. Some youth migrate, others become street beggars, and some are sold into servitude (see, e.g., Friedman 1996). In many developing countries youth move from rural to urban areas to earn money to send back to their parents (Lim 1991). Whereas men find somewhat varied employment opportunities, women are most likely to work in domestic services, entertainment, health care, or sex work. Migrant domestic workers are vulnerable to domestic violence and abuse, because they are frequently indebted to their employer for the costs of transportation, room and board, and because labor laws rarely protect domestic workers (e.g., in East Asia and the Middle East) (Cheng 1996; Osakue 1998). A huge increase has occurred in the number of Cambodian children, many of them trafficked, caught begging in Bangkok in recent years as a result of wretched economic conditions in Cambodia (Anonymous 1998d). Most trafficked children are sold or given away by parents who believe false promises of jobs and money. It is estimated that every year more than 2 million children, mostly girls, though the number of boys is increasing, are trafficked and sold for sexual purposes (Ralston, Murphy & Muldoon 1998). The scale of trafficking appears to be the greatest in Asia, although there is little reliable information on this topic. Trafficking exploits youth in every way, providing them with less than nothing for their education, health, well-being, or the quality of their future.

National Preparedness

The tremendous investments required by this unprecedented generation of young people affirm a recent assessment of the education, employment, and health needs of the nearly 1 billion teenagers in the world today as "one of the most important policy challenges in coming decades" (Gelbard et al. 1999, 37). Yet the needs vary by region. Governments must consider age structure, population growth rates, and economic resources when planning for education, health spending, and managing labor markets (Figure 2.6). How, then, are countries planning for and responding to the demands of this large global youth cohort given their diverse demographic and economic circumstances? We find considerable variation in countries' preparedness for this generation of youth.

Acknowledging the importance of education in reducing individual and national poverty (United Nations 1997a), nations have attempted

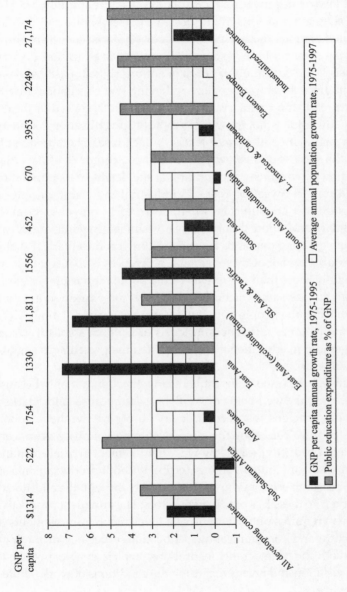

FIGURE 2.6. GNP per capita annual growth rate, annual population growth rate and public spending on education as a percentage of GNP. *Source:* UNDP 1999.

to increase education spending but are constrained by small budgets and competing budget priorities. In sub-Saharan Africa, South Asia, and Latin America and the Caribbean, where growth in GNP per capita has been low or negative, public expenditures on education are also low and stagnant and foreign aid decreasing (see Figure 2.6) (UNDP 1999; United Nations 1997a; UNESCO 2000). The large cohorts of youth entering the public school systems will send their education systems into a crisis if the education of youth is not prioritized. East Asia contrasts with these developing regions in having low population growth rates and already high primary and secondary enrollments; thus the demand for education is not growing as rapidly and educational systems are easily maintained at current levels. In fact, researchers frequently attribute the success of the newly industrialized countries of East Asia to the region's investment in education at the height of its population growth (Morris & Sweeting 1995). In industrialized countries, education expenditures are sufficient to support nearly universal primary and secondary education, though these investments in youth are threatened by the growing demands for expenditures on the elderly. What is most discouraging about these regional differences is that countries in which slightly more than *one-seventh* of the population is under age 15 spend roughly the same fraction of their GNP on education as countries in which young people constitute nearly *half* the population. Given the extreme national differences in levels of GNP, this constitutes an even bigger gap in educational spending than the percentages suggest (Figure 2.6).

We focus on the issue of investments in education not only because it contributes to the well-being of youth but also because labor markets in developing regions will face difficulty absorbing this huge cohort of young people. The labor force in developing countries is concentrated in low-productivity and low-wage employment in rural areas and the informal sector (United Nations 1997b). Without productive investments, increases in economic growth occur only through the addition of more workers to these less productive sectors. The growth of productive employment requires public and private investment, improvements in infrastructure and communications, education, especially at the high school level, and democratic institutions, which enable people to enforce legislation and norms regarding the conditions of work (United Nations 1997b).

Industrialized nations face a similar problem of training or retraining workers in new skills that are appropriate for growing areas of their economies, namely, finance, insurance, real estate, health care, and business services. The restructuring of industrial production, including the use of more capital-intensive production methods and the relocation of manufacturing production to developing countries, has left many low-skilled workers unemployed and unprepared for employment in growth sectors of these economies. During the 1980s and 1990s unemployment and income inequality grew in developed countries, due in part to this predicament (UNDP 1999). For this reason, tertiary education, particularly for adults outside of traditional school ages, is a high priority in industrialized countries.

We emphasize human capital development globally because it is key to reducing income inequality (World Bank 1995). A more educated labor force – that includes not only people who are already the most wealthy – can keep up with technological innovations in production and expand into information-based economic sectors, both critical to participation in the global economy. Furthermore, income and job growth propel the creation of "macroeconomic, legal, and broad institutional conditions that would lead to high savings and investment rates" (United Nations 1997b, 8). These conditions provide not only the capital for economic growth but also the basis for social protection for a nation's citizenry.

But education alone is not sufficient. It must be accompanied by guarantees of workers' basic benefits and rights, gender equity in employment, equal access to productive resources, especially credit, income transfers, and other social protections, especially during crisis and adjustment. In Latin America, austerity programs in the 1980s removed many of the social programs providing a safety net for those with the fewest resources. An Inter-American Development Bank (IADB) report concluded that "Of greatest importance is the need to maintain support for core education and health services to avoid irreversible losses in human investment; yet this was done poorly in Latin America in the 1980s" (IADB 1998, 122). This experience informs us that the long-term costs of doing away with social supports during economic crisis are greater than the short-term savings (UNDP 1999, 92). In addition, the process of globalization and the shift to market economies has been associated with rising inequality (UNDP 1999). In Russia, for example, income inequality has increased sharply since the start of its economic reforms (United Nations 1997b). The increasing decentralization of health and education in many countries has highlighted the inability of nongovernmental organizations and the private sector to compensate for services previously systematically provided by the government. The wealthy are able to purchase the best health and education for their children, thus increasing inequality in spite of widespread education.

Recent analyses of the relationship between inequality and development affirm that "gross inequities between people not only are unjust but represent a squandering of human resources and a potential brake on socio-economic development" (United Nations 1997a). Over the past 30 years, however, the gap between the rich and the poor has widened, both between and within countries. From 1960 to 1993, the gap between average per capita incomes in the industrialized and the developing countries tripled, and the richest one-fifth of the world's population went from taking 70 percent to taking 85 percent of global income (United Nations 1997a). Furthermore, a new and disturbing widening has occurred in the gap between the poorest developing countries and other developing nations (UNDP 1999). This gap could easily be closed if international lenders forgave the debt owed by developing countries, just as the German debt incurred during the Marshall program after World War II was forgiven.

Conclusion

The future prospects of youth ultimately depend upon the families, communities, and nations into which they are born. Today, as the population grows more rapidly in countries with fewer comparative advantages in the global economy, more children are being born outside of the few privileged corners of the world. For this reason we address issues of equity more than any other issue – equity within the family, within the community and nation, and between nations. Insofar as youth is a period in which parents and society invest in youth, developing their human capital, the inequalities of today are reproduced.

We've identified low dependency ratios resulting from the timing of fertility decline as potentially opening up a demographic window of opportunity for countries by creating a low youth and elderly dependency ratio. Of course, not all nations experience this demographic opportunity in the same way. It depends upon the speed at which mortality and fertility decline and the difference in the timing of the 2 declines. In general, this window is open only briefly in countries that experience relatively rapid and nearly simultaneous fertility and mortality declines. Although there are other factors that contribute to nations' growth potential, we emphasize the demographic opportunity because it is a major incentive for governments to invest in young people's health and education and to plan for their future employment. Nations with shorter-term priorities that focus, for example, on repaying international debt or engaging in civil or international conflicts that prevent them from investing in youth, will not reap the maximum benefits of the demographic opportunity, nor will youth receive the investments that they deserve.

The world's regions share some challenges in investing in youth: primarily reducing poverty and inequality. Making health, education, and labor market opportunities universally available is critical to promoting the well-being of all youth and fostering their hope for the future. Under any circumstances this is difficult, particularly when countries must contend with international debt and economies in transition, as in Latin America and the Caribbean and eastern Europe and the Commonwealth of Independent States. When the population is growing but the economy is not growing much, as in the case of sub-Saharan Africa and South Asia, the challenges are even greater. However, income inequality has increased even in the countries best positioned to reduce it as a result of reforms in income redistribution programs in countries subject to structural adjustment conditions and those opening their economies (UNDP 1999). This is one of the dangers for youth of the overreliance on markets to distribute what should be public goods: health, education, and equal opportunities for employment.

Gender equity is also an important component of inequality, though we have only described its relationship with education and household composition here. The need for equitable domestic relations between men and women has come to the fore in international discussions of population and development policy. No manner of programs or investments in women can overcome the resistance of the men in their lives – and indeed some women in their families – to the kinds of social changes that women's education and labor force participation bring about (United Nations 1995). The central role of women in transmitting to their children the benefits of their good health, education, and ability to mobilize resources is critical to investment in future generations. Yet in most parts of the world, the intersection of youth and sex keeps girls from accessing the resources they need, such as education, employment, and autonomy, for the development of their full potential (Mensch, Bruce, & Greene 1998).

We close with a review of issues that are likely to be salient for specific regions in the next decades, focusing on how the dependency ratios might influence investments in youth, but also speculating on particular regional issues. Forward-thinking policy makers in East Asia took advantage of the "demographic gift" of low dependency ratios that they began experiencing in the 1970s by investing in health and education programs and fostering growth based on mass employment. The economic expansion the region experienced in the 1970s and 1980s encouraged both private and public investment in youth. In general, countries in Southeast Asia and the Pacific are following the example of East Asia in trying to industrialize based on greater participation in world markets, but they are hampered by lower levels of development and the history of military conflicts in the region. Nevertheless, the area receives substantial development assistance and is experiencing high rates of per capita GNP annual growth, which look promising for both public and private investments in youth (UNDP 1999).

South Asia is an economically disadvantaged region facing significant obstacles to investing in youth. South Asia has experienced a slow decline in fertility, delaying and weakening the potential of low dependency ratios. Economic growth per capita in the region is low compared to many other developing countries. However, this region has experienced greater growth in primary and secondary enrollment ratios than other regions, suggesting a commitment to investing in education. But in South Asia, the educational and health systems do not do as well by women as by men and are further undermined by widespread poverty, inequality, and corruption. One indication of the barriers individuals face to improving their circumstances is that there is a significant migration flow between India, Bangladesh, Pakistan, and destination industrialized countries. This may signal the promise of remittances from the relatively educated people who leave, but it also indicates a significant loss of human capital to other countries. Although the incidence of AIDS is currently not terribly high, it is increasing rapidly due to a reluctance to mobilize comprehensive prevention programs. These trends bode ill for coming generations of youth in South Asia.

Countries in the Middle East and North Africa have invested in education, infrastructure, and resources that will expand labor market opportunities (Bloom & Canning 1999b). This should pay off as the large generation of young people moves into the labor force. However, inequity in distribution as evidenced by low gross enrollments in primary and secondary schools and the emphasis on more costly tertiary education may hamper the outcome. Some of this inequality is also due to the fact that education and health services are not fully extended to girls. Thus the future of youth may be marked by regionally characteristic inequalities.

Latin America and the Caribbean may be able to take advantage of their lower dependency ratios, but the debt burdens and austerity programs that many nations took on during the 1980s and 1990s have diminished their investments in youth. The lack of growth in educational enrollments in Latin America and the Caribbean suggest, that nations in this region are missing the opportunity presented by low dependency ratios. The already high education enrollments attained there and a prolonged period of youth have sustained a relatively high level of resources devoted to youth. However, job creation is critical in this region. Furthermore, the region is beset with high levels of income inequality that prevent its countries from making the most of their wealth. If formal employment with good wages cannot be created for the youth cohorts entering the labor market, these young adults may become discouraged, turning against themselves and against their communities and countries.

Eastern Europe and the Commonwealth of Independent States are expected to experience very low dependency ratios in the near future due to the stagnation or even reversals in life expectancy, accompanied by low fertility. The governments and economies of these regions are changing so rapidly that it is difficult to assess how well prepared they are to invest in youth. It depends largely on whether these countries are able to maintain a tax base with which they can continue to provide public health and education to the population.

Europe and North America, both industrialized regions, share the challenge of growing elderly dependency ratios. These regions long ago experienced gradual fertility declines and more recently a baby boom that provided a small "demographic gift." The baby boom resulted from the concentration of births, particularly in allied countries after World War II. This allowed for a brief period of low dependency when the baby boom cohort entered the market; as they retire the population will quickly age, however, creating a burden on the working population. These regions need to create well-paid, relatively low-skilled employment as their economies restructure, and they need to retrain the existing labor force to meet the needs of their economies. Furthermore, the aging of their populations presents a situation in which the elderly have unprecedented economic, demographic, and political influence over youth. Without enlightened public policy, direct competition between the interests of the young and the old will arise in the allocation of public resources (Preston 1984; Fussell 2002).

Youth in sub-Saharan Africa face a significantly different set of circumstances. The proportion of youth in these countries is huge and the

56   *Elizabeth Fussell and Margaret E. Greene*

resources scarce. Other regions are able to devote resources to education and job creation since the health and other basic needs of their
populations are being met. Many nations in Africa, in contrast, must
devote resources to all of these areas simultaneously while also focusing on the acute health crisis of HIV/AIDS. The AIDS epidemic has
devastated the region, not only by taking the lives of adults who might
otherwise be working from the population, but by depriving millions
of young people of the parental support they need to navigate youth to
a healthy and well-equipped adulthood.

To conclude, we return to our observation about the exceptional conditions faced by today's young people as a result of their absolute and
relative numbers. There is little that is predictable about the future, but
one thing we do know is the numbers of young people coming of age
in the next few decades. The absolute size of their cohorts is a direct
indication of future demand for schools, health care, and employment
training. The size of their cohorts relative to other population age groups
suggests the competition youth will face for public resources. National
ability to prepare for these youth cohorts depends on each country's
place in the global economy, the international assistance, and the attention it gives to planning for the future of its young people.

Notes

1. Because the data for this chapter are derived from various sources with
diverse dates, names, and classifications, there is some understandable
inconsistency between some tables and graphs. For details about the categories used to describe regions, levels of schooling, or other concepts, please
contact the authors or refer to the cited data sources.
2. International Conference on Population and Development in Cairo, 1994;
Fourth World Conference on Women in Beijing, 1995.
3. The data are difficult to compare and sometimes to quantify because of
national variation in the age ranges for which data are collected, the definitions of labor force participation (full-time, part-time), and the extent to
which informal or black market employment is measured.

References

Anonymous. 1998d. A new kind of trafficking: Child beggars in Asia. Scared,
hungry, enslaved. *World of Work*. 26:17–19.
Akukwe, C. 1999. HIV/AIDS in African children: A major calamity that deserves urgent global action. *Journal of HIV/AIDS Prevention and Education for
Adolescents and Children*. 3(3):5–24.

Baggaley, R., J. Sulwe, M. Chilala, & C. Mashambe. 1999. HIV stress in primary school teachers in Zambia. *Bulletin of The World Health Organization.* 77(3):284–287.

Berne, L. & B. Huberman. 1999. *European approaches to adolescent sexual behavior and responsibility.* Washington, D.C.: Advocates for Youth.

Bledsoe, C. 1980. *Women and marriage in Kpelle society.* Stanford, CA: Stanford University Press.

Bledsoe, C. H. & B. Cohen. 1993. *Social dynamics of adolescent fertility in sub-Saharan Africa.* Washington, D.C.: National Academy Press.

Bloom, D. E. & D. Canning. 1999b. The demographic transition and economic growth in the Middle East and North Africa. Paper presented at the Fourth Annual Conference of the Middle East Institute and the World Bank, April 14.

Brown, L. R. & B. Halweil. 1999. Breaking out or breaking down. *World Watch.* September/October: 20–29.

Case, A., Li, I. F., & McLanahan, S. 1999. Household resource allocation in stepfamilies: Darwin reflects on the plight of Cinderella. *American Economic Review Papers and Proceedings.* 89(2):234–38.

Cheng, S. J. 1996. Migrant women domestic workers in Hong Kong, Singapore and Taiwan: A comparative analysis. *Asian and Pacific Migration Journal.* 5(1):139–52.

Csillag, C. 1999. Sex education is key to combatting AIDS in Brazil. *Lancet* Jun 26; 353(9171):2221.

Desai, S. 1995. When are children from large families disadvantaged? Evidence from cross-national analyses. *Population Studies.* Jul; 49(2):195–210.

De Vos, S. & K. Richter. 1988. Household headship among unmarried mothers in six Latin American countries. *International Journal of Comparative Sociology.* 24:214–229.

De Vos, S. 1995. *Household composition in Latin America.* New York: Plenum Press.

Farley, R. 1996. *The new American reality: Who we are, how we got there, where we are going.* New York: Russell Sage Foundation.

Friedman, R. I. 1996. India's shame. *Nation.* Apr 8, 262(14):11–20.

Fussell, E. 2002. Youth in aging societies. *The changing adolescent experience: Societal trends and the transition to adulthood,* eds. Jeylan Mortimer & Reed Larson. New York: Cambridge University Press.

Gelbard, A., C. Haub, & M. M. Kent. 1999. World population beyond six billion. *Population Bulletin.* March; 54(1). Washington, D.C.: Population Reference Bureau.

Greene, M. E. & A. E. Biddlecom. 2000. Absent and problematic men: Demographic accounts of male reproductive roles. *Population and Development Review.* 26(1):81–115.

Hirsch, J. S. & G. Barker. 1992. *Adolescents and unsafe abortion in developing countries: A preventable tragedy.* Washington, D.C.: Center for Population Options.

Inter-American Development Bank (IADB). 1998. *Facing up to inequality.* Washington, D.C.

Jejeebhoy, S. J. 1995. *Women's education, autonomy, and reproductive behaviour: Experience from developing countries.* Oxford: Clarendon Press.

Joint United Nations Programme on HIV/AIDS. 1998. How HIV affects children. AIDS Alert. Jan, 2:13(1 Supplement).

Jones, E. F., J. D. Forrest, N. Goldman, S. K. Henshaw, J. Silverman, & A. Tores. 1989. *Pregnancy, contraception, and family planning services in industrialized countries.* New Haven, CT: Yale University Press.

Kaijage, T. J. 1990. Schoolgirl pregnancies in Tanzania. In *Maternal mortality and morbidity: a call to women for action,* [compiled by] Women's Global Network for Reproductive Rights and Latin American and Caribbean Women's Health Network/Isis International Women's Global Network for Reproductive Rights:15. Amsterdam, Netherlands.

Kulin, H. E. 1988. Adolescent pregnancy in Africa: A programmatic focus. *Social Science and Medicine.* 26(7):727–735.

Lesthaeghe, R. 1995. The second demographic transition in Western countries: An interpretation. In *Gender and family change in industrialized countries,* eds. K. Oppenheim Mason and A. M. Jensen. Oxford: Clarendon Press.

Lim, L. L. 1991. The structural determinants of female migration. Internal migration of women in developing countries. Proceedings of the United Nations Expert Meeting on the Feminization of Internal Migration. Aguas Calientes, Mexico, October 1991:22–25. New York: United Nations.

Lloyd, C. B. & S. Desai. 1992. Children's living arrangements in developing countries. *Population Research and Policy Review.* 11:193–216.

Lloyd, C. B. & A. J. Gage-Brandon. 1994. High fertility and children's schooling in Ghana: Sex differences in parental contributions and educational outcomes. *Population Studies.* 48(2):293–306.

Lloyd, C. B. & A. K. Blanc. 1996. Children's schooling in sub-Saharan Africa: The role of fathers, mothers, and others. *Population and Development Review.* 22(2):265–298.

Massey, D. S., J. Arango, G. Hugo, A. Kouacouci, A. Pellegrino, & J. E. Taylor. 1999. *Worlds in motion: Understanding international migration at the end of the millennium.* Oxford: Clarendon Press.

McLanahan, S. & G. Sandefur. 1994. *Growing up in a single parent home: What hurts, what helps.* Boston, MA: Harvard University Press.

Mensch, B. S., J. Bruce, & M. E. Greene. 1998. *The uncharted passage: Girls' adolescence in the developing world.* New York: The Population Council.

Morris, P. & A. Sweeting. 1995. *Education and development in East Asia.* New York and London: Garland Publishing.

Nanda, P. 2000. Health sector reforms in Zambia: Implications for reproductive health and rights. Takoma Park, MD: Center for Health and Gender Equity, working paper.

Ono-Osaki, K. 1991. Female headed households in developing countries: By choice or by circumstances? Paper presented at the Demographic and Health Surveys World Conference, August 5–7, 1991. Washington, D.C.

Organization for Economic Cooperation and Development. 1998. Education at a glance, OECD education indicators.

Osakue, G. 1998. Exposing age-old problems: Trafficking in women in Nigeria. *Women's World.* (32):25–6.

Preble, E. A. 1990. Impact of HIV/AIDS on African children. *Social Science & Medicine.* 31(6):671–80.

Preston, S. H. 1984. Children and the elderly: Divergent paths for America's dependents. *Demography.* Nov: 21(4):435–457.

Ralston E., E. Murphy, & B. Muldoon. 1998. Sexual trafficking: An international public health problem. Women's reproductive health initiative. Global Healthlink. Nov–Dec:10, 12.

Raymundo, C. 2000. Salud ocupacional y el significado del trabajo para los jovenes. Presented at the seminar, Trabajando con hombres jovenes: Salud, sexualidad, genero y prevencion de violencia. March: Queretaro, Mexico.

Sen, G., A. Germain, & L. C. Chen. 1994. Reconsidering population policies: Ethics, development, and strategies for change. In *Population policies reconsidered: Health, empowerment and rights,* eds. Sen, G., A. Germain, and L. C. Chen, Boston, MA: Harvard University Press.

Sinding, S. W. 2000. Policies at the end of the demographic transition: A speculation. Paper presented at the Population Association of America Annual Meeting, Los Angeles, CA, March: 22–25.

Standing, G. 1999. Global feminization through flexible labor: A theme revisited. *World Development.* 27:583–602.

Tzannatos, Z. 1998. Women's labor incomes. In *Women in the third world: an encyclopedia of contemporary issues,* ed. N. P. Stromquist, New York, NY: Garland Publishing.

United Nations. 1990. World population prospects, sales no. E.91.XIII.4. UN: New York.

United Nations. 1993. Age structure changes in 1950–1990. *Demographic yearbook special issue: Population ageing and the situation of elderly persons.* New York: United Nations.

United Nations. 1995. Report of the international conference on population and development, Cairo, September 5–13, 1994. New York: United Nations.

United Nations. 1997. Report on the world social situation. New York: United Nations, Department of International Economic and Social Affairs.

United Nations. 1997a. *Critical trends: Global change and sustainable development.* New York: United Nations, Department for Policy Coordination and Sustainable Development.

United Nations. 1997b. *Aspects of world employment strategy.* New York: United Nations, Department of Economic and Social Affairs.

United Nations. 1998. *World population prospects: The 1998 revision.* Volume III, Department of Economic and Social Affairs, Population Division. New York: United Nations.

United Nations Development Program (UNDP). 1999. *Human development report.* New York: Oxford University Press.

United Nations Education, Scientific, and Cultural Organization (UNESCO). 1995. *Statistical yearbook.* New York: United Nations.

United Nations Education, Scientific, and Cultural Organization (UNESCO). 2000. *Statistical yearbook.* New York: United Nations.

United Nations Education, Scientific, and Cultural Organization (UNESCO). 2000. Education for all, 2000 assessment. Dakar, Senegal, April 2000:26–28. New York: United Nations.

United States Census Bureau. 1999. International data base. www.census.gov.

Williamson, J., 1998. Growth, distribution, and demography: Some lessons from history. *Explorations in Economic History.* 35:241–271.

Wolf, D. L. 1992. *Factory daughters: Gender, household dynamics, and rural industrialization in Java.* Berkeley, CA: University of California Press.

Woodhall, M. 1994. The context of economic austerity and structural adjustment. In *Coping with crisis: austerity, adjustment, and human resources,* ed. J. Samoff. London: Cassell.

World Bank. 1995. Priorities and strategies for education: A World Bank review. Washington, D.C.: The World Bank.

Worthman, C. & J. W. Whiting. 1987. Social change in adolescent sexual behavior, mate selection, and premarital pregnancy rates in a Kikuyu community. *Ethos.* 15:145–165.

3

Adolescence in Sub-Saharan Africa

An Image Constructed from Africa's Triple Inheritance

A. Bame Nsamenang

Introduction

Adolescent psychology is a Eurocentric enterprise. Western social scientists, for example, have demonstrated remarkable ethnocentrism and have, with few recent exceptions, presented their findings as relevant to the human race (Lamb 1992; Munroe, Munroe, & Whiting 1981). Most of them have not had the motivation or the opportunity to consider the implications of their Eurocentrism. The ethnocentrism has been so overwhelming that the majority of both scholars and lay persons are unaware that the field would have been different had adolescence been "discovered" within the cultural conditions and life circumstances different than those of Europe and North America, say, in Africa.

The history of the discipline translates virtually into a tale of how research on adolescence emerged, developed, and consolidated as a Eurocentric project, of which the American model now dominates the field. This means, regrettably, that research efforts have so far failed to capture what adolescence truly is in its global context. Instead, scholars have tended to create, or more accurately, to recast, the African or other non-Western images of adolescence in the shadow of Euro-American adolescence. With this lopsided state of the field, the most compelling scientific project becomes the development of inclusive perspectives, which attempt to bring together the diverse ways by which all societies seek to understand and handle the challenges posed by their budding adults, adolescents, and youth. In so doing, it is perhaps instructive to act on the notion that adolescent psychology is a subjective and culturally diverse subject matter that traverses several disciplinary boundaries. Adolescence is a cultural process in the sense that adolescents everywhere develop in niches that have been constructed through centuries of cultural evolution (Nsamenang 1999). Indeed, between the "universal humanity" and "special individuality" of every adolescent, and indeed every human being, lies the large part "that is created by the culture handed down" by his or her society (Maquet 1972, 5).

This chapter attempts to summarize what sub-Saharan Africans regard as adolescence and how they handle adolescent life. As they seek to pass on what they know and have learned throughout history, their hope is to ensure not merely the survival and preparation of the next generation, but also that of their culture. In the chapter, I present "glimpses" of adolescence on the subcontinent from the literature available, rather than provide a comprehensive picture of national trends, which would require much more space and effort. Nevertheless, an attempt is made to assess the subcontinent's standing and prospects on some key indicators of adolescence relative to other world regions. The main shortcoming of the chapter is the limited geographical reference of the literature, albeit with greater focus on Cameroon, Kenya, and South Africa. In spite of the diversity that is said to characterize sub-Saharan Africa, the relevant literature on other countries was not available to permit, at least, an overview of the diversity. In a sense, this chapter is a selective summary of some important themes on adolescence in some sub-Saharan African countries.

Four key themes run through this chapter. First, the distinction between features of adolescence for rural versus urban youth is evident. Second, countries in the subcontinent display considerable ecological and socioeconomic diversity and cultural heterogeneity, but they are not elaborated upon. For instance, it is common knowledge that the physical differences between the towns of former French and British colonies (Gale n.d.) reflect differences in their colonial heritages, and eventually their effects on civic involvement, access to educational and economic opportunities, especially for girls in particular, and youth in general. Such differences are magnified in Cameroon, a melting pot of over 240 ethnicities, whose common German experience and separate British and French colonial legacies, in LeVine's (1976) view, provide marked contrasts not only in language, law, administration, and education, but also in much less tangible matters as political style and expectations. Of course, such differences are expected to, and indeed do engender divergent perceptions and opportunities for youth. The 3rd theme, imported images of adolescent development, emerges from Africa's history. The impact of foreign influences is perceptible throughout the chapter but not fully instantiated with specific data, due to word limitation and the nonavailability of the relevant literature. Finally, the pervasive theme is the coexistence of a dual set of realities, the indigenous and the exogenous.

In spite of the heterogeneity of sub-Saharan Africa, Maquet (1972) perceived "a certain common quality" inherent in Africa's patterns of adaptation to the ecology, the colonial experience, and the process of acculturation. To her, "Africanity" refers to "the totality of cultural features common to the hundreds of societies of sub-Saharan Africa" (Maquet 1972, 54). This perhaps justifies Diop's (1960) notion of the cultural unity of Africa. Accordingly, it may not be totally wrong to think about an African culture because there exist peculiarly African ideas, practices, and issues that stand in sharp contrast to the group of cultures loosely known as Western (Serpell 1992).

My hope is that an Afrocentric perspective on adolescence will begin to inform the psychological community, especially in the West, to rethink current assumptions and norms, and to become more open to alternative viewpoints on adolescent matters. Thus, the goal of this chapter is to introduce a perspective against which to gauge the extent to which some normative elements of adolescence constructed within Euro-American worldviews are inappropriate for Africans (Nsamenang & Dawes 1998) and the global nature of adolescence. One modest contribution in this direction is perhaps this author's (Nsamenang 1992a) characterization of African social ontogeny as a cumulative process of social integration into the family and community that Serpell (1994) claimed differs in theoretical focus from the more individualistic perspectives on ontogenesis that dominate Western paradigms. Readers are more likely to gain from this chapter because an Afrocentric view on adolescence is ordained by a worldview that constitutes a very different frame of reference from that which informs contemporary developmental psychology (Serpell 1994). Thus, an African view of adolescence and adolescent life can enrich the discipline, informing it about what are, or are not, universal aspects of adolescence (Nsamenang 1999). More specifically, it invites Euro-American social scientists and Western-trained social scientists of all nations to critically question their motives for neglecting or undermining sub-Saharan African or similar psychologies and views on adolescence (Holdstock 2000).

General Indicators for Adolescent Development in Sub-Saharan Africa

Sub-Saharan Africa stretches from the northern borders of Senegal and Sudan to South Africa. It houses a population of over 500 million people shared unevenly by about 45 nation-states that differ markedly in physical and demographic profile, colonial experience, political structure, and other important cultural traits. About half of this population is children under the age of 15 years, while less than 5 percent are over the age of 60 (Serpell 1984). Thus, sub-Saharan Africa is a young subcontinent; its child and adolescent cohorts make up over 60 percent of the total population. For instance, persons 35 years of age and younger constitute 75 percent of the population of South Africa (Mokwena 1999). In the vast majority of African countries, females and youth outnumber the rest of the demographic cohorts. Age structure determines national demands, labor needs, the dependency ratio, and patterns of personal and public expenditure (Nsamenang 1992a), hence the necessity to understand adolescence and youth, the future hope of any nation.

Development assistance was meant to set in motion a "modernization" process to assist Africa to catch up with "progress." Development, referring to the changes over time in demographic and societal, rather than individual, phenomena, has been monitored in terms of Westernized socioeconomic indicators – per capita income, accessibility to potable water, life expectancy, nutritional status, literacy and mortality rates, incidence of diseases, etc. In its 4th development decade, sub-Saharan Africa is performing much worse than any other world region on these and other indicators. For instance, living standards have declined to levels much lower than at independence, and there is an absolute increase in the number of people living in abject poverty (United Nations Development Program 1996; UNDP). Paradoxically, Africa is a rich continent whose people are poor and are growing poorer (Nsamenang 1998). Associated with or caused by inadequate water supply and poor sanitation, some 80 percent of illnesses are preventable.

In spite of the poor resource bases for and constraints to adolescent life in Africa, it is essential not to lose sight of the indigenous perspectives Africans deploy in facing their adversities. For instance, when the people of Darfur in Western Sudan faced drought and famine, their primary concern was not to ward off starvation, but instead to preserve social cohesion, the basis of their way of life (De Waal 1989). The point here is that Africans *do* come to terms with severe disasters and extreme poverty with indigenous strategies. Thus, when addressing the undesired condition of African adolescents, it seems advisable not to ignore or dismiss outright indigenous inputs, but to focus on how traditional ways of life continue to have relevance alongside the new (Ellis 1978).

Theoretical and Methodological Considerations

The purpose of this section is to draw attention to the conceptual complexity of constructing or reconstructing adolescence and adolescent life in Africa's multicultural, hybrid contexts. In so doing, it also briefly identifies some methodological shortcomings in the literature that has been reviewed.

Africa has irreversibly been drawn into a global culture that is essentially Eurocentric. The process of acculturation and globalization has bestowed on contemporary Africa a dual politicoeconomic and cultural system of old indigenous traditions and imported legacies. Accordingly, adolescence and adolescent experiences in Africa today are shaped by the "acculturative stress" and "behavioral shifts" incidental to the coexistence of the endogenous and the exogenous. The enculturative, acculturative, and globalizing forces have wrought profound changes on institutions, value foundations, and the perceptions of Africans, but nowhere have they led to the total extinction of indigenous systems (Bradley & Weisner 1997; Nsamenang 1992a). This has, however, produced a marginal population whose adults, teenagers, and children are groping desperately to reconcile within individual and collective psyches the ambivalences and contradictions of a confusing cultural braid.

This cultural braid is a more complex theoretical reality than has hitherto been articulated and presented. It is difficult to address this overlay of cultures without being polemical about the apparent neglect of the indigenous component that differs markedly from alien fragments, which unfortunately tend to be more valued and preferred.

Theoretical Complexity: A Triple Cultural Heritage of the Indigenous and the Exogenous

Undoubtedly all African societies have been exposed to external influences (Ellis 1978), albeit to varying degrees across rural and urban communities. Thus, in sub-Saharan Africa today, indigenous and foreign forces and images exist together in the same communities and individuals, in what Mazrui (1986) has termed a triple heritage. Africa's triple inheritance pertains to the extent to which exogenous influences now coexist or have penetrated and transformed or stagnated the institutional frameworks, social thought, knowledge systems, and values as well as customary practices of preexisting, indigenous Africa. It is a restive, hybrid cultural character produced by the interaction of a deep-seated indigenous component with fragments of alien forces, dominated in places by Arab-Islamic influences or Western-Christian legacies (see Figure 3.1). The Western-Christian strand contains an intrusive Darwinian, scientific motive, whereas the Eastern-Arabic input includes a fundamentalist-jihad element.

The cultural braid occurs in diverse shades across nations, families, social classes, and individual lives as well as across rural and urban settings. Secular, religious, economic, and other dimensions of the braid inspire multiple images of the human person and adolescent experience. Consequently, adolescent life becomes much more complicated as these multiple images overlap; they may coexist harmoniously in the same community, household, and individual life, or they may sometimes conflict and transgress each other. Thus, a conceptualization that ignores or trivializes how various strands of Africa's rich cultural braid mesh to shape and sharpen adolescence and adolescent life in the city or countryside can portray only an incomplete picture.

Methodological Issues

Efforts to obtain the relevant literature revealed that a good portion of the printed literature on Africa has been written by foreign authors and that it is easier to access from abroad than from inside the continent. Some of the studies that have been reviewed can be faulted on conceptual and methodological grounds, and much of the research was conducted within the framework and shadow of current research trends in Europe and North America. In this direction, Macleod (1999a) points out how, with few exceptions, the South African literature on teenage pregnancy reverberates early American and British research. This implies that aspects of phenomena peculiar to Africa have been ignored or improperly attended to, given the differentness of African social reality. One major methodological problem facing South African research, like research elsewhere on the continent, is the nonuse of comparative or control groups in quantitative studies (Macleod 1999b); the bulk of research is exploratory.

Furthermore, there are few longitudinal studies, meaning that fluid variables like self-esteem, family functioning, and many others are measured only once. As Breackwell (1993) points out, this is problematic

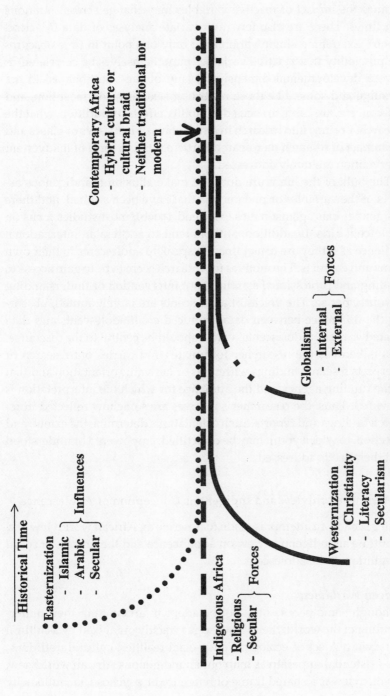

FIGURE 3.1. The externalization of African outlooks: Africa's cultural braid. *Source:* Nsamenang 2000

Historical Time →

Easternization — Islamic / Arabic / Secular } **Influences**

Contemporary Africa
- Hybrid culture or cultural braid
- Neither traditional nor modern

Globalism
- Internal } **Forces**
- External

Westernization
- Christianity
- Literacy
- Secularism

Indigenous Africa
- Religious } **Forces**
- Secular

because the impact of reactive variables may change across situations and times. There are also few multivariate analyses of data (Macleod 1999b). Examining single variables at only one point in time obscures the possibility that reactive variables may themselves be correlated or have a developmental dimension. Many of the questions asked are sensitive and some, like those regarding sexuality, contraception, and self-concept, are liable to social desirability effects. In addition, what the researcher brings into research in terms of his or her views or biases and the impact of research on research participants as a form of inadvertent intervention are rarely addressed.

The bulk of the literature does not make allusion to indigenous aspects of the variables or phenomena that have been studied, and there is a gender bias against males (Macleod 1999b); most studies focus on adolescent girls. In addition, authors tend to address an international audience as if they are constrained to speak to adolescents in their own terms and contexts. The motives for research seem to be to gain access to funding and professional standing, not intervention or understanding of youth, per se. The voices of adolescents are largely muted, obscuring the difference between data produced *about* adolescents and data created *by* them. Adolescents' voices should be central to the discourse. This is because the researcher formulates and carries out research or interprets research findings within his or her value orientation and that of the funding agency and the audience for which the interpretation is provided. Thus, the researcher's motives are somehow reflected in research findings and reports. Such orientations determine the extent, and direction, to which youth may be objectified, empowered or understood and their needs addressed.

African Worldview and Indigenous Conception of Adolescence

In this section an attempt is made to describe an African worldview and to outline an indigenous view on adolescence and the process of social integration of the adolescent.

African Worldview

Although some people may not be adept in articulating their understanding of the world, their knowledge is tacitly organized by a cultural worldview. A set of ecological and social realities, cultural traditions, and existential imperatives map out an indigenous African worldview. A worldview is a shared frame of reference or psychosocial outlook by which members of a particular culture perceive or make sense of the universe and the place of the human being in it (Nsamenang 1992a). Social representations shape social interactions and impose an imperative on members and, for our purpose, on adolescents to adopt a particular social and cultural identity.

Worldview is psychologically salient because its central concern is the fate of the individual. But African notions of individuality and autonomy are essentially relational and interdependent, not individualistic and independent. Thus, the African worldview visualizes the child as an active agent, developing in a sociocultural field in which full personhood is a matter of assent, acquired by degrees during ontogeny (Nsamenang 2000). In this sense, becoming an adult is a gradual process of incremental maturation. In their assent to adulthood, adolescents construct and modify their social identities through successive interpersonal encounters and experiences that make up their ontogenetic history. For example, adolescents are obliged to construct a gender and ethnic identity consistent with the cultural scripts and gender demands of their worldviews and economic obligations.

Indigenous Conceptions of Adolescence
In visualizing the human person in terms of its "becoming" (Erny 1968), the African worldview conceives of the adolescent or socialized neophyte as growing out of childhood and poised for an adulthood that lies in the future. In African social ontogeny, then, adolescence is a "way station" between the stages of social apprenticeship in childhood and the full social integration into adult life. It begins with social entrée, a brief transitional period that may be approximated to puberty, that marks the beginning of definitive priming into and preparation for adult status and roles (see Nsamenang 1992a).

A useful metaphor in African social thought that addresses a gradual ontogenetic progress is the *seed*, nursed to maturity in a sociological garden (Nsamenang 1992a) in which roles are shared among adults, adolescents, and children. Broadly conceived, indigenous African socialization can be regarded as cultivation into and through pivotal roles at different points of life. Inherent in each developmental stage is a distinct task, conceptualized in terms of important transitions between patterns of social participation that address the culture's definition of children, family, and their welfare. Adolescents are offered different opportunities to begin to make sense of the adult roles toward which they are directed. Adolescence, thus, is not an ambiguous stage; it is a distinct phase of development within African social ontogeny. Until about the age of 6, socialization is organized such that both boys and girls are cared for by the mother or other female adults; thereafter, the socialization of preadolescent boys and girls increasingly comes under the guidance of the same-sex parent or older sibling. This gender division of labor permits preadolescent and teenage children to learn from elder siblings and adults of the same sex, assisting them and copying their roles as they share their work.

The most formal phase of socialization or education is during the ritual celebration of puberty. Thus, new roles are assumed by degree, causing minimal strain. The social internship that precedes this *rite de passage* or developmental transition is designed to cultivate virtuous character and instill values of cooperation and generosity. Typically, the initiation of adolescent boys (*wonle ntsum* for the Nso of Cameroon), including circumcision, is a collective affair that marks the transition from the company of children and women to that of adult men. In some societies, the initiation of adolescent girls (*wonle ngon* in Nso) is subtler and less public as it focuses on training for proficiency in housekeeping and societal reproduction. The puberty rite marks the point at which adolescent boys and girls begin to take their place in the jural, cultural, and ritual affairs of the society, first, as their parents' representatives and later, in their own right, particularly for boys (Erny 1987). The specific form the rite takes varies across societies and has been reported in great detail by a vast but critical anthropological literature (e.g., Burton & Whiting 1961; Erny 1968; Harrington 1968; Jahoda 1982; Whiting 1965) that attests to the rite's social significance to the teenager's development.

At maturity, an African adolescent takes on the adult roles for which he or she was being primed. An adolescent does not, however, automatically attain adult status; full adulthood status requires being "married with children" (Nsamenang 1992a). The socialization of African youth is somehow changing, being affected by the consequences of schooling and the exigencies of urbanization and commercialization. For example, today's adolescents have more alternative opportunities for which their traditional socialization may be an inadequate preparation, more so than for past generations, and most schoolchildren combine schooling with sharing family maintenance chores.

Adolescents' Family Relationships and Life Experiences

The African does not think of the family in its nuclear form. In Kenya, as in much of Africa, the family can be defined as persons connected by blood, marriage, adoption, and shared cultural, economic, and *psychosocial tools for adaptation* (Bradley & Weisner 1997). For example, the concept of family in Senegal is so fluid as to include friends (Vandewiele 1981); sometimes multiple wives, relatives, as well as friends are part of the African family. This dense social network constitutes the extended or joint family. In most African societies, the legitimate way to procreate and have socially integrated children is through marriage. Accordingly, Bamileke and Beti adolescents in Cameroon perceive children as the fruit of marriage (Yana 1998). The conjugal pair is the core of the extended family, the major socioeconomic unit and primary agent that shares the socialization, care, and education of the young.

The contemporary African family can be seen from a variety of perspectives and levels of analysis. The variety notwithstanding, it is better seen "as an intergenerational, multilocal, psychosocial community linked to local, national, and global economies and polities" (Bradley & Weisner 1997, xxvi) in which the adolescent plays a changing role. African countries do not lack an awareness of the world order in which they exist. As Moore (1993, 4) remarked, "The global political-economy is in sight even from the food gardens of the most peripheral settlements" in Africa. Globalization, Western interests, the African nation state, and the world economic order – these matter to the contemporary, partially delocalized African family, but they do not in any way replace the importance of the values of African familialism. Thus, aspects of the family described in this section suggest that the institutional structures and functions of African families are becoming more diversified, but indigenous precepts are still emotionally salient. The family's functions, such as child care, concern for and care of the elderly, and the distribution of family nurturance and support (Weisner 1997) have not gone away, although they are changing in form and are becoming more heterogeneous. African family adaptation has been an ongoing struggle, a historically continuous cultural project to create a meaningful, sustainable, and coherent pattern of everyday life. The forces responsible for this state of flux include endogenous family dynamics, the change inherent in nature and sociohistorical contexts, and the delocalizing forces of intrusive world systems (Bradley & Weisner 1997).

Relationships, Roles, and Family Experiences of Adolescents

Adolescent experiences foreshadow the state of families, adolescents' roles, and adolescent-parent relationships. The family type and the resource allocation system shape family relationships and roles. Although polygyny is not universal, at least in Cameroon (e.g., Nsamenang 1992a), a 1984 survey in the Kisumu, Siaya, and South Nyanza districts of Kenya showed the percentages of married women in polygynous unions to be 38 percent, 47 percent, and 41 percent, respectively (Republic of Kenya 1986). The wide gap in the ages of male and female spouses created a large number of widows (Ssennyonga 1997). The practice of levirate, or the marriage of a widow to the brother of her deceased husband, was a traditional arrangement that partly solved this problem. It is important to caution that levirate is not universal throughout sub-Saharan Africa. It is thus clear that the structure and function of the family is an important factor in family relationships, particularly those involving the welfare of children. For instance, in polygynous families, wives have unequal access to resources, relative to that of husbands. This is because some societies use the temporal order in which the wives were married to the husband as a basis for allocating resources. Thus, using uxorial rank as a criterion for allocating resources certainly disfavors some wives and their offspring (Ssennyonga 1997). Such resource-allocation systems now tend to stir up considerable rancor and conflict in many an African family.

Another key determinant of adolescent experiences is the number of children per family, which in West Africa is estimated to range from 4.5 in Cameroon to 7.0 in Côte d'Ivoire (Ware 1983). In Swaziland it is 6.6 for women married by civil rite (Maphalala 1996) and 7.3 for those married by customary law (Gule 1991). The vast majority of sub-Saharan adolescents live in peasant households, which are productive units wherein a gender division of roles among adults and the young eases the integration and inclusion of children, especially adolescents, into the productive and social life of the family and the community. For example, a feature of African families of special significance for youth is the ubiquitous participation, manifested across the continent, of siblings in caregiving (Nsamenang 1992b), performance of errands and domestic chores (Ogunnaike 1997), and contribution to family income through street trading (Oloko 1994). Given children's contribution to family subsistence, Yana's (1998) claim of a high dependency index in Cameroon is quite surprising as the substantive economic inputs of adolescents are expected to either offset or reduce that index.

In the absence of effective publicly organized social security services, Africans rely on intrafamilial schemes that comprise parental insurance for children in spite of grinding poverty and, conversely, filial insurance for parents in the domestic services children render and the support they provide when parents are old (Nsamenang 1992a). A powerful determinant of parent-adolescent relationships, family interactions, and the dependency index is thus parental expectations. African parents expect their children, especially adolescents and youth, to serve them and sometimes to compensate for the parents' disappointments and failures. To make good such expectations, parents spare no effort to support and educate their adolescents in order to raise their status and potential to improve the welfare and resource base of the family. The mutuality and social support systems that pervade African family traditions permit equally the incorporation of children and teenagers into the homes of relatives or friends to provide service and/or to be apprenticed or educated (Laosebikan 1982). Adults who have elderly parents and children at school now face competing financial obligations. Nevertheless, some relatives are more significant to some adolescents than their biological parents because their assistance improved the life circumstances of those adolescents. The impact of placing children outside their biological homes on adolescent development is yet to be fully assessed. However, impressionistic evidence shows that children who were so placed have experienced some material deprivations, academic underachievement, and emotional distress (Laosebikan 1982; Nsamenang & Laosebikan 1982).

Family Functioning
Family satisfaction refers to the extent to which individual members are satisfied with the situation of their family in terms of its resource base, adaptability, and cohesion (Pillay 1998). Two markers of family satisfaction, family structure and parenting style, have been explored by researchers. Mboya (1995), for one, investigated the effect of gender-of-child on parenting and reported variations in parental practices among Black South Africans as a function of the gender and age of the adolescent. He concluded that social competence was more significant for girls and that although younger adolescents were closer to their parents, older ones sought to be distant and more independent. These findings are consistent with parental expectations that children acquire appropriate gender roles and become socially competent.

Pillay (1998) also reported that pregnant South African adolescents experienced their families as significantly less functional than did nonpregnant teenagers, attributing the dysfunctionality to poor control of adolescent behavior by parents, unclear ethical standards, conflicting family values, and lack of encouragement for autonomy. Regarding communication within the family, Anagnostara (1988) demonstrated that adolescents who reported closed patterns of family communication were more likely to have attitudes conducive to early childbearing than were teens whose families had open communication. A review of research on suicidal adolescents in South Africa revealed very low levels of family satisfaction among teenage suicide victims (Kerfoot 1987; Pillay & Wassenaar 1997).

Although popular literature and the mass media generally portray African parents as authoritarian, African adolescents accept their parents' "right to deal with them" in their best interest (Jahoda 1982). This apparently supports an African maxim that, "If a person is trained strictly then that person becomes a good person" (Ellis 1978, 48).

Continuities and Discontinuities in Family Life and Adolescent Experiences

Visible even to the casual observer of the African social landscape is the fact that the family is in a state of flux. The continuities and discontinuities in family structure and function partly reflect the extent to which adolescents and their families are coping with the competing values of traditionalism, modernity, and globalization. The degree to which the changes find expression depends, in large measure, on the type of family, roles of its members and their personalities, and the family's resources and how they are deployed.

The rural family still retains some homogeneity and familialism, but the size of the household is shrinking as the exodus of youth from rural settings is eroding its cohesion, further differentiating rural and urban communities (Weisner, Bradley, & Kilbride 1997). The urban family has become a group of individuals pursuing such disparate goals as farming, paid work, schooling, commerce, etc. at their own pace instead of staying together on the family production line, as families did previously. Schooling has reduced levels of adolescents' participation in the family economy. Increasing numbers of teenagers are growing up in divorced and single- or absent-parent homes – homes that have traditionally been regarded as incomplete. The family pattern most problematized is the single-parent, female-headed household. South African research with single parents has correlated Black teenage pregnancy with family disorganization (e.g., Boult & Cunningham 1993). This conclusion is questionable, however, because the study did not provide comparative data and single parenthood does not necessarily imply family "disorganization."

Opportunities for adolescent boys and girls and their parents are increasing; they are taking on roles that were either unavailable or not expected to be performed by them. One change that has altered family relationships profoundly is the increasing number of females in the paid labor force. Lifestyles and economic demands that require parents to spend more time away from home reduce parental visibility and availability, thereby limiting parents from being guides, mentors, and companions to their teenagers (Nsamenang 1992a). For example, long-distance trade, migrant labor, and commerce take some parents away from home, thus increasing the family responsibilities of other members. The migrant labor system in southern and West Africa has induced some migrant husbands to befriend teenage students (Du Toit 1983, cited in MacLeod 1999b), placing their wives back in family homes at risk for infidelity. Another drastic change is sleeping arrangements. With previous generations, spouses slept in separate households, but today many spouses sleep in the same household with their children.

In intergenerational relations, the parent, especially the father, is the net loser. His once undisputed authority is declining as teenagers and their mothers find their ways around the world without depending on his guidance or intervention. For example, parents are finding it difficult to provide guidance as they did with previous generations because they cannot apprentice or guide youth on career lines about which they are most ignorant.

Adolescents' Experiences in Dislocated Families
Images of Africa in crisis appear in the literature, art, academic writing, and the media (Bradley & Weisner 1997). Indeed, African families are in crisis (Weisner, Bradley, & Kilbride 1997), caused by social change, wars, and armed rebellions.

Historically, "lumpen youth" have been used in Africa's multiple wars and armed conflicts (Abdullah 1998). Some examples include the Union des Populations du Cameroun (UPC) resistance in the Cameroons, the Mulele rebellion in the Congo, the Movimento Popular de Libertacao de Angola (MPLA) in Angola, Frente de Libertacao de Mozambique (FRELIMO) in Mozambique, and Zimbabwe African National Union (ZANU) and Zimbabwe African People's Union (ZAPU) in Zimbabwe. Others are the Chad and Somali civil wars and the African National Congress's struggle against apartheid in South Africa. Youth and child soldiers are now fighting in Angola, Sierra Leone, Eritrea, and the Congo Democratic Republic, where a 29-year-old soldier has just replaced his assassinated father as president. Together with famine and lack of economic opportunity, war and political instability have produced a pattern of migration associated with dislocated families and rising numbers of adolescents and children living in urban informal settlements and on the streets (Aptekar 1998).

Wars have produced millions of child and teenage refugees, with an estimated 200,000 child and adolescent refugees in Mozambique alone. At least half of all of the refugees, returnees, and displaced persons in Ethiopia were children and adolescents (Children Youth and Family Welfare Organization 1992). Angola has one of the highest rates of displaced children and child amputees in the world, due to mine injuries. While 250,000 Kenyan children were estimated to be on the street as victims to AIDS and poverty by the year 2000, the estimate for Zambia was 1 million.

Children's street life is a continent-wide, urban phenomenon. The two categories of children on the streets include those who are working for their families (children in the streets) and those who are working for their own support (children of the streets) (Aptekar 1994). These groups have different problems, but because both are often poor, the tendency is to lump them together as street children. Street children also have to be differentiated from the rapidly growing numbers of child and adolescent refugees. This is particularly relevant if many adolescents from poor families work on the streets as a normal part of their family duties in the home division of labor (Aptekar 1994). Through her study of children's street work and schooling in urban Nigeria, Oloko (1994) discussed the transition from child as a responsible contributor to family subsistence to child as economic asset because he or she had to fend for resources to support his or her own education, and often his or her family.

Besides poverty and the factors identified above, other indicators of street life were family discord, abuse, or neglect. Studies show that the majority of the children found on the streets live at home but participate in the street economy in order to earn money for their families (Aptekar 1994). In one sense, the street economy highlights the acute sense of responsibility and resourcefulness African adolescents have in coping with family poverty and deprivations. The conditions that cause and sustain the existence of street children pose major challenges to economists, policy planners, and practitioners wishing to improve the life circumstances of African youth. The psychosocial cost of street life obviously is enormous, but its exact impact on adolescents' overall development remains to be assessed.

Peer Relationships and Adolescent Sexuality

We assume that peer relationships during adolescence can influence development in complex ways because they provide peer-controlled learning environments, particularly as peers are agents of their own socialization (Nsamenang 1992b). For instance, peers may play a more critical role than parents in shaping their social skills and sharpening identities. Furthermore, a multi-age peer setting can foster intergenerational transfer of cultural knowledge and skills. Adolescents' experiences with their peers may also have major effects on later development, including their orientations toward friendship relations and sexuality, issues that are central to the quality of adolescents' lives. It is essential to see peer influence in terms of both positive values and potential dangers, however.

Peer Relationships

The peer group is a ubiquitous institution in sub-Saharan Africa. Generally it is constituted by age, gender, or neighborhood. In some societies peers "mature" out of one activity setting to another, sometimes with a rite of passage. When parents are away on the farm, in the marketplace, or at work in either rural societies or poor urban communities, a multi-aged team of toddlers and older children come under the care and supervision of two or more teenagers who monitor their security and welfare (Nsamenang 1992b). The peer group is effective because a mechanism of self-regulation exists within the peer culture "due to the power inherent in the word of the adult, whose direct intervention is no longer needed" (Zempleni-Rabain 1973, 233). Once children become members of the peer group, they must carve out their own niche in terms of secure and reliable friends from whom to abstract appropriate rule systems and a sense of security. As children and adolescents keep together, older ones begin to "boss" the young, acting as *father* or *mother*. They share responsibility, play hide-and-seek games, and make their own playthings from local materials, often in imitation of adult models. Perhaps the rich traditions of African pottery, sculpture, weaving, and woodworks evolved through such practices.

While much of the developmental literature available for Africa is not quantitative, research on who spends time with whom in East African and West African rural settings shows that, by comparison with Western societies, preadolescent children spend a relatively high proportion of their time in the company of peers. In fact, parental values have been observed to guide Nso adolescents and preadolescents within their peer culture to notice and satisfy the needs of their younger charges (Nsamenang & Lamb 1995). During adolescence, Cameroonian boys and girls expand and diversify their personal relationships, which in childhood were centered primarily on the family (Songue 1998). Considering the intensity of peer-to-peer exchanges, it has been hypothesized that peer group interactions may be developmentally more significant than adolescent-adult dyads (Nsamenang 1992b). Peers do create their own culture in pretend play, and many adolescents mature, literally by themselves, through the influence of the peer culture. In rehearsing and enacting adult roles, adolescents use the peer culture to readdress and resolve some of the problems, confusions, and uncertainties raised in their interactions with adults (Nsamenang & Lamb 1995). In so doing, they attempt to "transform confusions and ambiguities from the adult world into the familiar routines of peer culture" (Corsaro 1990, 12). Thus, peers do not merely accommodate adult scripts, but are creative producers of meaning in their own right, and this deserves serious consideration.

It can be surmised from Songue's (1998) description of gender role socialization in Cameroon that an individual's first peer relations are formed with the same-sex partners. As children mature into adolescence, they begin to increase interaction and form peer groups with members of the opposite sex. Songue further pointed out that Cameroon, perhaps like much of sub-Saharan Africa, is a "dichotomous" society in insisting on sex-role differentiation. She also intimated that heterosexual relationships may be tolerated only in late adolescence or early adulthood as children "are encouraged to delay sexual relations while still in school" (Songue 1998, 165). In a survey of 665 Cameroonian adolescent students, adolescent boys expressed a preference to start sexual activity earlier than girls (Nsamenang & Tchombe 1998). The peer group was a preferred source of information on sexuality for adolescents both in this study (Nsamenang & Tchombe 1998; see also Songue 1998) and in the Central Africa region (Lloyd 1994) and South Africa (e.g., Macleod 1999b; Preston-Whyte & Allen 1992).

Adolescent Sexuality and Reproductive Health
The amount of speculation and street talk of sexuality in Cameroon, as in other countries, stands in stark contrast to the lack of reliable empirical

evidence on this subject. In general, sex is taboo and sexual matters are usually not discussed in the family. It is perhaps for this reason that parents were ranked by a sample of adolescent students in Cameroon as the fourth source of their information on sexuality (Nsamenang & Tchombe 1998). Thus, there is a general lack of understanding of sexuality and its expression, hence the general paucity of data regarding the sexual behavior of adolescent boys and girls and their knowledge concerning sexual matters. Leke (1998), for example, claims that fewer than 30 percent of African teenage girls correctly know their fertile period.

In much of sub-Saharan Africa, sexual socialization occurs through indirect traditional routes, associated with learning about gender roles and personal hygiene. The enculturation restricts sexuality to procreation, with special stress on girls' future roles as wives and mothers, albeit with only minimal focus on the role of boys as fathers and husbands (Songue 1998). Adolescent boys are encouraged to delay sexuality until they have a means of livelihood and teenage girls until they have become proficient in housekeeping and food production. In some traditional societies, a more formal route uses the *rite de passage* at puberty to give definite lessons in sexuality and gender roles to teenagers. Meanwhile, in Cameroon, as in much of the continent, school courses on human reproduction are not taught in a manner that reflects the lives and concerns of the rapidly growing and developing students. There is an apparent conspiracy of silence on adolescent sexuality, and the courses exclude the majority of teenagers. The most disadvantaged group, of course, is the out-of-school youth. Thus, without accurate information and guidance, most adolescents figure out for and by themselves the place and significance of sexuality in their lives – a state of affairs fraught with potential dangers. Some authors (e.g., Kuate-Defo 1998a; Tchombe 1998) have intimated that some parents do not appreciate nor condone sex education on the claim that it liberalizes sexual attitudes, thereby promoting sexual promiscuity.

In spite of the dearth of research data on the determinants and motivation for sexual activity, impressionistic evidence (Kuate-Defo 1998a) shows variability in adolescent sexual knowledge and practices. For example, the expected premarital fertility goal of a sample of young Cameroonian adults was 4, while it was 6 for their teenage peers. Urban youth expressed a desire for lower fertility, but the desire of rural girls was tempered more by economic considerations than traditional precept (Yana 1998). In general, in most societies on the continent, tradition discourages premarital sex and inserts sexuality into the life course as follows:

Heterosexual relationship > Marriage > Sexuality > Procreation
(Parenthood)

This implies that romantic love is not a traditional precept. Sexual relationships are permitted primarily within the institution of marriage, and premarital sex is proscribed. However, in particular circumstances in some cultures, sexual relations may be tolerated before marriage. The primary purpose of marriage is procreation, not sexual intercourse or the mere satisfaction of erotic or biological desire. Thus, some Cameroonian teens expressed the view that "marriage cannot work well without children" (Yana 1998, 103). Adolescent girls more than boys linked sexuality to procreation; such views are consistent with attitudes in West Africa, which regard infertility as a personal tragedy (Fortes 1950).

Under the influence of various cultural factors, some African parents marry off their daughters during adolescence and expect pregnancy soon thereafter. Although early marriage, sometimes soon after puberty, is possible in some cultures, the average age at first marriage is rising, due to advocacy and valorization of education over early marriage (Yana 1998). Although early marriage and the lower status of women increase the risks of poor reproductive health, childbirth confers on teenagers the valued status of motherhood. As Preston-Whyte and Allen (1992) have contended, parenthood is perhaps a credible pathway to acceptable adult status in cases where nuptiality is impossible or undesirably delayed by lack of money or other resources. Having observed sexuality handled naturally in traditional Africa, Erny (1972, 25) cautioned against projecting "erotic obscenity into African reproductive life."

In spite of the taboos that surround sexual matters, there is an increasing incidence of adolescent sexuality in Africa today, perhaps in response to early sexual maturity, greater opportunities for sexual contacts due to increasing mobility and openness (Tchombe 1998), and globalizing sexual values and practices. Moreover, the exposure of adolescents to sexual stimuli in magazines, television, movies, and video clips, without prior preparation to handle such sexual stimulation, either at home or at school, has produced many casualties as a result of sexual experimentation and blissfully innocent promiscuity (Tchombe 1998). In fact, Leke (1998) has claimed that some 50 percent of Cameroonian adolescents are sexually active. In a sample of 265 sexually active white

South African teenagers, Van Coeverden de Groot and Greathead (1987) found that the 37 percent of those who had first experienced coitus before age 17 came from single-parent families, compared with 12 percent of those for whom coitus was delayed until over 19. On their part, Boult and Cunningham (1992) found that 35.9 percent of the sampled 145 pregnant teenagers lived with their single mothers, 18.6 percent with kin, 4.1 percent with siblings, and 3.4 percent with single fathers.

Adolescent sexuality and reproductive health deserves keen attention, because adolescents are at great risk of compromising their futures (Songue 1998). This need is reinforced by a number of factors. First, teenagers are maturing at younger ages and starting sexual activity much earlier than in previous years (Kuate-Defo 1998b; Yana 1998). Second, the provision of family planning and health education services to adolescents is inadequate and ineffective throughout the continent (Nasah 1998). Third, the risk of sexually transmitted diseases (STDs) and unwanted pregnancies compromises the future of many teenagers (Nsamenang & Tchombe 1998). Fourth, in almost all sub-Saharan countries, HIV infection is growing rapidly among youth (United Nations International Children's Emergency Fund 1999; UNICEF). Finally, Africa's pronatalist values, myths, misconceptions, and religious beliefs about fertility complicate and confuse HIV/AIDS preventive messages to adolescents. In point of fact, as more and more adolescents become victims of STDs and HIV/AIDS, unplanned pregnancies and abortion, or are ignorant of the basics of their reproductive and mental health, we ought to become more concerned about the urgent need for education on reproductive health for this age group (Tchombe 1998).

Rural/Urban Differences in Sexual Behavior
There are rural-urban differences in fertility trends in adolescents on the continent. Yana (1998), for instance, claimed that urban Cameroonian teen students were more open-minded in discussing sexuality and procreation than were rural students. He also noticed differences with respect to number of children desired; urban teenagers preferred a smaller family size. Younger teenagers, though moderately receptive to pronatalist values, were quite perceptive of their parenting responsibilities and perceived procreation more traditionally in terms of personal affirmation, continuation of descent, social memory, and filial service to parents. Older adolescents, young adults, and urban youth, on the other hand, being more reality-oriented, tempered traditional

valorization of fertility with economic realities (Yana 1998). The 1991 Cameroon Demographic and Health Survey revealed that 39.8 percent of rural adolescent girls have had coitus, compared with 28.5 percent of their urban counterparts (Balepa, Fotso, & Barrere 1992). The fact that urban girls were more exposed to sex education and fertility control services and that they were more likely to stay in school longer than did their rural peers might have accounted for the surprising difference.

Buga, Amoko, and Ncayiyama (1996) and Richter (1996) found that 20 percent and 10 percent, respectively, of their sexually experienced sample indicated that they became sexually active because of peer pressure. Wood, Maforah, and Jewkes (1996) felt that peer pressure is effective because it takes the form of exclusionary practices such as sending sexually inexperienced teenagers away when discussing sexual matters. An important distinction to make, however, relates to pressure to have sex and pressure to prove fertility by becoming pregnant (Macleod 1999b). Preston-Whyte and Zondi (1989) contended that peer pressure pushes adolescent girls to early sexual activity, thereby increasing the risk of teenage pregnancy. In a household survey of the general teenage population in South Africa, Richter (1996) found that only 12 percent of the respondents wanted to have a baby within the next year or two; their main reason was the desire to prove fertility. Most teenagers did not, however, want babies out of wedlock, citing lack of preparedness or a desire to complete school as the main constraints. Some pregnant South African teenagers expressed a cultural viewpoint common throughout Africa, that pregnancy is essential for womanhood; hence the teenagers did not desire the humiliation of being infertile (Preston-Whyte & Zondi 1989). Anagnostara (1988) posited that some men, especially those whose wives were infertile, preferred teenage girls whose fertility had been proven as insurance against infertility in marriage.

Craig and Richter-Strydom's (1983) survey of students reported a gender discrepancy in sexuality. In their study, the girls did not regard proving fertility as crucial, but 30 percent of the boys expressed a preference for girls who had proven their "fruitfulness." This implies that premarital pregnancy increases a teenage girl's marital prospects. The basic message that teenagers in urban South Africa, as elsewhere in Africa, receive is that premarital pregnancy leads neither to unpopular marriage nor to ostracism from home (Nsamenang 1992a; Preston-Whyte & Allen 1992) or school. Many pregnant teenagers seldom stay out of school for more than an academic year (Preston-Whyte & Allen 1992), though in some countries government policy prohibits pregnant schoolgirls from attending classes. This increases the incidence of criminal abortion and other social ills associated with teenage pregnancy. Preston-Whyte and Allen (1992) have reported, however, that in South Africa most pregnant adolescents had left school before conception, and thus the dropout issue did not arise.

Adolescent Sexual Behavior and HIV/AIDS

Eastern and southern Africa is the epicenter of the HIV/AIDS epidemic. The region houses over 50 percent of the world's HIV-positive people and accounts for 60 percent of all deaths due to AIDS. Following a relatively slow start, South Africa now has one of the fastest-growing HIV-infection rates in the world. Families, communities, and health systems are responding to the pandemic with limited knowledge and scarce resources. It has so badly overwhelmed South Africa, especially youth, that some public hospitals are turning away victims, limiting treatment, and forcing doctors to make hard decisions about whom to save (AIDS Weekly 2000). In Cameroon, although 88.9 percent of a sample of 665 adolescent students perceived personal susceptibility to HIV, they did not report unsafe sexual practices and substance abuse as potential risk factors. In general, teenagers who were older, male, and in higher grades of schooling had more knowledge of HIV/AIDS than students who were younger, female, and in lower grades (Nsamenang & Tchombe 1998). The gaps and misconceptions in their knowledge of transmission, prevention, and adolescent sexuality were similar to those observed among Ivorian adolescent students (Dedy & Tape 1994).

As the leading killer in sub-Saharan Africa, AIDS has taken the lives of 16.7 million people since the epidemic began (*Washington Post* 2000), most of them youth and people in the prime of their lives (UNICEF 1999). AIDS patients in sub-Saharan Africa are said to die of their first opportunistic infection within one year of diagnosis due to general poor health and lack of treatment (Chin 1990). Neither words nor statistics can adequately capture the human tragedy of children grieving for dying or dead parents. "These children endure overwhelming and largely unmitigated losses, living as they do in communities already weakened by underdevelopment, poverty and the AIDS epidemic itself" (UNICEF 1999, 2). More children and adolescents have been orphaned in sub-Saharan Africa than anywhere else, and the number of AIDS orphans is expected to be 13 million as of the end of 2000. The enormity of the problem has already strained the age-old social safety net of the extended African family that has long proved itself resilient to other major calamities. Children who have been orphaned by AIDS are at a higher risk of malnutrition, illness, abuse, and sexual exploitation than those orphaned by other causes. In addition, AIDS orphans face stigma and discrimination, leaving them socially isolated and emotionally deprived. They are often the first to be denied education when extended families cannot afford to educate all the children of the household (UNICEF 1999).

The Role of Cultural Factors in Sexuality and
Perceptions of Procreation
Some traditional African practices exert a sexual control element. Although sex was, and is still, a taboo subject, traditional education did prepare the adolescents in their age group better than it does today. One explanation for this is that cultural practices that used to serve as mechanisms for the transmission of information about sexuality and its consequences are deteriorating (Tchombe 1998).

Amod and Shmukler (1986) investigated differences in sexual attitudes in a sample of South African Indian adolescents from traditional, transitional, and modern backgrounds and reported modern adolescents to be significantly more permissive in sexual attitudes than traditional adolescents. Most authors, however, treat culture as static, perceiving teenagers as victims whose "adequate" traditions are either replaced by nothing or by "inappropriate" foreign versions (Macleod 1999b). Songue (1998) exemplified this trend as she explained how the traditional ideal of premarital virginity in Cameroon became obsolete in the face of overwhelming sexual stimuli introduced by Western media and lifestyles. Preston-Whyte and Louw (1986) are among the few researchers who examined the dynamics of culture. By providing a case study of the strategies used to tackle the crisis precipitated by teenage pregnancy, they highlighted the ways in which South African cultural traditions were adapted to cope with contemporary realities. These included the payment of damages to the girl's family and a purification ceremony of *umgeto*.

Acculturation seems to be downgrading the significance of initiation, vaginal inspection (Bodibe 1994), and infibulation, cultural practices that were powerful sources of sexual control in adolescents as they marked specific developmental transitions (Serpell 1992). In addition, traditional education through initiation rites, chaperones, folklore, and the orientation of adolescents to acceptable sexual behaviors by grandparents, through oral traditions, seems to be losing its relevance rather rapidly.

The Education of Africa's Youth

Education, as deliberate teaching or preparation of the young, is a specific form of enculturation and socialization, widely referred to as schooling. It has been characterized as instructed learning (Tomasello, Kruger, & Ratner 1993), school learning, formalized or institutional education that is often contrasted with participatory learning, home learning, and societal or nonformalized education. Teaching and learning are not the monopoly of schools; they occur in and out of school throughout life. In some cultures, learning is organized primarily through didactic instruction in schools, with considerable cognitive stimulation. In African family traditions, children are guided and encouraged, with little or no instruction, to observe and participate in ongoing cultural and economic activities that emphasize socially distributed norms (Nsamenang & Lamb 1995). African schools tend to give the impression that African homes are culturally deficient dungeons to be escaped from or obstacles to overcome (Serpell 1993). Thus, the role of the school is to help Africans overcome their backwardness. This deficit model fails to realize that the education so far imparted in Africa has had limited or no relevance to the life paths of Africans.

My intention in this section is to describe the state of attempts to educate Africa's youth, the future hope of the continent. It is rather unfortunate that formal education, or schooling, is in a sorry state. My emphasis is on indigenous efforts. This is not to ignore or minimize the value of the school. Instead, it is because, so far, schooling systems on the continent have not outgrown deficit models that fail to incorporate African educational thought and practices that inform and shape the productive capacities of the vast majority of the population. In light of the difficulty being faced by African countries, or their seeming failure to design relevant schools for their citizens, I regard the substantive quantitative expansion of schooling in Africa as a certain dimension of progress that has, unfortunately, not critically improved the life circumstances of most Africans. The school has promoted cognitive, cultural, societal, and other forms of progress that are largely out of reach to the majority of Africans and have somehow incapacitated them in the face of the stark realities of their African world. In other words, as it stands today, the school is not yet fully suited to the agrarian life paths of the bulk of the continent's peoples, as its quality has been declining and its relevance to the life journeys of Africans (Serpell 1993) is increasingly being questioned. Thus, the African school is in dire need of drastic reforms. Accordingly, I consider it necessary to stress the nature of indigenous educational traditions as the basis for determining which of its positive elements could best inspire a more appropriate and fruitful education system for Africa in an era in which the imperatives of localization and globalization are both salient.

Indigenous African Educational Thought and Practice
The adolescent is being prepared to mature into an adult participant in family reproduction and societal productivity. The appearance of secondary sex characteristics is a marker of social entrée into the adult world (Nsamenang 1992a). From this point accentuated efforts are directed to more definitely induce and probate the neophyte into the life of the family and community. The role of parents and other mentors is (i) to guide adolescents to accept and understand the appropriate adult identity and models toward which they are being prepared; (ii) to communicate standards of valued behavior and virtue; and (iii) to prime and ensure their acquisition. The input of the peer group of all ages is significant in that, from toddlerhood, children spend more time and interact more within the peer culture than in adult-adolescent dyads (Nsamenang & Lamb 1995; Jahoda 1982). For example, when adolescents meet, play, exchange ideas, and resolve conflicts by themselves or interact with kin and others, the social identities asserted in the encounters and the values deployed therein evoke social representations and locate youth and their interlocutors as social partners.

The aim of indigenous education is to socialize responsible participation in the life of the family and community – a highly valued moral quality that is relatively ignored in the curricula of most schools in Africa (Serpell 1993). Most productive and moral lessons imparted to adolescents are tacitly woven into the texture of everyday social and economic activities. Through them, adolescents are apprenticed not only to learn useful economic skills but also to acquire prosocial attitudes and values of generosity, cooperation, and nurturance. For example, adolescents and older children perform chores and take care of younger siblings to reflect the principle of sharing family responsibility (Serpell 1992) and the priming process of learning the caretaker role from an early age (Nsamenang 1992b). Whereas international advocacy tends to characterize this role of the African child as exploitative child labor, it is important to realize that in the subsistence economies of Africa, such labor is legitimately interpreted as "an indigenous educational strategy that keeps children in contact with existential realities and the activities of daily life" (Nsamenang 1992a, 152). Ogunnaike (1997) has provided evidence that such participation stimulates cognitive development, by demonstrating how Yoruba children who were sent on errands or performed domestic duties scored higher on an adapted Bayley Mental Scale (Yoruba Mental Subscale) than their peers who did not participate. In Weisner's (1987) view, African parents use evidence that an adolescent can give or receive social support and notice and satisfy the needs of others as markers of cognitive and general developmental level, in much the same manner as American parents assess the academic ability of their children. However, African school curricula continue to ignore such forms of responsibility and cognitive functioning. Thus, the education so far dispensed by schools in much of Africa is qualitatively and quantitatively inadequate, as schools deny African adolescents the constructs that form the building blocks of their daily life and identity. That is, the education of African youth has failed to connect appropriately with their everyday cognition and life journeys (Serpell 1993).

The boy or girl is expected to complete his or her physical, social, intellectual, and practical education by the end of adolescence (*Encyclopédie de la République unie du Cameroun* 1981). The education has 3 stages: observation, imitation, and creative action. After observing, then imitating, the adolescent is able to perspective-take and act (Nsamenang & Lamb 1995), to create personally, and to exercise his or her trade or art (*Encyclopédie du la République unie du Cameroun* 1981). Learning is organized to enable the adolescent to master his or her language and rule systems by participating in proverbs, mental arithmetic, and listening to dilemma tales, legends, and adult conversation. Subtly modulated to fit the adolescent's emerging competence, participatory learning, in spite of its pitfalls, is free of the emotional pressure inherent in the Western system of explicit instruction and stringent certification (Serpell 1992). This education is effective because of its close relationship with life; it is through social acts (production) and social relationships (family life, social activities) that the education occurs. To the extent that the teenager learns everywhere and all the time, instead of learning only in predetermined circumstances as to place and time, outside of the productive and social world, the adolescent is truly in the "school of life" (Moumouni 1968, 29). The learners discover their talents and limitations and improve on their capacities, especially within the activity settings and free spirit of the peer culture. The onus to learn rests on the teenagers, with consequences or sanctions for those who fail to learn.

First, continental, then, maritime colonization brought into Africa new forms of education – Islamic/Arabic and Christian/Western education. The new systems did not incorporate African social thought, construction of knowledge, or interpersonal relations, etc., hence the tendency to undermine African educational thought and practice. While most African families continue to rely on indigenous education, African countries have implemented education systems in which adolescents receive didactic instruction from adults outside the context of skilled activity. The content and process of indigenous education is consistent with the values and skills required for subsistent, agrarian life. But the imported systems only intermittently and uncommittedly attempt to gain from the social intelligence and responsibility training inherent in African educational traditions. In some countries adolescents are subjected to traditional patterns of education, alongside Western schooling and Islamic training.

Patterns of Schooling and Institutional Education
African countries embarked on a massive and expensive expansion of their inherited colonial systems of education, but they are largely unsuitable for contemporary African needs and realities (Basu 1987). The progress recorded so far has been transient and varied across countries (Hubbard 1994). For instance, while the literacy rate in Mauritius is 80 percent, Mozambique's is 38 percent and that of Congo Democratic Republic is only 15 percent. Zimbabwe records a secondary school enrollment rate of 52 percent, Ethiopia 23 percent, and Rwanda's is 2 percent, just behind Tanzania's 4 percent (UNICEF 1997). But in Namibia, over three-quarters of urban dwellers and nearly one-half of rural residents have at least an 8th grade education, and 95 percent of youth aged 11–14 years and 73 percent of those aged 15–18 years are enrolled in school (UNICEF 1997). Cameroon's illiteracy rate of 40.5 percent (Republic of Cameroon 1993) compares with 24 percent for Black South African adults.

The expansion in education led to numerous initiatives of dubious quality (Brock 1996), as schools in Africa vary widely in terms of facilities, content, process, and quality of instruction. On one side there are expensive private schools with the best provisions. On the other side are the government schools charging little or nothing but nearly devoid of basic facilities. The group sizes are large, the syllabus is heavy, and teachers hardly update their skills. The textbooks used are foreign and are not oriented to African perspectives. Rote learning dominates the pedagogical system. These and other factors make school dismal and evoke limited flickers of interest among adolescents, hence the high rates of school dropout. Flisher and Chalton (1995) have revealed the following alarming school dropout rates for South Africa's racial groups: whites, 17.1 percent; Asians, 32.3 percent; Coloreds, 60.2 percent; and Africans, 72.1 percent. The reasons for school dropout include: (i) lack of resources to support schooling; (ii) poor academic ability; (iii) disinterest in school or wrong orientation; (iv) psychological consequences of malnutrition (Richter & Griesel 1994); (v) adverse conditions in the schools themselves (Gilmour & Soudien 1994); (vi) pregnancy or discipline problems; (vii) education imparted has no relevance to life circumstances; and (viii) inflexible school timetables. To illustrate the last point, the demand for adolescents' participation in agrarian activities causes a conflict of interests (Serpell 1993), and as some parents decide in favor of family subsistence they either use the teenagers intermittently for economic activities or withdraw them from school for full-time agrarian life.

Patterns of schooling also reflect the deeply gendered nature of African societies. In Cameroon (Republic of Cameroon 1993), for instance, 44.9 percent of males versus 37.3 percent of females received primary education, and 14.6 percent of boys compared with 8.9 percent of girls attended secondary schools. At the same time, 73.1 percent of Cameroonians aged 6–11 years were schoolchildren, while 20.7 percent of the adolescent population has had no schooling, the rate being higher for girls. In 1982 in Senegal, only 270 of the 1,006 teenage high school students were girls (D'Hondt & Vandewiele 1982), and in Liberia 756 boys compared with 306 girls were enrolled in high school (Fricke 1979). Although educational opportunities for girls are increasing, Africa still has the lowest female literacy rate in the world. There are 26 million African girls out of school, most of them in rural areas, and estimates show that this figure was expected to increase to 36 million in the year 2000 (UNESCO 1993). The fact that the girl child bears the brunt of both household chores and the care of siblings more than the boy child may account for this state of affairs.

Positive and Negative Consequences of Schooling

Schooling separates teenagers from parents, thereby increasing peer influence and further dividing generations. It has also reduced adolescents' availability and contribution to the family economy. Accordingly, the activities of adolescents have been reorganized to make time to attend school as well as participate in some of the activities for family subsistence and welfare (Bekombo 1981). In urban settings throughout the continent, for example, preadolescent and adolescent schoolchildren can be seen active in street trading, as an after-school activity that sometimes fetches the sole income for some families.

In one sense, the school is a "golden key of our new world" (Fricke 1979, 117). For example, education has expanded the horizons and experiences of Liberian adolescents beyond their ethnic frontiers and produced "multicolored expectations, hopes and desires" (Fricke 1979, 124). It has been a source of enlightenment and liberation, with a potential to transcend the limitations of the forms in which it was packaged (Serpell 1996). Yet the impact of Western literacy in Africa has been ironically termed "the domestication of the savage mind" (Goody 1977). The supposed intellectual empowerment the school confers also serves to recruit its African converts to lifestyles that are better-suited to the technology and value orientations of the West than to the African. Thus, in another sense, the school has decontextualized its African learners by failing to mesh with the local context. It has, for instance, taken away the bulk of the able-bodied population from agrarian life (Mkhize 1995).

Schooling in the contemporary world, according to Serpell (1993), has a multiple agenda of promoting economic and technological progress, transmitting culture across generations, and cultivating children's intellectual and moral development. Our analysis reveals that the extent to which this agenda satisfies African needs is at best doubtful. This is because the school has largely ignored or trivialized African knowledge systems, values, and technologies, but instead promoted foreign ones. The school is expected to serve as the process for acquiring the requisite skills and responsible values to ascertain technological progress and a favorable human development index, which, regrettably, seems to have eluded Africa. There is no doubt that schooling has initiated progress in Africa. Unfortunately, almost everywhere on the continent, this progress seems inconsistent with the value foundations and basic needs of Africa's agrarian livelihoods.

To conclude, it is clear from the foregoing analysis that, "The school is neither a miraculous medicine for all societal diseases nor an all-powerful poison," destroying Africa's adolescents (Freitag 1996, 2). To be relevant and productive, the curriculum of the African school of the 3rd millennium will need to delicately balance the processes of the participatory learning of indigenous education with the cognitive reflection of didactic instruction. And it will make good sense to follow new vistas by extracting its content, primarily from stark local and national realities, and supplementing it with the appropriate elements of globalization. The curriculum should be designed to produce graduates with suitable knowledge, skills, and responsible values to face the increasingly competitive local and global job markets with confidence. In brief, it is essential to focus educational effort on the cultural roots of Africans as the springboard and secure base from which to adapt to globalization.

Combating Unemployment and Exclusion: Creating Value for the Inclusiveness of Adolescents

Employment, or at least, meaningful participation in community affairs, is an important marker of social integration and active citizenship. In this sense, most adolescents in Africa are excluded from the life of their communities. Planning their engagement becomes more problematic, if the youth is seen as any person between 14 and 35 years of age, as in South Africa (Mokwena 1999). Osei-Hwedie (1991), citing an unemployment rate of 34 percent for Zambia, sees youth as an ambiguous term with different meanings in different contexts. The lack of gainful employment and an apparent absence of meaning in the continent's despondent youth are an index of progressive exclusion and marginalization of the bulk of the population (Kopoka 1999; Mokwena 1999). This is either a symptom of socioeconomic crisis and decay, a negative response to globalization, or an inability to deal with these issues.

Given that African economies are overwhelmingly agrarian with minimal technological inputs, the danger is that the skills adolescents acquire through indigenous education will become obsolete by the time they reach adulthood or will leave them unable to subsist. Although such youth find it difficult to cope with globalization, they at least subsist with their indigenous skills, unlike their schooled but unemployed peers who remain totally dependent. This is because agricultural land and indigenous craft and art production are more readily available than wage employment, such that the prospect of unemployment is surprisingly more likely with schooling than with indigenous education. In fact, the school system in much of Africa has so spiraled out of control that it mainly churns out unemployed youth who can read and write, but who are totally dependent and cannot even create or utilize local knowledge (Hoppers 1981). These serious shortcomings do not, however, obviate the value of the school and some of its positive contributions to personal and national development.

Progress in a nation's wealth begins with work, the input of every citizen being an essential factor for economic progress and societal development (Nsamenang 1998). Unfortunately, most African countries no longer consider their youth as a resource, but as a problematic statistical category (Wallace & Weeks 1972). For instance, today's youth no longer participate actively in the family economy and societal life as they once did. In African family traditions, the adult, the adolescent, and the child, each according to ability, contributed to the welfare of the family. It is equally crucial to note that it takes more than economic growth to underwrite exclusion, unemployment, and poverty. African nations, to varying degrees, implement various forms of nonformal education and vocational training for out-of-school youth, school dropouts, and disabled persons in different types of institutions. They do engage youth in self-help and rural development activities for personal progress and national development (Agere 1986). These services are provided by government, political parties, and nongovernmental agencies (e.g., Walla 1998), as well as by private initiatives in a variety of hands-on apprenticeship facilities (e.g., Tanon 1994). Some countries – Cameroon, Malawi, Nigeria, Zambia, Zimbabwe, to cite but a few – have specific ministries or departments that organize sports, build capacity, and attempt to generate employment opportunities for youth. In some nongovermental organizations (NGOs), such as the Catholic Youth Group, Young Women's Christian Association (YWCA), and in similar initiative groups, youth assume leadership roles by making decisions and organizing which projects to undertake.

These initiatives have not, however, been as successful as desired, as most of them have not been sustainable. In fact, the common denominator of the projects and services is a proclivity to failure as Africa's experience instead betrays precocity to diminishing returns. The World Bank has attributed Africa's failure to enlist and sustain youth in civic activities and create employment opportunities to excessive government intervention and lack of good governance and planning to meet rapid population growth. An imported dimension of the failure is the condemnation of the productive role of children in families as child labor by international advocacy (Nsamenang 1992a). As a result, many African governments have outlawed the street economy, instantly forcing thousands of youth into idleness and inactivity when the goal should be to create more new jobs (Bugnicourt, Ndiaye, & Sy 1994).

The most urgent challenge is to create opportunities for young people to learn to develop and maximize their potentials. There is a need to carry out an in-depth exploration of exclusion and how youth can be placed at the center of the development process (Kopoka 1999) by creating value and meaning and giving youth a definitive role in families, communities, and national life. The key to social inclusion is participation, respectful dialogue, and peaceful communication, which are remarkable by their absence in the experiences of today's youth. It is essential to open new channels and develop fresh strategies for youth to find creative ways to responsibly raise their voices and bring their concerns and aspirations, from their own perspectives, into the regional and national agenda.

Satisfying Needs and Providing Services to African Youth

The quantity and quality of services in Africa remain the lowest and the poorest in the world and underline an unfortunate tendency to inefficiency and decline. The services tend to be oriented toward children and adults to the detriment of adolescents, or the services only marginally refer to them. Even where they are meant for the young, adolescents do not have easy access to them.

Potential Threats to the Needs of African Adolescents
The demographic and development indicators identified earlier in the chapter evidently exert psychosocial and ontogenetic impact on the quality of adolescent lives. Accordingly, the needs of sub-Saharan African youth are likely to be compromised by: (i) a dense social network; (ii) endemic diseases and frequent ill health; (iii) recurrent episodes of hunger, even starvation; (iv) wars and armed conflicts; (v) low life expectancy and frequent experiences of bereavement; and (vi) conflict emanating from the imperatives of indigenous and imported realities. These and other indicators frustrate the efforts of most African teenagers, but may not be obvious to Western researchers or service providers framed by Darwinian or "psychologized" mentalities.

The Health Care Service Delivery Systems
Throughout the continent, adolescents suffer from inadequate access to and use of health care and family planning services (Macleod 1999b; Nasah 1998). In fact, most health systems provide contraception only to married women (e.g., Macleod 1999a), doing little to provide basic

screening services, which most adolescents need to safely manage their gender needs and reproductive health (Kuate-Defo 1998b; Walla 1998). By 1988, about three-quarters of all African countries had family planning programs, some of which set up strategies for population control. Fertility appears to be declining in a few of the states that established family planning services. However, modern contraceptive methods are used only by 6 percent of couples in sub-Saharan Africa, as compared to 30 percent in India and 70 percent in China (Hubbard 1994). Such population control programs meet with serious difficulties because of Africa's pronatalist values (Nasah 1998), as rural families still want and tend to have more babies.

Health service systems should promote physical, mental, emotional, and spiritual well-being, which is determined not only by the physical disease process, but also by social, cultural, and material conditions (Freeman & Pillay 1997). Understood thus, health becomes a broader concept (Petersen 1998) that incorporates mental and spiritual well-being. This requires a broader vision than is the case in Africa today. But for most countries, vision and policy principles are overwhelmingly centered on physical health, with mental well-being seen as an issue outside the mainstream of health care service. In South Africa, for example, adolescent sexuality and reproductive health were not seen within a more comprehensive framework of mental health (Pillay 1998). Mental health services can be of tremendous benefit to adolescents, particularly teenagers with emotional difficulties and conduct disorders (Kerfoot 1987; Pillay 1998). Unfortunately, in much of Africa, mental health tends to be limited to psychiatric care, while spiritual and emotional well-being are seen as a separate matter, beyond the domain of health care, to be addressed by a cadre of spiritualists. The AIDS pandemic is further worsening Africa's precarious health situation.

Like everything else, health care services are unevenly distributed across Africa, most of them ending at the fringes of towns. Namibia is an exception in one sense; over two-thirds of births occur in hospitals (Stanton et al. 1999). The indigenous and modern health care systems coexist. In order to be certain about treatment, many people revert to both systems, as do the Baoule of Côte d'Ivoire (Dasen et al. 1978). Given this confusing duality, it is time to begin to revise the therapeutic models in order to reduce the hegemony of biomedicine over ethnomedicine. This should be done in a manner to extract the positive aspects of each system with the goal of evolving to a more comprehensive, holistic health care system that is in tune with the health and illness behavior of the people.

Adolescent Perceptions of Their Own Future

The young are any country's greatest resource and hope for the future. The evidence reviewed here points to adverse circumstances confronting African adolescents, some of whom expressed awareness of their responsibility (Songue 1998; Yana 1998) and unfortunate fate (e.g., Fricke 1979; Osei-Hwedie 1991). For example, some teenagers perceived personal risk to HIV infection and pregnancy. Some boys and girls stated their fertility goals and normative responsibility in procreation (e.g., D'Hondt & Vandewiele 1982; Yana 1998) and endorsed personal ability and proper education as the means to achieving life goals (Fricke 1979; Osei-Hwedie 1991). There were also noticeable differences in perceptions by age, gender, and rural-urban dichotomies. However, faced with nonexistent or limited opportunities, it might be difficult to realize such hopes. On the other hand, other youth seemed to proceed as if tomorrow did not count. Some Cameroonian adolescents echoed such a sentiment by pointing out that life will not stop because there is a fatal disease, AIDS (Nsamenang & Tchombe 1998). They would rather live their life, regardless.

Toward a Theoretic and Methodological Insight

The purpose of this chapter is to sketch an outline of adolescence in sub-Saharan Africa and to discern the trends in adolescent life indicators. Although the conceptualization of most studies reviewed did not specifically address Africa's hybrid cultural character, findings are unambiguous in pointing to the coexistence of local and foreign images. Young Africans navigate between the demands and values of traditionalism and modernity fairly well. They are emotively African, striving to "cover" the depth of their Africanity with a veil of modernity (Obiechina 1975). The emerging picture is that of a continent in search of a future for its young.

The disturbing concern is whether today's youth possess the potentials and responsible values to sustain and propel technological progress and the human growth index in the 21st century. The heart of the matter is globalization, which tends to be regarded, albeit lopsidedly, as the extent to which Westernization influences humanity.

Adolescents do create a peer culture. A futuristic African youth culture should derive from the imperatives of both localization and globalization, necessitating global thought and localized action. As they play an important part in brain drain, supply of migrant labor and addictive drugs, or as they consume products of the transnational marketplace like tobacco and the media, African youth need to learn how and when they are being exploited. Such awareness and knowledge is empowering.

A plausible theoretic caveat is not to pit "traditionalism" against "modernity" because this does little to advance understanding of the phenomenon. It instead presupposes an inherent incompatibility of the two realities (Wallace & Weeks 1972) and imposes unilinear, externalized interpretation on the indigenous. This is empirically inappropriate and theoretically and methodologically limited and limiting. The conceptual challenge is to create the value on which to abstract a vision from the interface of competing indigenous and imported images of adolescence. The theoretical issue is to sensitize and train social scientists to the diversity that exists. The empirical problem is to incorporate adolescent voices. All this compels exploration of alternatives to the conventional views and approaches, not so that existing ones become necessarily displaced, but that we may "come to [a] wider, fuller understanding" (Wright 1984) of adolescence.

An appropriate understanding of adolescence in Africa is necessarily constructivist and is best undertaken through critical discourse within the hermeneutic circle of indigenous and imported psychologies (Nsamenang & Dawes 1998). Regardless of the nostalgia for the indigenous, or the insistent allure of globalization, we must resist seeing one image as the *right* one. The contemporary reality lies in the interface of the endogenous and exogenous. Given that adolescence interfaces several disciplines of the social and biomedical sciences, research is best conceptualized within a multidisciplinary framework that permits several disciplines to cross-fertilize and enrich theory, method, and practice (Nsamenang 1999). Sensitivity to the power of participation and of the fact that data *about* adolescents differ from data *by* them necessitates the inclusion into the research agenda of adolescents as knowers and creators of meaning. What is needed is research and practice that is grounded on our best understanding of the processes of behavioral change prior to, during, and after adolescence. To understand and tackle contemporary adolescent issues best, it is critical to know how adolescents themselves understand and cope with their multiple and sometimes conflicting role obligations (Edwards 1997).

Conclusion

The future of Africa is in its children, and adolescents are the bridge to that future. As an index of that future, the state of today's youth leaves us worried whether youth will handle competently the challenging expectations of the 3rd millennium. This compels understanding of Africa's inability to fully utilize its youth potential. The multiple needs, talents, and knowledge base of youth can be assessed in order to articulate strategic goals and policy principles that can support and nurture Africa's youth. The solicited role of the international community in this regard is stimulation and respectful support.

The vision is to craft value and meaning on which to place youth at the center of development efforts. It will be essential, in so doing, to bring into sharper focus stark local realities as they confront the imperatives of globalization. It is equally important to realize that change in the status and circumstances of the adolescent generation will not depend solely on government or organized efforts (Mokwena 1999). Most citizens are "invisible people" who continue to do what has to be done, regardless of whatever programs or strategies are in place (Mokwena 1999). Their efforts must be crafted into the agenda.

References

Agere, S. 1986. Participation in social development and integration in sub-Saharan Africa. *Journal of Social Development in Africa*. 1:93–110.
AIDS Weekly. 2000. AIDS overwhelms South Africa hospitals. *AIDS Weekly*. Jan. 17:1–2.
Amod, Z. & D. Shmukler. 1986. Sexual attitudes and behavior of Indian South African students. *South African Journal of Psychology*. 16:21–26.
Anagnostara, A. 1988. The construction and evaluation of a scale for assessing the sexual attitudes of black adolescents. Unpublished master's thesis. Rand Afrikaans University.
Aptekar, L. 1994. *Environmental disasters in global perspective*. New York: Hall/Macmillan.
Aptekar, L. 1998. Adolescence and youth among displaced Ethiopians: A case study in Kaliti camp. Paper presented at the 4th ISSBD African Regional Workshop. April. Windhoek, Namibia.

Balepa, M., M. Fotso, & M. Barrere. 1992. Enquete demographique et de sante au Cameroun, 1991 [*Demographic and Health Survey in Cameroon, 1991*]. Direction Nationale du Deuxieme Recensement General de la Population et de l'Habitat. Macro International.

Basu, A. 1987. Rethinking education in the third world. *Africa Quarterly.* 27:89–95.

Bekombo, M. 1981. The child in Africa: Socialization, education and work. In *Child work, poverty and underdevelopment*, eds. G. Rodgers & G. Standing, 113–129. Geneva: ILO.

Bodibe, C. R. 1994. Investigating the sexual knowledge, attitudes and behavior of black adolescents. Unpublished doctoral thesis. University of the Free State.

Boult, B. E. & P. W. Cunningham. 1992. Black teenage pregnancy: A socio-medical approach. *Medicine and Law.* 11:159–165.

Boult, B. E. & P. W. Cunningham. 1993. Black teenage pregnancy: An African perspective. *International Journal of Adolescence and Youth.* 3:303–309.

Bradley, C. & T. S. Weisner. 1997. Introduction: Crisis in the African family. In *African families and the crisis of social change*, eds. T. S. Weisner, C. Bradley, & P. L. Kilbride, xviii–xxxii. Westport, CT: Bergin & Garvey.

Breackwell, G. M. 1993. Psychological and social characteristics of teenagers who have children. In *The politics of pregnancy: Adolescent sexuality and public policy*, eds. A. Lawson & D. L. Rhode, 159–173. London: Yale University Press.

Brock, C. 1996. Changing patterns of teacher education in Sierra Leone. In *Global perspectives on teacher education*, ed. C. Brock, 103–121. Wallingford: Triangle Books.

Buga, G. A. B., D. H. A. Amoko, & D. J. Ncayiyama. 1996. Adolescent sexual behavior, knowledge and attitudes to sexuality among school girls in Transkei, South Africa. *East African Medical Journal.* 73:95–100.

Bugnicourt, J., R. Ndiaye, & E. H. Sy. 1994. Clear the streets and start again. *The Courier.* 143:54–55.

Burton, R. V. & J. W. M. Whiting. 1961. The absent father and cross-sex identity. *Merrill-Palmer Quarterly*, 7:85–95.

Children Youth and Family Welfare Organization. 1992. Addressing the situation in children in especially difficult circumstances: Draft national program of action, 1993–2000. Addis Ababa, Ethiopia: Author.

Chin, J. 1990. Current and future dimensions of the HIV/AIDS prevention in women and children. *Lancet.* 336:221–224.

Corsaro, W. A. 1990. The underlife of nursery school: Young children's social representations of adult roles. In *Social representations and the development of knowledge*, eds. G. Duveen & B. Lloyd, 11–26. Cambridge: Cambridge University Press.

Craig, A. P. & L. M. Richter-Strydom. 1983. Unplanned pregnancies among urban Zulu schoolgirls. *South African Medical Journal.* 63:452–455.

Dasen, P. R., R. Inhelder, M. Lavallee, & J. Retschitzi. 1978. *Naissance de l'intelligence chez l'enfant Baoule de Côte d'Ivoire [Birth of intelligence among Baoule children of Ivory Coast].* Berne: Hans Huber.

Dedy, S. & G. Tape. 1994. *Jeunesse, sexualité et SIDA en Côte d'Ivoire: Le cas d'Abidjan [Youth, sexuality, and AIDS in Ivory Coast: The case of Abidjan].* Abidjan: Comité Nationale de Lutte contre le SIDA.

De Waal, A. 1989. *Famine that kills: Darfur, Sudan 1984–1985.* Oxford: Clarendon Press.

D'Hondt, W. & M. Vandewiele. 1982. Attitudes and behavior at the time of adolescence as perceived by secondary school students in Senegal. *Journal of Genetic Psychology,* 140:319–320.

Diop, C. A. 1960. *L'Unité culturelle de l'Afrique Noire [The cultural unity of Black Africa].* Paris: Presence Africaine.

Edwards, C. P. 1997. Morality and change: Family unity and paternal authority among Kipsigis and Abaluyia elders and students. In *African families and the crisis of social change,* eds. T. S. Weisner, C. Bradley, & P. L. Kilbride, 45–85. Westport, CT: Bergin & Garvey.

Ellis, J., ed. 1978. *West African families in Britain.* London: Routledge and Kegan Paul.

Encyclopédie de la République Unie du Cameroun [Encyclopedia of the United Republic of Cameroon]. 1981. Douala, Cameroon: Eddy Ness.

Erny, P. 1968. *L'énfant dans la pensées traditionelle de l'Afrique Noire* [The child in traditional African social thought]. Paris: Le Livre Africain.

Erny, P. 1972. *Les premiers pas dans la vie de l'enfant de l'Afrique Noire: Naissance et premiere enfance* [First Steps in the life of a black African child: Birth and early childhood]. Paris: L'Ecole.

Erny, P. 1987. *L'Enfant et son milieu en Afrique Noire [The child and his environment in Black Africa].* Paris: L'Harmattan.

Flisher, A. J. & D. O. Chalton. 1995. High school dropouts in a working class South African community: Selected characteristics and risk-taking behavior. *Journal of Adolescence.* 18:105–121.

Fortes, M. 1950. Kinship and marriage among the Ashanti. In *African systems of kinship and marriage,* eds. A. R. Radcliffe-Brown & D. Forde, 259–271. Oxford: Oxford University Press.

Freeman, M. & Y. Pillay. 1997. Mental health policy – plans and funding. In *Mental health policy issues for South Africa,* eds. D. Foster, M. Freeman, & Y. Pillay, 32–54. Cape Town: Medical Association of South Africa Multimedia Publications.

Freitag, B. 1996. The role of the school in child development. *ISSBD Newsletter.* 1(29):1–3.

Fricke, R. 1979. Orientation towards the future by Liberian schoolchildren: A contribution to the understanding of young West Africans. *Human Development.* 22:113–126.

Gale, T. S. (n.d.). Segregation in British West Africa. *Cahiers d'etudes Africaine, 80.* 22(4):495–507.

Gilmour, D. & C. Soudien. 1994. Disadvantage in South African education: The issue of transformative policy and research. In *Childhood and adversity: Psychological perspectives from South African research,* eds. A. Dawes & D. Ronald, 122–135. Cape Town: David Philip.

Goody, J. 1977. *The domestication of the savage mind.* Cambridge: Cambridge University Press.

Gule, G. 1991. Fertility, mortality and migration in Swaziland. In *Proceedings of the national workshop on population and development focus on Swaziland*, ed. A. Okore. Department of Statistics & Demography: University of Swaziland.

Harrington, C. 1968. Sexual differentiation in socialization and some male genital mutilations. *American Anthropologist*. 70:952–956.

Holdstock, T. L. 2000. *Re-examining psychology: Critical perspectives and African insights*. Hampshire: Routledge.

Hoppers, W. H. L. M. 1981. *Education in a rural society: Primary pupils and school leavers in Mwinilunga, Zambia*. The Hague, The Netherlands: Nuffic.

Jahoda, G. 1982. *Psychology and anthropology*. London: Academic Press.

Hubbard, D. 1994. Economic trends in Africa 1985. In *Africa south of the Sahara*. 15:56–59. London: Europa Publications Limited.

Kerfoot, M. 1987. Family therapy and psychotherapy following suicidal behavior by adolescents. In *Suicide in Adolescence*, eds. R. F. W. Dickstra & K. Hawton, 95–111. Dordrecht: Martinus Nijhoff.

Kopoka, P. A. 1999. The political economy of youth marginalization. Paper presented at a colloquium on understanding exclusion, creating value: African youth in a global era. July: Cape Town, South Africa.

Kuate-Defo, B. 1998a. Emerging patterns in adolescent sexuality: Fertility and reproductive health in Africa. In *Sexuality and reproductive health during adolescence in Africa*, eds. B. Kuate-Defo, 15–35. Ottawa: University of Ottawa Press.

Kuate-Defo, B. 1998b. Trends and determinants of regional differences in sexual initiation during adolescence. In *Sexuality and reproductive health during adolescence in Africa*, ed. B. Kuate-Defo, 59–75. Ottawa: University of Ottawa Press.

Lamb, M. E. 1992. Foreword. In *Human development in cultural context*, A. B. Nsamenang (Author), ix–xi. Newbury Park, CA: Sage.

Laosebikan, S. 1982. A commentary for clinical psychology in Nigeria: Implications for training. Paper presented at the 2nd Annual Convention of the Nigerian Association of Clinical Psychologists. Nov: Benin City, Nigeria.

Leke, R. J. I. 1998. Reproductive health of adolescents in sub-Saharan Africa. In *Sexuality and reproductive health during adolescence in Africa*, ed. B. Kuate-Defo, 255–260. Ottawa: University of Ottawa Press.

LeVine, T. V. 1976. Political integration and United Republic of Cameroon. In *The search for national integration in Africa*, eds. D. R. Smock & Bentsi-Enchill, New York: Free Press.

Lloyd, C.B. 1994. Adolescent fertility in sub-Saharan Africa. *Population dynamics of sub-Saharan Africa*. 20:194–199.

Macleod, C. 1999a. Teenage pregnancy and its "negative" consequences: Review of South African research – part 1. *South African Journal of Psychology*. 29(1): 1–7.

Macleod, C. 1999b. The 'causes' of teenage pregnancy: Review of South African research – part 2. *South African Journal of Psychology*. 29(1):8–16.

Maphalala, T. P. 1996. *Street children in Swaziland*. Paper presented at the ISSBD Africa Regional Workshop. Lusaka: Zambia.

Maquet, J. 1972. *Africanity*. New York: Oxford University Press.

Mazrui, A. A. 1986. *The Africans.* New York: Praeger.

Mboya, M. M. 1995. Variations in parenting practices: Gender and age-related differences in African adolescents. *Adolescence.* 30(120):955–962.

Mkhize, Z. M. 1995. Social needs of teenage mothers in the rural communities of Ongoye and Enseleni districts. Unpublished master's thesis. University of Zululand.

Mokwena, S. 1999. A perspective on youth and social justice in South Africa. *New Designs for Youth Development.* 15(3):1–5.

Moore, S. F. 1993. Changing perspectives on a changing Africa: The work of anthropology. In *Africa and the disciplines: The contributions of research in Africa to the social sciences and humanities,* eds. R. H. Bates, V. Y. Mudimbe, & J. O'Barr, 3–57. Chicago: University of Chicago Press.

Moumouni, A. 1968. *Education in Africa.* New York: Praeger.

Munroe, R. H., R. L. Munroe, & B. B. Whiting. 1981. Preface. In *Handbook of cross-cultural human development,* eds. R. H. Munroe, R. L. Munroe, & B. B. Whiting, ix–xiii. New York: Garland STPM Press.

Nasah, B. T. 1998. Family planning and adolescent sexuality and reproductive health in sub-Saharan Africa. In *Sexuality and reproductive health during adolescence in Africa,* ed. B. Kuate-Defo, 205–217. Ottawa: University of Ottawa Press.

Nsamenang, A. B. 1992a. *Human development in cultural context: A third world perspective.* Newbury Park, CA: Sage.

Nsamenang, A. B. 1992b. Early childhood education and care in Cameroon. In *Child care in context,* ed. M. E. Lamb, 419–439. Hillsdale, NJ: Erlbaum.

Nsamenang, A. B. 1998. Work organization and economic management in sub-Saharan Africa: From a Eurocentric orientation toward an Afrocentric perspective. *Psychology and Developing Societies.* 10(1):75–97.

Nsamenang, A. B. 1999. Eurocentric image of childhood in the context of the world's cultures: Essay review (1996) of images of childhood. Eds., Philip C. Hwang, Michael E. Lamb, and Irving E. Sigel. *Human Development.* 28:159–168.

Nsamenang, A. B. 2000. African view on social development: Implications for cross-cultural developmental research. Paper read at the 5th ISSBD African Regional Workshop. Sept.: Kampala, Uganda.

Nsamenang A. B. & A. Dawes. 1998. Developmental psychology as political psychology in sub-Saharan Africa: The challenge of Africanization. *Applied Psychology: An International Review.* 47(1):73–87.

Nsamenang, A. B & M. E. Lamb. 1995. The force of beliefs: How the parental values of the Nso of Northwest Cameroon shape children's progress towards adult models. *Journal of Applied Developmental Psychology.* 16(4): 729–739.

Nsamenang, A. B. & S. Laosebikan. 1982. Father-child relationships and the development of psychopathology. Paper presented at the 10th Annual Conference of the Nigerian Psychological Society. Apr.: Jos: Nigeria.

Nsamenang, A. B. & T. M. Tchombe. 1998. Perceptions of HIV/AIDS among a sample of teenage students in Northwest Cameroon. Unpublished manuscript.

Obiechina, E. N. 1975. *Culture, tradition, and society in the West African novel.* Cambridge: Cambridge University Press.

Ogunnaike, O. A. 1997. Yoruba toddlers: Relating cognitive performance to family: Sociodemographics and mediating factors in the child's environment. Unpublished doctoral dissertation. Tufts University, Medford, MA.

Oloko, B. A. 1994. Children's street work in urban Nigeria: Dilemma of modernizing tradition. In *Cross-cultural roots of minority child development,* eds. P. M. Greenfield & R. R. Cocking. Hillsdale, NJ: Erlbaum.

Osei-Hwedie, K. 1991. Work attitudes and life goals of Zambian youth. *Journal of Social Development in Africa.* 6(1):63–73.

Petersen, I. 1998. Comprehensive integrated primary mental health care in South Africa: The need for a shift in the discourse of care. *South African Journal of Psychology.* 28(4):196–203.

Pillay, A. L. 1998. Perceptions of family functioning in conduct disordered adolescents. *South African Journal of Psychology.* 28(4):191–195.

Pillay, A. L. & D. R. Wassenaar. 1997. Recent stressors and family satisfaction in suicidal adolescents in South Africa. *Journal of Adolescence.* 20: 155–162.

Preston-Whyte, E. & J. Allen. 1992. Teenage pregnancy in the coloured community. In *Questionable issue: Illegitimacy in South Africa,* eds. S. Burman & E. Preston-Whyte, 208–225. Cape Town: Oxford University Press.

Preston-Whyte, E., & J. Louw. 1986. The end of childhood: An anthropological vignette. In *Growing up in a divided society: The contexts of childhood in South Africa,* eds. S. Burman & P. Reynolds, 360–392. Evanston, IL: Northwestern University Press.

Preston-Whyte, E. & M. Zondi. 1989. To control their own reproduction: The agenda of black teenage mothers in Durban. *Agenda.* 4:47–68.

Republic of Cameroon. 1993. *Indicateurs démographique sur le Cameroun [Demographic indicators for Cameroon].* Yaounde, Republic of Cameroon: Author.

Republic of Kenya. 1986. Kenya contraceptive prevalence survey (Provincial report, Central Bureau of Statistics). Nairobi: Nairobi Government Printer.

Richter, L. M. 1996. A survey of reproductive health issues among urban Black youth in South Africa. Unpublished reports: Medical Research Council of South Africa.

Richter, L. & R. Griesel. 1994. Malnutrition, low birth weight and related influences on psychological development. In *Childhood and adversity: Psychological perspectives from South African research,* eds. A. Dawes & D. Donald, 66–91. Cape Town: David Philip.

Serpell, R. 1984. Research on cognitive development in sub-Saharan Africa. *International Journal of Behavioral Development.* 7:111–127.

Serpell, R. 1992. Afrocentrism: What contribution to science of developmental psychology. Paper presented at the 1st ISSBD Regional Workshop on the Theme Child Development and National Development in Africa. Apr.: Yaounde, Cameroon.

Serpell, R. 1993. *The significance of schooling: Life-journeys in an African society.* Cambridge: Cambridge University Press.

Serpell, R. 1994. An African social ontogeny: Review of A. Bame Nsamenang (1992): Human development in cultural context. *Cross-Cultural Psychology Bulletin.* 28(1):17–21.

Serpell, R. 1996. Commentary on Freitag's lead article: The role of the school in child development. *ISSBD Newsletter.* 1(29):5.

Songue, P. B. 1998. Social influences on adolescent sexuality and reproductive behavior in Southern Cameroon. In *Sexuality and reproductive health during adolescence in Africa,* ed. B. Kuate-Defo, 162–173. Ottawa: University of Ottawa Press.

Stanton, B. F., A. M. Fitzgerald, X. Li, H. Shipena, I. B. Ricardo, J. S. Galbraith, N. Terreri, J. Strijdom, V. Hangula-Ndlovu, & J. Kahihuata. 1999. HIV risk behaviors, intentions, and perceptions among Namibian youth as assessed by a theory-based questionnaire. *AIDS Education and Prevention.* 11(2): 132–149.

Ssennyonga, J. W. 1997. Polygyny and resource allocation in the Lake Victoria Basin. In *African families and the crisis of social change,* eds. T. S. Weisner, C. Bradley, & C. P. Kilbride, 268–282. Westport, CT: Bergin & Garvey.

Tanon, F. 1994. A cultural view on planning: The case of weaving in Ivory Coast. *Cross-cultural Psychology Monographs,* 4. Tilbury, The Netherlands: Tilbury University Press.

Tchombe, T. 1998. School-based approach to adolescent sexuality and reproductive health. In *Sexuality and reproductive health during adolescence in Africa,* ed. B. Kuate-Defo, 301–319. Ottawa: University of Ottawa Press.

Tomasello, M., A. C. Kruger, & H. H. Ratner. 1993. Cultural learning. *Behavioral and Brain Sciences.* 16:405–552.

United Nations Development Program (UNDP). 1996. *Human development report.* New York: Oxford University Press.

United Nations Education, Scientific, and Cultural Organization (UNESCO). 1993. *Ouagadougou Declaration on the Education of the Girl Child.* Ouagadougou: Author.

United Nations International Children's Emergency Fund (UNICEF). 1997. *The state of the world's children.* London: Oxford University Press.

UNICEF. 1999. *Children orphaned by AIDS: Frontline response from eastern and southern Africa.* New York: UNICEF/UNAIDS.

Van Coeverden de Groot, H. A. & E. E. Greathead. 1987. The Cape Town teenage clinic. *South African Medical Journal.* 71:434–436.

Vandewiele, M. 1981. Influence of family, peers, and school on Senegalese adolescents. *Psychological Reports.* 48:807–810.

Walla, G. 1998. The organization and management of youth groups for promoting adolescent sexual and reproductive health. In *Sexuality and reproductive health during adolescence in Africa,* ed. B. Kuate-Defo, 333–350. Ottawa: University of Ottawa Press.

Wallace, T. & S. G. Weeks. 1972. Youth in Uganda: Some theoretical perspectives. *International Journal of Social Science.* 24:354–365.

Ware, H. 1983. Male and female life cycles. In *Male and female in West Africa,* ed. C. Oppong, 6–31. London: Allen & Unwin.

Washington Post. An unequal calculus of life and death. December 27, 2000.

Weisner, T. S. 1987. Socialization for parenthood in sibling caretaking societies. In *Parenting across the life span: Biosocial dimensions,* eds. J. B. Lancaster, J. Altman, A. S. Rossi, & L. R. Sherrod, 237–270. Hawthorne, NY: Aldine de Gruyter.

Weisner, T. S. 1997. Support for children and the African family crisis. In *African families and the crisis of social change,* eds. T. S. Weisner, C. Bradley, & C. P. Kilbride, 20–44. Westport, CT: Bergin & Garvey.

Weisner, T. S., C. Bradley, & C. P. Kilbride, eds. 1997. *African families and the crisis of social change.* Westport, CT: Bergin & Garvey.

Whiting, B. B. 1965. Sex identity conflict and physical violence: A comparative study. *American Anthropologist.* 67:123–140.

Wood, K., F. Maforah, & R. Jewkes. 1996. Sex, violence and constructions of love among Xhosa adolescents: Putting violence on the sexuality education agenda. Unpublished report: Medical Research. Cape Town.

Wright, R. A. 1984. Preface. In *African philosophy,* ed. R. A. Wright, xiii–xv. Lanham, MD: University Press of America.

Yana, S. 1998. Sexuality and procreation among the Bamileke and Beti. In *Sexuality and reproductive health during adolescence in Africa,* ed. B. Kuate-Defo 91–107. Ottawa: University of Ottawa Press.

Zempleni-Rabain, J. 1973. Food and strategy involved in learning fraternal external exchange among Wolof children. In *French perspectives in African studies,* ed. P. Alexander, 221–233. London: Oxford University Press.

4

Adolescence in India

Street Urchins or Silicon Valley Millionaires?

Suman Verma and T. S. Saraswathi

Introduction

The Indian adolescent? A kaleidoscope of images flits through the mind's eye – the jeans clad 18-year-old, dressed ever so casually in designer clothes, attending an elitist institution in technology; the veiled young girl of 15, her first child tucked on her hip, trudging to the village well with two shining brass pots on her head; the stunted 14-year-old boy, who toils at the roadside restaurant from dawn to dusk so he can live on the footpath and send his meagre earnings home to a sick mother in the village; the doe-eyed Bengali refugee girl, sold to prostitution by parents too poor to feed her or themselves and other children; the bejewelled and bedecked bride all of 17 years, waiting for her groom who will come riding in on a white horse ... kaleidoscopic images – images of dreams for a rosy future, of dreams that died before they took shape, of privileges and deprivations, of leisure and toil, of hope and despair.

The same problem that confronts the respondent when asked, "What is Indian?" leaves one baffled when asked to describe the situation of the "Indian adolescent" at the dawn of the 21st century. The contrasts are so vivid that any attempt to generalize needs to be tempered with

The author extends grateful thanks to Nandini Manjrekar, Research & Programme Officer, Women's Studies Research Centre, M. S. University of Baroda, for preparation of the section on education; to the faculty of the National Institute of Mental Health & Neuro Sciences, Bangalore, particularly Prof. Srinivasa Murthy, and the Post Graduate Institute of Medical Research, Chandigarh, for the materials and suggestions for the mental health section; and, to Mahesh Soni, who typed the manuscript several times with friendly cheer (I mean without beating me up !!).

a caveat. Against the backdrop of social and economic disparities that characterize Indian adolescents and youth, this chapter examines the trends shaping adolescence in India. More specifically, the chapter examines what is known about Indian adolescents in the areas of family dynamics, peer relations, experience of schooling, and their physical and mental well-being. Issues concerning adolescents' political participation, community involvement, employment status, and the services available to them are also addressed. Standing at the crossroads of technological advancement and a global market economy, it is an opportune time to examine how tradition and modernity in sociopolitical and cultural factors have shaped and continue to influence adolescence in India.

In preparing the chapter, we drew primarily from culture-sensitive literature (excluding a majority of published work that only replicates Western studies, usually using culturally inappropriate measures) and extrapolated, where appropriate, from our own experience and others' observations. Second, in view of what Arnett (1998) describes as "emerging adulthood," or the lengthening age span of 'adolescence' from early teens to mid-20s or even later, we have included information on older youth (i.e., 20 to 25+ years) where pertinent. Lastly, we make reference to caste differences only when pertinent and where reliable information was available, as this is a politically sensitive topic.

Demographic Profile

There are currently about 200 million adolescents in the 10–19-year age group, constituting 22 percent of the total population (United Nations Population Fund 1998; UNFPA). There are about 300 million adolescents between the ages of 10 and 24, accounting for approximately 30 percent of the population (Institute of Applied Manpower Research 2000; IAMR). There are marked variations in the situation of adolescents, qualified by gender and setting. The census data show a declining ratio of females to males in the total population in the last 5 decades, with a decrease from 946 females per 1,000 males in 1951 to 933 in 2001 (Registrar General & Census Commissioner, India 2001; RGCC). Due to sociocultural pressures, adolescent marriage and fertility rates are high. According to the National Family Health Survey (International Institute for Population Sciences & ORC Macro 2000; IIPS & ORC), 34 percent of girls aged 15–19 years were married. The mean age at marriage is about $2\frac{1}{2}$ years lower in the rural areas than in the urban areas for both males and females. About 19 percent of the total fertility in India is attributed to women in the 15–19 age group. However, there has been a general decline in the fertility rate across ages 15–45. In the 10–19 age group, 86 percent of boys and 72 percent of girls are literate. Though the literacy rate has gone up steadily, there is a 14 percent gap between the literacy of boys and girls in this age group. Enrollment of rural girls is lower and their dropout rates higher compared to their urban counterparts (IIPS & ORC 2000). For every youth living in a city, 3 live in the countryside, although this picture varies from state to state. Projections indicate definite trends toward a significant increase in the proportion of urban youth on account of migration and urbanization (IAMR 2000).

In modern India, while 'adolescence' is a comparatively new term, the word 'youth' is better known, particularly at the national and policy-making levels (Singh 1997). The terms *Kumara* and *Brahmachari*, which refer to the stage of celibacy and apprenticeship or acquisition of knowledge, were used in the traditional texts of the *Dharmashastras*, especially with reference to the training of young males of the upper castes, and are still familiar, though not commonly used. (The *Dharmashastras* prescribe the code of conduct for each stage of development and assign a crucial place for adolescence in the process of enculturation. Belief in these codes is deeply rooted in the Indian psyche and continues to influence cultural practices in a powerful manner.) In the Draft National Youth Policy (DNYP; Government of India 1997), youth refers to all people between the ages of 10 and 35. The policy recognizes that all the people within this broad age range are not "one homogeneous group but a conglomeration of various subgroups with differing roles in the society and different needs and aspirations" (2). The DNYP recognizes youth as an important asset for developing human resources. It recommends better opportunities and support systems to empower the youth.

Family Relations

A brief description of the traditional Indian family and a gender perspective on the status of girls and women serves as an introduction to this section. These descriptions contextualize the cultural milieu in which adolescent development takes place and provide the backdrop against which social change and its consequences assume significance and meaning.

The unique characteristics of the traditional joint family in India are a composition that includes the patriarch of the household and his spouse, children, married sons, their spouses and children, as well as other members of the extended family such as single brothers, sisters, widowed aunts and other dependent kin, who share the same roof and hearth; common production and consumption, be it through farming, business, or craft production; interdependence among the members with more emphasis on the family than the individual; and absolute authority of the head of the household regarding all major decisions from arrangement of marriages to the sale, purchase, or management of property (Sinha 1994). While composition and living arrangements within families are rapidly changing in India, the joint-ness, in terms of interdependence in major family decisions, remains for a majority of families (Khatri 1972). This has direct consequences for adolescent development in India, since most young people stay with the family until early adulthood or even later in the case of joint families. In keeping with the code of conduct prescribed by the *Dharmashastras*, becoming a householder and procreating are still considered obligatory in the Hindu world view. *Samskaras*, or sacred and ritualistic ceremonies, are still performed to mark the stages of individual and family life cycle in most homes (Kakar 1979; T. S. Saraswathi & Pai 1997).

In the patriarchal setting of the Indian family, growing up as a female child carries with it the connotation of inferior status and lesser privileges when compared to the male child (Dube 1988; Kakar 1979). The picture of gender discrimination, with the scales tipped clearly in favor of the male, cuts across the entire life span, from conception to old age (Indian Council of Social Science Research 1974; ICSSR). Females across social classes are encouraged to develop an interdependent and even sacrificial self and to prepare for their roles as good wives and mothers. The picture is not too different even among the increasing number of career-oriented young women, who clearly prioritize family obligations (T. S. Saraswathi 1999).

The family continues to play a major role in socialization despite the fast pace of social change. As mentioned earlier, the family itself is undergoing structural and functional modifications that have a direct bearing on adolescent socialization and parent-child relations. Research regarding specific psychological outcomes is sparse. For discussion in this section, we selected two topics that have been more frequently and systematically examined: 1st, child-rearing practices and their implications for adolescent identity, autonomy, and decision making; and 2nd, family variables that influence the impact of social change and create stress.

Child Rearing and Implications for Adolescence

Parental beliefs regarding child rearing reflect the traditional emphasis on familialism, interdependence, and respect for elders (T. S. Saraswathi & Ganapathy, in press). In practice, one observes a relaxation in the patriarchal hierarchy, especially among the educated middle-class, professional families. Marked gender differences, however, continue to prevail. Girls perceive parental control more in the area of their social and household activities, whereas boys perceive it in relation to their academic work reflecting dominant patterns of gender socialization in India (Hegde & Gaonkar 1991). In the case of boys, occupational success is closely related to academic achievement and warrants close supervision during the adolescent years (T. S. Saraswathi & Dutta 1988). Evidence of social transition, especially in the upper-middle-class urban population, comes from an interesting study using the Experience Sampling Method (Larson, Verma, & Dworkin 2001). Fathers, mothers, and 8th graders in 100 urban middle-class families took part in the study. Results indicate that fathers spent almost 22 percent of their time with children (as compared to 31 percent of mothers' time) and, of this, 7 percent was time alone with children with no difference in time spent with sons and daughters. This lends support to the impression that, among the urban middle class, fathers are becoming more involved in parenting and the gender differences in their interactions with children are less marked than before.

Parental involvement and control is very high, especially in the middle class. Parents set high career aspirations and become active participants in adolescents' academic achievement. Psychoanalysts have commented on the implications of a high degree of emotional dependence on parents for mate selection and assumption of independent responsibility in job management (T. S. Saraswathi 1999).

A characteristic feature of a patrilineal system has been the closeness of the mother-son bond, especially the first-born son (Kakar 1978). More often than not, the mother is a stranger to the conjugal family and is not always welcome. The establishment of a close bond between the newly wed is not encouraged, especially in joint family households. The birth of the male child, who will carry on the family name, raises the young mother's status, resulting in a high degree of emotional investment in the son, who is seen as her savior now, and again in old age, when he will care for her. Psychoanalysts have speculated on the ambiguous resolution of the male adolescent's identity because of this intense mother-child bond (Kakar 1978; Ramanujam 1979).

Another feature that characterizes Indian families is the interdependency among family members, be it mother-son, parents and children, or brothers and sisters. Some of these are ritualized as part of one's *dharma*, or duty. These include the son's obligation to care for parents in their old age; the position of power and responsibility accorded to the eldest son; the brothers' duty to protect sisters before their marriage and extend help when needed after their marriage. The brother-sister bond is accorded much social significance and is ritualistically renewed every year in northern India through the observance of a festival called *Rakhi*, wherein sisters tie an artistically woven wrist band on their brother's wrist to socially proclaim their interdependency even after raising their own conjugal families. Roland (1988) observes that Indians are geared toward the rich interdependencies of hierarchical relationships. He sees Indian identity evolving around 'we', 'us', and 'ours' rather than 'I', 'me', or 'mine', reflecting a relational self.

The continued prevalence of traditionalism and familialism is evident in various facets of family life, even among educated Indian adolescents from both rural and urban settings (Bhende 1994; Pathak 1994; Pebley, Delgado, & Brineman 1980). Attitudes of adolescent respondents toward marriage and the female role, largely conformed to traditional norms with 63 percent of males and 72 percent of females – even among the privileged, 'Westernized' upper middle class – preferring arranged marriages (Pathak 1994). There is also a general acceptance of double standards for males and females in matters related to premarital sex and selection of marriage partners, with considerably more freedom for males (Uplaonkar 1995). Social change is evident in the distinct preference for small families among adolescents of all social classes, as well as in increasing individualism and materialism as perceived by parents and other significant adults who interact with young people.

Stressors Associated with Social Change
The fast pace and all-embracing character of sociopolitical and economic changes in India has significant consequences for the individual and the family (Sinha 1988). The fast pace of change and the discordant sequence of changes contribute to individual stress. The ambiguity of values adolescents observe in the adult world, the absence of powerful role models, increasing gaps between aspirations and possible achievement, not

surprisingly, lead to alienation and identity diffusion (Singh & Singh 1996).

Parents themselves appear ill-prepared to cope with social change, having grown up in hierarchically structured and interlinked social groups and collectives, such as the extended family, kinship network, and caste groups that provided stability and solidarity (J. B. P. Sinha 1982, cited in Singhal & Misra 1994). The conflict between parents' desire to help their adolescent children cope with the competitive demands of the market economy and achievement orientation and their own rootedness in the safety of tradition expresses itself in the "cold feet syndrome" when things go wrong (T. S. Saraswathi & Pai 1997). Parents who seem 'modern' in their child rearing practices get anxious when their adolescent child breaches established social codes. Intergenerational conflicts related to marriage, career choice, or separate living arrangements result in the tendency to fall back on tradition. A key concern is the stress created by the changing composition and dynamics of the family with differential expectations, values, competencies, and coping styles between parents and adolescents. Clinical practitioners have expressed concern regarding implications for mental health, especially the tensions experienced by the weakening of social supports from kinship groups and the community. Increasing numbers of educated and employed women with consequent expectations of greater gender egalitarianism in a highly patriarchal society is yet another issue that will continue to challenge Indian families in the coming decades. Yet, across the Indian subcontinent, in both rural and urban locales, even while the outward forms of the family are changing, strong traditional family values prevail and create a vital family life for adolescents and youth.

Peer Relations

The class-based and gendered nature of adolescence in India is most evident in peer relations. Traditionally, families provided a rich web of peers inside the family. Even today there are joint families that have more than 50 members residing under the same roof wherein a dozen cousins may be adolescents. Peers, as a segregated non-kin group, become increasingly prominent as one moves up the social class scale. In contrast to Western and African countries, outside peer groups play a less significant role in the lives of most Indian adolescents (the exceptions being the rich with leisure time; the very poor, especially those employed in wage labor; or socially deviant males, who get involved in drug use, delinquency, and black marketing).

What follows is a predominantly impressionistic account of the role of peers in adolescent development in India, substantiated by limited empirical information where available. Peer relations in India must be understood in the context of cultural restrictions related to interactions with the opposite sex, especially for girls after puberty; and extended and extensive family relations with plenty of scope for within-family peer relations with siblings, cousins, even uncles or aunts of the same age.

Assessment of time spent with family and nonfamily peers indicates the significance of these people in adolescents' lives. Verma and Saraswathi (1992) present systematic data from a short-term longitudinal study of 90 upper-middle-class college students' time use in the city of Chandigarh. Male and female students were found to spend about the same amount of time with peers, with residents in dormitories spending nearly 3 times as much as nonresidents. In a study using a similar design, college girls in Baroda reported that time spent with peers, classmates, or friends was emotionally satisfying (T. S. Saraswathi & Sridharan 1991).

In contrast, adolescent girls in urban slums spend less than 30 minutes a day with peers only, even though they spend nearly 2 hours in mixed groups composed of family members and peers (T. S. Saraswathi & Dutta 1988). Mothers in slum settings expressed concern regarding the negative influence of peers and restrained their adolescent girls from spending time with their peer group. Adolescent girls in rural communities represent yet another pattern, spending nearly 3 hours a day in the company of peers. Rarely was this time spent with a single peer. Typically, a group of neighborhood girls assembled together for domestic work in the courtyard or for agricultural work in fields near the village, accompanied by siblings, cousins, and other female family members of a similar age (T. S. Saraswathi & Dutta 1988). These studies highlight the variation by social class, locale, and gender of the role of peers in adolescents' daily life experiences.

Except for school-based activities, the role of peers is subservient to that of family. Among Indian families, both in India (T. S. Saraswathi & Dutta 1988) and abroad (e.g., Switzerland, Sapru 1999; U.S., J. Mistry, personal communication November 2, 2000), peers often become an integral part of family gatherings and even address each other's family members by kinship terms. There are special festivals wherein peer group activity assumes predominance. Three examples are presented here. In the state of Gujarat, Midwest India, the festival of *Navratri*, or

9 nights, is celebrated in September/October with 9 nights of dancing. Young boys and girls decked up in traditional costumes and jewelry, dance in circles all night to the lively tunes of folk songs. The 2nd occasion is the kite flying festival in January, when citizens of entire towns, cities, and villages are on rooftops or streets, witnessing teenagers fly kites by the thousands, competing to win. Peers also play a dominant role in the festival of *Holi*, celebrated to welcome spring, especially, in the northern parts of India. Colored powder or water is thrown profusely on peers of both sexes, providing a socially sanctioned license in the otherwise strict gender divide in social relations. In both cases, family members and neighbors are present either as participants or as spectators.

Evidence of a distinct peer culture is more clearly present in the upper middle and upper social class than among those lower on the scale. The characteristic features of the subculture include distinct styles in attire, hairstyle and grooming, music, and the use of slang; and having preferred "hang-outs." Access to resources, available leisure time, and parental permissiveness account for the emergence of the peer culture in this class of society. Compared to other social classes, heterosexual interactions and dating, as well as romantic involvement, are also more evident in the upper class. Popular Hindi films are the main form of entertainment for youth across India and portray the recurrent theme of romantic love, garnished with songs and dance numbers. The recent emergence of music video cassettes reinforces this imagery. A point of interest is that romantic love takes a back seat when it comes to marriage in the majority of cases and parents' choice is considered most appropriate and preferred (Pathak 1994; Uplaonkar 1995).

In sum, time spent with peers is limited – in most cases, parents monitor peer choice, and peer influence is moderate and mainly limited to overt expressions of peer culture. When it comes to long-term and value-based decisions, such as career choice or mate selection, adolescents usually opt for parental influence, letting tradition take precedence over the modernity depicted in the popular Indian cinema.

Role of Religion and Caste

Even though, constitutionally, India defines itself as a secular state, religion and caste are deeply entrenched in the identity of Indians across ages and play a direct or indirect role in the daily lives of young people. Hindus predominate, with Muslims and Christians as well as other religious groups, such as Zorastrians and Jews, forming about 20 percent of the population. The distribution of the minority groups varies in different parts of the country. It must be mentioned that Hinduism is usually defined as a way of life, rather than as a religion, and has a strong philosophical base. Considered more than 5,000 years old, it has a history of religious tolerance, accepting Buddhism, Sikhism, Islam, Christianity, and Zorastrianism with no major problems. In recent decades, however, there have been expressions of religious fundamentalism, especially among the Hindus and Muslims, leading to communal clashes among adults and young people. Other than these extreme expressions of religiosity, religion plays a low-key role in daily life, though it is a significant part of a young person's cultural experience and is omnipresent. Most homes have a place of worship (maybe even an entire room in larger houses) and youth do participate in a brief period of daily worship, most marked during examination weeks! Temples, churches, and other places of worship are a regular feature of the local scene, and, except for a small minority, adolescents and their families do visit them and offer prayers to the several deities, at least during religious festival days. For the Hindus, there is 1 major festival practically every month; for other religious groups, there are at least 2 or 3 major religious occasions a year. These, and the public holidays associated with the festivals, keep religion alive in daily life. Most Hindu adolescents have little hesitation in going to the church or mosque as they attend Christian missionary schools or have friends among Muslims. The same is not true in the reverse, as some of the religions do not sanction worship of a deity with a human form. The majority of the schools admit students of all religious faiths, though there are a few that cater only to children of Islam. In sum, religion is ever present in the lives of adolescents, though it plays more of a social than religious role in most cases.

The role of caste in adolescents' lives is much more complex. The constitutional proclamation of secularism has diluted the role of caste in public life. The rigid boundaries of trade and vocation that characterized and defined castes in the past have weakened. Traditionally, the Brahmins were priests and teachers; the Kshatriyas the warriors; the Vaishyas the traders and businessmen; and the Untouchables performed the menial tasks such as being sweepers. Formal schooling and industrialization have loosened the vocational barriers to a great extent. Religion and caste are not barriers to friendships. However, when it comes to marriage partner selection, the embeddedness of caste in the Indian psyche is transparent. In marriages arranged by parents (and most marriages are so arranged) the choice is made from within the immediate caste or a sect very close to it. If a young person's own choice of partner transgresses religious and caste barriers the whole family, especially in rural areas, risks social ostracism. But resisting young people's choice of their own partners can at times have tragic consequences, for example, suicide.

Role of Media

Two general observations regarding the role of media in adolescents' lives merit attention. The 1st observation relates to the high popularity of the Hindi films produced by Bollywood, the Bombay, India, equivalent of Hollywood in the United States, and their regional language counterparts in southern India. The 2nd concerns television serials or soap operas, especially those produced indigenously. India enjoys the dubious distinction of producing the highest number of films in the world (United Nations Development Program 1999; UNDP). These are popular especially among adolescents and youth, not only in India, but also in the Middle East, South and Southeast Asia, some parts of Russia, and among the Indian emigrants in the United States, Canada, and the United Kingdom.

From the perspective of adolescent life experiences, these films offer a rich and colorful fare. They are often filmed in scenic locations abroad, are emotionally charged, and have romantic love as a central theme. The lilting music with poetic wording adds to the attraction. Films are a major and much sought after life experience of adolescents, cutting across class and gender. Many adolescents view films several times in the theater, and many can recite lengthy dialogues from memory. Adolescents imitate the young heroes and heroines in dress and hairstyles, and at times, in romantic love affairs. Media projection of youth, both in films and television, are either as romantic and dreamy or as rebellious and modern, in contrast to adults, who are portrayed as more traditional and conforming. Most parents worry about the negative effects of such media models. Faced with a daily life full of hassles, uncertainties, and corruption, the world of Indian cinema offers make-believe hope to adolescents in the form of heroes and heroines who surmount all problems to reach their goals.

One perceived negative consequence of the celluloid world that has caused much social concern is the increase in the incidence of rape across the country. Since so many factors, including increases in reporting, play a role in the increased incidence of rape and social violence, it is difficult to attribute the contribution of films and imported television programs.

A second outcome popularly attributed to the cinema is the incidence of romantic love affairs among adolescents and youth. In a cultural context of marriages arranged by the family, such romantic love mostly leads to major family conflict and disruption resulting in elopement or, in extreme cases, suicide by the young couples. While reliable statistics are hard to find, almost daily the local papers carry news stories of such love affairs wherein the families feel betrayed by the new generation. Films and even television provide an excellent medium to contrast the idealized traditional roles of obedient and respectful youth, and duty-bound parents and grandparents, with the romantic image of modern youth happy and free, reaching out to the next century. The serial programs televised on the small screen are more by way of family dramas, though many project unconventional themes, such as extramarital affairs, even while idealizing traditional roles. These have not in any way lessened the immense popularity of Indian films. Other media, such as the Internet, play a minuscule role at present because access is limited.

Contexts and Constraints of Education and Schooling

Caste, class, gender, religion, and location constitute the social landscape for Indian adolescents and frame their expectations, ambitions, and aspirations from education. We will review briefly in this section the historical legacy of the Indian educational system, the levels and types of schooling, especially in light of their significance for future employment, and the major hurdles in accessibility of basic education for all.

The historical bases of educational inequalities in India lie in the development of the public education system under the colonial regime in the mid-19th century. As in other British colonies, introduction of the formal education system displaced systems of indigenous education (based predominantly on the oral tradition and close teacher-pupil relations) with mass-based examination systems and a "textbook culture" (Kumar 1991). The colonial educational system enabled the creation of a selective demand for education from those sections privileged by class (upper), caste (high), and gender (male).

This colonial legacy has had far-reaching effects on Indian society. By the time of Indian independence in August 1947, formal education had come to be accepted as an ideal by upper- and middle-class people in India, who have since dominated the bureaucracy and major professions. Central to this dominance has been the perception of English as a language of prestige and power, a symbolic status marker that has

TABLE 4.1. *Age-Specific Rural-Urban Illiteracy Rates by Gender, India (1998–99)*

Age Group	Rural M	Rural F	Urban M	Urban F
10–14	15.0	28.6	7.0	9.6
15–19	17.0	38.7	8.8	13.4
20–29	23.7	55.2	9.1	21.6
Total	18.5	40.4	8.3	14.7

Source: Computed from International Institute for Population Sciences (IIPS) & ORC Macro 2000. *National Family Health Survey (NFHS-2), 1998–99: India*: 26–27; Table 2.7. Mumbai: Author.

outlived colonial domination and struggles for language supremacy in a multilingual society.

Despite a constitutional commitment by the state to ensure universal, free, and compulsory elementary education, and despite having one of the largest schooling systems in the world, India also has the largest concentration of children and adolescents not enrolled in school, and the largest number of nonliterate adults between the ages of 15 and 35 (PROBE 1999; UNDP 1999, 2000). It has been estimated that the number of children who have never been to school is around 100 million (Tilak 1999).

Urban-rural and gender disparities in literacy are evident in Table 4.1. Age-specific illiteracy rates in the 10–29 age group are 12 percent in urban areas and 30 percent in rural areas. In both rural and urban areas, the proportion of literate females in the population decreases with age. Cohort differences indicate that some progress has been made over time in reducing gender inequalities in education although gaps remain. Gender differences in completion rates in favor of males are more evident in rural schools, and particularly in the older age groups. Only 10 percent of females have at least a high school education, in contrast to 18 percent of males (IIPS & ORC 1995).

Educational inequalities form a pyramidal structure of relative disadvantage with the rural, tribal, and low-caste girls in the most backward states being the most disadvantaged in literacy and years of schooling (UNDP 2000). In 1991, literacy rates among the Scheduled Castes and Scheduled Tribes were at least 20 percent lower than those in other categories. Five out of 6 tribal women were illiterate (Government of India 1991; GOI).

Elementary education, the first tier of 8 years, is supposed to be universal and mandatory but is not so in practice. Schools mirror, and largely reproduce, patterns of class stratification. About 70 percent of children attend public or government schools where no fees are charged; another 22 percent attend government-aided schools that charge moderate fees; and less than 10 percent attend private schools that charge high fees and offer high-quality education as well as extracurricular activities (National Council of Educational Research and Training 1992; NCERT). Private schools predominantly have English as their medium of instruction and cater to the upper middle class and upper-class elite. Public schools offer instruction in the local languages and draw their pupils mainly from the lower middle class and the poor. Despite affirmative action policies that provide incentives to disadvantaged groups, including the girl child, gross disparities continue to exist. More than half the children aged 6–14 drop out before completing 8 years of school (GOI 1998). For children belonging to Scheduled Caste and Scheduled Tribe communities, dropout rates are even higher (Nambissan 1996). These children belong to the lowest rung in the caste structure (Scheduled Caste) or indigenous ethnic groups (Scheduled Tribes) and have been officially identified in the constitution as backward classes targeted for affirmative action at all levels of education and employment.

Structural factors coupled with sociocultural pressures keep participation in schooling low. For young girls and boys, going to school is a function of their location (rural/urban) and gender. Data from 1998–99 National Family Health Survey (IIPS & ORC, 2000) indicate that in the age group 10–19 years, 29 percent complete primary school; 18 percent middle school; and 9 percent high school. Social discrimination, economic deprivations, and lack of facilities translate into low participation of lower caste and tribal children in schooling (Nambissan 1996).

Higher Education
University education, which caters to the age group 18–24 years, is highly subsidized by the government. The medium of instruction at this stage is predominantly English. A network of prestigious engineering and management institutes offers facilities of international standards that screen students on highly stringent criteria. There is a high social and market demand for a college degree, and only 5 percent of high school graduates opt for vocational courses (Tilak 1999). Since the 1980s, privatization has been growing in the higher education sector, more so

in the information technology and management areas, to the advantage of richer students.

Gender and other social disparities are also seen at the higher education level. Although women make up 24–50 percent of those enrolled, across different states of India (Karlekar 2000) only 1 in 3 students in science courses and 7 in every 100 engineering students are women. By contrast, women make up more than 50 percent of students in education courses. Affirmative action policies have been more for young men in the higher education sector. For the country as a whole, male Scheduled Caste students constitute 9 percent of total enrollment and male Scheduled Tribe students 3 percent, which is not inconsiderable given their total representation in the national population (17 percent and 8 percent respectively). However, the proportion of Scheduled Caste and Scheduled Tribe women in total enrollment was only 2.4 percent and 0.9 percent respectively (Chanana 2000). This only confirms the confounding of caste and gender, making girls and women from the lowest caste the most educationally disadvantaged.

Continuing Concerns
The persistence of educational inequalities and the sheer growing numbers of out-of-school children continue to be causes for concern, buttressing the debate on making education a fundamental right going beyond the constitutional recognition of education. The share of elementary education in national budget allocations has always been low; in 1995–96, only 1.5 percent of the 3.2 percent of gross national product (GNP) allocated to education was earmarked for elementary education (PROBE 1999). It has been argued that for achieving the most modest goals of education, at least 8 percent of GNP will be necessary. This seems remote since public expenditures on education have been reduced in the last decade under policies of economic liberalization (Tilak 1999). The strains of the transition to a market economy are being passed on to children and youth in India via education. For those in school, more young people are reporting signs of academic stress (Verma, Sharma, & Larson 1999); competitive individualism based on achievement makes the scenario even more complex (Roland 1988). Making education more meaningful to young people in contemporary India will entail a powerful dismantling of ideologies that privilege dominant elitist voices over the marginalized. Overcoming the colonial legacy of an education that is not culturally embedded and that does not have meaning in the daily lives of most adolescents is a Himalayan

task. This presents a challenge to progressive educators committed to seeing a more humane society and more equal opportunities for education.

Employment

Child and adolescent labor is part of India's historical tradition (Dube 1981). What exist today are pernicious variants of a socially supportive tradition, wherein young people were apprenticed for their adult occupations as teachers, priests, farmers, or artisans. This contrasts with the exploitative labor of the industrial and postindustrial eras (Verma 1999).

The Indian subcontinent has the largest number of working children in the world. The IAMR *Yearbook* (2000) estimates that 10 million children aged 0–14 are out of school and put to some work, in the home or outside. The labor force participation rates as per the Census of India (Registrar General and Census Commissioner 2001) are 5 percent for the 10–14-year age group, and 36 percent for the 15–19-year-old adolescent population (44 percent for males, and 26 percent for females) (UNFPA 1998). Burra (1997) estimates that children constitute 10 to 33 percent of the total workers in different industries. Most studies point to the gross underestimation of child labor due to varied definitions and the need for more reliable assessment measures (Rodgers & Standing 1981; UNICEF 1991). Further, labor in the informal family or street economy often remains unremunerated. In contrast to the poor who are forced to work early in life because of poverty and unstable home conditions, employment for middle-class adolescents is delayed until early adulthood, as they are encouraged and financially supported by parents to pursue their education and prepare for a better career.

Policy makers have justified the existence of child labor with the argument that the family needs the wages of the child to supplement its income. Two major policies arose out of this conviction, the Child Labor Prohibition & Regulation Act (CLPRA) of 1986 and the National Policy on Education (NPE; GOI 1986). The Indian government considers child labor a 'necessary evil' and the CLPRA does not completely ban but only seeks to 'protect' working children. Recognizing the need for giving access to elementary education to those sections of the population who cannot be enrolled in local schools, the NPE announced the continuance of nonformal education for working boys and girls as a major thrust. The issue has been openly debated with two schools of thought emerging: one supports the government position of regulation, the other favors a complete ban on child labor (Burra 1997). Research in the area of child labor has primarily focused on the magnitude of the problem, areas of work, working conditions of children, indicators of exploitation and its consequences on the health, education, and psychosocial well-being of children. Availability of disaggregated data and life experiences of the 10–19-year-old adolescent group is sparse, since children start work early in life in unskilled and semiskilled jobs in the unorganized sectors, which do not get recorded in census data.

Child labor is deeply embedded in the Indian tradition of home-based or family work, where the children are expected to learn the father's craft or, in the case of girls, to share the responsibility of housework. The idea also fits in with the historical reality of being born into a role (Dube 1981). Another reason for children joining the workforce is a lack of faith in the existing education system, which does not necessarily lead to employment or upward social mobility (Kanbargi 1988). Migration of families, broken homes, parental abuse, and abandonment are other reasons for children and adolescents joining the workforce (Fonseka & Malhotra 1994). Employers prefer children as they are cheap, productive, and obedient (Burra 1997). Child labor gets its legitimacy when officials and employers argue that children work as apprentices, acquiring needed skills for adult employment, contribute to the family income, and are mainly employed as part of family labor, and thus sustain India's traditional craft-oriented industries (Weiner's *Foreword*, in Burra 1997). Burra's case studies (1997) refute each of these arguments by showing that children are not working alongside their parents, and children are employed in spite of high levels of adult unemployment.

Children and adolescents work as main and marginal workers, both in the organized and unorganized sectors of rural and urban economies. A majority is employed in agriculture, on plantations, in mines, and in the match and fireworks industries. Other industries where they work include cigarette manufacturing, gem polishing, lock manufacturing, handicrafts, carpet weaving, brassware, woolen hosiery, and glass factories. Adolescents also work in gas stations and restaurants, or they may be self-employed as porters, vendors, or car park attendants, or as bonded laborers where they are exchanged for settlement of debts incurred by fathers. Health problems in young adolescents abound due to performance of adult-level tasks, for long hours, in hazardous, unhygienic conditions, with a high risk of physical and sexual abuse.

Children and adolescents working in small-scale industries and business establishments are to some extent covered by the law. However, those working and living on the streets are outside the purview of the legislation. There are approximately 11 million children and adolescents in India who fend for themselves in the streets of metropolitan cities and large townships (Phillips 1992). Adolescents on the streets resort to rag-picking, begging, shoe-shining, and selling balloons and fruits and vegetables. A number of studies on street youth, sponsored by UNICEF and carried out in different cities, reveal that they come from households that experience repeated crises of health, unemployment, criminality, strained family relations, and alcoholism. These situations increase the prospects of an adolescent being led into antisocial activities, and/or may cause youngsters to leave home and to lead semi-independent lives (Institute of Psychological and Educational Research 1991; IPER). Harassed by middlemen and police officials, many children resort to begging, thieving, drug peddling, and pimping (Panicker & Nangia 1992). Verma (1999) observes that experiences on the street promote the development of self-preservation skills, a conformity orientation to the group to coexist, and to develop resiliency and independence. Yet the absence of the family in the case of adolescents who have no home to return to at night results in inadequate socialization, disruptive relationships, and negative developmental outcomes with adverse consequences on their psychosocial competence and well-being (Verma 1999). Although adolescent girls are more protected by families than boys are, when girls do break the bonds they are often worse off than boys are, as they are lured into prostitution.

Some of the remedial measures suggested and undertaken at the government level (Narayan 1988) and by several nongovernmental organizations (NGOs) working with this group are: to provide education, health, nutrition, recreational, and welfare services; to regulate work conditions; to provide on-the-job training and safety measures from hazards and accidents; and to encourage social intervention within the family and community (rather than advocating an institution-based approach). Given the sheer numbers of children and adolescents participating in the workforce, the problem of child labor will continue in the coming decades with children working in hazardous and exploitative conditions. A national labor policy that adopts a more comprehensive approach (with regulation as its short-term goal and abolition as its long-term goals), with strict enforcement machinery involving both the public and the private sectors, alone can help arrest and abolish child and adolescent labor.

It must be pointed out at this juncture that the grim picture of early entry into the labor force is characteristic essentially of the lowest one-third of the population who fall below the poverty line. The unemployed statistics for 1993–94 are approximately 4.9 percent for the rural males aged 20–24, and a high 12.6 percent for urban males of the same age (Kundu 1997). For the adolescents from the lower-middle and middle classes, the employment scenario is more positive and hopeful. Several factors contribute to this: (a) the parents in these social classes view education as a means to upward mobility and willingly make enormous personal sacrifices to see their sons through school and college; (b) there is a greater awareness regarding access to loans and scholarships for education; and (c) there is an ethos of literacy in the homes and the neighborhood contributing to supervision, support, and modeling.

In a highly competitive educational environment, strong educational qualifications and professional training are highly correlated with social class (and sometimes caste). Adolescents from the lower-middle class opt for vocational training after school or a college degree in arts or commerce, where entry is easy, ensuring a white-collar job as typist, clerk, accountant, postmaster, or similar position. The upper-middle- and upper-class adolescents, both boys and girls, compete for courses in professional training such as medicine, engineering, or finance and management, and more recently, in the computer sciences in elitist institutions like the Indian Institutes of Technology, Sciences, and Management. If unsuccessful in entering into these institutions with limited seats, they settle for similar programs of study in other institutions. Usually the training offered in technology and the sciences prepares students well for competitive job positions both on the national and multinational corporate scene. The same cannot be said of the arts and commerce streams, where preparation for employment is inadequate, resulting in large numbers of educated unemployed. As mentioned in the section on education, high talent in technology and computer sciences has opened up the world labor market for the Indian adolescent, making training in other disciplines comparatively far less lucrative and appealing. While individuals and families cope as best as they can depending on their resources and cognitive skills, at the macrolevel the conflict between tradition and modernity is apparent. A subsistence economy apprenticed their adolescents in the vocations cut out for them. Today the options are many, but for a majority of adolescents, the means to achieve them are not so clear.

Political and Civic Participation

Participation of Indian youth in political movements came to the fore during the struggle for independence, inspired by Gandhi's charismatic leadership. Thousands of students discontinued their studies to join the Quit India movement in 1942. Some of them became prominent political leaders during the 5 decades that followed (Chowdhury 1988; S. Saraswathi 1988).

The early years following independence in 1947 saw youth involvement in the fight for social justice. The 1950s also saw the emergence of youth power in junior colleges and universities, supported by political parties that harnessed student power to serve their own ends, by creating a power base on campuses (Adsule 1996). The 1960s and '70s saw youth movements propelled by high unemployment (Deva 1992), a flawed system of education (Sajid 1992), and ineffective governance and university-state relations (Upreti 1987). Students became active agents of opposition and change, using protests, demonstrations, strikes, boycotts, and other deterrents to achieve their ends, which ranged from the cessation of fee hikes to the dissolution of state assemblies. Student agitation in the northeastern state of Assam presents an excellent case study of assertion of student power, initiated as a rebellion against the flow of immigrants into the state, a demand for use of Assamese as an official language, and reservation of key jobs for state domiciles. The All-Assamese Students' Union eventually succeeded in forming the first ever student government in the country (Kumari & Sree 1992). The negative spinoffs from this movement continue to plague state politics even today, luring unemployed youth into terrorist activities through threats or monetary rewards.

The last decade has seen degeneration in youth politics, once inspired by powerful role models governed by values of equity and social justice. Regional aspirations and religious conflicts, combined with diminished economic opportunities in some regions of the country and for some segments of the population, have changed the course and quality of youth movements. Subversive activities in the northeastern states of

Kashmir and Punjab exploit young people's frustration, harnessing it for militancy and violence. With the recent lowering of the voting age from 21 to 18, older adolescents can make a difference in who is voted for and who stays in power in the government. Unfortunately, few make the effort to become informed voters and many do not vote.

Civic Participation

Productive civic activity of both student and nonstudent youth is visible by their participation in various community development activities through schemes of both the government and NGOs. The governmental programs, such as the National Cadet Corps, National Service Scheme, Nehru Yuvak Kendras, and the National Service Volunteer Scheme, have been instrumental in arousing social consciousness among the youth while engaging them in community work and in the promotion of national integration (Chowdhury 1988). Spread across colleges and universities, such activities have resulted in students doing extensive work in villages by engaging in income-generating projects, medico-social surveys for need assessment, and running vocational training centers for rural women. In the urban areas, activities include slum development projects, literacy, mass immunization, sanitation drives, and nonformal education for the weaker sections of the community. Religious groups such as Buddhists, Jains, and Christians also foster civic participation in their congregations and encourage social welfare programs for the economically disadvantaged and physically challenged. It is interesting to observe the traditional belief of service and philanthropy merge with the contemporary concept of volunteerism, especially when natural calamities like cyclones or earthquakes occur. Schoolchildren and adolescents respond to the call for help with alacrity and commitment. High schools foster civic participation through a required course called "Socially Useful Productive Work." To instill a sense of social obligation, schools encourage adolescents to work with the less economically privileged and the physically and mentally challenged. Campaigns to promote literacy, such as "Each one teach one," have witnessed enthusiastic participation. And, NGOs use adolescent volunteers both from schools and colleges to serve various humanitarian causes. Quantified data on rate of voluntary participation is not available. What is noteworthy is that, in general, there is greater participation in civic activities among the middle- and the lower-class adolescents than among the very well-to-do.

Delinquency and Crime

A general impression among the lay public holds that there is a disturbing trend of increase in crimes by young offenders. Reasons offered include political instability in the country, high rates of unemployment and frustration, exploitation by politicians and gang leaders, and the tendency of youth to take up crime as a short cut to a good lifestyle and fast money (Adsule 1996). Partly these may reflect the model provided by the popular Hindi film world. The underworld in many cities thrives on young recruits without police records; and politicians, often linked to the underworld, use young men to influence the electoral process (Bhagbanprakash 1997). In the section on political participation, we had mentioned exploitation of unemployed youth by political parties, especially in the disturbed regions of the country. The reality is, however, that the recorded juvenile crime rate has shown a steady decrease from 1971 to 1998 (National Crime Records Bureau 1998; NCRB). During this period girls' contribution to juvenile crime has increased from 6 percent in 1986 to 26 percent of the total juvenile crime in 1998; and, while there is a proportionately high involvement of youth from the lower social classes in crime, recent evidence suggests rising involvement of middle- and upper-middle-class youth. Anecdotal evidence of murder, robbery, kidnapping, and extortion by middle-class adolescents is highlighted by the popular press as the malaise of consumerism.

The Juvenile Justice Act (1986) provides for care, protection, treatment, and rehabilitation of delinquents or the neglected, and also for adjudication of matters that are related to the conduct and disposition of delinquents. A juvenile, as per this act, is defined as a male below 16 years and a female below 18 years of age. Going by the statistics of the NCRB (1998), among those arrested under the Indian Penal Code and the Special Laws & Local Laws, adolescents aged 12–16 account for 61 percent of arrested young offenders, those aged 16–18 account for 22 percent, and those aged 7–12 for 18 percent.

Substance Use

No accurate figures are available to catalogue the extent of adolescent drug abuse in India. Nevertheless, the India Country Paper (GOI 1998) revealed that most of the abusers are 16 to 35 years of age, with abuse being more prevalent among the 18 to 25 age group. Rates of current abusers are low in early adolescence and are high during the early 20s.

In 1989, an exhaustive survey covering 33 cities reported that a large number of drug addicts come from the lower social class and are unemployed laborers, transport workers, and students, especially in the northeast bordering Burma and the golden triangle, and those from metropolitan cities (Ministry of Welfare 1992; Shastri 1996). Tobacco consumption, especially smoking, is considered to be a starting point in getting initiated into other drugs from marijuana to harder ones. The average age at which young people start smoking could be as early as 12 years (Jha 1994), and street children are particularly vulnerable. Entry of multinational corporations and trade is expected to have adverse consequences because of their compelling advertisement campaigns. There have been public debates expressing concern.

Crimes Against Adolescents

There is no separate classification of offenses categorized as offenses against adolescents. Data available from the NCRB (1998) indicate a high incidence of rape, kidnapping and abduction, and domestic violence. Voluntary organizations have played a very supportive role in empowering girls, women, and families seeking redress. The media have been used extensively to reach out, and many television channels address the issue.

Forced prostitution looms large as a social problem. Thapar (1998) reports from a study conducted by the Central Social Welfare Board in 1991 in 6 metropolitan cities, wherein 40 percent of prostitutes were inducted before 18 years of age. The *devadasi* practice in Karnataka, a system in which daughters of lower castes are dedicated before puberty to the village deity and are later made available to the priests and other men (Chatterjee 1990; Rath 1991), is yet another example of child prostitution and abuse by parents and caregivers. Further, the gaining popularity of 'child sex workers' especially among street and working children, is alarming.

In sum, adolescent exposure to abuse and violence is influenced, not only by the strengths and vulnerability of individual adolescents, but also by the character of the settings in which they live and the ways in which they connect to their social world. Changes in social policy, effective law enforcement, evaluation of rehabilitation programs, and improved training can help combat the problem to some extent. A multilevel effort to improve the capacity of families and communities in building safety nets, social controls coupled with positive school experience, and reduced opportunities for engaging in crime and other risk behaviors can prove beneficial in the long run.

Physical and Mental Well-Being

It is only recently that adolescence has drawn the attention of program planners and policy makers, mainly out of concern for reproductive health and its impact on fertility control. Problems in obtaining reliable data on the physical health and nutritional status of adolescents and on their mental well-being are manifold. First, documentation is inadequate. Second, access to documents such as census data is delayed by several years. Third, most of the statistical profiles do not use adolescence as a marker, but current data for 0 to 5 years, 5+ to 15 years, and 15+ to 45 years, thereby aggregating adolescent data with data on either children or adults. This applies to both physical and mental health data.

Physical Development and Nutritional Status

There are marked social class differences in stature, from childhood through adolescence and mature adulthood, with undernutrition appearing to affect all growth parameters (longitudinal data, Satyanarayana et al. 1992; Kanade, Joshi, & Rao 1999; crosssectional studies, Tripathi et al. 1985). Early height deficit is partially compensated for by the longer span of years in which height increments are observed in adolescents from lower socioeconomic groups due to later puberty. However, the maximum potential is never achieved, leaving them stunted when compared with their peers from the higher social classes (Srikantia 1989).

The relationship with social class is also evident in the age of menarche. The all-India mean age of menarche among lower socioeconomic groups is reported as 14.5 years, which is 1.3 years older than that of the higher socioeconomic group (Indian Council of Medical Research, 1972 cited in Srikantia 1989). A secular trend of decline in age of menarche has been observed in the higher socioeconomic group, wherein, currently, menarche occurs around 12 years (Prakash & Pathmanathan 1992). The observed mean weight at menarche is around 38 kgs, which is much lower than the 46–48 kgs reported in the West (Srikantia 1989).

Stunting, under- and malnutrition, early marriage, and early pregnancy have adverse implications for maternal and child health, placing them at high obstetric risk (CEDPA/UNFPA/PRERANA 1996). Gopalan (1993) rightly terms the high incidence of teenage pregnancies in India as "child labor at its worst." To quote, "we witness the sad spectacle of millions of 'children' (girls 14–18 years) compelled to engage in child-bearing and child rearing even before they have had a chance to complete their own physical growth and development and attain adulthood.... It is 'labor' which carries greater risks than some other forms of child labor over which there is public outcry" (2). Interventions through the nationwide Integrated Child Development Services have only made a marginal difference (Sharma 1992). In sum, the health scenario of more than 40 percent of adolescents in India is plagued by undernutrition. Problems due to lifestyles such as overeating or improper food habits affect only a minuscule segment.

Sexuality and Reproductive Health
While documentation of evidence on this taboo subject is only now beginning to appear, informal discussions with college students and the experiences of NGO volunteers working with adolescents in the urban slums make one suspect that premarital sex among adolescents in India was and is not as rare a phenomenon as adults would like to believe. This has been substantiated by anecdotal evidence from medical practitioners and counselors, and by popular magazine surveys. If anything, despite the AIDS scare, sexual activity is on the increase and there is a steady lowering of the age of initiation of sexual activity into the early teens. Further, more than 50 percent of youth are married by the end of the teenage years and hence engaged in socially accepted (and expected) sexual relations.

As mentioned earlier, about 22 percent of the Indian population is between the ages of 10 and 19, which means there were approximately 200 million adolescents at the end of the year 2000 (Jejeebhoy 1996). Of these, more than 40 percent of girls are married by 17 years or earlier, and of these, nearly 58 percent are mothers or pregnant (IIPS & OCR 1995). Twenty to 30 percent of all unmarried males (17 to 24 years) are sexually active (Goparaju 1993; Savara & Sridhar 1994; Sharma & Sharma 1995; Watsa 1993). Self-report figures for females are much lower, i.e., 6 to 9 percent (Bhende 1994; Savara & Sridhar 1994). An exceptionally high incidence of 40 percent is reported in the case of tribal girls in one unique study by Bang and colleagues (1989) using direct clinical examination of all adolescent girls in the area.

Double standards exist, whereby unmarried adolescent boys are far more likely than adolescent girls to be sexually active. Furthermore, boys are also far more likely to approve of premarital sexual activity for themselves, and have far more opportunities to engage in sexual relations, but are more disapproving of girls' freedom to engage in sexual activity (Bhende 1994; Jejeebhoy 1996). The girls also concur with the view of dual standards (Bhende 1994; Kumari 1985). Commercial sex workers seem to be the most frequently cited sex partners in the case of males (Bhende 1994; Goparaju 1993; Sharma & Sharma 1995) though older married women in the community, friends, relatives, and fiancées figure in that order of frequency (Goparaju 1993). Homosexual relations are reported as ranging from 2.5 to 25 percent among the rural and urban students surveyed (Watsa 1993). The wide range in prevalence rate reflects variation in interpretation of homosexuality, from serious relations (very low) to casual contacts (on the higher end).

Condom use and accurate information regarding proper use is absent or irregular among both the sexually active (Sharma et al. 1996) and the general population of school-going adolescents (Tikoo, Bollman, & Bergen 1995). This, combined with reluctance on the part of parents and schools to talk more freely about sex (Tikoo et al. 1995; Sharma 1996), is particularly disconcerting, considering the reported increase in sexual activity, incidence of STDs, and clinical abortions among unmarried adolescents.

HIV/AIDS

HIV/AIDS has been singled out for attention among physical health problems because of the current concern regarding its epidemic spread. Adolescents and youth are particularly vulnerable because of possible infection through commercial sex or drug use, or because they have to assume care of AIDS-infected parents and/or orphaned siblings.

Analyzing the epidemiological data in India, Satpathy and Shaukat (1997) report that: (i) the highest number of HIV infections are among Injectable Drug Users (IDU) in the northeastern state of Manipur; (ii) males account for 79 percent of AIDS cases; (iii) the majority of the patients (89 percent) are 15 to 44 years old; (iv) HIV infection is spreading from urban to rural areas; from individuals practicing risk behaviors to the general population; and from mothers to children; and (v) tuberculosis is spreading rapidly among AIDS patients, and the chances of a dual epidemic of TB and HIV is likely in the future. Lowering of social control by community members along with greater scope for experimentation has increased adolescent risk behaviors.

Findings related to awareness and knowledge about HIV/AIDS among adolescents are mixed. Some studies with urban school and college-going adolescents report a high degree of awareness and knowledge (Francis, Gill, & Chowdhury 1997). Most others report average or poor levels of knowledge, with many misconceptions about methods of transmission, high-risk groups, and preventive measures (Bahulekar & Garg 1997; Wadhva et al. 1997). Awareness levels increased with age and males were better informed than females (Tikoo, Bollman, & Bergen 1995). Common sources of knowledge reported were TV, radio, magazines, newspapers, friends, and, rarely, parents and teachers (Aggarwal et al. 1997). College students from rural areas (Rahate, Zodpey, & Bhalkule 1997) and out-of-school adolescents (Kalra & Kalra 1996) report less awareness and AIDS knowledge, with 60 to 70 percent having grave misconceptions. Interventions among school students have proved to be effective in enhancing awareness and dispelling misconceptions regarding the disease.

Mental Health
Reliable studies, at the population level, of the incidence of psychiatric disorders in children are hard to find. As reported in an extensive review of the prevalence of psychiatric disorders in schoolchildren in India, Malhotra, Kohli, and Arun (1999) present figures ranging from 8 to 36 percent. The wide range is accounted for by the nature of sampling and methods used for assessment. Studies reviewed by Kapur (1992), Sarkar, Kapur, and Kaliaperumal (1995) and Sitholey and Chakrabarti (1992) report prevalence rates of 6 to 20 percent, the incidence being higher among older adolescents and among boys compared to girls. Epidemiological studies of the general population report a prevalence rate of 5 to 15 percent, which is lower than the estimates of clinic-based studies (Sitholey & Chakrabarti 1992). Recurrent diagnosis across studies indicate mental retardation, neurotic disorders, conduct disorder, enuresis, and epilepsy to be the common problems. Kapur (1992) points out that community surveys pick up conditions such as enuresis, stuttering, sleep disorders, mental retardation, and epilepsy, while school surveys identify scholastic problems, emotional disturbance, and conduct disorders as major problems. Scholastic underachievement was found to be inversely related to mental health, highlighting the importance accorded to school success, by both teachers and parents.

Health Care
One of the most positive outcomes of the initiatives taken by the national mental health institutes is the integration of the traditional healing

practices with community psychiatric care. This is particularly significant because modern psychiatric care is neither accessible nor affordable
for a majority of the population.

Problems associated with physical and mental health of Indian adolescents and expression of sexuality need to be understood in their cultural context. A distinct hierarchy based on caste, class, and gender
characterizes Indian society. This, combined with large-scale poverty,
exacerbates the condition of the vulnerable, namely, the poor, low caste,
and female. The problem is made more acute by associated factors such
as absence of safe water sources and sanitation facilities, and low access
to education and health facilities (World Bank 1998).

Provision of basic public health facilities has been expanding since
independence in 1947 and systematically so since 1975 when the Integrated Child Development Services (ICDS) was initiated. The ICDS aims
to improve the quality of life of children, adolescents, and mothers of
reproductive age through early interventions for nutrition, health, and
education. Every family is supposed to have access to health and primary education services within walking distance from home (e.g., 1 to
1.5 kms). Of course the reality is that, even when the physical building
may be present, the quality of and access to services varies. States like
Kerala and West Bengal, with high literacy and public awareness, claim
100 percent coverage. Other states, like Bihar and Rajasthan, perform
poorly.

Several policy documents at the national level exemplify the central
government's awareness of the significance of issues related to health.
Three of the policies deserve special mention: (i) The National Health
Policy (1983) aims to provide primary health care with special emphasis on the preventive, promotive, and rehabilitative aspects of health;
(ii) The National Policy on Education (GOI 1986) envisages reorganiza-
tion of education at all levels, including education of the handicapped
and minority populations; and (iii) the National Mental Health Program for India (Director General of Health Services 1982) aims to ensure
availability and accessibility of basic mental health care to all (Murthy
1992).

As we move into the new millennium, we cling to the hope that the
health sector will be more successful in the coming 50 years than it
has been in the past 50. Such a hope can be actualized only in the context of overall socioeconomic development, education for awareness,
better access to public health care including safe drinking water and

environmental sanitation, as well as controlled food prices. Similarly, fertility control through rigorous implementation of the legal age for marriage, nutritional and sex education, and protection for the unmarried pregnant adolescent demand urgent attention. At present, all these services and interventions are available in a piece-meal fashion with nonoptimal consequences for adolescent health.

The National Youth Policy & Development Programs for Adolescents

The Draft National Youth Policy (GOI, 1997) has as its main objectives developing a respect for the principles and values enshrined in the constitution, promoting awareness of historical and cultural heritage, and helping develop qualities of discipline, self-reliance, justice, and fair play. The policy expects to achieve its goal by providing, among other things: (i) education commensurate with abilities; (ii) access to employment that matches abilities; (iii) food and nutrition adequate for overall development; (iv) basic and constitutionally guaranteed rights; and (v) full access to places and facilities for cultural, recreational, and sporting activities. The policy has been critiqued on several grounds ranging from focus on too broad an age range (10 to 35 years) to absence of a concrete action plan. Yet it provides a broad conceptual umbrella for several government action programs.

Within and outside the DNYP framework a number of programs have been implemented both by government and by NGOs. Government-sponsored programs, referred to briefly in the section on civic participation, include the National Cadet Corps, the National Service Scheme, and the Nehru Yuvak Kendra Scheme (Chowdhury 1988). The latter focuses specifically on rural youth (S. Saraswathi 1988). Gender-sensitive empowerment programs such as Mahila Samakhya focus on life skills development and promote development of competencies including functional literacy, health, nutrition, sanitation, reproductive health, and rights among young girls (Population Council 1999). Work by NGOs has been geared to educational, recreational, health services, vocational training, empowerment, and self-development (GOI 1998).

Despite these clearly articulated policies, the government programs are often plagued by the absence of a sense of direction and clear commitment combined with bureaucratic rigidity. The NGOs have succeeded well on these counts, though sustainability is curtailed by funding problems. With political commitment, better governance, and more coordination among the service sectors, the impact can be tremendous.

Conclusion

Where do we go from here? How do we conclude? By painting the picture of Indian adolescents dropping out of school, entering and exiting the labor market before their time, physically stunted, not adequately covered by social welfare measures, tempted by drugs, crime and violence? That would hardly be fair. Because alongside these pictures are more than a million young people climbing heights their parents could not have dreamt of. They are physically fit, educationally successful (even on the international scene), professionally sought after by multinationals in the United States and Europe for their training, expertise, and productivity (Nerd Mentality 2000), and with more money to spend and more leisure to spend it, they are the apple of the eye of the consumer market. The truth, as always, lies somewhere in between the welfarists' nightmare of widening economic disparities that could result in frustration and consequent negative social fallouts and the economists' dream of unlimited opportunities and the pathways to reach them.

Using the vernacular of the stock market, "The scene is volatile." It would be folly to spell doomsday, for there is hope and promise. One sees hope in the smiling eyes of the street vendor; hears hope in the carefree laughter of a bevy of high school graduates; and senses hope in the adolescent glued to the new computer program, dreaming of becoming a dot.com millionaire. For as they face the future, regardless of life's challenges, most of them can draw strength and sustenance from traditions that have stood the test of time.

References

Adsule, J. 1996. Indian youth and crime. *Perspectives in Social Work.* XI(1):19–21.
Aggarwal, K., A. T. Kannan, V. Grover, P. Kumar, & A. K. Puri. 1997. Knowledge and attitude towards AIDS among college youth of East Delhi. In *HIV/AIDS Research in India,* eds. O. P. Aggarwal, A. K. Sharma, & A. Indrayan, 84–85. New Delhi: National Aids Control Organisation, Ministry of Health & Family Welfare, GOI.
Arnett, J. J. 1998. Learning to stand alone: The contemporary transition to adulthood in cultural and historical context. *Human Development.* 6:295–315.
Bahulekar, P. V. & B. S. Garg. 1997. AIDS awareness in school children. In *HIV/AIDS Research in India,* eds. O. P. Aggarwal, A. K. Sharma, & A. Indrayan,

181–188. New Delhi: National Aids Control Organisation, Ministry of Health & Family Welfare, GOI.

Bang, R. A., A. T. Bang, M. Baltule, Y. Choudhary, S. Sarmukaddam, & O. Tale. 1989. High prevalence of gynecological diseases in rural Indian women. *Lancet*. 1(8629):85–88.

Bhagbanprakash. 1997. Youth in urban areas: Problems and prospects. Paper presented at the National Symposium on Youth in Urban Areas. Feb: Chandigarh, India.

Bhende, A. A. 1994. A study of sexuality of adolescent girls and boys in underprivileged groups in Bombay. *The Indian Journal of Social Work*. LV (4): 557–571.

Burra, N. 1997. *Born to work: Child labor in India*. Delhi: Oxford University Press.

Center for Development and Population Activities/United Nations Population Fund/Prerana (CEDPA/UNFPA/PRERANA). 1996. Expanding partnerships for adolescent girls. Working Paper. New Delhi: Author.

Chanana, K. 2000. Treading the hallowed halls: Women in higher education in India. *Economic and Political Weekly*. XXXIV(12):1012–1022.

Chatterjee, M. 1990. *A report on Indian women from birth to twenty*. New Delhi: National Institute of Public Co-operation and Child Development.

Chowdhury, D. P. 1988. *Youth participation and development*. Delhi: Atma Ram.

Deva, I. 1992. Youth in third world countries. In *Global youth, peace and development, Vol. II*, ed. Y. C. Simhadri, 44–62. Delhi: Ajanta Publications.

Director General of Health Services. 1982. *National mental health program of India*. New Delhi: Ministry of Health and Family Welfare.

Dube, L. 1981. The economic roles of children in India: Methodological issues. In *Child work, poverty, and underdevelopment*, eds. G. Rodgers & G. Standing, 179–213. Geneva: International Labor Organization.

Dube, L. 1988. On the construction of gender: Hindu girls in patrilineal India. In *Socialization, education and women: Explorations in gender identity*, ed. K. Chanana, New Delhi: Orient Longman.

Fonseka, L. & D. D. Malhotra. 1994. India: Urban poverty, children and participation. In *Urban children in distress*, ed. C. S. Blanc, 161–215. Luxembourg: Gordon & Breach.

Francis, P. T., J. S. Gill, & S. Chowdhury. 1997. Knowledge, beliefs and attitudes regarding AIDS, STDs and human sexuality among senior secondary students in New Delhi. In *HIV/AIDS research in India*, eds. O. P. Aggarwal, A. K. Sharma, & A. Indrayan, 162–165. New Delhi: National Aids Control Organisation, Ministry of Health & Family Welfare, GOI.

Gopalan, C. 1993. Child care in India – emerging challenges. *Bulletin of the Nutrition Foundation of India*. 14(3):1–3.

Goparaju, L. 1993. Unplanned, unsafe: Male students' sexual behavior. Paper presented at the Workshop on Sexual Aspects of AIDS/STD Prevention. Nov.: Bombay, India. Resource Development, Department of Education.

Government of India. 1986. *Juvenile justice act*. New Delhi: Delhi Law House.

Government of India. 1986. *Child labour and prohibition act*. New Delhi: Ministry of Labor.

Government of India. 1991. *Census of India*. New Delhi: Author.

Government of India. 1997. *Draft national youth policy.* New Delhi: Ministry of Human Resource Development, Department of Youth Affairs and Sports.

Government of India. 1998. India country paper. Paper presented at the South Asia Conference on Adolescents. July: New Delhi, India.

Government of India. 1998. *Annual Report 1997–98.* New Delhi: Ministry of Human Resource Development, Department of Education.

Hegde, B. & V. Gaonkar. 1991. Perception of parental control by adolescents. *Indian Psychological Review.* 36(5–6): 19–24.

Indian Council of Social Science Research. 1974. *Towards equality: Report of the committee for the status of women in India.* New Delhi: Author.

Institute of Applied Manpower Research. 2000. *Manpower profile India yearbook 2000.* New Delhi: Author.

Institute of Psychological and Educational Research. 1991. *A composite report of situational analysis of urban street children in India: Study reports of six major cities in India.* Calcutta: Author.

International Institute for Population Sciences (IIPS) & ORC Macro. 1995. National Family Health Survey (NFHS–1), 1992–93: India. Mumbai: Author.

International Institute for Population Sciences (IIPS) & ORC Macro. 2000. National Family Health Survey (NFHS–2), 1998–99: India. Mumbai: Author.

Jejeebhoy, S. J. 1996. Adolescent sexual and reproductive behavior. A review of the evidence from India. International Center for Research on Women, Working Paper No. 3.

Jha, S. S. 1994. Lifestyle related problems of youth. *The Indian Journal of Social Work.* LV (1):3–12.

Kakar, S. 1978. *The inner world: A psycho-analytic study of childhood and society in India.* Delhi: Oxford University Press.

Kakar, S. 1979. *Identity and adulthood.* Delhi: Oxford University Press.

Kalra, R. M. & S. Kalra. 1996. *Adolescents and AIDS: A new generation at risk.* New Delhi: Vikas.

Kanade, A. N., S. B. Joshi., & S. Rao. 1999. Undernutrition and adolescent growth among rural Indian boys. *Indian Pediatrics.* 36:145–156.

Kanbargi, R. 1988. Child labor in India: The carpet industry of Varanasi. In *Combating child labor,* eds. A. Bequele & J. Boyden, 93–108. Geneva: International Labor Organization.

Kapur, M. 1992. School mental health in India. In *Child mental health in India,* eds. S. Malhotra, A. Malhotra, & V. K. Varma, 179–188. New Delhi: Macmillan.

Karlekar, M. 2000. Women's studies and women's development. In *Third survey of research in sociology and anthropology,* ed. M. S. Gore, 117–220. New Delhi: Indian Council of Social Science Research.

Khatri, A. A. 1972. The Indian family: An empirically derived analysis of shifts in size and types. *Journal of Marriage and the Family Living.* 34(4):725–734.

Kumar, K. 1991. *Political agenda of education: A study of colonialist and nationalist ideas.* New Delhi: Sage.

Kumari, M. K. & K. J. Sree. 1992. Role of youth in religion and politics of India. In *Global youth, peace and development, Vol. II,* ed. Y. C. Simhadri, 97–103. Delhi: Ajanta Publications.

Kumari, R. 1985. Attitude of girls towards marriage and a planned family. *The Journal of Family Welfare.* 31(3):53–60.

Kundu, A. 1997. Trends and structure of employment in the 1990s. Implications for urban growth. *Economic and Political Weekly.* XXXII(24):14–20.

Larson, R., S. Verma, & J. Dworkin. 2001. Men's work and family lives in India: The daily organisation of time and emotions. *Journal of Family Psychology.* 15(2):206–224.

Malhotra, S., A. Kohli, & P. Arun. 1999. Prevalence of psychiatric disorders in school children in India. Unpublished manuscript. Chandigarh, India: PGIMER.

Ministry of Welfare. 1992. *Drug abuse – Summaries of research studies sponsored by Ministry of Welfare.* New Delhi: National Institute of Social Defence, GOI.

Murthy, R. S. 1992. Policies relating to children in India: Focus on mental health. In *Child mental health in India*, eds. S. Malhotra, A. Malhotra, & V. K. Varma, 66–90. New Delhi: Macmillan.

Nambissan, G. B. 1996. Equity in education: The schooling of Dalit children in India. Paper series number 15. Thiruvananthapuram: UNDP/GOI/IDRC Research Project, Centre for Development Studies.

Narayan, A. 1988. Child labor policies and programs: The Indian experience. In *Combating child labor*, eds. A. Bequele & J. Boyden, 145–160. Geneva: International Labor Organization.

National Council of Educational Research and Training. 1992. Fifth all India educational survey: National tables. New Delhi: Author.

National Crime Records Bureau. 1998. Crime in India. New Delhi: Ministry of Home Affairs. Government of India.

Nerd Mentality: Europe begins to covet Indian brains under watchful US eyes. 2000. *Indian Express* (Ahmedabad edition). April 15:9.

Panicker, R. & P. Nangia. 1992. *Working and street children of Delhi.* Noida, India: Child Labor Cell.

Pathak, R. 1994. The new generation. *India Today.* Jan 31:72–87.

Pebley, A. R., H. Delgado, & E. Brineman. 1980. Unmarried adolescent females in rural India: A study of the social impact of education. *Journal of Marriage and the Family.* 42(2):427–436.

Phillips, W. S. K. 1992. *Street children of Indore.* Noida: Child Labor Cell.

Population Council. 1999. *To light a candle: Case study of Mahila Samakhya, Karnataka, Andhra Pradesh.* New Delhi: Author.

Prakash, S. & G. Pathmanathan. 1992. Age at menarche and its prediction in the well-off northwest Indian girls. *Journal of Human Ecology.* 3(2):133–137.

PROBE. 1999. *Peoples' report on basic education.* New Delhi: Oxford University Press.

Ramanujam, B. K. 1979. Toward maturity: Problems of identity seen in the Indian clinical setting. In *Identity and adulthood*, ed. S. Kakar, 37–55. Delhi: Oxford University Press.

Rahate, N. P., S. P. Zodpey, & P. R. Bhalkule. 1997. AIDS awareness amongst rural junior college students. In *HIV/AIDS research in India*, eds. O. P. Aggarwal, A. K. Sharma, and A. Indrayan, 222–223. New Delhi: National Aids Control Organisation, Ministry of Health & Family Welfare, GOI.

Rath, S. 1991. Dynamics of child abuse: Role of parenting behaviour. In *Research on families with problems in India: Unit for family studies, Vol. II, ed.* M. Desai, 462–471. Bombay: TISS.

Registrar General & Census Commissioner, India. 2001. Census of India 2001. Provisional Population Totals, Paper 1 of 2001, Series 1. New Delhi.

Rodgers, G. & G. Standing. 1981. The economic roles of children: Issues for analysis. In *Child work, poverty and underdevelopment*, eds. G. Rodgers & G. Standing, 1–45. Geneva: International Labor Office.

Roland, A. 1988. *In search of self in India and Japan: Towards a cross-cultural psychology*. Princeton, NJ: Princeton University Press.

Sajid, S. M. 1992. Youth unrest in India with special reference to student youth. In *Global youth, peace and development: Vol. II*, ed. Y. C. Simhadri, 21–32. Delhi: Ajanta Publications.

Sapru, S. 1999. Parental practices and the identity development of adolescents. A study of Indian families in Delhi and Geneva. Unpublished doctoral dissertation. University of Geneva, Switzerland.

Saraswathi, S. 1988. *Youth in India*. New Delhi: ICSSR.

Saraswathi, T. S. 1999. Adult-child continuity in India: Is adolescence a myth or an emerging reality? In *Culture, socialization and human development*, ed. T. S. Saraswathi, 214–232. New Delhi: Sage.

Saraswathi, T. S. & R. Dutta. 1988. *Invisible boundaries: Grooming for adult roles*. New Delhi: Northern Book Centre.

Saraswathi, T. S. & H. Ganapathy. (in press). The Hindu world view of child and human development: Reflections in contemporary parental ethnotheories. In *Between biology and culture: Perspectives on ontogenetic development*, eds. H. Keller, Y. Poortinga, & A. Scholmerich. Cambridge: Cambridge University Press.

Saraswathi, T. S. & S. Pai. 1997. Socialization in the Indian context. In *Asian perspectives in psychology*, eds. H. Kao & D. Sinha, 74–92. New Delhi: Sage Methodology Series.

Saraswathi, T. S. & A. Sridharan. 1991. Time use by college youth: A methodological study. *Perspectives in Education*. 7(1):41–54.

Sarkar, A. B., M. Kapur, & V. G. Kaliaperumal. 1995. The prevalence and pattern of psychological disturbance in school going middle childhood children. *Nimhans Journal*. 13(1):33–41.

Satpathy, S. K. & M. Shaukat. 1997. HIV/AIDS in India: The present scenario. In *HIV/AIDS Research in India*, eds. O. P. Aggarwal, A. K. Sharma, & A. Indrayan, 1–4. New Delhi: National Aids Control Organisation, Ministry of Health & Family Welfare, GOI.

Satyanarayana, K., A. Suresh, M. G. Radhaiah, & S. S. Rao. 1992. Role of growth curve fitting and computerization in India. *Proceedings of national workshop on adolescence: Need for critical appraisal*. Mar: 21–41. Pune: Agarkar Research Institute.

Savara, M. & C. R. Sridhar. 1994. Sexual behavior among different occupational groups in Maharashtra, India, and the implications for AIDS education. *The Indian Journal of Social Work*. LV(4): 617–632.

Sharma, A. 1992. *National evaluation of integrated child development services*. New Delhi: National Institute of Public Co-operation and Child Development.

Sharma, N. 1996. *Identity of the adolescent girl*. New Delhi: Discovery Publishing.

Sharma, V. & A. Sharma. 1995. The letter-box approach: A model for sex education in an orthodox society. *The Journal of Family Welfare.* 41(4):31–34.

Sharma, V., A. Sharma, S. Dave, & P. Chauhan. 1996. Sexual behavior of adolescent boys: A cause for concern. *Sexual & Marital Therapy.* 11(2):147–151.

Shastri, S. S. 1996. Medical aspects of tobacco, alcohol, and substance abuse. In *WHO-TISS Workshop: Involvement of youth in health education and health promotion: Tobacco, alcohol and substance abuse,* eds. U. S. Nayar & L. Narayan, 28–33. Mumbai: TISS.

Singh, L. B. & A. K. Singh. 1996. Alienation: A symptomatic reaction of educated employed youth in India. *International Journal of Psychology.* 31(2):101–110.

Singh, S. 1997. Adolescent reproductive and sexual health needs in India. Paper presented at the Workshop on Youth across Asia, Kathmandu, Nepal.

Singhal, R. & G. Misra. 1994. Achievement goals: A situational-contextual analysis. *International Journal of Intercultural Relations.* 18(2):239–258.

Sinha, D. 1988. Some recent changes in the Indian family and their implications for socialization. *The Indian Journal of Social Work.* XLV(3):271–286.

Sinha, D. 1994. The joint family in tradition. *Seminar.* 424:20–23.

Sitholey, P. & S. Chakrabarti. 1992. Child psychiatric research in India: Epidemiology, assessment and treatment. In *Child mental health in India,* eds. S. Malhotra, A. Malhotra, & V. K. Varma, 66–90. New Delhi: Macmillan.

Srikantia, S. G. 1989. Pattern of growth and development of Indian girls and body size of adult Indian women. In *Women and nutrition in India,* eds. C. Gopalan & S. Kaur, 108–149. New Delhi: Nutrition Foundation of India.

Thapar, V. 1998. Family life education in India: Emerging challenges. Background paper for the National Convention on Family Life Education: Emerging Challenges. New Delhi: National Institute of Public Co-operation and Child Development.

Tikoo, M., S. R. Bollman, & B. Bergen. 1995. Knowledge level of youth in India regarding human sexuality and AIDS. *Journal of Sex & Marital Therapy.* 21(4):248–254.

Tilak, J. B. G. 1999. National human development initiative: Education in the union budget. *Economic and Political Weekly.* XXXIV(10):614–620.

United Nations International Children's Emergency Fund (UNICEF). 1991. *Children and women in India: A situation analysis 1990.* New Delhi: UNICEF India office.

United Nations Development Program. 1999. *Human development report.* New York: Oxford University Press.

United Nations Development Program. 2000. *Human development report.* New York: Oxford University Press.

United Nations Population Fund. 1998. Socio-economic, demographic, and reproductive health profile of adolescents in SAARC countries. July: South Asia Conference on the Adolescent, New Delhi.

Uplaonkar, A. T. 1995. The emerging rural youth: A study of their changing values towards marriage. *The Indian Journal of Social Work.* 56(4):415–423.

Upreti, H. C. 1987. *Youth politics in India.* Jaipur: Printwell Publishers.

Verma, S. 1999. Socialization for survival: Developmental issues among working street children in India. In *Developmental issues among homeless and working street youth*, eds. M. Raffaelli & R. Larson, 5–18. San Francisco: Jossey-Bass.

Verma, S. & T. S. Saraswathi. 1992. At the crossroads: Time use by university students. Project report submitted to the International Development Research Centre, Canada.

Verma, S., D. Sharma, & R. Larson. In press. School stress in India: Effects on time and daily emotions. *International Journal of Behavioral Development*.

Wadhva, S. K., S. N. Wahab, S. C. Gupta, G. S. Tibdewal, & J. S. Deshmukh. 1997. Knowledge and attitudes of secondary students towards HIV/AIDS. In *HIV/AIDS research in India*, eds. O. P. Aggarwal, A. K. Sharma, and A. Indrayan, 184–188. New Delhi: National Aids Control Organisation, Ministry of Health & Family Welfare, GOI.

Watsa, M. C. 1993. Premarital sexual behavior of urban educated youth in India. Paper presented at the Workshop on Sexual Aspects of AIDS/STD Prevention, Bombay, India.

World Bank. 1998. World Bank country study: Reducing poverty in India. Options for more effective public services. Washington, D.C.: Author.

5

Adolescence in China and Japan

Adapting to a Changing Environment

Harold W. Stevenson and Akane Zusho

There is probably no group about which stereotypes are stronger than those concerning children and youth in Japan and China. Part of this situation can be attributed to the eagerness with which the media have presented the most dramatic examples they can find rather than attempting to provide an objective, rounded picture of the adolescent years in these countries.

The image of Japanese or Chinese teenagers as conforming to and being controlled by society, as being devoted to their studies at the cost of participating in other activities, and as being prone to suicide and psychological problems as a result of their devotion to their studies is obsolete and probably never was an accurate portrayal of these teenagers' lives.

We attempt in this chapter to present research findings that dispel such myths and that are helpful in interpreting the rapid developments taking place in these 2 countries. In particular, we focus on how recent societal and economic changes have affected the lives of youth in China and Japan. To accomplish our goal, we cover a wide array of topics, from adolescents' changing relations with their families to their assumption of a role in the civic life of their country.

Background

We chose to focus our discussion on these 2 countries despite the fact that there is vastly more information available about Japan than there is about China. The reason is clear: research in the social sciences was abandoned in China during the years of the Cultural Revolution

(1966–1976) and only recently has attention been directed to topics relevant to a discussion of adolescence. Nevertheless, it is of interest to present an overview of the information that is available. At the same time, however, it is important to note that while parallels exist in the trends in China and Japan, differences should be expected. After all, China and Japan operate under different political and economic ideologies; and while Japan is considered to be among the industrialized nations of the world, China is not.

A few additional words of explanation should be helpful to the reader before the results of various studies of Chinese and Japanese adolescents are discussed. A review of the research literature dealing with adolescence in China and Japan cannot possess the methodological sophistication and rigor that is expected in reports from countries with longer histories of an interest in this topic. It is especially difficult to study adolescents in China because such a large proportion are not in school or are busy preparing for university entrance exams. Furthermore, whereas school plays a central role in the life of adolescents in many industrialized societies, many adolescents have dropped out of school in China in order to become entrepreneurs in the new market economy (Chinese Adolescent Research Center Project 1995).

Adding to the difficulties is the fact that access to primary sources is much more difficult than it is for reviewing the Western literature. Even when primary sources are available, there are linguistic problems. Terms are often difficult to translate, and it is often hard to find English terms that carry the same nuances of meaning held by the original terms in Chinese or Japanese.

One of the first issues raised by a consideration of Chinese and Japanese adolescents is what the term means in those cultures. This is not a simple question, and a brief discussion of why this is the case suggests the confusion that surrounds references to this period of development. In contrast to English, where either "teenager" or "adolescent" would be widely understood, the use of one of these terms in Chinese and Japanese is likely to devolve into an extended discussion of its meaning. The difficulty results in part from the fact that this period has not been of great interest in the past. There was childhood and there was adulthood. But in itself adolescence did not attract much attention; it was not considered to be a defined period of development.

The period between childhood and adulthood has been given many names and many different meanings. In Japan, "adolescent" can be roughly translated as *"seishonen"* and *"seinen."* Both of these terms are typically used to describe the younger generation, young people, or the youth at large. The terms most commonly used for the period of adolescence, however, is "*seinenki*" or "*jyudai*." Another word, "*shishunki*," is often associated with adolescents but does not necessarily mean adolescent. It is most often used to refer to puberty, and as such, it implies a period of potentiality, freedom, and reason, with overtones of the anticipation of an interest in sexual experience.

Problems of definition in China are equally complex. Most persons would understand the term "*qing shao nian*," the Chinese equivalent of the Japanese *seishonen* (Z. X. Zhu 1990). There are still other terms that would be used by officials, including *shaoninan qui, qing nian,* and *shichun qui* (Chang 1993).

Because of these problems and ambiguities, most Japanese and Chinese would avoid using any one specific term for adolescence or adolescent (an exception are Japanese writers for research journals; their choice term for adolescence seems to be *seinenki*). Nor would they cite age, for there are disagreements among both professionals and lay persons concerning the age range covered by the various terms. For example, in Japan, there is a ceremony of "*seijinshiki*" held when the individual is 20 years old to signal the time when he or she becomes a member of adult society. This is a legal term that marks the beginning of the possession of legal rights of an adult. It does not, however, necessarily indicate the end of adolescence. As a result, the general practice is to refer to a person's institutional identity and to speak, for example, of a "middle school student" or "a high school student." For that reason, many of the targets of the studies we reviewed for this chapter varied widely in age, from elementary school students to even college students. Accordingly, we use the term "adolescent" somewhat loosely in this chapter, to include individuals as young as 4th graders to those as old as 21 or 22 years of age.

Overview

For the past several decades East Asia has been known as the most rapidly developing area in the world. Over the past 2 decades, members of both Chinese and Japanese societies have experienced rapid transformations from conditions fostering interdependence to those emphasizing individualism, changes stimulated by the growing interaction with the West, and by the dramatic changes in the economic traditions of the 2 East Asian countries. As a consequence of these changes, Chinese and Japanese children and adolescents experienced advances in their everyday lives, including opportunities for healthy development, easier access to education, and more frequent opportunities for interaction with their peers in other parts of the world.

More recently, however, economic conditions have clouded these remarkable achievements. Some segments of Chinese society benefited greatly from the transition from a socialist to a market economy, but others, less well trained, have not been able to benefit so greatly from these advances. Peasants and unskilled workers in China face a bleak future as unprofitable state-owned factories and other enterprises have been shut down. Millions of citizens have found themselves without a job, and new jobs are hard to find. China's fabled iron pot is not available to everyone who is hungry. At the same time, large segments of Chinese youth now have disposable incomes, which make them an economic force within the country (Tien 1996). In contrast to the plight of the unskilled worker, the transformation from a socialist to a market economy has been accompanied by greater opportunities for Chinese adolescents who have the skills needed in a rapidly expanding, technologically oriented society. As a result of these changes, differences in the economic status of families within the nation have rapidly increased (Wen 1996).

Trends in China and Japan have differed, but some parallels exist. The situation in Japan has also been tumultuous. Again, as a result of economic changes, the lifetime security expected by Japanese when they were first employed has been severely challenged and unemployment has become a national problem (Asahi Shimbun 1998). Competition from other countries and various unwise decisions made in the Japanese financial world have combined to produce profound changes in the Japanese economy. As a result, Japanese teenagers who have not yet established themselves as members of adult society have been a group whose lives have been most strongly affected by these rapid and unpredictable developments.

Family Life

Modeling
The concept of child rearing differs in China and Japan from that which is evident in the West. Parents in China and Japan subscribe to a modeling theory of learning whereby they believe that children learn most effectively on the basis of emulating models. Such beliefs promote a strong environmentalist position (Y. X. Zhu 1997). Chinese and Japanese are

confident of the ultimate emergence of appropriate behavior by children if parents display early tolerance, provide a positive environment, and function as desirable models. Children's disruptive behavior is tolerated during the early years of childhood, but by the time children enter elementary school, they are expected to be capable of reasoning and of acquiring appropriate social behavior (Stevenson and Stigler 1992).

Fundamental to the mutually satisfying relations between parent and child is the belief in the natural benevolence of children. Chinese and Japanese parents assume that children are basically good and readily malleable – 2 views that depart radically from the long-held views in the West of offspring needing redemption in environments that permit the appropriate display of natural talents and weaknesses. This set of beliefs means that parents and teachers have high basic confidence in children's ability to develop into healthy adults if they live in a healthy environment while they are growing up (Suen 1997).

Parent-Child Relations
In both China and Japan, the family has traditionally been considered to be one of the most important segments of society (Takahashi & Takeuchi 1994). However, the recent social and economic aspects of family life in East Asia have taken a toll on parent-child relations. One important change has been the weakening of the extended family and the emergence of more and more nuclear families devoid of grandparents or other family members. This new family organization is markedly different from the organization that existed for many years in both China and Japan (Shao 1996). In the past, in addition to the members of the immediate family, relatives and members of the broader society were more directly involved in the rearing of children and adolescents than is the case in many other countries. It was commonly assumed that child rearing was the responsibility of other villagers, as well as the biological parents. This has for the most part disappeared, but even today a neighbor might reprimand a misbehaving child. In Japan, however, rather than relying on neighbors, parents are more and more likely to turn to the school or to teachers in matters concerning their children's upbringing. Japanese teachers, rather than parents, are often held responsible for instilling habits normally considered in the West to be at the sole discretion of parents, such as those related to discipline and comportment (Peak 1991).

Perhaps the biggest change in family life in Japan, however, concerns the increasing trend among Japanese mothers to take jobs outside the home (Takahashi & Takeuchi 1994). Although these jobs are mostly part-time, Japanese parents nevertheless report having less time to interact with their children. For example, according to a recent governmental poll, Japanese parents on average only spend 1 hour per day with their adolescent child, with fathers spending even less time than mothers (Somucho 1996). Despite this minimal contact with their children, however, Japanese parents seem to be satisfied with the current amount of interaction. Part of the explanation, as mentioned previously, is likely to lie in the transfer to schools of many of the functions formerly accomplished by the parents. Approximately 65 percent of the mothers in a government poll and 40 percent of the fathers said that the amount of time they spent with their children was sufficient, although most parents seem to acknowledge that this minimal contact with their children remains a problem (Shimizu 1999). Indeed, these current reports of working mothers and absent fathers signal different conceptions of child rearing from the one conveyed by the intensely motivated "education mom" (*kyoiku mama*) of previous decades (Kojima 1996).

The perceptions Japanese youth have about their relationships with their parents, on the other hand, seem largely favorable. Japanese teenagers report communicating with their parents on a "fairly regular basis," especially on topics that deal with various aspects of their future. Moreover, approximately 80 percent to 90 percent of the respondents described their family life as being "fun" or "pleasant." At the same time, only 10 percent of males and 20 percent of females reported that they thought their parents truly understood them (Somucho 1996).

The One-Child Family

Most of the recent literature on family relations in China focuses primarily on the long-term consequences of the Chinese government's adoption of the one-child family policy initiated in response to the extraordinarily rapid growth of the Chinese population during and after the 1950s. Children who were born following the widespread application of this policy are just now entering adolescence. They are faced with restricted opportunities for employment, families of reduced size, and demands by older groups in the population for appropriate social and health benefits provided by funds obtained from the young workers (Su & Hu 1997).

Chinese parents have been worried that the one-child family policy would produce egocentric, spoiled children. During the children's preschool years there were indications that these fears were justified.

Preschool children appeared to be spoiled and were quickly labeled the Little Emperors and the Little Empresses. Worry was reduced when the children started elementary school. Through the socialization that occurred during their interactions with their age mates, children thought to be spoiled no longer displayed such self-centered behavior and demands. More recently, worries of another type have appeared. The only-child adolescents appear to place greater emphasis on their own satisfaction than on making contributions to society or to other persons. This has become evident to other members of Chinese society. When individuals over 20 years old were asked if parents overindulged their only children, 54 percent agreed that they did. Among 13- to 19-year-olds, 22 percent agreed. A matter of current concern is whether the only-child adolescents possess the self-discipline necessary to keep their jobs (Su & Hu 1997).

It is paradoxical that a nation that has placed great value on the family for centuries is now faced with a one-child family in which the child appears to be so strongly interested in self-advancement. Adding further to the breakdown of the traditional extended Chinese family is the opinion of many young people that a family of two adults is preferable to one that includes the single child permitted by the one-child family policy (Shao 1996).

The worries described in Japan are similar to those heard in China. Even without a national policy defining the number of children permitted in a family, Japanese family size also is declining. This has occurred in Japan as a consequence of social factors rather than on a government decree. The self-centered Japanese adolescents are addressed as members of the "me generation" and display the types of behavior associated with Chinese only children. The philosophy of social interdependence that characterized the Japanese is also undergoing a change to a more individualistic philosophy that emphasizes the rights, rather than the obligations, of members of Japanese society. It appears that the self-centeredness of Japanese adolescents is related to their efforts to adapt to a rapidly changing society that has come to emphasize one's self rather than social relationships.

Other than the one-child family policy, no contemporary problems related to Chinese family life have resulted in greater change than those initiated following the Cultural Revolution. This social movement began as an effort to strengthen the role of the Chinese Communist Party. However, it also resulted in a new type of interaction between parents and children. In establishing their form of revolution, schools were closed, universities only admitted workers recommended by their peers, and efforts were made to destroy all vestiges of classical Chinese life. Moreover, it changed adolescents' relationships with their parents. Not only were adolescents urged to report the behaviors of their parents, young people in general had more important roles in the movement itself, and the youthful leaders kept China in a state of disruption for a decade. Many adolescents left home and took advantage of free train rides throughout China or were sent to the countryside for rectification of attitudes, beliefs, and practices that characterized China before liberation; that is, before 1949 when the government of Mao Zedong replaced that of Chiang Kai-Shek, thereby creating a separation between 2 factions, 1 with the goal of strengthening family relations and the other seeking to switch loyalty from the family to the government. This conflict continues, but has a less obvious impact today than it did during the years of the Cultural Revolution.

Divorce

In terms of other family-related problems, such as divorce, approximately 1 in 5 couples in Japan is getting divorced (Ministry of Health & Welfare 1999). Interestingly, the divorce rate in Japan was relatively high until the middle of the Meiji Era (1868–1912) as a result of the lax enforcement of the family system under the old civil code. Following the Meiji Era, however, the divorce rate gradually declined and was lowest in 1963 (rate per 1,000 was 0.73). Since 1963, however, the rate of divorce has been steadily increasing, although the divorce rate in Japan is still considered by many to be low by international standards. Comparable statistics for China could not be located, although it is our opinion that the rate of divorce in China is also increasing.

Peer Relations

The adolescent years typically are characterized as a time when activities shift from the family to the peer group. Research on peer groups in Japan supports such a notion (Okamoto & Uechi 1999; Omi 1999). During the transition from elementary school to junior high school, Japanese teens appear to learn to rely more strongly on friends and peers than on parents for advice. One study also suggests that these students do not consider their regular public school teachers (or their teachers in after-school classes) to be a major part of their social support network (Omi 1999).

As for Chinese adolescents, surprisingly little basic research has been conducted on the structure and function of Chinese peer groups, with the exception of the research on the usefulness of participation in school-related clubs and interest groups in reducing the likelihood a member will later experience adjustment problems (Chen in press). Such peer groups, where students must interact with their peers, are widely encouraged in China and Japan, and membership in at least one of these organizations is often required in most schools. Moreover, it is believed that these clubs provide the most significant source of friendships for adolescents attending schools in these 2 countries (LeTendre 1998).

In terms of adolescents' romantic relationships, most Japanese junior high and high schools forbid dating; however, this does not necessarily preclude Japanese adolescents from dating, or at the very least, expressing an interest in dating (LeTendre 1998). While dating at the junior high school level is strongly discouraged, it is not uncommon to find high school students on dates. Nevertheless, it often is difficult to locate accurate statistics on dating trends among Japanese adolescents, given that most schools in Japan prohibit dating. However, a 1993 survey of Japanese 11th graders' sex-related behaviors found that approximately 16 percent of males and 25 percent of females reported having a boyfriend or girlfriend. Among these students, approximately 25 percent of males and 30 percent of females reported having been sexually active (Satoh 1996). In marked contrast to China a decade ago, heterosexual dating has also become increasingly frequent in China.

Other influences on peer interactions, such as "face" or the quality or scope of long-enduring interactions and friendships with neighborhood peers, reciprocal obligations among friends, and an emphasis on tranquility – all characteristics of social interactions among Chinese and Japanese youth – should lead to further provocative research findings.

Schooling

Schools provide the central core around which the lives of Chinese and Japanese adolescents revolve. It is useful, therefore, to describe the formal and informal aspects of the learning and teaching environments in which they study.

The Education System
While differences exist in the schooling experiences of adolescents in China and Japan, the similarities are striking. Among the major

accomplishments of the 20th century have been the widespread improvements in the education systems instituted by the Chinese and Japanese governments. In fact, efforts at educational reform are currently underway in Japan, including a move to the 5-day-a-week system (as opposed to the current system of $5^1/_2$-day-a-week), which should be in place by 2002.

Both China and Japan require 6 years of attendance at elementary school followed by 3 years of junior high school. The 3 years of high school are optional. Both countries have met the goal for elementary school education, but China has not yet attained universal attendance at the junior high school level (Chen, Lee, & Stevenson 1996). The percentage of students who go on to high school in Japan has increased steadily since the end of World War II. In recent years, the percentage has stabilized to approximately 95 percent for both male and female students (Asahi Shimbun 1998). In terms of actual enrollment, there has been a continuous decline since 1980 in the number of elementary school students and an increase in the number of university students (Shimizu 1999). This decline in the number of elementary school students and an increase in the number of university students is most likely due to the declining birth rate.

The situation in China is reported in a slightly different fashion. In 1998, 94.3 percent of the graduates of primary schools were enrolled in junior high schools and 50.4 percent of the graduates of junior high schools were enrolled in senior high schools. The educational enterprise is obviously a large one, and efforts to provide education for a high percentage of qualified or needy candidates is a large expense for the Chinese at both local and national levels.

Children in China and Japan attend elementary and junior high schools in their own neighborhoods. This is not the case with high schools, which are organized hierarchically according to the level of achievement demonstrated by students in entrance examinations. Both governments support vocational high schools as well as regular academic high schools. In fact, over half of the high school students in China currently are enrolled in vocational high schools (Chinese Adolescent Research Center Project 1995). The corresponding percentage of high school students in Japan who are enrolled in vocational schools has declined during recent years to around 20 percent (Shimizu 1996).

Admission to Chinese and Japanese universities is restricted to the most able youths as reflected in their prior academic achievement. The limited number of places, the preeminence of a small number of private and public universities, and the strong role that the university attended has on subsequent opportunities for employment produces intense competition for admission to these universities.

Flexibility in gaining admission to a Japanese university was unheard of until recently. Although it is possible to enter a university on a basis other than the college entrance examination, the score obtained on the examination still plays the primary role in determining whether or not a student will be admitted. Educators discuss such issues and attempt to help those who do not obtain admission to a school or college of their choice find alternative educational plans.

University attendance in China is growing, but it still remains very low. In 1994, national statistics for educational level in China are as follows: illiterate, 7.2 percent; only elementary school education, 31.3 percent; middle school education, 45 percent; high school education, 13.5 percent; and college education, 2.4 percent (Chinese Adolescent Research Center Project 1995). These data are in sharp contrast with those from Japan, where, among males in 1997, 99.5 percent graduated from high school (Asahi Shimbun 1998).

Academic Achievement
The Third International Mathematics and Science Study of achievement in science and mathematics has received worldwide attention. In this study, a total of 500,000 students from 41 nations participated. Included were representative samples of 3rd and 4th graders, students from 7th and 8th grades, and from the final year of high school. Two aspects of the study have received the greatest attention among Americans: the low average scores of the American participants and the high average scores of those from East Asia. As citizens of one of the countries making the greatest investment in education (4.02 percent of the Gross National Product) the U.S. students are not competitive with their peers from many countries. The financial investment of East Asian countries is below that of the United States (2.8 percent for Japan; and 1.4 percent for Hong Kong). It is discouraging, however, to find little relation between test scores and the country's financial support of education. The top 5 countries among the middle-school students were, in order, Singapore, Korea, Japan, Hong Kong, and Thailand. China did not participate in the study.

The argument is commonly made that Chinese and Japanese students learn the skills of reading by reliance on rote learning and memorization. The basis for learning in this fashion is evident when one looks at the skills and content to be mastered in learning to read these languages. Chinese students enter middle school with a repertoire of approximately 3,000 Chinese characters that can be combined to form over 7,000 words. Japanese, on the other hand, acquire skill in reading and writing the 1,000 characters used in written Japanese and 2 syllabaries in Japanese writing (*hiragana* and *katakana*). Learning the Roman alphabet adds to the tasks that must be mastered by the skilled reader. Despite the complexity and extensiveness of these tasks, Chinese and Japanese adolescents are among the world's best readers.

Gender Differences

Despite recent efforts in Japan to curtail the widening gender gap (Takahashi & Hatano 1999), adolescent females still do not have access to levels of higher education equal to those of males. Although the actual percentage of females entering 4-year universities or colleges is on the rise, it still lags behind that of males by almost 10 percentage points (males = 34.9 percent, females = 24.4 percent). Moreover, a significant percentage of females (22.8 percent) still choose to attend 2-year junior colleges and major in subjects such as early childhood education, thus limiting their career opportunities (Shimizu 1999). As a result, there is an imbalance between males and females in their attendance and graduation rates from 4-year colleges. In China, too, the percentage of females attending colleges is significantly lower than males. In 1998, approximately 27.3 percent of the adolescent population were enrolled in a university or college in China. Of this percentage, however, males accounted for over 63 percent of the college student population (Zhang 1999). Because the financial investment in the education of males and females continues to rise, it is likely that the gender gap will continue for at least the next several decades.

Conditions that exist for both Chinese and Japanese women are not limited to education. Bleak economic conditions have generally had other negative consequences for females. The egalitarianism in terms of gender implied by Mao Zedong's saying that "women hold up half of the sky" is unlikely to be reinstated. When cutbacks are introduced in large businesses or industries it is often females whose jobs are eliminated first. Furthermore, Confucian edicts and Confucian conceptions of behavior and lineage are still honored in the Chinese family. Sons are preferred because they can continue the family name, are expected to contribute to the support of their parents, and can be of greater assistance to their parents in some types of labor than females (Soled 1995).

Racial and Ethnic Differences
Despite the high degree of racial and ethnic homogeneity in Chinese and Japanese societies, both nations are faced with problems involving minority populations. In Japan, this primarily refers to Koreans and the Burakumin, an "outcast" group which consists of descendants of Japanese who were involved in trades or jobs that have been shunned by the rest of the Japanese population since medieval times; but there are also other minority groups, such as the Ainu, Chinese, and Brazilian and Iranian Japanese. Coping with these minority groups has posed problems. Burakumin teenagers attend regular schools, but school authorities are forbidden to disclose their status. Through such means schools have been increasingly effective in creating conditions conducive to the assimilation of these minority groups into Japanese society. Koreans and Chinese have been assimilated to a high degree, often leading, for example, to the adoption of Japanese names. Even so, antipathy remains against these long-term residents of Japan. Moreover, there is some evidence to suggest that these minority students typically fare worse academically than nonminority Japanese students (LeTendre 1998).

In China, only 8 percent of the population are not members of the majority "Han" group (Soled 1995). The minority groups are concentrated in western and southern China. These groups range from the Moslems and Kazaks of Xinjiang in the west to the Miao of southern China (Zhang 1995). As is the case in Japan, these minority groups often have their own schools. In fact, some of the most impressive vocational high schools in China are those serving minority students.

Students in many of the vocational high schools are given high levels of training. Rather than being educated as seamstresses, efforts are made to train them as clothing designers; rather than being trained as cooks, they learn how to be chefs in tourist hotels; and rather than learning to be guides, they are taught the essentials of becoming tourist agents. Because of the schools' efforts to promote equal treatment for minority and nonminority students, there have been few problems associated with minority status of Chinese students in urban schools (Wong 1996).

Gifted Children
The education of gifted children poses problems for both China and Japan because of the possible reinstatement of the elitism that existed in these societies in the past. Earlier in this century college attendance was confined to the upper classes, and it was difficult for anyone else to gain admission to post-secondary education. This worry is balanced by

the recognition of a need for well-educated citizens if the societies are to develop and remain competitive during the coming decades. Whether these students should be given special treatment remains a source of contention, but the practice has been to reduce attendance at schools for gifted and talented youth.

China established several types of special schools and programs during recent decades. Olympic schools were aimed at the preparation of gifted students for the international Olympics in areas such as mathematics and science. "Key" schools brought high academic achievers together with a demanding curriculum, especially skilled teachers, and highly motivated students. Special schools for cultivating athletic abilities were also founded. However, by the late 1990s movements were underway to close Olympic schools and "key" schools, with the explanation that they are undemocratic and have the unfortunate consequence of fostering elitist education (Stevenson 1998).

Japanese educators have seldom proposed special schools or programs for the gifted. Rather than foster the development of what they consider to be unhealthy tracking programs, they have promoted the formation of mixed-ability heterogeneous groups during the elementary and junior high school years. When students reach the high school level, however, they are permitted to enroll in high schools according to their high school entrance examination scores. The closest the Japanese have come to tracking is to allow fast learners to master 2 semesters' work in a single semester, thereby allowing such students opportunities for studying advanced topics during the 2nd semester (Stevenson 1998).

Another approach to the education of gifted students is currently underway with the recent liberalization of the education systems in both China and Japan. China has announced a program of "education for quality" to replace "education for tests" (Suen 1997). Japan has introduced several education reforms, including a vaguely defined individualized education, life-long learning, greater freedom in selecting elective subjects, and an emphasis on creativity and problem solving. The programs in both countries remain to be fully developed.

Exceptional Adolescents

Educators and parents in both Japan and China have been perplexed about how to respond to the needs of exceptional students. In an effort to provide an education for students with various types of disabilities, education authorities of the central governments in each country have initiated discussions of special education. Special education programs for the blind, deaf, and mentally and/or emotionally handicapped have been available for some time in Japan, but they often operate sporadically and fail to serve a high percentage of disabled students. In part, this is a result of parents' wishes; many parents of exceptional children in Japan would rather have their child placed in regular classrooms of regular schools. As a result, the disabled children remain in regular school classrooms, where they are expected to follow the regular curriculum if given special help.

Creative Adolescents

Among the views often expressed during the course of a conversation with Chinese and Japanese adolescents is that neither they nor many of their peers are endowed with "natural" creative ability. Others have disagreed, however, and have offered alternative interpretations. These interpretations typically indicate the lack of creativity as being due to a lack of support from members of society. Members of East Asian societies are more likely to favor repetition and rote learning over innovation and elaboration than are members of Western societies. The distinction is especially clear in an activity such as painting. A painting "in the style of" a famous painter is more likely to be praised than a painting in which new elements have been introduced. The same contrast is evident in other areas, such as sculpture, architecture, dance choreography, industrial design, and novels. When applied to the content of tests, the argument is that a high score should reflect the answer in all aspects that were included in the initial explanation of topics and organization of the test. It is expected that with a change in social attitudes a new expressive period will emerge. This has occurred in the past 2 or 3 decades in East Asia.

After-School Activities

Extracurricular Programs

Visitors to China and Japan often criticize what they perceive to be excessively long hours that the students spend in school. Teenagers may be seen on public transportation or walking home long after the time the rest of the family has finished dinner. What the observers do not realize is that most of the after-school time is taken up in participation in a wide variety of after-school clubs and programs. The degree to which the students can choose among these offerings varies. In Japan, some schools require students to join at least 1 club, but many students choose to participate in several. Some programs may actually take place during school hours, but the majority are after-school events. Similarly, Chinese students remain at school, interacting with classmates, collaborating on school work, and enjoying other after-school programs (Stevenson 1994).

It is assumed that these after-school programs foster creativity, increase cooperative behavior, and enhance students' efforts at self-direction. Other rationales for clubs and programs are offered: they (a) keep students occupied, (b) promote health and leisure time activities, (c) supplement the regular curriculum with courses in such activities as martial arts, foreign languages, and computer programming, (d) provide knowledge and skills related to their own culture, such as flower arranging, calligraphy, and use of the abacus, (e) sponsor team sports, and (f) prepare students for entering the adult world through participation in political events.

Participation in extracurricular events is most popular during the high school years in Japan. In addition to the school-based clubs and after-school activities, high school students spend time watching television (an average of 12 hours per week), talking with friends (12 hours), dating (1 hour), or working (1.5 hours) (Shimizu 1999). At school, there are breaks of at least 10 minutes after class, long lunch hours, and large amounts of time spent in studying and in extracurricular activities.

Private Preparatory Schools: Juku and Yobiko

Correspondents from the West who visit Japan often seek to explain the high level of academic success that exists among Japanese students on the basis of attendance at *juku* and *yobiko*. Both are after-school academies devoted, among other things, to the preparation of students for high school and college entrance examinations. What is often not mentioned is the fact that many adolescents attend *juku* because of their social function. Students enjoy spending after-school time with their friends; attending *juku* makes it possible for them to do their studying in a friendly social environment.

Perhaps contrary to expectations, *juku* attendance is greatest during elementary school years and lowest among the high school years. For example, in a recent survey, 70 percent of high school students reported *not* attending *juku*, in comparison to 30 percent of junior high school students, and 15 to 20 percent of elementary school students. However, such findings can be attributed in part to the large percentage of elementary school students attending nonacademic *juku*, often called *"okeiko"* or *"naraigoto,"* which includes activities such as sports, calligraphy, English conversational classes, abacus, and music (Somucho 1996). Thus, the observer of Japanese education should realize that what may seem to be excessive amounts of time spent at *juku* may reflect time spent in self-improvement and relaxation rather than in formal academic classes.

The results are different, however, when the question concerns attendance at academic *juku*. Enrollment in academic *juku* is highest among junior high school students (50 percent). Only 25 percent of elementary school students reported attending academic *juku* (Somucho 1996). This relatively high rate of attendance at *juku* during the junior high school years occurs because it is the time when students must take the critical high school entrance examinations. Chances for admission to one of Japan's more prestigious colleges or universities are dependent upon being admitted beforehand to one of the city's highly ranked high schools. Thus, *juku* assume their greatest importance during the junior high school years. Although *juku* serve many needs, attendance at *juku* drops markedly between the high school and college years. During the senior high school years students are more likely to stay at home and study on their own.

Yobiko have a mission similar to that of *juku*: however, they are aimed at helping students who have had, or anticipate having, trouble passing the college entrance examinations. During this period the students are unattached scholars (*ronin*), spending full time studying for the examinations.

Both *juku* and *yobiko* have been subject to criticism. A major complaint is that only families with financial resources are able to afford their adolescent's attendance. The fear here, as it is in other aspects of Japanese education, is that these institutions foster the development of an elite cadre of students and graduates, a consequence that is unacceptable to Japanese.

Bushiban are the formal counterparts in China to the Japanese *juku*. Parents are aware of the necessity to provide extra help for their children, and attendance of *bushiban* is becoming increasingly popular in serving this function (Interviews, Beijing, July 2000). This usually takes the form of hiring a tutor or paying teachers to provide extra help. Before the economy developed to the point that families could afford the fees for *bushiban*, teachers offered supplementary classes to help students prepare for the entrance examinations.

Leisure Time

Japanese adolescents have recently changed their attitudes about money. The emphasis in Japan during previous years was to save money that had been earned rather than spending it. Leisure-time activities could then be supported by the money that was saved. However, with the currently faltering economy there is a strong social impetus now to spend, rather than to save.

In addition to the increase in their purchasing power as a result of the country's economic growth, Chinese adolescents have greater amounts of leisure time. Chinese adolescents spend most of this time indoors, watching television (30 percent of the time) and reading (37 percent). Teenagers were generally not dissatisfied with the amount of leisure time they had available: one-third said they were satisfied; 50 percent were neutral; and only 18 percent said they were not satisfied. The major complaint was not so much one of dissatisfaction, as of the fact that leisure time tended to be spent indoors (Tien 1996).

It is common for students to remain at school after school hours to study with their friends. In this way, schools assume strong social functions at the same time they are meeting the students' needs for studying. Beyond these opportunities for self-improvement and for service to the school, such as cleaning the school yard, the activities have become important for admission to colleges and universities. Because 1 in 5 high school students in Japan is admitted to college on the basis of teachers' and schools' recommendations, adolescents hope to impress their teachers with their participation in a variety of activities. Teachers worry, however, that extracurricular activities may be crowding out some of the more important academic functions of high school and that students may enroll in certain easy classes to display their well-roundedness rather than enrolling in more difficult classes to advance their education.

Employment

During the past decade both China and Japan have had to reconsider the state of their economies, with the outcome that the studies have had strong effects on the opportunities available to adolescents for employment (Somucho 1998). The tighter economy in Japan has meant fewer jobs for teenagers, leaving them to engage in other activities to fill their time, such as extending their education, remaining at home, or taking temporary positions. For example, only 23 percent of high school students in Japan entered the workforce upon graduation in 1998. It is unclear, however, what impact the recession has actually had on Japanese high schoolers, given that part-time work is generally forbidden by most high schools in Japan. Nevertheless, in a recent poll, 27 percent of Japanese high school students reported having part-time jobs after school, but it is likely that others also have jobs but hold them in secret. Little is known about part-time employment among high school students in China, but it would appear to be quite low.

In terms of full-time work, adolescents in Japan typically obtain employment through 2 main avenues. Students planning on entering the workforce upon graduation from vocational and/or technical high schools often rely on their school's "*shinro shidou shuji*," or head of placement teacher. This teacher acts as a liaison between students and local businesses searching for students to fill positions within their establishment. Generally, these businesses approach the schools directly on an annual basis. The teacher, in turn, recommends 2 or 3 students to these companies. The responsibilities of the *shinro shidou shuji* often vary by school type; for example, the teacher who serves as head of placement at an academic high school performs duties that are comparable to those of a guidance counselor in the United States. In such cases, the *shinro shidou shuji* would provide information to students about certain colleges or universities, or about the college admissions process in general, rather than about specific employment opportunities.

As for those adolescents attending colleges, most students begin their job search, or "*shushokukatsudo*," approximately 1 or 2 years prior to graduation. The process is similar to those in most industrialized countries; students attend job fairs and/or obtain employment information through their institution's "*shushokuka*," or career planning and placement center. It is now also possible for students to find similar information on the Internet. In recent years, the precarious economic situation in Japan has adversely affected the employment opportunities available to students upon graduation from college. It has become increasingly difficult for college graduates to obtain employment upon graduation; for example, the employment rate among graduates of both 2-year and 4-year colleges in 1998 was 66 percent, an all-time low, in comparison to the employment rate in the late 1980s and early 1990s of 87 percent (Shimizu 1999).

Again, we were unable to locate comparable statistics for Chinese adolescents. However, within our own research, we have come across a number of Chinese youths who profess a desire to study abroad in the

United States and elsewhere, rather than actually enter the workforce in China upon graduation. As for those adolescents living in the rural areas of China, it is not uncommon for these youths to move to the cities and become transient workers. Some Chinese adolescents in the late 1990s also expressed characteristics that would influence their choice of an occupation that is different from those mentioned in the early 1990s. The characteristics mentioned in the earlier reports were, in descending order, high income, matching one's interests, fostering creative activity, permitting independence, and developing good human relations. In the later survey, receiving a high income dropped to last place and was superseded by matching interests, independence, equality between workers and management, creativity, and human relations.

Mental Health

Suicide

The negative perception of the mental health of Chinese and Japanese adolescents appears to be widely shared among both foreign professionals and nonprofessionals. The image commonly portrayed is of suicide-prone, excessively tense, and depressed young people. These images are not borne out by the statistics. The most recent report from the *Japan Almanac* (Asahi Shimbun 1998) indicates a rate of suicide per 100,000 of 4.4 for adolescents between the ages of 15 and 20 and a rate of 11.0 for 20–24-year-olds. These percentages are either similar to or notably lower than those in the United States (approximately 12.0 per 100,000 adolescents). When broken down by age, the rate for Japan rises with increasing age, and the incidence of suicide is greater for boys than for girls at all ages. The suicide rate has also been found to vary, depending on the sample and age range; for example, Johnson, Krug, and Potter (2000) report an 8.6 (per 100,000) suicide rate among 15–24-year-olds in Japan.

No comparable data could be located for China, but other data do reveal a low rate of serious mental disorders, ranging from 0.5 per 1,000 for 10–14-year-olds, 2.7 for 15–19-year-olds, to 16.2 for 20–24-year-olds (Shek 1996).

Psychological Adjustment

Just as there is very little evidence reported in support of a high suicide rate among Japanese youth, there is little evidence of maladjustment. In a study of Chinese and Japanese 11th graders, no indications were found for a high rate of self-reported indices of maladjustment. Self-ratings made on 5-point scales ranging from "never" to "every day" revealed low frequencies of occurrence for stress, depressed mood, academic anxiety, aggression, and psychosomatic problems (Crystal et al. 1994).

No relation between stress and academic achievement was found for the Chinese or Japanese students. Among U.S. students, in contrast, the higher the students' performance on a test of mathematics, the higher were their reported feelings of stress. Similarly, the highest level of stress was found for U.S. students attending a high school of science and technology with especially rigorous admission requirements. The major source of stress reported by the students was school. Several reasons appear to be associated with the relation between stress and achievement. East Asian students are told repeatedly by their parents that their major task during childhood and adolescence is to do well in school and to get a good education. U.S. students complain that they are given a mixed message, one that implies that they must not only do well in school, but also must have a healthy social life, engage in sports and exercise, find a job, and help around the house. Stress, then, appears to be a consequence of the conflict that the students report as a result of being faced with all of these demands.

The message that appears to be contained in these self-reports is that high levels of academic achievement can be attained without stress if the student is given a clear message of parental expectations and understands that studying and doing well in school are activities supported by their parents and by society in general. However, knowing the results of studies apparently does little to reduce Chinese and Japanese parents' worries about what they perceive to be excessive stress on the part of their children. The stress appears to be attributed to the large amount of time spent studying for the college entrance examinations, an important issue in both Japanese and Chinese societies.

School-Related Behavior Problems

Japanese have become increasingly concerned about the growing prevalence of violence and other behavior problems in schools. During the 1997 academic year, 28,526 incidents of violence were reported in Japanese schools, of which 1,300 occurred in elementary schools; 18,000 in junior high schools; and 4,000 in high schools (Shimizu 1999). School violence occurs against fellow students, as well as teachers, and as indicated by the above statistics, primarily during junior high school. For example, in terms of specific acts of aggression toward teachers, there were nearly 200 cases reported in elementary schools, over 3,000 in junior high schools, and 430 cases in high schools. This incidence represents a large increase over the frequencies reported in 1985, when, respectively, 67 and 434 reports were made of high school and junior high school students' violence against a teacher (Shimizu 1996).

Bullying, or "*ijime*," a form of misbehavior often reported in the Japanese press, is primarily an elementary and junior high school phenomenon. The number of bullying cases hit an all time high in 1986, when there were over 96,000 cases reported among elementary and junior high school students. Following this, the number of cases declined dramatically. In recent years, however, the trend again seems to be on the rise. The number of bullying cases, for example, more than doubled during the 1993 and 1994 academic years from over 12,000 cases to over 26,000 cases. We were unable to find parallel data from China, nor have we ever heard of reports of other types of violence in Chinese schools.

Physical Health

General Health

According to the 1998 School Health Statistics Survey (Shimizu 1999), the height statistics of Japanese boys aged 9–13 years and Japanese girls aged 10–13 years were the highest since the start of data collection. In comparison to their parents (statistics from 1968), present-day Japanese boys are anywhere from 8 cm (5-year-olds) to 6.5 cm (12-year-olds) taller. Japanese girls, too, are taller: the difference in heights range from 1.9 cm (5-year-olds) to 5.3 cm (11-year-olds). Similarly, the weights of present-day Japanese students are also greater than years past. In comparison to statistics from 30 years ago, Japanese males are approximately 9 kg (5-year-olds) to 7.0 kg (12-year-olds) heavier. Japanese females are also slightly heavier; the difference in weight statistics is from 1.0 kg (5-year-olds) to 5.3 kg (11-year-olds). Despite these trends, students' physical fitness and/or stamina has hit a 10-year low. Japanese experts typically attribute such findings to lack of exercise in general and to the demands of college entrance exams.

Additionally, students' dental health seems to have deteriorated, with 80 percent of elementary, junior, and high school students reporting having at least 1 cavity in comparison to 40 to 50 percent of students in 1953. Japanese students' visual acuity has also decreased, most likely as a result of the increase in video game usage. The percentage of overweight elementary school students also seems to be increasing, as well as the number of students afflicted with asthma. National trends concerning physical health in China are very complex to interpret, for they would likely vary greatly between the urban and rural populations, region of the country, and measure of physical health.

Drugs, Smoking, and Alcohol

Drug abuse among Chinese youth is growing. In 1980, 3.7 percent of all crimes in China were committed by adolescents; by 1993 the percentage had nearly doubled to 6.2 percent (Hsiao & Xiu 1996). Most of this delinquency was related to drugs – primarily to the use of drugs by transient workers or rural youth, who committed 80 percent of these crimes (Tsang 1997). Drug abuse by Japanese junior high school students is low (2 percent), but it increases 5-fold among high school students (10 percent) (Somucho 1999). According to Wada, Price, & Fukui (1997), use of volatile solvents, primarily toluene and paint thinner, has been a well-recognized drug problem among Japanese adolescents.

Society's attitudes about smoking and drinking in China and Japan are more relaxed than in many other contemporary societies. In Japan, for example, cigarettes and alcohol in various forms are readily available. The attitude in Japan appears to be that smoking and drinking are permissible if the adolescent has sufficient funds and chooses to spend them on cigarettes or alcohol. Although the legal age for drinking and smoking in Japan is 20 years, easy access to these substances leads to frequent violations of the law. One study, for example, found that approximately 60 percent of Japanese junior high school students and 70 percent of Japanese senior high school students have had some experience with alcohol (Suzuki, Minowa, Osaki 2000). Moreover, Chinese and Japanese adolescents, like most adolescents, also appear to pay little attention to the research indicating the potential negative consequences for health and safety of the frequent use of either substance.

Sexual Activity

Attitudes and practices among Chinese and Japanese youth regarding premarital sexual activity differ markedly from those of the West. Partly because neither China nor Japan has a codified or religion-based set of rules for proper conduct, discussions about teenage sex often end as efforts to reach social definitions of what is permissible and what is unacceptable. Sexual activity among youths is considered by many adolescents to be permissible if it is handled discreetly, and contraceptives are used to prevent pregnancy, although most adults continue to treat teenage pregnancy with great concern. For example, among

Chinese adolescent males, 46 percent thought that premarital sex was normal or understandable, 30 percent thought it was immoral, and 24 percent were undecided. The corresponding percentages for Chinese adolescent girls were 29 percent, 41 percent, and 9 percent, respectively (Tien 1996).

Accurate data related to sexual activity among Chinese and Japanese adolescents are generally hard to find, especially those from Japan. As mentioned previously, this is related, in part, to the fact that many Japanese schools forbid their students to date; thus, schools most likely do not keep track of such statistics. However, most Japanese surveys of adolescents' sexual behaviors typically find that approximately one-tenth of adolescents are sexually active (LeTendre 1998; Satoh 1996). We were unable to locate comparable statistics for China.

In terms of sex education, a need for more-widespread sex education for premarital youth was voiced by 92 percent of the females and 90 percent of the male adolescents polled in China (Qiang 1997). Currently, information about sex comes from parents (2 percent), school (20 percent), books (60 percent), television (3 percent), and other sources (15 percent). Fewer than 15 percent of Chinese adult males thought that premarital sex should be forbidden (Qiang 1997). In Japan, sex education is not considered part of the formal school curriculum. However, the Ministry of Education has published a sex education manual in light of the increasing number of people in Japan being diagnosed with the AIDS virus (in 1998, 1,757 people were newly diagnosed with the AIDS virus; 4,118 were HIV-positive). On the other hand, it is unclear as to whether the schools are actually using this manual (Shimizu 1999). In China, AIDS has generally been too sensitive a topic for publication in the media, and accurate statistics regarding the incidence of AIDS are difficult to find. According to governmental officials, 20,711 persons tested positive for the HIV virus in China in 1999, although Chinese health officials privately estimate that the number is closer to 500,000 (Rosenthal 1999). It seems likely that AIDS is a problem that adolescents in both China and Japan will have to confront more extensively in the coming years.

Consumerism

Economic development has obviously brought about large changes in adolescents' lifestyles and in their standards of morality. One guiding principle appears to be that everything depends on money and that self-fulfillment is dependent on having the opportunities made available by money. What a few years ago was enthusiasm about political reform in China has been transformed into enthusiasm about economic reform, and consumerism, especially among adolescents, has become rampant (Tien 1996).

One index of Chinese adolescents' aspirations is the nature of the purchases they would like to make. In the 1970s, it was a bicycle, watch, and sewing machine; in the 1980s, a television, refrigerator, and washing machine; and in the 1990s, it was a computer, telephone, high tech stereo, and automobile. A stroll down a street in downtown Beijing indicates the degree to which the teenagers' desires are being met. Stores feature popular books and magazines, CDs and DVDs, and luxury goods, such as pearl necklaces, gold rings, cameras, cordless telephones, leather jackets, and personal beauty aides – unheard of purchases a few years ago, but now items that are readily available to those with the necessary money (Tien 1996).

Civic Engagement

Every 5 years, the Japanese Youth Affairs Administration conducts a study in which approximately 1,000 adolescents from each of 9 countries, ranging in age from 18 to 24 years, respond to an extensive survey. The primary objective of the study is to gain an accurate picture of Japanese adolescents' contemporary life so as to inform future policies concerning youth. Consequently, the interview covers a broad range of topics. The ones of concern to us here are their reactions to politics and their responses concerning their involvement in the community (Youth Affairs Administration 1999).

Japanese adolescents currently display little interest in civic engagement or other forms of political activity. This is surprising in view of the intensity of the movement for greater participation and involvement in these affairs during previous decades. According to the Youth Affairs Administration study, in response to the question, "How much interest do you take in the politics of your country?" approximately 60 percent of Japanese respondents indicated little to no interest in Japanese politics. In contrast, the majority of youth in Thailand, Philippines, Korea, and the United States expressed interest in their country's political system. In another question, respondents were asked whether they were proud to be a citizen of their country and whether they would like to do something for their country. While 77 percent of Japanese respondents said they were proud to be Japanese, fewer than half indicated that they actually wanted to do something for Japan.

Despite such statistics, a number of Japanese adolescents participate in some form of involvement or assistance to the community, although much of this activity has been delegated to schools. Schools and other agencies sponsor demonstrations, such as visiting homes for the elderly or assisting in preschools. Indeed, when asked if they are interested in volunteer activities, over 60 percent of Japanese youths expressed some interest in volunteering. At the same time, however, fewer than 3 percent of the respondents were currently involved in any kind of voluntary activity, although 22 percent indicated that they had participated in such activities in the past (Youth Affairs Administration 1999). Typically, it is not until a major event or disaster occurs, however, that today's adolescents respond vigorously to the need for their participation and help. Several reasons account for this state of affairs. First, adolescents point out that things generally are going well, thereby reducing the need for their involvement. Second, the current leadership seems to be successful, thus the adolescents would argue that there is no need for widespread participation in political activities by individuals.

In reaction against these views of adolescents is the help they have provided when there is a national disaster such as an earthquake or social event such as an antinuclear protest. Finally, adolescents' participation is limited because they lack relevant experience and fail to understand various aspects of the social and economic structure, such as banking or women's suffrage. Thus, despite their appearance of involvement, adolescents in both countries have adopted a conservative stance. How long and in what form this will be maintained is not clear (Takahashi & Hatano 1999).

Services for Youth

It is hard to imagine how a relatively poor nation such as China with a yearly cohort of millions of births could provide adequate services for youth. The rapid advances made in health and education in China have been remarkable, however, although both areas require expansion. Health in terms of breadth of coverage, and education in terms of level and availability of offerings, will require further extension in the coming years. A 2nd problem is that many jobs held by survivors of the Cultural Revolution will be vacated, but the number of openings is insufficient to provide opportunities for the large numbers of youths seeking them. Youths, therefore, will be likely to make demands their governments cannot fulfill. The question – and it is a profoundly difficult one – concerns the kinds of responses that can be made to youths' needs and desires. The strength of the economic, social, political, and moral domains of society will be put to a difficult test.

Nevertheless, in terms of health care services for adolescents, China offers free annual physical exams for all children enrolled in school, as does Japan. Typically, these exams are comprehensive; students receive vision and hearing tests, as well as immunization shots. All expenses for these exams are incurred by the government. In Japan, the law not only requires that these exams be administered, they must also be completed by June 30 of each year.

Conclusion

In summary, the discussion of adolescence in China and Japan presented here offers a generally positive picture of a cohort of young people who have been able to live through and for the most part benefit from the political and social tranquility that has characterized most of the past decade. During this time it has been possible for adolescents to experience conditions that are very favorable for ensuring their integration into East Asian societies. More recently, however, some of the negative consequences of these conditions have become evident. Serious problems have emerged in both societies in terms of their faltering economies and the constraints this places on the efforts of adolescents to establish themselves as productive members of adult society. In China, corruption, bribery, and environmental pollution have raised questions about the cost of rapid economic development. Continuing problems in the Japanese economy have led some observers to ask whether Japan can ever regain its vitality and avoid periods of anxiety and instability. Resolution of these problems will depend in part on the behavior and motivation of each nation's adolescents, who, in turn, will have strong influences on their own growth and development.

References

Asahi Shimbun. 1998. *Japan almanac*. Tokyo: Asahi Shimbun.
Chang, R. S. 1993. *Qinnien xinlixue (Adolescent psychology)*. Beijing: Beijing Normal University Press.
Chen, C. S., S. Y. Lee, H. W. Stevenson. 1996. Academic achievement of Chinese students: A cross-national perspective. In *Growing up the Chinese way: Chinese child and adolescent development*, ed. S. Lau, 69–91. Hong Kong: The Chinese University Press.

Chen, X. (In press). Peer relationships and networks and socio-emotional adjustment in Chinese children: A cross-cultural perspective. In *Social networks from a developmental perspective*, eds. B. Cairns & T. Farmer.

Chinese Adolescent Research Center Project. 1995. 1994–95 Zhongguo qinnien shehuei fazhan yianjiou baogao (1994–95 Chinese youth social development research report). *Chinese Youth Research.* (Beijing) 1995: 6:13–16.

Crystal, D. S., C. Chen, A. J. Fuligni, H. W. Stevenson, C. C. Hsu, H. J. Ko, S. Kitamura, & S. Kimura. 1994. Psychological maladjustment and academic achievement: A cross-cultural study of Japanese, Chinese, and American high school students. *Child Development.* 65:738–753.

Hsiao, C. G. & C. Xiu. 1996. Ershiyi shiji Zhongguo qinshaonien falu baohu de zouxiang. [Direction of legal protection for 21st century Chinese adolescents]. *Adolescence Deliquency.* (Shanghai) 1996: 4:4–8.

Interviews, Beijing, July 2000.

Johnson, G. R., E. G. Krug, & L. B. Potter. 2000. Suicide among adolescents and young adults: A cross-national comparison of 34 countries. *Suicide and Life-Threatening Behavior.* 30:74–82.

Kojima, H. 1996. Japanese childrearing advice in its cultural, social, and economic contexts. *International Journal of Behavioral Development.* 19(2): 373–391.

LeTendre, G. 1998. The role of school in Japanese adolescents' lives. In *The educational system in Japan: Case study findings*, ed. U.S. Department of Education, 79–136. Washington D.C.: Office of Educational Research.

Ministry of Health and Welfare. 1999. White Paper: Annual report on health and welfare. (Online) Available: http://www.mhw.go.jp/english/white_p/book1/p1_c1/c1_sect5.html

Okamoto, K. & Y. Uechi. 1999. Adolescents' relations with parents and friends in the second individuation process. *Japanese Journal of Educational Psychology.* 47:248–258. [Japanese].

Omi, Y. 1999. A cross-sectional study of the social support network of children and adolescents. *Japanese Journal of Educational Psychology.* 47:40–48. [Japanese].

Peak, L. 1991. *Learning to go to school in Japan: The transition from home to school life.* Berkeley: University of California Press.

Qiang, S. C. 1997. Jioulin niendai chenshi weihuen qinnien xinguannien, xinxingwei diaocha [Survey of sexual concept and behavior of urban unmarried youth in the 90s]. *Chinese Population Science.* (Beijing) 1997: 2:50–52.

Rosenthal, E. 1999. AIDS finally is described by the Chinese as an epidemic. *The New York Times.* Dec.:12, 17.

Satoh, R. 1996. Teenager's sex-consciousness and sex behavior. *Journal of Mental Health.* 42:13–17. [Japanese].

Shao, R. M. 1996. Dangdai jiatin de yanbian yu qinnien shehueihua [Contemporary family change and youth socialization]. *Chinese Youth Research.* (Beijing), 1996: 1:38–39.

Shek, D. T. L. 1996. Mental health of Chinese adolescents: A critical review. In *Growing up the Chinese way: Chinese child and adolescent development*, ed. S. Lau, 169–199. Hong Kong: The Chinese University Press.

Shimizu, K., ed. 1996. Kyoiku Dataland '97–'98 [1997–1998 Databook of Educational Statistics]. Tokyo: Jijitsushinsha.

Shimizu, K., ed. 1999. Kyoiku Dataland 1999–2000 [1999–2000 Databook of Educational Statistics]. Tokyo: Jijitsushinsha.

Soled, D. E., ed. 1995. *China: A nation in transition*. Washington, D.C.: Congressional Quarterly Inc.

Somucho Seishonen Taisaku Honbu. 1996. Seishonen no seikatsu to ishiki ni kansuru kihonchosa (gaiyou). [Management and Coordination Agency Youth Affairs Administration. An investigation into the lives and opinions of youth]. Tokyo: Okurasho.

Somucho Seishonen Taisaku Honbu. 1998. Heisei 10-nendoban seishonen hakusho no gaiyo. [Management and Coordination Agency Youth Affairs Administration. A summary of the 1998 white paper on youth.] (Online) Available: http://www.somucho.go.jp/youth/haku10

Somucho Seishonen Taisaku Honbu. 1999. Hikou geiin ni kansuru sogouteki kenkyu chosa (daisankai) no gaiyou. [Management and Coordination Agency Youth Affairs Administration. A summary of the comprehensive research report on the causes of delinquent behavior.] (Online) Available: http://www.somucho.go.jp/youth/990615c.htm

Stevenson, H. W. 1994. Extracurricular programs in East Asian schools. *Teachers College Record*. 95:387–407

Stevenson, H. W. & S. Y. Lee, in collaboration with S. Carton, M. Evans, S. Meziane, N. Moriyoshi, and I. Schmidt. 1997. International comparisons of entrance and exit examinations: Japan, United Kingdom, France, and Germany. Commissioned paper by Jacob Javits Center for Gifted and Talented, U.S. Department of Education, Washington, D.C., U.S. Government Printing Office.

Stevenson, H. W. 1998. Cultural interpretations of giftedness: The case of East Asia. In *Gifted Children: Vol. 2*, R. Friedman & B. M. Shore, eds. 61–77. Washington, D.C.: American Psychological Association.

Stevenson, H. W. & J. W. Stigler. 1992. The learning gap. New York: Summit Books.

Su, S. X. & P. T. Hu. 1997. Diyidai dushen tsenu nen shiyin shehui ma [Can the first generation only child adjust to society?] *Wen Hui Journal*. 1997:3:1.

Suen, B. H. 1997. Zhongguo dushih qinshaonien tsai shehui zhuanxingqi de daode kunhou ji qi jiaoyu dueiche [Morality crisis and education policy of Chinese urban adolescent in the changing societies]. *Contemporary Youth Research*. (Shanghai) 1997: 4/5:93–97.

Suzuki, K., M. Minowa, & Y. Osaki. 2000. Japanese national survey of adolescent drinking behavior in 1996. *Alcoholism: Clinical and Experimental Research*. 24:377–381.

Takahashi K. & G. Hatano. 1999. Recent trends in civic engagement among Japanese youth. In *Roots of civic identity: International perspectives on community service and activism in youth*, eds. M. Yates & J. Youniss, 225–244. Cambridge University Press.

Takahashi, K. & K. Takeuchi. 1994. Japan. In *International handbook of adolescence*, ed. K. Hurrelmann, 234–245. Westport, CT: Greenwood Press.

Tien, K. W. 1996. Quanyu Zhongguo qinnien shenhuo fangshi de miaoshu [General lifestyle of Chinese youth]. *Chinese Youth Research* (Beijing) 1996: 4:35–38.

Tsang, J. C. 1997. Wailai qinshaonien yu dangdi qinshaonien tuanhuo fanzhuei de bijiao [Adolescent delinquency: Comparison between local and transient adolescents]. *Adolescence Delinquency* (Shanghai) 1997: 1:26–28.

Wada, K., R. K. Price, & S. Fukui. 1997. Cigarette smoking and solvent use among Japanese adolescents. *Drug and Alcohol Dependence.* 46:137–145.

Wen, S. L. 1996. Dangdai Zhongguo qinnien guannien wenhau de zhuanxing [Conceptual and cultural changes of contemporary Chinese youth]. *Chinese Youth Research.* (Beijing) 1996: 4:33–34.

Wong, J. 1996. *Red China Blues.* Toronto, New York, London: Doubleday Books.

Youth Affairs Administration. 1999. *In comparison with the youth of the world, the Japanese youth: A summary report of the sixth world youth survey, 1998.* Tokyo, Japan: Management and Coordination Agency.

Zhang, X., ed. 1995. *China statistical yearbook.* Beijing: China Statistical Publishing Co.

Zhang, X., ed. 1999. *China statistical yearbook.* Beijing: China Statistical Publishing Co.

Zhu, Z. X., ed. 1990. Zhongguo ertong qinshaonien hsinli fatsan jiaoyu [Psychological development and education of Chinese children and adolescents]. Beijing: Zouyue Publishing Co.

Zhu, Y. X. 1997. Dangdai qinshaonien renshen jiazhi guan de tedian yu jiaoyu dueiche [The characteristics of contemporary adolescence value and the implication for education policy]. *Education Science.* (Da-Lian) 1997: 1:42–44.

6

Youth in Southeast Asia

Living Within the Continuity of Tradition and the Turbulence of Change

Madelene Santa Maria

Introduction

For the last 2 centuries the peoples of Southeast Asia (SEA) experienced rapid changes in their societies brought about by the influx of political and religious influences from other nations and by global breakthroughs in technology. SEA states have shown, in varying degrees, their capacities for change. But beneath the rapid social and material transformations, traditional beliefs and life patterns continue to provide the framework that guides most of people's life activities. Some may view this continued reliance on 'what has always been' as resistance to progress. However, historical accounts show that the ability of the SEA peoples to absorb and accommodate various influences, while not allowing these influences to radically transform their societies, has been the major source of stability and resiliency (Vatikiotis 1996).

The youth of SEA embody both their societies' vulnerability to the turbulence of rapid change and their societies' strength that emanates from the bedrock of tradition. In SEA societies, youth are viewed as the hope of the family's survival and as the symbol of passion and vitality in society. At the same time, youth are viewed as victims of modernization, the sector most vulnerable to the rapid progress in society. These images interact with lives of youth, structuring their relations with others and enabling them new degrees of autonomy.

SEA states generally accept the United Nations (UN) definition of youth as those who do not have the full legal status and roles of adulthood, and consequently, unlike adults, they do not have access to family, professional, and political rights (UN 1997a). Guided by this general

TABLE 6.1. *Youth Population Ratios in 8 Southeast Asian Countries*

Country	12–17 age group	18–23 age group	Total
Cambodia	14.6	8.2	22.8
Indonesia	12.1	11.8	23.9
Malaysia	12.1	11.1	23.2
Myanmar	12.5	12.5	25.0
Philippines	13.2	11.9	25.1
Singapore	7.7	7.3	15.0
Thailand	11.1	11.5	22.6
Vietnam	13.3	12.1	25.4

Source: United Nations, 2001, 131.

definition, SEA states prescribe varied age ranges in identifying who belongs to this age category. In the Philippines, youth are legally defined as those who are 15 to 30 years old. In Thailand, youth are those who are 15 to 25 years old (UN 1997a). In Malaysia, the state's Youth Council defines youth as those from 15 to 40 years of age (UN 1997a).

The life of youth in SEA is best understood in terms of the waves of change occurring within the region over the last 30 years. One of the most significant changes happening in SEA between the 1970s and the mid-1990s is the phenomenal growth of its population. Uhlig (1988) reported that it increased from 210 million in 1972 to 380 million in 1982; and it was 506 million in 1998 (Wright 2000). Although the strategies that have been undertaken to control population growth are now considered to be successful, overpopulation remains a problem in some SEA countries. This population explosion may be said to be an explosion of the youth population. To illustrate, a Philippine population census in 1995 recorded 13.7 million youth, signifying that their number doubled over the previous 25 years (Berja 1999). By 1990, youth between the ages of 10 and 24 composed one-third of the entire Philippine population (Go 1994). Table 6.1 presents the youth population ratios in 8 countries in SEA.

Across these 8 SEA countries youth compose an average of 22.9 percent of the population. This huge and expanding number of young people puts greater pressure upon the income earners who feed them. It also puts pressure on society to establish more educational institutions and to create more jobs. Differing projections occur as to whether this growth will continue. Some recent reports project a decline in the youth population after the 1990s (Mehta, Groenen, & Roque 1998).

However, UN data (1997b, 2001) show that the proportion of youth in the population has been continuing to increase; at the extreme, the number of 15–25-year-olds in Vietnam rose from 20.0 percent in 1995 to 25.4 percent in 2001.

A related phenomenon in modern SEA is urban growth, turning former predominantly agrarian cultures to more urbanized ones within a 2 to 3 decade period (Vatikiotis 1996). For example, the Thai capital of Bangkok had a population of 3.5 million in the early 1970s, which ballooned to 10 million in the mid-1990s. The population of the Indonesian capital, Jakarta, was estimated to be 4.5 million in 1970, and it increased to 11 million some 20 years later (Osborne 1997). Cities draw in rural dwellers with the lure of a more materially comfortable life. What is notable is that the movement from rural to urban areas is largely a youth phenomenon, and it is more common among young women. A UN report (2001) revealed that female migration from rural to urban areas is particularly noteworthy in the SEA region, with a large number of young, unmarried females moving independently, or with their families. The large number of female urban migrants has been specifically noted in Thailand (UN 1997a) and the Philippines (Xenos & Raymundo 1999), where it is contributing to a gender imbalance in both rural and urban areas. In much of the region the urban migration of young women and men has become so rapid that it has far outpaced the creation of available work and educational opportunities.

Population growth in the region and the growth of urban centers are accompanied by social transformations in young people's lives. Youth have a capacity to experience the new while still absorbing the enduring influences of SEA traditions. We therefore find SEA youth straddling dualities of old and new, stability and change. They have to deal actively with the expectations and role definitions of groups and institutions from both sides of these dualities. The consequences on their lives are revealed in concerns that have become a focus in the region. For example, attention is currently being given to the plight of youth who are left to survive on their own in the city streets, and to increased incidence of dissidence and delinquency. Concerns are also focused on young people's increased proneness to reproductive health risks, resulting from their heightened sexual experimentation.

In the following account, I attempt to describe the transformations in the contexts and life worlds of SEA youth. Examination of young people's experiences in these contexts will allow us to better understand their sense of self, as well as their relations with others. A description will also be given of the impact of social and economic demands on the youth's health, their forms of civic participation, as well as the assistance provided by groups and institutions to address the problems faced by the youth. By presenting an account of the current state of youth life within these contexts, I hope to provide a sense of how youth achieve a coordination of cultural dualities that exist in SEA life.

The goal of this chapter is to capture as comprehensive a picture of youths' life as possible in the entire region. I had limited access, however, to the work of local researchers in many SEA nations, thus I relied more heavily on documents produced by international agencies that provide more general assessments of youth. I also conducted interviews with social scientists in the region to obtain a more detailed picture of the youth situation in their respective countries. Because I am Filipino and have greater access to published Philippine materials, I often give a particular focus to the situation of Filipino youth. This chapter does not therefore hope to provide the reader with an exhaustive review of the literature, but rather with a general overview of the lives of SEA youth.

Background

The SEA region is made up of 10 states: Myanmar, Thailand, Laos, Cambodia, Vietnam, Malaysia, Brunei, Indonesia, Singapore, and the Philippines. In the mainland portion of the region, one finds the countries of Myanmar, Thailand, Laos, Cambodia, and Vietnam. These countries are located east of the borders of India and Bangladesh, and south of the borders of China. The rest of the countries are found straddling the islands to the south. The state of Malaysia geographically consists of the Malay peninsula, Sabah, and Sarawak in the island of Borneo. Negara Brunei Darussalam is situated on the northwest coast of Borneo. Indonesia, the largest country in the region, is that volcanic island arc that stretches from the Indian Ocean to the Pacific Ocean. The city-state of Singapore occupies one main island and some tiny islets at the southern end of the Malacca Strait. Finally, situated in a remote eastern corner of the region is the Philippines, an archipelago of over 7,100 islands.

One is exposed in SEA to a world where 2 great cultures meet – the Indian culture from the west and the Chinese culture from the north. Influences from these 2 great cultures are of significance partly through their introduction of the universal religions of Hinduism, Buddhism, and Islam. These great religions dynamically interplay with local indigenous life patterns and belief systems to produce a unique SEA identity. The coming of European colonial powers during the late 1500s added to this blend of influences, including Christianity. But before the Europeans influenced the political and cultural lives of the people of SEA, Buddhism and Islam were already strongly rooted in most of these countries. The majority of the population in Myanmar (85 percent), in Laos (80 percent), and in Cambodia (95 percent) is Buddhist (Neher & Marlay 1995). The Muslim religion is followed by a larger proportion of the population in Indonesia (87 percent), in Malaysia (53 percent), and in Brunei (60 percent) (Neher & Marlay 1995). It was only in the Philippines where Spanish colonial rule managed to firmly establish the Catholic religion over most of the islands. A total of 83 percent of the population in the Philippines are now Catholics (Neher & Marlay 1995). Despite these variations in faiths, tolerance for the practice of different religions exists throughout the region.

Scholars stress the extent to which various peoples of the region have given importance to their own needs and values as they adapted themselves to foreign ideas and influences. This common pattern of adaptation has paved the way for an interest in SEA as a geographic and cultural unit. In his historical account of SEA, Osborne (1997) enumerates a bulk of evidence indicating this unity. Throughout the region, for instance, one may observe the predominance of the nuclear family, which differs markedly from the importance given to the extended family in India. SEA countries also share greater recognition for the status of women within the family and society, as contrasted to the place allotted to women in Indian and Chinese societies. There are also commonalities in the languages of the SEA region that cut across the national boundaries set by colonial powers. For example, the variants of the basic Indonesian/Malay language are spoken throughout Indonesia, Malaysia, Brunei, in the southern part of the Philippines, and along the southern coastal regions of Cambodia, Vietnam, and Thailand.

The commonalities across the region are most evident in cities, where one is bound to see a combination of the still vibrant "old" and the inevitable "new." Alongside the precolonial and colonial lifeways are the postcolonial influences, having visible impact. As Osborne (1997) further observed, a person's life does not necessarily change as a result of adopting modern styles of living. Beneath the appearance of great change and modernity in the cities lies the traditional world of rural life.

In summary, the peoples of SEA continue to rely on tradition while embracing the possibilities of modern change. We will see this tendency in its clearest form in the urban centers where youth flock to avail themselves of the opportunities for material advancement. Let us now have a closer look at one of the more enduring institutions of SEA life – the family. We will see that this institution provides a stable background for youth as they make their way through changes in modern life.

Family Organization and Relations

Family life in SEA may be characterized from a child's point of view as "many-peopled." This label, used by Shimizu (1984) for the Filipino family organization, aptly describes the family environment in most SEA societies. Although households are increasingly nuclear, extended family members often live nearby and are often included in daily activities and practices. In this kind of environment, an individual grows up surrounded by, and frequently and closely interacting with, a number of adults and children who are relatives or are recognized as relatives. There is an appearance of the family as extended, but in reality, there are relatives as well as nonrelatives with whom the family may be maintaining frequent face-to-face interactions (Shimizu 1984, 109). Thus, while growing up, the child learns to deal with different types of people of varying ages. It is possible to assume that the youth leave their childhood equipped with people-skills that allow them to adapt in varying social situations.

In the SEA family, we may observe a certain amount of freedom given to the individual to exercise his or her choices, within the bounds of relationships that serve as systems of support and cooperation in times of need. In the Philippines, we find this system of family relations characterized by mutual cooperation. Within the household, we are likely to find grandparents, aunts or uncles, and older siblings sharing the responsibility of caring for children and assisting in household work. The individual is said to learn this expectation of assistance early in life. Socialization is thus focused on the development of young people's ability to relate well with others and to demonstrate concern for others. According to Ventura (1999), the first important concept acquired by the Filipino child in his/her social development is *pakiramdam* or sensitivity to others' feelings and intentions.

In Malaysia, where nuclear family arrangements are also common, the same pattern of extended family cooperation can be observed (Dube 1997). For instance, newlyweds may choose to live with parents for economic reasons, and more frequently, the young wife will prefer that they live with her parents because of the strong affective ties and well-established cooperative patterns that exist between mother and daughter. Here, it is evident that choices made in marriage are dictated by considerations of remaining within the network of mutual help and cooperation.

Socialization Within the Family
In most SEA societies, despite social change, the family remains the context in which most of the influences affecting youth are found. This is reinforced by the high value of family solidarity held by youth in the region. Among Filipino adolescents, there is a commonly held belief that close, warm ties among family members must be maintained, and that sacrifices should be made for the good of the family (Go 1994). For them, a show of support and loyalty to the family is very important. This support is demonstrated, for example, in the way an older brother or sister may stop schooling or postpone marriage in order to help support or educate younger siblings.

What is important to emphasize here is the nature of relationships that young people learn to value as they grow up. For most SEA societies, the growing child assumes an important place in an open, nonisolated form of nuclear family organization. The terms used in the local Malay-Indonesian and Filipino languages to name that grouping called the family show close similarities in meaning. In Filipino, family is referred to as *mag-anak*; in the Malay-Indonesian language, a close counterpart would be the term *beranak*. When translated, the root word *anak* means "child." This implies, as far as the Malay-Indonesian-Filipino realm is concerned, that the center of family relations is the child, or that all of the family's preoccupations are focused on the child.

Shimizu (1984) emphasized that young people learn to accept dependence and reliance on other family members in a way that makes the growing process become less stressful and less dissatisfying. Children are thus not expected to develop rapidly, nor are they harshly disciplined. They are taught to get along well with others, and any expression of aggression is discouraged. Children therefore learn to exhibit "sociable-intimate" behaviors in order to maintain their social relations for the purpose of realizing their goals. Exposed very early to open, complicated, and diverse relationships, Filipino youth learn the art and behaviors needed to maintain, strengthen, and extend relationships.

Youth are also assigned the important role of improving the family's situation. In Indonesia, youth are expected to take on responsible roles in the family, and are called upon to take the lead role in advocating for needed societal changes (Prof. Lambang Trijono, personal communication 2001). Parents also encourage young people to seek better opportunities in the cities. Youth's success in these endeavors is seen as the family's success; the youth's failure is the family's failure. Youth and families in Malaysia share the same expectation. Failure in one's educational and work pursuits would bring shame and disappointment to the family (Dr. Kamarulzaman Askandar, personal communication 2001). Likewise, Filipino families view their children in terms of their economic utility, as well as the psychological security they bring to the family (Liwag, de la Cruz, & Macapagal 1996).

Impact of Social Transformations on the Family
While families remain central, they are also changing with the modern world. As mentioned earlier, young people are more mobile, sometimes living and working in distant cities, often to send money home to families. As will be mentioned later, the age of marriage is coming later to accommodate further education and this urban employment pattern. A related change is the slow disappearance of the "extended" family organization and an increase in isolated nuclear families in urban areas (UN 1997b). These transformations have contributed to changing family life patterns and relations.

One important transformation is the diminishing of young people's traditional participation in family activities. A McCann-Erickson study (1993) on Filipino youth revealed that youth are spending less time with their parents. Other family members, too, are becoming more and more independent in their activities. As one Filipino youth mentioned, "It's hard to get the family together because everyone's got their own thing to do." The McCann-Erickson study further revealed that the marked absence of shared activities among family members is leading Filipino youth to make more decisions on their own, and to become more dissatisfied with family life.

Recent data also indicate that a high percentage of Filipino youth are reporting an increasing life world of experience outside the family (Xenos & Raymundo 1999). Young people show a trend to move out and seek other contexts of interaction. This includes youth that live at home but spend more time away and youth who leave home. Xenos and Raymundo report that more youth are moving, leaving their household base to form a household themselves or converge in other households headed by nonyouth. This movement is more prevalent in Philippine rural areas where the youth-to-household ratio is smaller (0.96 youth per household) than in urban areas (1.28 youth per household). To ensure greater stability during adulthood, young people are choosing to leave their families at an earlier age and to establish a family at a later age. Xenos and Raymundo point out, however, that the observed mobility among young Filipinos is transitory and does not undermine the fundamental stability of the Filipino household and family.

When there is a serious threat to family unity, or when difficulties are faced by any of its members, return to the family household base for support remains the usual practice. In fact, in the Philippines, the percentage of married older youth living with parents is noticeably rising (Xenos & Raymundo 1999), indicating that this temporary living arrangement is resorted to when economic independence cannot be sustained. Typically, youth turn to their mothers for support, which Dube (1997) indicates has strong cultural approval across SEA. The deep cooperative relationship between mothers and daughters makes for enduring cooperative links within the nuclear family base. In the Philippines, mother-headed single-parent households are growing, resulting in an increasing proportion of youth living with, or returning to, their mother's household (Xenos & Raymundo 1999). Dube explained this central role of mothers as arising from the matrilineal and matrilocal nature of SEA families, which contrasts with the patrilineal, patrivirilocal, and more authoritarian family patterns found to predominate in other Asian societies.

Gender Socialization and the Changing Role of the Female
This general inclination toward matrilineality and matrilocality of the SEA family organization has resulted, according to Dube (1997), in egalitarian relations between males and females – a quality of gender relations that may be assumed to have predated the advent of Islam and influences from the West. This quality of gender relations is also reinforced by the relatively nongendered way of assigning roles and tasks to increase family productivity inputs. This has important consequences on young women's lives in SEA. According to Dube, women have gained considerable autonomy in their social and economic lives. In view of the form of family arrangement and kinship organization in SEA, Dube observes that the region offers women a variation of choices, for example, in marital partners, residence, and household composition. Women, thus, hold more bargaining power in interpersonal relationships and are presented with choices and opportunities in income-earning

activities. Women exercise these choices and opportunities, however, within the framework of family needs and aspirations.

A short description of the gender socialization process in Filipino families provides us with an understanding of how girls and women have gained more autonomy in the midst of rapid social change. In the traditional life of the Philippines, no formal initiations are experienced by youth as they take leave of childhood. It is in the period of adolescence when the family emphasizes gender differences. The beginning of adolescence for males is marked by a change in voice and by circumcision. Among females, the period is marked by first menstruation. Boys are said to be physically stronger and are supposed to exhibit more aggressive behavior. Girls are now more "ladylike," modest, and gentle. Boys are given greater freedom, while girls are restricted in their movements (Medina 1991).

According to Liwag and her associates (1996), when the female enters the period of menarche, it is the mother's principal role to instruct the daughter about hygiene matters and proper behavior because – the daughter is told – she has now become a lady. The restrictions the girl experiences in childhood are now intensified, conveying to her that she needs to exercise control in her deportment and in her relations with the opposite sex. The son, on the other hand, continues to enjoy the freedom he was given throughout childhood.

As a form of responsibility training, Filipino girls are expected to assist in housework. They become more independent and are able to take care of themselves at an early age (Liwag et al. 1996). In poorer families, girls usually serve as mother- or father-surrogates by assisting in the care of younger siblings. Girls are also expected to assist in family income-earning activities. Boys, on the other hand, are expected to assist in carrying out household jobs that necessitate physical strength. In rural families, boys assist their fathers in farm and fishing activities. Boys may also be given tasks usually assigned to girls, especially when girls are unavailable. The rationale for the assignment of specific tasks for each gender is that girls should receive training for their eventual role as housewives; boys have to be trained for their eventual role as "head of the family." Liwag and her associates are quick to point out, however, that the task boundaries are not so rigid and there is considerable male and female crossover of responsibilities.

On top of household demands, young women in families are given a major role in augmenting family income. They provide critical income support to cushion the stresses experienced by the family at a time of rapid change, as well as to help with the increasing material family needs that come with modernization. In the Philippines, daughters feel more obligated than sons do to work abroad for the family (Tacoli 1996, as cited in Liwag et al. 1996). Likewise, in Indonesia it is daughters, rather than sons, who leave home to work overseas (Prof. Lambang Trijono, personal communication 2001). Sons are expected to stay close to home to better fulfill their obligation of "protecting" the family. While females are more likely to marry at an earlier age, they are also more likely to be living away from home while they are single. Males, on the hand, generally marry later, but are more likely to remain at home with the parents while they are still single (Xenos & Raymundo 1999). This implies that young women are now being socialized to be independent in their activities even before marriage.

In summary, we can observe that transformations, resulting from new social and economic conditions, are affecting youth's engagement in the family. But, although relations in families are changing, the basic cooperative bonds are preserved – primarily by the female members. Female youth are given the main task of ensuring that the system of support continues, including protecting the family from difficulties brought about by increasing economic demands. She is now enjoying more freedom and autonomy, but the freedom she enjoys is to be used for the purpose of carrying out her duty of caring for the family. We may thus observe that, on the one hand, youth feel the excitement and push of modern life focused on values of material prosperity and the freedom of expression and mobility. On the other hand, they continue to place great value on the psychological and material support derived from traditional cooperative relations nurtured within the family.

Peer Relations and Sexuality

Little is known about the peer relations of SEA youth, and much of the information that exists has been gathered in studies of youth problems, such as drugs, delinquency, and illicit sexuality. To my knowledge, the most comprehensive description of youth's peer relations was a study by Mendez and Jocano in 1979 of youth in the Philippines. Their study showed that, in their selection of friends, a majority of the respondents placed a high value on personality traits, similarity of interests, and their confidence in the other's ability to provide assistance. These are factors that strengthen cohesive relationships within a peer group. The study also revealed that youth consult with friends mainly about school and matters concerning the opposite sex. Friends were described as providing comfort and confidence during the initial stages of courtship. Mendez and Jocano concluded that youth learn new peer group norms in adolescence, which create new patterns of behavior distinct from childhood. Socialization within the peer group helps develop a sense of freedom and independence. The extent of self-expression and openness to changing moral values exhibited by Filipino youth is, in turn, calibrated against the rules of expression and standards of morality within one's peers (Rimando 1981).

The McCann-Erickson study (1993), also in the Philippines, provided further information about the expanding peer world. Their data showed that the temporary or permanent parental absenteeism, experienced by some youth, has led them to turn to their peers, not only for companionship and friendship, but for nurturing, guidance, intimacy, and security. Some respondents in this study reported that it is their friends who understand them. This study also found that sports, eating out, and music-related activities were the most frequent forms of youth activities, and shopping and "malling" (i.e., spending time inside shopping malls) were new additions to this list of activities. These new additions are an indication of the growing consumerism and material preoccupation among youth. A 1996 study undertaken by the Social Weather Stations (SWS) in the Philippines showed that more youth (74 percent) listen to the radio than watch television (57 percent), while 31 percent read books, magazines, and newspapers. Despite the growing influence of peers, only 28 percent reported getting together with their friends every day (SWS 1996).

Romantic involvement and sexual activities are usually facilitated and supported by peers. According to Raymundo (1999) group dating, usually involving one's peer group members, is a common practice among Filipino youth to initiate acquaintances with the opposite sex. Rimando (1981) pointed out that peers are also those who are first approached for consolation and protection when premarital pregnancies happen.

Sexual Behaviors

The incidence of premarital sexual activity among Filipino youth has been increasing (Rimando 1981; Medina 1991). This has occurred despite a traditional double standard of morality in Philippine society, which required females to be faithful and chaste, but which condoned premarital sexual activities among males. By this moral standard, females are made to feel guilty of their sexuality, whereas males are encouraged to engage in sexual activities as a prerequisite to manhood. Most Filipino youth consider it natural for males to have many partners (Silayan-Go 1997). Tied to the notion of females' premarital virginity has been the ownership by males of that virginity. There is no equity of responsibility in a heterosexual relationship. According to Silayan-Go, the female is supposed to control and set limits to male sexuality. If unplanned pregnancy should happen, the female is often faulted for not taking the proper precautions.

Thai society imposes the same prescriptions on female youth. According to Soonthoundhoda (1996), sexual promiscuity has been strongly forbidden for girls, and cohabitation is only allowed upon marriage. This is considered as a standard of good upbringing by Thai parents. A daughter's marriage is an important event in the family since it is supposed to bring economic benefits to the family in the form of a bride price. In the Philippines, with the general social disapproval of premarital sex, females who are sexually active are careful to keep it under wraps in order not to arouse societal stigma (Medina 1991).

In Thailand, the traditional view that men should be given more sexual freedom than females is changing (Gray & Satsara 1999). Research findings suggest that more youth in Thailand now tend toward early and premarital sex with a noncommercial partner (Gray & Satsara 1999). In Malaysia, studies also reveal that from 18 percent to 25 percent of youth are engaged in premarital sex (Huang Soo Lee 1999). These changes reflect a new generation's more open attitude toward sexuality. Medina (1991) reported that many Filipino youth see sex as a natural, spontaneous act. Virginity was still found to be important, although premarital sex was permissible when there is love and an intention to marry. Among Filipino youth, this new morality was not viewed as promiscuity, but was labeled as "permissiveness with affection." This new morality accepts sex with someone one loves and expects to marry, or someone with whom one has a stable relationship (Medina 1991).

The average age at first sexual encounter is 18.0 among Filipino males and 18.3 among females (Berja 1999). Estimates show that some 18 percent of youth (26 percent among males and 10 percent among females) are engaging in premarital sex (Berja 1999). Silayan-Go also noted the prevalence of short-term relationships among Filipino youth, which are initiated without courtship and which usually include sexual intimacies. Anecdotal evidence suggests that there is an increased incidence of premarital cohabitation among SEA youth. The decision to live together before marriage is common among couples who have stable relationships and are planning to marry at a later time. This practice is usually observed among youth who live distant from their parental homes (Prof. Lambang Trijono, personal communication 2001), and parents are also usually kept in the dark (Dr. Suwit Laohasiriwong, personal communication 2001).

Thus increased sexual activity among Filipino youth is interrelated with the widespread migration of youth to urban areas, as well as with disruptions in parental supervision sometimes attributed to mothers working outside the home (e.g., Medina 1991). There is also a prevalent notion that the introduction of "Western" ways of life and values, as propagated in media especially in urban areas, is contributing to increases in premarital sexuality and pregnancies. However, there is reason to believe that the "modern" values of self-realization, self-expression, and independence, as well as the need for economic security, have a more direct impact on the age of marriage, which in turn influence youth's ideals and views about sexuality and relationships.

Delaying Marriage

More and more Filipino youth are reported to favor delayed marriage and having fewer children (Medina 1991). For these youth, early marriage may be seen as leading to more children, and, in turn, to economic strains. They believe later marriage makes them better prepared for marital life. Trends show an increasing proportion of unmarried young Filipinas in both the 15–19 and 20–24 age groups, although a tendency to marry early is still observed among the low educated, rural dwellers, and the poor (Berja 1999). Youth in Thailand also appear to be marrying at later ages (Gray & Satsara 1999).

The decision to delay establishing one's own family may be indicative of the growing pragmatism among the young. They may not necessarily be viewing family as irrelevant in their future lives as adults, but are acknowledging that having a family entails responsibility and requires maturity and economic stability. Most youth may now be of the opinion that adulthood can be assumed later. The result is that the duration of adolescence is becoming longer.

In conclusion, the movement of SEA youth away from their families brings with it a measure of behavioral autonomy, achieved, to a certain extent, in their romantic and sexual relationships. Although the adult world does not deny the existence of sexual experiences among youth, these are still under wraps and young people are not allowed to assume full responsibility for these experiences. Nonetheless, peers are quite influential in the regulation of youth's sexual behaviors. And many youth affirm responsibility and are guided by values on stability, preparedness, and love to make their decisions about sexual relations prior to their assumption of adult roles through marriage.

Trends in Education

Since the colonial period, there have been continuous, energetic efforts to establish and develop schools in SEA (Uhlig 1988). Nations have mandated free and compulsory education, especially at the primary levels. In the Philippines, free and compulsory primary (6 years) and secondary (4 to 5 years) education is now provided to all children. In Thailand, free education is available for 12 years in many locales, with opportunity for schooling at the secondary level expanding to the villages (Dr. Suwit Laohasiriwong, personal communication 2001). In Indonesia, free education is provided only at the primary level (Prof. Lambang Trijono, personal communication 2001); however, numerous state schools were established in the past years, primarily through a decree by former President Suharto. Because of these efforts, literacy rates have increased across countries of the region. During the mid-1990s, literacy rates were reported to achieve between 80 percent to over 90 percent across countries, except in Cambodia (50 percent) and Laos (40 percent) (Neher & Marlay 1995).

Enrollment Rates

Enrollment ratios at the secondary level have increased in most SEA countries within the last 2 decades. Table 6.2 shows comparative ratios at the secondary and tertiary levels in SEA for the period from 1980 to 1997. The most favorable pattern is seen in the Philippines, which has one of the highest enrollment rates in the region. Increased participation in education is observed especially among single female Filipinas aged 20–24 (Berja 1999). Data also revealed that there are consistently more female youth in the Philippines enrolling in the tertiary educational level than males (Berja 1999). This further indicates that women's later age at marriage over the past decades is interrelated with later ages of school-leaving and higher educational attainments (Xenos & Raymundo 1999).

At the other extreme, Table 6.2 shows rates of enrollment to have been falling in Cambodia. More-recent data in the same report indicates upward trends in both Cambodia and Laos for the 1-year span between

TABLE 6.2. *Gross Enrollment Ratios at the Secondary and Tertiary Levels from 1980 to 1997*

	Enrollment Ratio (1980)		Enrollment Ratio (1997)	
	Secondary Level	Tertiary Level	Secondary Level	Tertiary Level
Brunei	61	1	77	–
Cambodia	32	1	24	1
Indonesia	29	4	56	11
Laos	21	0	28	3
Malaysia	48	4	64	–
Myanmar	22	5	30	5
Philippines	64	24	78	–
Singapore	60	8	74	39
Thailand	29	15	59	–
Vietnam	42	2	57	–

Note: Dashes indicate that data are not available.
Source: United Nations 2001, 152.

2000 and 2001. This may indicate an expansion of educational opportunities in this part of the region. On the other hand, downward rates for the same 1-year period in Thailand, a country having one of the lowest levels of educational attainment among SEA nations (Gray & Satsara 1999), does not bode well for that country. However, the recent mandate in Thailand for compulsory education to at least the junior secondary level (Gray & Satsara 1999) may improve the situation.

Educational Survival Rates

Although many countries show dramatic increases in student enrollment in recent years, low educational survival rates – the rate of staying in school – are observed especially among the poorer countries in SEA. In Thailand, many youth are only able to complete 6 years of schooling. They withdraw from school to work on farms or as unskilled labor in factories, or many migrate to the cities for employment (Dr. Suwit Laohasiriwong, personal communication 2001). Following the pattern in other countries, in the Philippines, the largest number of these out-of-school youth are females and are living in rural areas (United Nations Population Fund 1997b; UNFPA). Out-of-school youth in Philippine urban areas end up living in the streets doing odd jobs or are likely to join the informal labor force as street and market vendors. Research showed that most of the out-of-school youth either search for employment or stay at home to assist in household tasks (UNFPA 1997b).

To account for dropout rates among Philippine youth, both school-related and nonschool-related factors are cited (De los Angeles-Bautista & Arriola 1995). Among school-related factors are inadequate facilities and materials, overcrowded classrooms, and overworked teachers. Nonschool-related factors have to do with poverty and the accompanying required participation of youth in household work and income-generating activities, the attitude of parents to education, family mobility, and the child's poor health. The Philippine National Youth Council commissioned survey in 1996 also revealed that major concerns include the quality of education and the lack of access to education, particularly in the secondary levels (UNFPA, 1997b). The low quality of education is evidenced by the poor results of national achievement and assessment tests at the primary and secondary levels. The remoteness of schools and the high costs of education highlight the problem of access. Dropout rates are highest among poor students at the primary and secondary levels. Unequal access to tertiary schools is caused by the concentration of these schools in the bigger cities.

Educational survival rates at the secondary level are higher in Malaysia than in most other SEA countries (Huang Soo Lee 1999). Educational survival rates are higher in Malaysia partly because of the greater financial capacities of most Malaysian families. High survival rates are also due to students not being allowed to drop out of school in spite of their poor academic performance. However, 2nd and 3rd generation urban poor youth frequently drop out of school, lured away by increased opportunities for part-time employment (Dr. Wazir Karif, personal communication 2001). Those youth who stay in school often carry heavy burdens helping their parents to care for the household, which means they do poorly and become less motivated for schoolwork. Many Malaysian youth are also becoming aware that, whether they study hard or not, they will eventually be able to obtain well-paying jobs (Dr. Kamarulzaman Askandar, personal communication 2001), which has negatively affected their motivation and achievement levels in school.

In summary, while vigorous efforts in most SEA countries has been moving them toward the goal of providing universal education at the primary and secondary levels, that goal is yet to be achieved. Many youth drop out, due to poverty, poor access to education, the limited quality and relevance of education, as well as the increased opportunities for factory employment available for youth at a very early age. An ominous sign is that for some youth, secondary and further education is being viewed more as a convenience than a necessity, and their motivation to stay in school and to achieve is negatively affected.

Employment Trends

Many things are shaping SEA youth's experience in the world of work: state development plans, poverty levels, labor market demands, and educational training. My account of the employment trends among Filipino youth, given here, does not hope to provide a representative picture of the experience of young people in the entire region. In some countries where poverty is almost eradicated, the situation will be entirely different. Youths' employment situation in Malaysia, for example, shows encouraging trends, as more employment opportunities are available due to economic progress in the country over the past two decades. In most SEA countries, where poverty and unemployment remain as society's ills, underemployment and exploitation are among the problems that confront youth.

Labor Force Participation Rates

In the Philippines, young people aged 15–30 years comprise almost half of the country's labor force (UNFPA 1997a). Relatively high labor force participation rates (LFPRs) are found in the agricultural sector, where a majority of working youth are employed (Berja 1999). A greater number of the male youth participate in this sector, while more employed females participate as sales or service workers in urban areas (UNFPA 1997a). About 0.6 percent of Filipino youth hold administrative, managerial, and executive positions (UNFPA 1997a). These youth and those who work in the service sector receive higher wages (UNFPA 1997a). One-third of young workers hold part-time jobs, that is, they work less than 40 hours a week and are therefore underemployed.

Lower LFPRs were also found among young Filipino females. Their lower participation rates are due to the following reasons: i) female youth often work as unpaid family labor, ii) agricultural work, where most youth find employment, is male-dominated, and iii) females experience interruptions in their life cycle due to reproductive and child-bearing periods (UNFPA 1997b). Aside from these factors, lower LFPRs among females are due to the fact that many of them join the informal labor sector, finding intermittent work opportunities, for example, as street or market vendors.

TABLE 6.3. *Philippine Rural-Urban Labor Force Participation Rate by Sex and Age Group (1996)*

Males	Urban 67.2%		Rural 79.7%
15–20 Age Group		38.6%	62.7%
21–25 Age Group		85.7%	91.6%
26–30 Age Group		96.6%	98.6%
Females	**45.2%**		**40.9%**
15–20 Age Group		32.4%	33.4%
21–25 Age Group		56.8%	48.3%
26–30 Age Group		54.4%	46.6%

Source: UNFPA 1997a, 4.

The traditional sex differences that appear in employment trends, however, are now being altered by marked changes in the participation rates of older Filipino female youth in the last 2 decades (Xenos & Raymundo 1999). The rise in female participation rates is indicative of the greater autonomy experienced by females, as discussed above. It is important, however, to note that many employed female youth have more years of schooling than employed males (UNFPA 1997b), although female youth earn less. The current reality is that even unschooled males are sometimes able to get jobs, while for females, lack of schooling can be a disadvantage in the labor market (UNFPA 1997b).

Relatively high participation rates of youth are also found in urban areas. Table 6.3 shows rural-urban LFPRs among male and female youth in the Philippines. It is evident that the LFPR is higher in rural areas for the 15–20 age group. This is indicative of the lack of accessibility of secondary education in these areas (UNFPA 1997a), forcing these youth to seek employment while they are out of school. Another apparent trend shows that the LFPRs of females in the 21–30 age group are higher in urban areas. This trend mirrors the large number of females engaging in low-paying jobs in these areas (UNFPA 1997a). It is also explained by the fact that most youth who are able to find employment as agricultural workers in the rural areas are males. This causes females to seek jobs in urban centers, where most jobs are in community and social services or manufacturing.

In terms of job aspirations, a majority of Philippine youth have indicated that they intend to have their own business (SWS 1996). Among Thai youth, an opportunity to get a job in government is still preferred because of the stability and benefits these jobs offer (Dr. Suwit Laohasiri-wong, personal communication 2001).

Large numbers of youth also aspire to work abroad (SWS 1996). Statistics show that many youth in the Philippines, especially females, are joining the overseas labor market (UNFPA 1997a). An increasing number of Indonesian and Thai youth are seeking employment abroad, in international agencies, and in nongovernmental organizations (NGOs). Many Indonesian female youth are obtaining jobs through placement agencies as domestic helpers in Malaysia and Saudi Arabia (personal communication, Prof. Lambang Trijono 2001). After finding it difficult to get factory jobs during the economic crisis, many Thai youth worked overseas as construction workers or domestic helpers (Dr. Suwit Laohasiriwong, personal communication 2001).

Problems and Issues in Youth Employment
Both national development plans and the nature of educational training received by youth have direct bearing on their employment opportunities, and these often do not match. In most cases, the educational training youth receive is not related to the manpower needs of the country (UN 1997b). As a result, youth with academic training often are not able to obtain employment commensurate to their qualifications and training. Youth often end up accepting jobs below their level of educational training. Another problem is that government plans for development have largely focused on moving resources from the agricultural to the industrial sector (Dixon & Kim 1985), which leaves rural youth with fewer opportunities. Thus, in the first quarter of 2000, the industrial sector grew by 4.8 percent, while growth in the agricultural sector was a measly 0.2 percent. For these and other reasons, a recent report showed that 77 percent of the total number of unemployed in the Philippines comes from the 15–34 age bracket (Press release 2000).

Conditions of employment are also affected by the number of youth entering the labor force, which is dependent on a nation's fertility rate. This number of youth may continue to rise in the Philippines, where population growth, especially in rural areas, is still a problem, as compared to countries like Thailand, where the population problem is successfully being controlled (UN 1997a). Rural youth, aged 15–19, tend to start working on farms before they try out other activities (UN 1991). But when farm opportunities are scarce, and as increasing numbers of youth leave school, the service sector in urban areas gets overloaded and incomes fall, therefore, more and more youth are limited to working as street vendors, domestic helpers, and the like.

Lack of employment in rural areas, inadequate training or preparation for work in their communities, and the inability on the part of parents to support their children's education are among the factors that influence Philippine youth to seek employment in cities. The decision to migrate to the cities is also made because of a dislike for farmwork and an inability to find other types of work within their own communities or in nearby rural areas (Go 1994). Whether in rural areas or in urban centers, most youth suffer various forms of exploitation in the work context. Many youth – especially those employed in rural areas – are not protected by minimum wage provisions (UNFPA 1997a). Working youth also have poor access to social security benefits and do not enjoy job security rights (UNFPA 1997a). Moreover, youth have become easy victims of recent developments in the Philippine labor market resulting from globalization and the recent economic crisis. These developments include the extensive use of subcontracting arrangements and the extensive use of child labor (UNFPA 1997a). In these forms of labor practice, employers take advantage of the cheap labor offered by those who are under- or unemployed among the youth. The practice of subcontracting does not provide job security, while violations against minimum wage levels and against provisions for overtime pay are usual features of child labor practices.

Youth Unemployment
Young workers are also the most adversely affected by unemployment. In the Philippines, the unemployment rate is the highest among those who have completed or have some tertiary education, because there are fewer jobs at this level (UNFPA 1997a). For those who have little schooling, unemployment rates are lower because jobs that require less educational training and offer less pay are easier to find. As stated above, females are especially likely to suffer from this kind of labor market discrimination. Table 6.4 presents the Philippine unemployment rate among youth in 1996. It is evident that unemployment rates among males and females are almost equal in urban areas. In rural areas, however, there are more unemployed females than males. This is again due to the fact that males have greater access to agricultural work. Another cause is that farm work done by females often goes unrecorded in employment statistics (UNFPA 1997a).

Madelene Santa Maria

TABLE 6.4. *Philippine Youth Unemployment Rate (%)*
by Age Group, Sex, and Rural-Urban Differences (1996)

Urban	Male	Female
15–20 Age Group	22.0	18.7
21–25 Age Group	17.7	17.4
26–30 Age Group	10.9	11.1
Rural	**Male**	**Female**
15–20 Age Group	7.8	17.8
21–25 Age Group	8.2	18.5
26–30 Age Group	4.2	7.1

Source: UNFPA 1997a, 14.

As documented in a UN (1991) report, unemployment may also be due to inefficient job hunting by youth. In Thailand, the duration of unemployment among youth is an average of 15 to 16 weeks. In the Philippines, it lasts for an average of 4 weeks. Given lack of experience with the labor market, many may employ ineffective strategies to look or have expectations that are too high. Youth between the ages of 15 and 19 tend to rely less on mass media and placement services and more on their family, friends, and relatives.

Social Consequences of Unemployment
Aside from the obvious economic consequences, there are important social consequences of youth unemployment that need to be addressed (UN 1991). One of these is the growing pessimism among youth who find themselves facing a bleak future of limited employment opportunities. Many may become indifferent to the changes and issues that confront them in their daily lives. For example, approximately two-thirds of the unemployed in the Philippines between the ages 15 and 19 believe that there is no work available for them. This frustration is felt more by rural youth than by their urban counterparts. Leaders in Philippine business noted recently that unemployment among young people may be the reason for the increase in the number of young people joining radical armed movements (Press release 2000). When youth lose hope for their future in the present society, they are more prone to act against it.

In summary, opportunities for well-paying and secure jobs for youth have become generally dismal over recent years in the less economically prosperous SEA countries, with these trends very apparent in the Philippines. The imbalance existing between the requirements of the labor market and the training provided to youth in schools has contributed to this situation. To avoid unemployment, youth are forced to accept jobs that require lower skills and training or that offer low wages. Some try to get employed abroad. The desperate choices some take, whether at home or elsewhere, make them vulnerable to exploitation.

To be able to enter the labor market and to obtain a sense of security in their jobs, youth creatively make use of many alternative strategies. These include making use of existing relationships or creating social networks. To achieve success in the work setting, many youth are realizing that it is the training one receives on the job and the capacity to innovate in rapidly changing conditions that have become more important than their educational degrees. It is therefore possible that most of the relevant training for a more stable career is not obtained by youth in educational institutions, but within their work settings. This reinforces the possibility that employment may not signify an end to adolescence in SEA, but may represent an important part of the new regime of preparation for adulthood.

In addition, it is important to note that tradition plays a crucial role in youth's life in the world of work, by providing them with tools to cushion the demands of employment – which for many youth comes very early in their lives. Culture nurtures these tools by giving continuing meaning to what it is to be a young person within the network of one's relations with others. For youth in many SEA countries, early employment may not necessarily be a burden but a privilege, since they are given the opportunity to participate actively in the system of cooperation within the family. At the same time, the family provides the needed support to youth by ensuring that the system of social relations will protect them against the possibilities and consequences of failure.

Health Concerns

As youth participate in the world of adult life, they bear the risks to physical and mental health that go with it, including the many consequences of societal change. Negative health consequences of employment and sexuality are increasing concerns. Across the entire SEA region, behavior problems – drugs, alcohol, delinquency, and organized crime – appear to be on the rise (UN 1997b).

The consistent growth in life expectancy indicates progress in the health status and health behaviors of youth, in the Philippines (Berja 1999) and other SEA countries. On the other hand, health hazards continue to threaten youth as they are exposed to unhealthy work environments (e.g., exposure to chemical fertilizers in agricultural work) and to irregular working hours. More and more youth are suffering from pulmonary and stomach-related diseases (ref. Berja 1999). One out of 5 (20 percent) Filipino youth smoke, with higher proportions among males than females (SWS 1996). About 15 percent of youth were found to drink alcoholic beverages once a week or more often (SWS 1996). Significant attention also is now being given to health risks that relate to the youth's sexual activities.

Reproductive Health
Focus on youth's reproductive health is in part due to the global concern about AIDS. Research indicates that many sexually active SEA youth do not take precautions against unfavorable consequences to their health and family life. This is primarily due to their poor knowledge of reproductive health issues. In the Philippines, young people were found to have a high level of awareness of HIV/AIDS and sexually transmitted diseases (STDs) but only a fair knowledge about how these may be transmitted (Berja 1999). Moreover, sex among Filipino youth is generally unprotected: 90 percent of sexual encounters among male youth is unprotected, 78 percent of their sexual encounters with commercial sex workers are also unprotected (Berja 1999). Berja (1999) enumerated the factors in the use of contraceptives among Filipino youth. Among males, use was higher among the more educated, those residing in urban areas, and those with greater religiosity. Among females, use was higher among those with urban exposure, more education, and greater religiosity.

In Thailand, only one-third of sexually active youth report using contraceptives when having sex (Soonthoundhoda 1996). The rest did not use any method of birth control, mainly because of their lack of knowledge about contraception. Thai youth also said they feared the side effects of birth control methods. Young Thai females believe that the use of contraceptives is the male's concern: because sex should be spontaneous and initiated by men, it is the man who should take the responsibility for precaution.

Among those who are most vulnerable to reproductive health risks are the youth who spend most hours of their day on the streets. Estimates indicate that approximately 600,000 of Philippine youth live and work on the streets (De los Angeles-Baustista & Arriola 1995). Some 60,000 of these youth engage in commercial and freelance sex work, exposing themselves to the risks of unwanted pregnancies and STDs. Accurate data regarding STD incidence among SEA youth are difficult to obtain because youth are generally shy about approaching clinics and centers about their problems (ref. Huang Soo Lee 1999). Providing contraceptive service is said to be equally difficult because of the legal and social restrictions on giving these services to unmarried youth in most SEA countries.

Juvenile Delinquency

In most SEA countries, juvenile delinquency is predominantly an urban phenomenon (UN 1989). The rising incidence of juvenile offenses is attributed to the disruption of the support functions of traditional social institutions without the replacement of alternative systems. In the Philippines, juvenile delinquency is particularly high among the growing number of urban out-of-school youth and those working and living on the streets. In most SEA countries, drug abuse is associated with juvenile delinquency (UN 1989).

Leones (1993) described the profile of the Filipino juvenile delinquent as often male, 14 to 17 years of age, and out of school. He has left school after some years at the primary level in a public school, may have repeated a grade, and his failure in school was due to truancy. His parents are usually engaged in nonskilled or semiskilled labor or engaged in odd jobs. He often resides in the slums without recreational facilities and lives in a rented house with other families. In Thailand, 90 percent of the juvenile offenders in 1990 were male, with nearly half not living with their parents at the time of arrest. The most frequent crimes committed are theft and the use of illegal drugs (Sriwana 1993).

Life Conditions of the Urban Poor Youth

To help address the problem of delinquency, researchers are beginning to examine the life conditions of street children and poor urban youth. De los Angeles-Bautista and Arriola (1995) reported that Filipino poor urban youth often live in conditions that lack basic facilities, lack privacy because of congestion, and that make youth vulnerable to infectious diseases. Moreover, children working and living in the streets are vulnerable to exploitation and are likely to fall into substance abuse. They are often recruited into prostitution and may thus be exposed to physical harm by clients. De los Angeles-Bautista and Arriola further mentioned that the parents of these children are usually the ones who have forced these children to work in the streets. To bear the consequences of their life situation, these children often turn to drugs and support from their peers. Risks increase when children go through their activities alone. The presence of family, peer, or adult support was reported to be influential in preventing youth from experiencing the dangerous consequences of street life (Szanton Blanc 1994, as cited in De los Angeles-Bautista & Arriola 1995).

In summary, it may be observed that efforts to document physical and mental health concerns among youth have largely focused on sexual activities, criminal behaviors, and exposure to unhealthy environmental conditions in urban areas. Very little is known about young people's health practices and the positive things they do to cope and take care of themselves. Information on their nutritional status is likewise in short supply.

Mental health issues have also received less emphasis, although research findings for Filipino youth suggest a more positive picture than one might have expected, given the conditions described in this chapter. A study by the International Labor Organization (ILO; 1996), for example, revealed that most Filipino street children possess positive self-perceptions, and likewise believe that others view them positively. Looking at the wider youth population, a survey commissioned by the Philippine National Manpower and Youth Commission (NMYC; SWS 1996) revealed that youth assessed their health as good, reported that they were generally happy, and felt more optimistic about the future than the average Filipino adult. A study by Church and colleagues (2000) on the emotional experience of Filipino youth also revealed a salience of positive emotions among the respondents; and another study found high levels of satisfaction (SWS 1996). Youth in the later study also gave high ratings to the way they got along with their parents and to their satisfaction with themselves, the people with whom they spend time, the neighborhood where they live, and to their lives as a whole.

Service Providers

The philosophy that underlies services for youth in SEA tends to be one of social control (UN 1997b). In this philosophy, youth are perceived to have "problems" – due to idleness, under- or unemployment, or limited schooling. There are numerous projects and programs spearheaded by both government and NGOs in the region focusing on social control efforts. Many of these are documented in a United Nations (1997b) report on youth. We find, for example, that in Malaysia there are several government agencies that are concerned with youth affairs. The Malaysian

Ministry of Youth and Sports, established in 1964, coordinates these agencies. The Rakan Muda project of the Ministry encourages out-of-school youth to involve themselves with peers in activities of similar interest (Huang Soo Lee 1999). In Thailand, the Child Welfare Association disseminates information and improves existing laws that have to do with the rights and welfare of children. The Association initiated a Child Welfare Laws Project in 1986. In the Philippines, the Family Planning Association started a project on "Development and Family Education for the Youth" in 1983, with the aim of providing youth with education, counseling, and reproductive health services to increase young people's understanding of the adverse consequences of teenage pregnancy and early marriage. The project also provides livelihood skills training for out-of-school youth.

Rehabilitation and noninstitutional supervision are also provided to drug-dependent youth. For instance, Malaysia's commitment to regional and international collaboration in drug abuse control is exemplified in the comprehensive research program undertaken by the University of Science in Penang. Moreover, in many countries, drug education for youth is integrated in primary and secondary school health education programs with curricula designed to improve lifestyles. It is assumed that knowledge of drugs and their adverse effects will help youth make mature decisions, which will then lead them to more healthy lifestyles. Educational programs are also targeted at other groups that have considerable influence on youth's behavior: teachers, health professionals, law enforcement personnel, the media, the judiciary, religious organizations, and community service groups.

Social welfare policies for youth in many SEA countries are usually charity-oriented and often involve youth activities that are recreational (UN 1997b). Increasingly, policies are being oriented to human development goals. For example, there is a conscious effort to engage youth in income-generating programs through skills training leading to employment. However, the products from these programs, such as handicrafts, have limited marketability, which often discourages efforts toward self-reliance.

Services Within the School System

Most youth programs that have a developmental orientation are within the school system. In addition to skills training and vocational preparation, services also include nonformal education, organizational leadership training, guidance and counseling for job placement and social adjustment, and community volunteer services. These social welfare programs are aimed at promoting the development of self-confidence and self-realization among youth, and at encouraging out-of-school youth to participate in self-and community development projects. In the Philippines, population control and sex education programs have long been a part of educational curricula. The training materials developed by the Population Education Program of the Department of Education and Culture have facilitated the implementation of these programs. Two modules from this set of training materials are devoted to the subject of sexuality, namely, Human Sexuality and Reproduction, and Family Planning. Career development is likewise now a recent focus in educational institutions. The Department of Education has also come up with a set of modules on self-awareness and family wellness, on relationships and ways of relating with others, and on decision making with regards to goal setting and career planning.

Government Services

The programs undertaken by governments usually address problems among youth that are consequences of poverty (e.g., malnutrition, school dropout, drug dependency, abuse and exploitation, unemployment and underemployment) (Dixon and Kim 1985). For example, Malaysia's Ministry of Education undertakes textbook loan schemes to alleviate financial difficulties. There are vigorous efforts on the part of the Philippine government through the Ministry of Culture, Youth and Sports to develop self-reliance, discipline, and responsibility among poor youth through vocational and technical training, campaigns against drug abuse, and healthy activities such as sports. Programs that are designed to decrease school leaving due to financial difficulties include the Accreditation and Equivalency program and the Study-Now-Pay-Later plans. In Thailand, there are similar efforts by the government to promote the health and welfare of youth.

There are also efforts by governments to enact special policies and programs to promote youth employment (UN 1997a). In Indonesia, for example, the Board of Volunteer Services of the Ministry of Labor has employed educated youth from the rural areas to assist in government development projects in these areas. These youth receive allowances from the government and are guaranteed civil service positions with lower educational requirements. In Malaysia, the government has, since 1986, temporarily attached 4,000 unemployed graduates to various government agencies and departments.

Services from Nongovernmental Organizations

Government efforts alone are seen to be limited in addressing youth-related problems. The participation of other organizations is now seen as a necessary component for effective program implementation. Efforts by NGOs have also been initiated in areas neglected by government. For instance, in the Philippines, as in many other SEA countries, health services for adolescents have been neglected (Cruz & Berja 1999). In particular, it has been found that information regarding sexually transmitted diseases, unwanted pregnancy, and risks of maternal mortality and morbidity, as well as premature birth is not getting to youth. This dearth of information may be attributed to a number of factors. One is the lack of a clear-cut government health program for the youth. Another is the current restriction on government spending on such projects. Another significant factor is the existing resistance in Philippine society and institutions in accepting that the adolescent should be held responsible for his/her sexuality. In other words, while the concern for reproductive health is widely accepted, the idea of an adolescent engaging in sexual activities outside of marriage is still quite a thorny issue in Philippine society, one that is only likely to be addressed by the nongovernmental sector.

Intervention efforts in many health issues for youth are now being initiated by a growing number of civil society organizations in the Philippines. For example, the Population Services Pilipinas, Inc. provides comprehensive reproductive health care through its clinics. Another organization is the Foundation for Adolescent Development, which has telephone hotlines to receive calls from troubled adolescents. The Foundation was set up to help youth develop their potentials so that they may become emotionally secure, self-reliant, and productive individuals and responsible members of the community. School-based counselors are also trained through the Foundation. Another organization, the Institute for Social Studies and Action, has programs for adolescents that provide: i) resource materials on adolescent health; ii) seminars and workshops on adolescent sexuality; and iii) educational campaign materials on reproductive health. The ReachOut AIDS Education Foundation, established in 1990, is one of the first organizations in the Philippines to address the AIDS epidemic. Their programs for adolescents include an AIDS helpline and seminars and workshops on "Empowerment Program for Young Adults." There are still a number of other organizations that cater to the needs of street children (e.g., Christian Children's Fund and the Education Research and

Development Assistance Foundation) and organizations assisting the youth who are employed as sex workers (e.g., End Child Prostitution in Asian Tourism, Tanikala and Buklod). The Visayan Forum is a non-government organization that assists migrant and trafficked youth in provinces in the central islands of the Philippines. Its strategy is to develop support and welfare facilities for children in domestic services through self-help groups and the strengthening of young people's abilities to cope with their situation.

Factors Contributing to Successful Interventions
The success of these youth programs appears to be greatest when there is effective collaboration between civil society organizations and government agencies. For instance, the Kamalayan Development Center, Inc. was set up in the Philippines to provide assistance to government agencies in monitoring the presence of illegally employed youth in factories. Successful government rescue operations were possible through nongovernment organizational assistance. Moreover, the lowering of drug use rates in the Philippines is said to be a reflection of coordinated efforts by government and nongovernment drug-watch programs.

Past experience in providing services for youth points to the need for more collaborative and coordinated efforts from various sectors of society. Success in attaining goals occurs most often when the government, nongovernment organizations, and communities are united in their efforts to address youth-related issues within a nation. The government alone is limited in its capacities because of the centralized nature of its operations and because of its adherence to policies that may be too general in scope and too restricted in orientation. Nongovernment organizations are generally more innovative in their orientations and strategies and possess a closer view of the youth's experience, but they usually have to rely on the resources of government to implement projects on a wider scale. Finally, change for the betterment of youth's condition is most possible when there is a commitment for this change from the community. Along with all these is the significance of the involvement of those people where remedies are initiated. Projects that are planned and implemented with the participation of youth are found to be better accepted and more successful (Berja 1999).

Civic and Community Engagement

The participation of youth in civic affairs and in promoting community welfare is generally recognized in most SEA countries. For instance, the new Philippine constitution underscores the vital role played by youth in nation building. Moreover, the new Child and Youth Welfare Code encourages the active participation of Filipino youth in civic activities. In Indonesia, youth leaders are increasingly motivated to get involved in civic affairs due to the growing number of welfare services for children and youth (UN 1997b). In SEA, we see organized youth engaging in activities with social and economic objectives, such as economic productivity, population and family planning, community improvement and reforestation, and physical fitness and sports. In countries like the Philippines, where economic and political crises loom, we may observe many youth joining other sectors of society in denouncing social injustice and in calling for the building of a society of peace and justice. The majority of Filipino youth were found to give priority to environmental protection and to consider economic matters, crime, and governance as the most important problems of the country (SWS 1996). Most youth, however, admit that they are not doing anything to solve these problems (SWS 1996).

Youth involvement in national politics appears to be most evident in collective actions directed toward issues of governance, desired social changes, and human rights issues (Bunthan 2000; Chrishandi 2000; Chua 2000). Unfortunately, this type of political involvement is being viewed by nations as an added "problem" that needs to be addressed through social control. Politically active youth are seen to create disruptive situations, and the general response is to isolate, pacify, and occupy the time of these dissidents (UN 1997b).

Youth involvement in civic activities seems to be more socially appreciated and accepted at the local and community level. For example, a form of apprenticeship is encouraged wherein youth from urban areas work with other youth to improve rural communities (UN 1997a). This partnership is said to result in practical skill enhancement, self-development between the two groups, and stronger ties between rural and urban communities. In Indonesia, youth's participation in street protests is supported by the community (Prof. Lambang Trijono, personal communication 2001). Youth are encouraged to take the initiative when community-level issues have to be addressed.

Some organizations and agencies help to prepare youth for civic engagement by providing leadership and citizenship training. Involvement from youth is also facilitated when opportunities are provided for social action, participation in community and development projects, and religious apostolate activities. In Indonesia, for example, the "Karang Taruna" Youth Centers mobilize media to encourage involvement of youth in development. At the local government level in the Philippines, youth are organized to participate in community planning. They are also encouraged to initiate their own projects that are relevant to their concerns in the community. Filipino youth, especially those from the urban poor and from rural areas, are also frequently included as representatives in civil society organizational coalitions. In these coalitions, the voice of the youth sector is allowed expression in discussions on societal issues, and in setting the agenda for social change.

In most SEA countries, however, the level of civic involvement by youth – and the support for this – is limited. There still exists a general lack of trained youth workers and leaders in voluntary organizations (UN 1997b). Youth continue to remain largely uninvolved in the formation of programs designed for their benefit. Their noninvolvement is apparent in development projects and in decision-making processes in society. There may be at least 2 factors accounting for this. One factor is the nature of youth involvement in many societies. Youth are viewed more as recipients rather than as initiators of programs that benefit them. Another factor has to do with the characteristics of the youth population in most SEA countries. The majority of youth comes from, or has lived in, rural areas. In contrast to their urban counterparts, they are less knowledgeable of their political rights and privileges due to the quality and level of education they receive and because of the inaccessibility of media in rural areas.

Conclusion

One of the striking features of life in SEA is the increased mobility of young people as they temporarily migrate to areas that they perceive will provide them with better educational and work opportunities. This mobility is urged on by the family, which expects and encourages youth to leave home in order to uplift the material well-being of the family. It becomes evident that for the SEA youth, marriage and the desire for greater freedom are not the most important considerations for leaving the nuclear family unit. As youth undertake this movement away from home, relations between them and among their family members are transformed. Research on adolescent life has not taken a closer look into these transformations, mainly because family relations are viewed as antecedents rather than consequences of the behavioral changes that occur. Related to this is the need for researchers to pay greater attention to the social transformations that are occurring among female youth in the region. We have seen that young SEA women are undergoing dramatic changes, which are likely to influence family and community life in very important ways.

It is likewise important to observe that youth life in SEA seems to be filled with contradictions. For instance, in this account, it becomes apparent that young people are pressured by society to pursue education, but at the same time, they may need to forgo educational goals to look for work because of economic difficulties. Youth are also encouraged to exhibit greater civic consciousness. But when they do express their views about social justice and change, they are labeled as "dissidents" by the state. Moreover, even as society recognizes the increased sexual activity among youth, sex education is limited to biological information and to responsibilities for family life. Themes that perhaps would be more relevant, such as emotional and relationship concerns, are often ignored. Another seeming contradiction is the increasing segregation of daily life between youth and adults, even as youth are now entering the adult world through employment.

There are apparent consequences that result from these contradictions. One such consequence is the vulnerability experienced by young people in this life period. Youth must now deal with their sexuality with limited emotional preparation. They may also have to suffer a lowering of their self-esteem as they enter a labor force that can only offer them unstable and low-paying job prospects. Another is that, despite greater autonomy in many ways, youth experience continued dependence on the social network that was built during childhood. To achieve both a sense of competence and the needed emotional support, they have to rely on this system of relations, which fortunately, they learned to use skillfully in earlier periods of their lives.

To deal with their vulnerability and continued dependency, youth have learned adaptive strategies. First, they continue to hold family-centered goals, which give them a sense of participation and competence within the family and community. Second, they develop greater cognitive and behavioral autonomy, which is evident in their assertion of their capability to make their own decisions within and outside of the family context. This achievement of autonomy in adolescence is facilitated by the economic demands on the family and the opportunities for employment early in life. Finally, youth make use of traditional practices in dealing with the stresses and strains of modern life. It is not uncommon, for example, to observe a young person dressed in a business suit offering joss sticks in a temple during an office break. This image speaks profoundly of youth's ability to coordinate and utilize the resources from both worlds of continuity and change.

References

Berja, C. L. 1999. Communication and advocacy strategies: Adolescent reproductive and sexual health (Case study Philippines). Bangkok: UNESCO PROAP Regional Clearing House on Population Education and Communication.

Bunthan, M. 2000. Cambodia. In *The 5th forum of democratic leaders in the Asia-Pacific leaders young workshop*, 43–44.

Chua, B. S. 2000. Thailand. In *The 5th forum of democratic leaders in the Asia-Pacific young leaders workshop*, 132–134.

Church, T. A., M. S. Katigback, J. A. Reyes, & S. M. Jensen. 2000. The structure of Filipino affect on emotional experience. In *Filipino personality: Indigenous and cross-cultural studies*, eds. A. T. Church & M. S. Katigback, 137–161. Manila: De La Salle University Press, Inc.

Chrishandi, Y. 2000. Indonesia. In *The 5th forum of democratic leaders in the Asia-Pacific young leaders workshop*, 74–81.

Cruz, G. & C. Berja. 1999. Reproductive health. In *Adolescent sexuality in the Philippines*, eds. C. Raymundo, P. Xenos, & L. Domingo, 58–69. Quezon City, Philippines: University of the Philippines Population Institute.

De los Angeles-Bautista, F., & J. C. Arriola. 1995. *To learn and to earn: Education and child labor in the Philippines: A country report*. Manila: International Labor Organization.

Dixon, J. & H. S. Kim. 1985. *Social welfare in Asia*. New Hampshire: Groom Helm.

Dube, L. 1997. *Women and kinship: Comparative perspectives on gender in South and South-east Asia*. Tokyo: United Nations University Press.

Go, S. 1994. The Filipino youth: Their views and values on marriage and family life. *Kaya Tao*: 13:1–27.

Gray, A. & S. Satsara. 1999. *Case study: Thailand*. Bangkok: UNESCO PROAP Regional Clearing House on Population Education and Communication.

Huang Soo Lee, M. 1999. *Case study: Malaysia*. Bangkok: UNESCO PROAP Regional Clearing House on Population Education and Communication.

International Labor Organization. 1996. *The child's inner and outer world: A study of the phenomenology of the child in prostitution*. Manila: International Program on the Elimination of Child Labor, International Catholic Child Bureau-Asia.

Leones, C. S. 1993. Philippines. In *Rehabilitation of juvenile delinquents in the ESCAP region*, 87–104. New York: Economic and Social Commission for Asia and the Pacific, United Nations.

Liwag, E., A. de la Cruz, & E. Macapagal. 1996. How we raise our daughters and sons: Child-rearing and gender socialization in the Philippines. *Philippine Journal of Psychology*. 28 (1–4):1–46.

McCann-Erickson Study. 1993. Portrait of the Filipino as a youth: The Metro-Manila findings. *AmCham Journal*. 53:22–24.

Medina, B. 1991. *The Filipino family: A text with selected readings*. Quezon City, Philippines: University of the Philippines Press.

Mehta, S., R. Groenen, & F. Roque. 1998. Implementation challenges of reproductive health, including family planning and sexual health: Adolescent reproductive health. Paper presented at the meeting of ESCAP and UNFPA. March: Bangkok, Thailand.

Mendez, P. P. & F. L. Jocano. 1979. *The Filipino adolescent in a rural and an urban setting: A study in culture and education*. Manila: Centro Escolar University Research and Development Center.

Neher, C. D. & R. Marlay. 1995. *Democracy and development in Southeast Asia: The winds of change*. Boulder, Colorado: Westview Press, Inc.

Osborne, M. 1997. *Southeast Asia: An introductory history*. St. Leonards, NSW, Australia: Allen and Unwin.

Press release on the Philippine economy. 2000. *Philippine Daily Inquirer*. July 20.

Raymundo, C. M. 1999. Introduction. In *Adolescent sexuality in the Philippines*, eds. C. Raymundo, P. Xenos, & L. Domingo, 1–4. Quezon City: University of the Philippines Population Institute.

Rimando, M. 1981. The changing morality of Filipino adolescents' sexuality and its effects on the family. *St. Louis University Research Journal*. 12(3):321–338.

Shimizu, H. 1984. Filipino children in family and society growing up in a many-people environment. In *The growing child in family and society: An interdisciplinary study in parent-infant bonding*, eds. N. Kobayashi & T. B. Brazelton, 95–112. Tokyo: University of Tokyo Press.

Silayan-Go, A. 1997. Fact sheet on adolescent sexuality problems of Filipino youth: Behavioral aspects. Paper presented at the Seminar-Workshop on the Philippine Population and FP Program for Community Journalists. August: Tagaytay City, Philippines.

Social Weather Stations. 1996. SWS-NYC study on the situation of the youth in the Philippines.

Soonthounhoda, A. 1996. *Sexual attitudes and behaviors and contraceptive use of late female adolescents in Bangkok: A comparative study of students and factory workers*. Institute for Population and Social Research, Mahidol University.

Sriwana, O. 1993. Thailand. In *Rehabilitation of juvenile delinquents in the ESCAP region*, 151–161. New York: Economic and Social Commission for Asia and the Pacific, United Nations.

Uhlig, H. 1988. *Suedostasien*. Frankfurt am Main: Fischer Taschenbuch Verlag GmnH.

United Nations. (UN) 1989. *Report of the Expert Group Meeting on Adolescence and Crime Prevention in the ESCAP region*. New York: Author.

United Nations. 1991. *Socio-economic aspects of youth unemployment in Asia and the Pacific*. New York: Author.

United Nations. 1997a. *Review of the youth situation, policies and programs in Asia and the Pacific*. New York: Author.

United Nations. 1997b. *Social welfare policies in Asian and Pacific countries with special reference to the development of children, youth and women*. New York: Author.

United Nations. 2001. *Economic and social survey of Asia and the Pacific*. New York: Author.

United Nations Population Fund. (UNFPA) 1997a. *Situation of the working youth in the Philippines*. Manila: Author.

United Nations Population Fund. 1997b. *Situation of the out-of-school youth in the Philippines*. Manila: Author.

Vatikiotis, M. R. J. 1996. *Political change in Southeast Asia: Trimming the banyan tree*. London: Routledge.

Ventura, E. 1999. Sikolohiya ng bata: Paghahambing ng mga pag-aaral noong 1966–1980 at 1980–1985. [Child psychology: A comparison of studies from 1966–1980 and 1980–1985]. In *Unang dekada ng Sikolohiyang Pilipino: Kaalaman, gamit at etika* [*The first decade of Sikolhiyang Filipino: Knowledge, application and ethics*], eds. E. Protacio-Marcelino & R. Pe Pua, 31–39. Quezon City, Philippines: Pambansang Samahan sa Sikolhiyang Filipino.

Wright, J., ed. 2000. *The New York Times 2000 almanac*. New York: Penguin.

Xenos, P. & C. Raymundo. 1999. The modern profile of Filipino youth. In *Adolescent sexuality in the Philippines*, eds. C. Raymundo, P. Xenos, & L. Domingo, 5–15. Quezon City: University of the Philippines Population Institute.

Interviews

Dr. Zeus A. Salazar, Filipino historian and ethnologist.

Prof. Lambang Trijono, Professor of Sociology and Political Science, Gadjah Mada University, Yogyakarta, Indonesia.

Dr. Suwit Laohasiriwong, Director of the Institute of Dispute Resolution, Khon Kaen University, Khon Kaen, Thailand.

Dr. Kamarulzaman Askandar, Professor of Political Science, Coordinator of Research and Education for Peace, Universiti Sains Malaysia, Penang.

Dr. Wazir Karif, Director-General of the Academy of Social Sciences in Malaysia, Director of Women's Development Research Center, Universiti Sains Malaysia, Penang.

7

Arab Adolescents Facing the Future

Enduring Ideals and Pressures to Change

Marilyn Booth

An Egyptian proverb says, "When your son grows up, make him your brother." Socialization in the Arab world recognizes the passage to adulthood as a transition to reflective, mature participation in society, maintaining the primacy throughout life of family ties, connectivity, and mutual responsibility. Adolescence in Arab societies – as varied as those societies are, both from each other and internally – is a process of learning responsibility and agency within a web of ongoing relationships. Traditionally, the transition from childhood to adulthood was marked by marriage. But economic and social pressures toward later marriage have lessened the salience of that marker, while contributing to increased recognition of adolescence as a stage with its own characteristics and challenges.

An ethos of connectivity and group primacy that puts the family at center stage need not conflict with achieving a mature self. Islam, the majority religion of the Arab world, offers a strong structure within which to define individuals' rights and duties. Arab Christians and Arab Jews also grow up with strong, communally supportive, structures. Yet, the family values with which today's Arab adolescents have grown up do not always seem to provide a helpful blueprint for the future, as those adolescents face local situations and a global environment that both seem increasingly to value economically defined contractual relations. And, as important as belief systems are to an adolescent's world view anywhere, neither those systems nor the impact they can

The author thanks Sharafuddin Malik and Susan Schaefer Davis for their important contributions to this chapter.

have are uniform, while many other factors shape social experience. Divergent national histories, demographic pressures and socioeconomic differentials, access to education and communication technologies – all mold Arab teenagers' lives.

In the Arab world, blind adherence to Westernization has never been acceptable and is increasingly criticized. It is a region where the pitfalls of a "modernization theory" that assumes convergence toward Western structures are well demonstrated and recognized. Arab adolescents, often drawn by – yet critical of – products and ideas generated by Western capitalist societies, respond in creative and varied ways, even as many feel left out by the directions their own societies are taking. The coping mechanisms of many are tightly constricted by economic, political, and ideological constraints.

The Arab World

Although the 22 nations situated in Asia and Africa that consider themselves Arab share much cultural homogeneity and historical experience, the diversity that marks their thousands of communities and subcultures precludes generalizations about a region holding 4.6 percent of the world's population. The majority of Arabs are Muslims, but several Arab nations have numerically and socially significant Christian populations; some had important Arab Jewish communities until after (sometimes long after) Israel's 1948 declaration of statehood. (Iran and Turkey, part of "the Middle East" – a term coined by Western powers – are majority-Muslim but not Arab countries. Their languages, Farsi and Turkish, are not linguistically related to Arabic, perhaps the most important defining factor of Arab identity.) Further religious diversity characterizes most Arab nations, for internal historical-doctrinal differences mark the Muslim and Christian communities both. But for most Arabs, religious identity has been a paramount aspect of community existence. Today's adolescents may find that both reassuring and constraining.

Population size and density vary hugely, contributing to problems relevant to adolescents' lives – from overcrowding and housing shortages, unemployment, and hunger to labor shortages and emigration outflows. For example, Bahrain and Qatar have fewer than one million inhabitants each, while Egypt's population exceeded 60 million by 1996. For oil-exporting countries, high immigration to meet employment needs has swelled the population and created social diversity, although immigration has slowed recently. These factors increase pressure on city infrastructures, for most Arab countries are highly – and relatively recently – urbanized. In 1996, urban population exceeded 40 percent in 15 countries and 70 percent in 7. Many Arab adolescents grow up in cities where rapid expansion far exceeds capabilities of city services and existing housing, and where extreme poverty is juxtaposed with new, conspicuously displayed, wealth. National wealth ranges widely, only some Arab countries produce oil; in 1996, per capita gross national product exceeded $21,000 in the United Arab Emirates (UAE) and $19,000 in Kuwait but in 9 Arab countries was under $1,000. Adolescents, therefore, live many different lives. As Davis and Davis remark for Morocco, "[u]pper-class youth in the large cities like Casablanca may live lives similar to urban Americans, with dating and discos a regular part of their experience. In more isolated rural villages, on the other hand, young people may attend only primary school, leaving early to help with the family land or herds" (1989, 10). In Egypt, children of the new business class enjoy flashy new cars and beach vacations in new tourist resorts along the Mediterranean and Red Sea coasts, while many more adolescents cannot even contemplate traditional expectations for transition to marriage and family, for they cannot afford even a tiny apartment.

Most Arab countries have greatly improved health care provision, and birth rates are generally declining, but disparities remain vast between countries and from city to countryside. Moreover, war conditions have taken or drastically affected many people's lives and health, the young disproportionately. Most Arab countries have a young population and a high ratio of dependent children to adults, a commonality with major repercussions for adolescent experience since it may entail overcrowded schools and lack of job opportunity. Over 40 percent of the region's population is under 15, climbing to 45 percent in Djibouti, Mauritania, Palestine, Syria, Somalia, and Yemen. Only 4 nations – Bahrain, Kuwait, UAE, and Qatar – have an under-15 population of less than 35 percent, mainly because so many adult laborers immigrate into these countries. In the 1990s, the 10–19-year-old population ranged from 20 to 26 percent across the Arab world (General Secretariat 1997; Makhlouf & Abdelkader 1997).

To what extent is "Islam" a dominant factor in shaping Arab societies? This is a controversial question that many have tried to answer, but the most important point to make is that no single answer holds. Islam is the established state religion in many (but not all) Arab countries; Islamic law is the dominant (but not the only) source of civil legal systems (and less so for criminal law). But Islam is not monolithic: throughout the region, citizens contest their state's particular construction of it.

Correlations between Islamic doctrine, prescribed social gender roles, and women's rights are especially contentious; various actors in the region (state officials, judges, independent intellectuals, opposition politicians, feminist activists) advance diverging and not always predictable interpretations of what religious sources actually say. For both allies of the state and those in opposition to it, "Islam" may symbolize an anti-imperialist, pro-"third world" way into modernity first and foremost.

While the very real and powerful religious devotion of Muslims throughout the world is not in doubt, we must recognize that the tremendous variety encompassed in Islam – as religion, legal system, social blueprint, oppositional ideology – makes it impossible to generalize about its impact across sectors of the population. Some groups – such as Bedouin in Egypt, even those settled now among the general population – see themselves as far more observant than the society in general (Abu-Lughod 1993). Moreover, many social practices and heirarchies in Muslim-majority societies predate Islam's coming. Religion does provide a set of behavioral guidelines – or long-accepted behavioral guidelines are explained as deriving from the religion. But this does not mean that Arab adolescents always conform to those guidelines or see them as essential to their own faith. And other social pressures can cause religiously sanctioned guidelines to change. What can be said is that Islam is one variable symbolic and social force that precludes total or unquestioning acceptance of "Western" lifestyles and values.

Being an Adolescent

The time preceding adulthood has not traditionally been seen as a separate stage: in Morocco, "adults perceive and describe the physical changes of puberty, but they tend not to label youth as distinct from childhood and adulthood unless moved to criticize adolescent misbehavior" (Davis & Davis 1989, 52). But language use suggests adolescence as a special if not totally separate stage of life. In Arabic, the term closest to naming "adolescence" is *murahaqa*, which signifies "puberty" and thereby has sexual connotations. The verb from which it comes means "to reach" or "to overtake," and in the context of human development, "to grow to the age of sexual maturity." Found in academic texts, the term is rarely encountered in ordinary language, since it is often construed as a negative attribute pertaining to sexuality. In everyday Arabic, other words refer to stages of growth, but not necessarily specifically adolescence. From about age 7 to 13, the growing person is a *sabiy*, if male, and *sabiya*, if female; the word's connotations emphasize "childishness" over growth. From about 14 to 17, the male is a *fata* and the female a *fatat* if unmarried, labels that signify a person on the way to adulthood, but not necessarily "adolescence" as a separate stage. Another term more generally signifies the growing person, from about 13 years into the late 20s: *shabb/shabba*. Embedded in the social expectations of Arab societies, these terms connote less a growing personal autonomy than a sense of responsibility and obligation toward others with whom one's specific relations are well defined, be they children or adults.

Understandings about adolescence and normative relationships with and among adolescents in Arab societies draw heavily on the authority of family and customary practices that are enmeshed in but not completely defined by religion. Whether Muslims or Christians, Arabs consider adolescence to be a time particularly fraught with sexual temptations, and both draw on religious authority to regulate children's lives during this period. Sexual contact outside of legally sanctioned marriage is strictly forbidden, and cohabitation before marriage is absolutely unacceptable. In practice, though, there exists a double standard; male adolescents gaining "experience" may be indulgently ignored (see Davis & Davis's (1989) subtle analysis of this in one context). In the past, to control adolescent sexuality and protect family honor Arab societies encouraged teen marriages, often drawing on religious precepts, although marriage age is not stipulated in religious texts. But this practice is disappearing from urbanized and even less urbanized areas of the Arab world, for myriad reasons: longer periods of formal education for both boys and girls, the high costs associated with marriage, and other socioeconomic factors (Hassan 1998; Obermeyer 1995; Davis & Davis 1989; Davis 1993; Abu-Lughod 1993; Moghadam 1993; Hoodfar 1997).

These transitions and pressures are creating a new stage of life, when youth are no longer children but not yet adults; when the connotations of *shabb/shabba*, *fata/fatat*, *murahaqa*, and new and changing elements of agency and responsibility combine to form a confusing collection of hopes and needs, images and experiences. In school, Arab teenagers are learning that adolescence is a life stage with its own contours, as for a Bedouin girl in Egypt: "Kamla now quoted from a book she had read at school [that said] it was natural as one entered adolescence to begin thinking about members of the opposite sex. She admitted that such things had never even crossed her mind before" (Abu-Lughod

1993, 214). In Morocco, "students in secondary school learn about a life stage called adolescence, so for some, school has 'created' the concept as well as the expectation of behaviors associated with it" (Davis & Davis 1989, 59). The Arab world is witnessing the emergence of a phase of adolescence, newly if only partially free from the confines of early adulthood within which it has long been tucked. It is easy to think so when one sees young people in public spaces in some cities intermingling freely and volubly, seeming to have their own modes of communication. As elsewhere in the world, the shopping mall is an adolescent meeting ground, while cyber cafes offer the newest meeting spaces, both physically and through chat rooms. This trend seems sure to continue, due to increased education, communications opportunities provided by new information technologies, and increased population mobility. Meanwhile, ideas about adolescent freedom are changing even outside the metropolis, for instance in small Moroccan towns, although norms about limiting friendships between girls and boys remain strong (Davis 1993). The uneven emergence of adolescence as a recognized stage of life was suggested by Davis and Davis's research in Morocco, where "urban parents had the same 'oh no' reaction as American parents when adolescence was mentioned, while rural parents needed the word *murahaqa* defined" (S. Davis, personal communication Jan. 30, 2001).

As longer periods of education, greater mobility, urbanization, and exposure to media become common, some Arab youth are beginning to have more say about when and how they become adults. And religiously sanctioned codes of conduct have become less salient for some. Yet these young people tend to be from the more economically privileged, and more urbanized, strata. And changes that bring mobility and opportunity to some increase the suffering and frustrations of others. This leads some youth to attach themselves to new oppositional activisms that are sometimes called "fundamentalism" and sometimes "Islamist" activism. These opposition groups shape their call for a "return" to traditional practices in terms of renewed allegiance to basic religious precepts. In reality, their call for "traditionalism" involves many modern assumptions; most Islamists, for instance, support continued formal education for girls as well as boys, although they prefer segregated education.

Islamists believe that the region's economic and political subordination to a West-dominated "new world order" is to blame for the breakdown of social boundaries, especially gender boundaries. Interestingly, they are producing a new literature on adolescence that utilizes these beliefs as an explanatory framework for adolescent behavior, thereby accepting the modern notion of adolescence as a separate life stage (see, for instance, Al-Husayni 2000). Describing the present as a time of social chaos and family dissolution, Islamists call for reassertions of control by the patriarchal family and the patriarchal state. Their assertions of indigenous cultural identity are reassuring to young people caught in contradictory circumstances. Whether they join an organized opposition group or not, many young people have taken up the visible signs of commitment to an Islamist outlook, expressed most obviously in styles of dress for both genders. Yet this commitment – like Islam itself – can mean many different things. And it can be a source of both self-expression and repression for adolescents.

Family Relationships

Gradual controlled change within a context of conservative social expectation expressed in religious terms seems a central theme in the recent history of the Arab family. Traditionally, families have been organized around a patriarchal system where power rests with elders, particularly males; younger males are socialized to assume control over female lives, in a system that emphasizes family over the individual. As anthropologist Suad Joseph explains it, "Arab sociocultural systems often have supported the primacy of the family over the person, the family of origin over the family of procreation. Children have been socialized to feel lifelong responsibility for their parents and siblings. Older children ... have been given parental responsibility for younger ones. Men have been encouraged to control and be responsible for their female kin. Women have been called upon to serve and to regard male kin as their protectors." But this is not immutable: "persons in these Arab families have often resisted, constructed alternatives, or created networks that crossed the boundaries" (1999, 11). Joseph describes this system as one of "patriarchal connectivity," where "persons do not experience themselves as bounded, separate, or autonomous" and where maturity is defined partly by how well the individual works within and maintains a web of kin and other relationships, yet where this is also shaped by "the privileging of males and seniors and the mobilization of kinship structures, morality, and idioms [of family] to legitimate and institutionalize gendered and aged domination" (Joseph 1999, 12).

The eldest son in particular and male children in general constitute a locus of power next to the father, to whom mothers and female children tend to defer, although older females often accrue considerable power within the family. Perhaps because fathers are the authoritarian figure in the family, adolescent boys in Saudi Arabia were found to report more positive feelings toward their mothers and mothers' relatives than toward their fathers and fathers' families (Malik 1990b). Mothers in Egypt, Rugh found, tend to have "more egalitarian" and "affective" rather than jural relationships with their children (Rugh 1985, 82, 96). As children – and especially boys – grow older, the father may take on a more distant role, retaining final authority (Davis & Davis 1989).

Even if this family system is common to Arab societies, it shapes family experience more strongly in some societies (or in some sections of some societies) than in others. For example, in Saudi Arabia, the family remains strongly hierarchical: male over female, older over younger. Traditionally, extended family and filial relationships are often more salient than marital relationships; sons are valued and educated, while daughters are submissive, dependent, modest, and reticent (El-Islam 1983). Elsewhere, the same pattern may be detected but in a more diffuse state, while in Saudi Arabia itself, change is evident in elite families' divergent attitudes across generations toward female education, employment, public visibility and freedom of movement, and marriage decisions (Altorki 1986). Abu-Lughod's work among Bedouin on Egypt's north coast shows strongly hierarchical families where younger members and females strongly assert their desires, and where formal education is shifting power relations but only very subtly (1993). Everywhere, class differences affect attitudes and practices. Rugh observed that "middle-class parents [in Egypt] work much harder controlling their children in the interests of the children's futures than do most lower-class parents who, despite their greater authoritarianism, often work more as a team with their children to satisfy the present needs of the whole family" (1985, 87; Hoodfar 1997). Finally, it must be remembered that the patriarchal hierarchy is a formal structure; while acknowledging its salience, less powerful family members, including adolescents, have strategies to subvert its claims on them. One of the newest strategies may be Internet use to skirt parental dictates on friendship, communication, and romance, just as the media of TV and films has given adolescents of decades past new social patterns to contemplate (Davis & Davis 1995).

In sum, while the patriarchal family system remains important both as a social ideal and as a shaper of family relations, the power structure and terms of interaction within Arab families are undergoing gradual but persistent change, while there has always been more room for negotiation than sociologists recognized in the past (Hattab & Mekki 1980; Sharabi 1988; Rugh 1985; Nawar, Lloyd, & Ibrahim 1995; Joseph 1996). These changes have of course been occurring for some time, as suggested by a large-scale study on shifting family values carried out decades ago, through interviewing adolescents from Egypt, Lebanon, Syria, Iraq, and Jordan (Nagaty 1974). More-recent but smaller-scale research suggests that trends toward greater parental permissiveness are on the increase, even outside major urban centers (e.g., Davis 1993). Yet directions for change are not always easily predictable. As Nawar and colleagues (1995) comment for Egypt, the "family is indeed changing.... [As] education, economic transformation, and modern communication bring new ideas into the smallest village, a trend toward religious conservatism sends contradictory messages rejecting change and calling for a return to more traditional social arrangements" (148). These contradictory changes are likely to have the greatest impact on adolescent females. For example, staying in school longer, girls may have more choice over marriage arrangements than in the past; at the same time, family control over marriage partners (for both boys and girls) remains strong, though it may vary according to socioeconomic status and geographic location.

Other variables are even less clearcut in their impact on adolescents' degree of control over their own lives. More than a quarter-century ago, Nagaty found that Christian parents tended to be more permissive toward adolescents of both sexes than were Muslim parents, explaining this as a result of Christian parents' greater exposure to modernization (Nagaty 1974). Yet, larger social and political contexts are crucial here; among Egypt's minority Coptic Christian population, Rugh (1985) suggests, "Christian parents exert strong controls over their children to assure that they not face temptations to convert or to marry outside the Christian community. These fears tend to deter efforts to encourage children to pursue their own interests as they approach adulthood" (209). In this case, community needs exert a pressure on families that counters trends toward increasing freedom. Moreover, in a sociopolitical context where minority Christian communities feel on the defensive as Islamist definitions of community hold increased appeal, Christian parents may try to control their children's choices even more tightly.

The complexity of age, gender, religion, and communal factors in determining parental permissiveness is clear, too, in Hattab and Mekki's (1980) field work on parental authority and compliance among Lebanese youth in the 1970s, during their country's civil war. While high-income parents tended toward more flexibility in controlling children's social activities, they exercised strong control over economic matters. But whether the adolescent child was male or female strongly affected his or her compliance with family norms, and so did a young person's level of participation in the war. In all areas of conduct, female adolescents were subject to stricter controls than were males. Yet, girls were more likely to comply with the controls, and the study argued that most Lebanese adolescents did not appear to suffer psychologically from conforming to parental norms. Those who were clearly nonconformists were the young people participating directly in the civil war. Under the various authorities of their combating political factions, they were no longer under parental control.

While Lebanon under civil war does not constitute a "normal" situation, it shows starkly both the strength of family authority and possible areas of tension for adolescents. For an ethos of connectivity may enhance family solidarity and the quality of emotional support, as studies elsewhere in the region suggest. A study of 710 10th-graders in the UAE found that adolescents generally perceived their families "to be operating more toward the functional than dysfunctional end of the scale," with no difference by gender (Alnajjar 1996, 436). In the Moroccan town they studied, Davis and Davis found that "[e]ven with widespread change, conflict is less characteristic of adolescent-parent relations ... than one might expect" (1989, 65).

The emphasis on connectivity suggests that socialization in traditional Arab culture has instilled ideals of loyalty to the group, to family and community honor, over individual goals. Studies on adolescents in war suggest some of the many implications this socialization has; witness the Intifadas of recent Palestinian experience, when young Palestinians faced the Israeli war machinery with rocks and slingshots (Barber 1998; Punamaki & Suleiman 1990). Could this collectivistic form of socialization deprive adolescents of their inclination to consolidate a selfhood marked by autonomy and individuation? Many scholars believe these to be the main prerequisites for the development of a healthy identity conducive to a sound transition into adulthood (Conger & Petersen 1984). But as Suad Joseph (1999) has argued, patterns of socialization in Arab societies challenge the very notion that "autonomy" as developed in Western social science literature is necessarily a marker of healthy adulthood. Studying Arab adolescents requires scholars to broaden notions of the self (Davis & Davis 1989).

Family, Gender Difference, and Social Expectation

Thus, family closeness and control, and nets of social obligation, remain extremely important shaping factors in adolescent lives. In general, Arab parents expect their children – of any age and either gender – to be kind, polite, submissive, modest, and truthful. Traditionally, though (and as illustrated by some of the studies discussed above), Arab societies have had 2 sets of expectations for adolescents' relationships with parents, one for boys and another for girls. In Arab families, boys are expected to demonstrate, in a socially measurable and conspicuous manner, un-questioning deference to their father's authority, respect for elders in general, love and care for their mother, and love and protection for their sisters. Rugh quotes one Egyptian woman as explaining, "Boys are ex-pected to give money to their parents once they're employed. They sup-port their parents in their old age and look after the well-being of their married sisters" (1985, 91). Muslim boys are trained early to perform religious rituals (prayers and fasting) in private and with their fathers publicly at the mosque. Before marriage, boys are to refrain from sexual performance and keep their distance from the opposite sex. They are expected to participate in family work and to run errands that might expose females to more of the outside world than their families wish. As young adults, boys are expected not only to support and nurture el-derly parents to the extent of their abilities, but also to extend the family line by producing their own offspring. The firstborn male grandchild is often named after his grandfather, especially if the latter is deceased. A son's failure to produce children often led traditionally to divorce and remarriage. Or it led to taking an additional wife, although polygyny, never as common in the Arab world as was believed in the West, has be-come even rarer, especially as economic pressures have mounted and as social expectations have changed. Thus, sons may have more freedom, but they also encounter strong "jural-social obligations" (Rugh 1985).

Female adolescents are expected to show deference to parental au-thority, to demonstrate love and obedience toward their mother and siblings, to show respect for elders, and to take on tasks of caring for younger siblings. They have been expected to refrain from mixing with boys, may be prohibited from walking about out of doors un-accompanied, and are expected to dress decently. Among Muslims, general strictures (on both females and males) to dress modestly have in recent decades given way in many countries to specific dress practices known as *al-zayy al-islami*, "Islamic dress," applied particularly strictly to females according to the laws of some governments and, elsewhere, by informal pressures and self-appointed nongovernmental "watchdogs." Yet, this practice is taken up selectively in most Arab countries; moreover, people have many different reasons to comply (or not to comply). On the streets of Cairo, one can see adolescent girls dressed in every way, from tight jeans to loose all-encompassing garments. Some leave their hair uncovered while others cover their entire face and wear gloves. This new, urban "Islamic dress" (in itself so variable) is different also from the traditional dress of rural and Bedouin girls and women (see Rugh 1986; Macleod 1991; Zuhur 1992). And "Islamic dress" can mitigate the difficulties girls encounter in urban environments; as a public statement of their modesty, it can paradoxically offer them *more* liberty of movement. But however they are dressed, girls find strong social pressure to appear modest and to act in accordance with norms of modesty and submissiveness. They are expected to refrain from loud talking or laughing, especially in public places where males are present, to avoid getting involved sexually with boys, to perform religious rituals, generally in the home, and to prepare diligently for marriage and motherhood, whatever other aspirations they may have.

These differently gendered expectations are evident in adolescents' evaluations of family experience. In the study of UAE teenagers cited previously, boys rated families highest for encouragement toward external relations and emotional fulfillment, while girls rated families higher on encouragement toward internal relations and behavioral control, and lower on emotional fulfillment. The authors concluded that family influence over teenage sexual behavior continues along traditional lines, while control is "directed more toward females" (Alnajjar 1996, 441). Some of the adolescent Moroccan girls whom Davis and Davis interviewed said they would have preferred, partly on this basis, to have been born male: "If I were a boy, I would be outdoors. . . . At the movies, taking a walk. . . . Not like a girl, as soon as it gets dark, she has to get back home and that's it. . . . It is also that the girl does a lot of housework. The boy gets up, has breakfast, and leaves. He does not care about anything. That is not the case for the girl. She has to do the laundry, sweep the floor, and cook. She gets exhausted by work" (Davis & Davis 1989, 139).

Although these expectations can be found in families of different religious origins, it is widely believed among the population that such gendered social expectations have their origin in the Qur'an and the Islamic tradition. As such, these behavior guidelines assume a sacrosanct status that renders their observance by individuals imperative. However, in addition to social factors that may dilute their observance, such as young people's increased mobility, social palliatives exist that facilitate fulfillment of these expectations by sometimes easing the restrictions that guide them. The central texts of Islamic belief and practice emphasize a rational tolerance of human behavioral needs and a positive acceptance of sexuality (within marriage) as important to human fulfillment as well as social order. One practical import of this recognition of human needs is a certain flexibility: moral and social improprieties can often be contained within the system, in a notion that we might call "permissible misconduct." This is one reason why the vast majority of Arab adolescents find it possible to comply with community norms and indeed are, more often than not, well adjusted to their communities. The precept of permissible misconduct stems from the public, communal cast of Islam as a religion and social system, which rules out means of judgment other than the public yardstick. When an act is personal and secret, it does not necessarily pose a problem to society unless conduct becomes public. This is also meant to afford protection to the accused. For example, an Islamic court cannot condemn an adulterer and adulteress to death unless 4 witnesses testify to seeing not merely indications of sexual misconduct, but the intercourse itself. Yet, it must be said that these rules are often applied unevenly, with disastrous consequences for the powerless.

As a matter of psychosocial well-being, Arab adolescents seem to have acquired early in life the skills and versatility that they need to juggle "ought-to's" and " realities," "do's" and "don'ts," without compromising behavioral norms. In the process, most adolescents find room to maneuver, shaping morality to personal inclinations to some extent. An adolescent in love – especially a girl – will hide her true feelings from her parents. If questioned, she may deny those emotions without feeling that she is lying. Rather, she will regard herself as being economical with facts that, if revealed fully, would upset her parents. Getting to know a love interest without parental permission might lead an adolescent girl to be not so much "concerned with the morality of the act itself as she is with violation of the trust her father has in her to proceed according to the appropriate conventions" (Rugh 1985, 162). Parents, in turn, may be aware of the situation but prefer to remain quiet, their eyes on the line that cannot be crossed without social delegitimization. Learning self-control becomes especially important. "Personal lapses in behavior, if kept secret, are of little consequence; it is only their public acknowledgment and association with the lowering of group status that causes an individual a sense of shame and personal guilt" (Rugh 1985, 33).

Peer and Sibling Relationships

Little research has been done on peer relationships in Arab societies, partly because, in the past especially, they may have been of comparatively less importance than in other societies. During early adolescence, peers have been traditionally mostly relatives, e.g., cousins. Parents usually encourage this type of relationship, for females in particular, as long as these are same-gender friendships. Rugh comments that "Egyptians... do not see the necessity of pairing their children with friends of the same age and sex as we in the West do. Children are first and foremost sisters and brothers with strong common interests; only secondarily do they cultivate interests of their own outside families" (1985, 153, 155).

Studying the Greater Beirut neighborhood of Camp Trad, Joseph (1997) described brother-sister relationships at length, a depiction that can characterize ideal sibling relationships throughout the region:

> For both brothers and sisters in Camp Trad, connective identities and mutual love were linked to family honor. The ideal of brother/sister relationships in Camp Trad was based on a cultural promise: a brother will protect his sister; a sister will uphold her family's honor. Men saw themselves as their sisters' protectors. Invested in their sisters' behavior, their sense of their own dignity and honor was tied to their sisters' comportment. They were permitted by their parents and the culture to see sisters as extensions of themselves and thus to be molded to fit their sense of self. This included the cultural sanction to discipline their sisters when their behavior was considered improper.
>
> Sisters identified with their brothers as their security. A woman without a brother was seen as somewhat naked in the world. A brother's achievements opened opportunities for their sisters, just as their failure closed doors. Sisters understood that to receive the protection and support of brothers, they had to address their brothers' expectations. They were socialized to accept their brothers' authority over their lives and to see it in their own interests to accept that authority. Even when they might have disagreed with their brothers, sisters acknowledged their brothers' "rights" over them as a central vehicle for maintaining family honor (238).

In the past, the valence of sibling relationships, and extended-family closeness, tended to reduce the salience of other peer relationships for young people, although with increasing formal education this is changing. It might remain most true of adolescents in traditional families residing in rural areas, where all except young children are perceived more or less as adults. In urban settings, where the generation gap between adolescents and their parents can be wider and is a more accepted part of life, peer relations may be more vivid. Urban adolescents are more likely to rely on peer groups for enhancing their self-identity and obtaining psychological support (Melikian 1981). Urbanization, the tendency toward nuclear families separated from extended kin groups, and increased time spent in school have tended to make non-kin friendships more possible, especially for older adolescents. In a sample of nondelinquent boys in Saudi Arabia, 4.8 percent of 13–15-year-olds spent 6 hours or more per day with friends, while this figure increased to 13.4 percent for 16–19-year-olds (Malik 1990b).

When adolescents do have friendships, they are intimate and close, perhaps especially for girls. A study of Saudi youth found that both girls and boys place a high value on friendship (Simmons, Simmons, & Habib Allah 1994). Another study found that Bedouin adolescents rated their intimate friendships highly on 3 measures of closeness (emotional closeness, conformity, control) and indicated great respect for friends. Bedouin adolescents also placed much value on conforming to friends' practices and standards and put high value on self-disclosure to friends (Elbedour, Shulman, & Kedem 1997). Davis's work in Morocco suggested that for girls, female peers are important in coaching acceptable social behavior and its limits (1993). As children stay in school longer, spending more time away from families, friendships take on greater importance to socialization and adolescent behavior. Modern Arabic novels portray adolescent friendships as central to the process of growing up; in Egyptian novelist Latifa al-Zayyat's 1960 novel *al-Bab al-maftuh* (*The Open Door*), peer friendships sustain middle-class adolescents as they confront their nation's coming-of-age and their own. Members of a *shilla* (friendship group) typically show strong sentiments of obligation toward other members (Rugh 1985); that is almost part of the definition of the term.

But peer relationships are sources of worry and targets of adult control, too. Arab adults warn adolescents, especially boys, against "companions in wickedness" (*rifaq al-su'*), peers who are regarded as "bad influences," responsible for deviance and antisocial conduct, and who undermine parental authority in ways different than do education or "modernity" in general. Studies on juvenile delinquency and drug abuse in Arab societies indicate that male delinquents and addicts spend more time with peers than nondelinquents do (Malik et al. 1995; Malik 1996; Soueif, El-Saadani, & Taha 1998). The issue of "peer pressure" tends to come up only in relation to deviant behavior among male adolescents. Initiation into smoking cigarettes and drug use by males is popularly blamed on peer influence, along with lack of parental supervision and weak religiosity (Ghaloum 1983; Malik 1990a). Malik (1990b) found that the peer culture of delinquent boys in Saudi Arabia incorporated elements of the clandestine furtive camel raids of their Bedouin past and the rowdy undisciplined lifestyle associated with the subculture of soccer hooliganism, imported from Europe. In a Moroccan town, it was girls and their parents who worried more about the impact of "bad companions" on behavior (Davis & Davis 1989, 100).

In general, peer relationships seem less of a threat to parental authority and social conformity in Arab societies than in many other societies. For example, a study involving a large sample of 14–19-year-old boys and girls in the UAE found most respondents of both genders perceiving their families as providing for their various needs (Alnajjar 1996). Such findings suggest that peer influence on Arab adolescents is limited, when compared with parental influence.

Yet, the rise of conservative religious movements may be increasing certain kinds of peer influence. An early study of young members of one group in Egypt observed that "the fundamentalist peer group served as a reference point by which the morally sure-of-themselves students became alienated from their center-of-the-road parents" (Rugh 1985). Yet these were by and large students of rural origin who had been living in the city away from their families, and to measure the influence of such peer groups requires more research.

It is a sensitive matter to study Arab adolescents' crossgender relationships, since at least ideally, adolescents are not supposed to have much interaction – and certainly not sexual interaction – with nonrelatives of the opposite sex. But these rules are becoming more flexible in much of the region, particularly in urban and semiurban areas, despite growing religious conservatism. In fact, religious activism is one way for young people to form crossgender friendships. At the same time, increased opportunities for social interaction create difficult situations for young people – especially females – who have been warned against it, and may lead to "greater ambivalence with regard to interpersonal relations" (Davis & Davis 1989, 103), possibly intensified by girls' growing literacy and access to magazines and television soap operas – let alone the Internet.

Education and Employment

Educating the young is a top development priority in the Arab world, but national education systems face profound problems in delivering education to ever-growing numbers of children. On average, Arab countries spend 5.2 percent of their national incomes on education compared with 3.9 percent for developing countries in general and 5.1 percent in industrialized countries (Al-Siheibani et al. 1998).This suggests the importance Arab governments place on education. Yet the systems in place are relatively recent, and cultural norms, social disparities, population distributions, political unrest, and states of war have all shaped the differential access of Arab youth to sustained educations. Moreover, to what does education lead? Many youth throughout the region wonder whether education will lead to better futures, where unemployment is high and national economies are vulnerable.

All Arab nations have comprehensive public schooling, although in some countries, such as Egypt, private schools have become more numerous and popular among those who can afford them, as public schools become more crowded and less effective. If we look at the systems of 2 Arab societies, we get a sense of educational organization and priorities, although of course these vary throughout the region. In Saudi Arabia, all schools are strictly segregated by sex (for students, teachers, administrators, and support services), while in Egypt elementary schools (ages 6–11) are usually mixed. Students then attend generally sex-segregated middle and high school for 3 years each, graduating at age 17. Specialized high schools, such as agricultural or hotel-administration schools, are open to both sexes, as are some experimental schools. Egypt's burgeoning new Islamic private schools often segregate by sex, while even in public schools some administrators or teachers now separate boys and girls into separate sections of the classroom, arguing that this conforms to "Islamic values." Whether separated or mixed, boys and girls study the same books and follow the same curricula. In contrast, in Saudi Arabia the curriculum differs according to the sex. Girls' curriculum comprises fewer academic subjects and has a heavier domestic-science component; in addition, teaching methods in girls' schools, reflected in schoolbooks, tend to be more traditional, while boys' curriculum shows the impact of contemporary pedagogical research; even the schoolbooks are more colorful. Girls, it has been believed in Saudi Arabia, find it harder to learn and therefore must submit to rote methods; and unfortunately, girls internalize these attitudes.

Before the 1930s, most formal education in the region was religious in content. Children of both sexes (though a higher number of boys) memorized parts or all of the Qur'an and then went on to learn reading and writing. But first in Egypt and then throughout the region, a secular education system was established (with religious components for both Muslims and Christians); even Egypt's venerable Al-Azhar – one of the world's oldest universities – added secular programs (medicine and engineering, for example) to its curriculum in the 1960s, while the Egyptian (now Cairo) University had offered secular higher education since early in the 20th century to Arab elites. This history means that educational ideals and expectations are deeply rooted, yet universal education is still recent and uneven. Given that fact, it is impressive that the large majority of youth in the region do receive at least some primary education; a majority go on to high school (Fussell & Greene this volume). Yet rates for school registration and attendance vary widely, reminding us of how wide the range of Arab adolescent experience is.

Despite improved access to education, illiteracy remains high though variable, ranging (among those aged 15 and over) from 90 percent in Djibouti, to 75 percent in Somalia, to only 19 percent in Lebanon. Within some countries literacy rates jump substantially from rural to urban areas. But the younger generation enjoys a much higher literacy rate than do their parents and grandparents. This creates generational gaps in experience with which many adolescents contend. While the gender gap in literacy narrows greatly from the older to the younger generations, gender disparities in education remain a problem even where girls' schools have long existed; in Egypt, as of 1993, 62.2 percent of women were illiterate compared to 37.8 percent of men (Kamphoefner 1996). Still, illiteracy rates have plummeted; in the region as a whole, from 1970 to 2000, the overall rate dropped from 70.7 percent (56.1 for males and 85 for females) to 38.8 percent (27.1, 51) (United Nations Education, Scientific, and Cultural Organization, 1999; UNESCO).

Where economic conditions are difficult or a state of warfare prevails, education is directly and adversely affected. In Sudan, both structural adjustment policies and civil war have decreased the resources available for education. The rate of school dropouts increased in the 1990s, and in the capital, a recent study claimed only 21.4 percent of 15–19-year-olds had primary education, while in rural areas many children have no access to education (Okeny 1999). Palestinian children in territories occupied by Israel have often experienced interruptions in their school careers, and during the Lebanese civil war a whole generation of adolescents, in some parts of the country, had no sustained schooling.

The gender disparity varies too: Egyptian schools register 82 girls for every 100 boys in school, while in Morocco only 69 girls for every 100 boys are registered, with higher gender disparities in rural areas (Courbage 1995). Although a majority of girls attend secondary school regionwide (52.3 percent were registered in 1997, according to UNESCO 1999), girls also have a higher attrition rate, with fewer completing high school and going on to college (Fussell & Greene this volume). In the Moroccan town Davis and Davis (1989) studied, fewer girls were in school partly because their household labor was needed. Moreover, families may facilitate boys' studying over girls' studying, providing "the appropriate environment" for the former, while "girls can always be interrupted to take care of certain demands of boys and to comply with household responsibilities. Girls can also be taken out of schools at any stage of education to be married regardless of their academic performance, ambitions, intelligence and personal needs" (Saeed 1996). This study concerned Sudan, but these issues are not unique to Sudanese families. It remains common in parts of the Arab world for girls to be taken out of school to marry in their teens; compared to other regions of the world, girls are less likely to delay family and make a transition from school to employment (Fussell & Greene this volume), although this has been changing recently. But girls often stay in school longer than they did in the past; this may contribute to (and also be a result of) the overall trend toward later marriages.

According to Arab League statistics, 15 million adolescents did not register for secondary school in 1995. In addition to gender factors, explanations include broad socioeconomic conditions and factors specific to national educational systems. High rates of poverty and illiteracy among parents, particularly in rural areas, negatively affect school registration. Lack of awareness and/or financial ability may deter parents from encouraging children, especially females, to pursue education, although many poor parents recognize education as the sole route to a better future and sacrifice to put children through school. State officials are aware of the problem; a recent national survey on adolescents in Egypt recommended that the government provide scholarships that would allow low-income families to secure school fees and other necessities (El Tawila et al. 1999), for parents incur expenses even in sending children to public schools. In Egypt, parents pay for school books, uniforms, and other supplies. In Morocco, similar costs keep many children from attending secondary school (Davis & Davis 1989). Even more daunting, in many countries, overloaded school systems and underpaid, undermotivated teachers mean that children's success often depends on private tutoring, an expensive proposition (Baradei 2000).

The education structure itself may increase attrition. In most Arab countries national examinations determine one's movement through the education system (Bluhm 1983), attainment of a degree, and employment (at least in the public sector). Whether one will get into college at all, and then into what degree program (medicine, law, business, etc. – all undergraduate degrees in the first instance) depends on obtaining high marks in the nationwide "general secondary" examination. This puts tremendous psychological and material pressure on pupils to compete in rote learning that will allow them to pass the examinations. In Egypt, Saudi Arabia, and Jordan, test anxiety among secondary school students is reported as significantly higher than in the United States and Brazil (El-Zahhar & Hocevar 1991). This structure also worsens classroom overcrowding by producing repeaters at all levels. And overcrowding produces a vicious circle. The system is so overloaded in Egypt, for instance, that many public school buildings must double up; some students attend in the morning, others in the afternoon, and there is literally not enough time to cover all the academic subjects in the curriculum – even though, in the end, the students will be tested on them. On the other hand, to return to our comparison, in Saudi Arabia overcrowding is not such a problem. And, unlike in Egypt, students in Saudi Arabia who do successfully finish high school, and certainly college, can anticipate a job at a good salary, thereby giving them more incentive to stay in school.

Critics lambaste the quality of education across the region as poor and out of focus (Ammar 1998). Bluhm (1983) laments that the educational and vocational future of many Egyptian adolescents is already determined by age 14–15, due to poor performance at the preparatory level. Students suffer from lack of professional guidance and the scarcity of in-school counseling services (Soitman 1986; Bluhm 1983). Pupils with special needs and those from unstable or poor families often fail to continue their education.

Teachers have much to complain of, too, such as insufficient professional training and low salaries. Those who opt to teach at the primary and intermediate levels are usually school graduates with the lower grades in national examinations; they often come from poor economic backgrounds. Frequently, they are not well-equipped intellectually to

teach. In 1995, only 7 percent of primary teachers in Egypt had university degrees (Baradei 2000). The rest – an overwhelming 93 percent –
had only 9 years of formal education; they were to teach at the primary
level, where they had been pupils not so long before.

In addition to institutional and economic impediments to strong education, there are often political factors that curtail adolescents' educational experience. Arab students have been at the forefront of political
change, and therefore educational institutions are watched closely by
the authorities of many countries. The Sudan today, where school attendance, attrition, and educational conditions are reported to be especially
worrying (Okeny 1999), provides an extreme but not unprecedented example. Knowledgeable observers believe that attempts by the current
Islamist government to debilitate youthful energies through suppres-
sion, coercion, or indoctrination are motivated by insecurity about
its own self-preservation. University and high school students could
claim much of the credit for toppling 2 earlier authoritarian regimes
(1964, 1985); they constitute a potential and troubling opposition for
the present government, as is true of student populations elsewhere in
the region – even though a small percentage of adolescents in the Arab
world attend university.

Where the percentage of university students is higher, as in Egypt,
universities suffer from overcrowding as the schools do. Vocational education and minor diplomas, available in some Arab countries, attract
a smaller portion of intermediate and secondary school graduates; in
Egypt, where public-sector employment cannot support a family, vocational education for private-sector work has become more popular
(Hoodfar 1997). Throughout the region, more private universities are
opening, but these are not available to everyone.

As imperfect as education systems may be, schooling shapes the tenor
of life for millions of Arab adolescents in ways that make their lives radically different, in many cases, from those of their parents. Spending
hours of the day away from home and with peers; walking or taking
buses to and from school; postponing marriage and work to achieve
training or a degree; participating in school-related political or other
interest groups; in these and other ways, education brings adolescents
into contact with new experiences, and in fact, "the availability of education has made the life stage we call adolescence both more common
and in some ways more problematic" (Davis & Davis 1989, 60, speaking
of Morocco but with relevance to the entire region). If this is especially
evident in increased mixing of the sexes and the stresses that the gap

between prescribed and actual behavior may cause, it is also clear in the new hopes that some adolescents express.

Yet, education often does not deliver what its recipients hope for. Educated or not, adolescents constitute a large proportion of the region's large unemployed workforce. In fact, in Morocco there is a union of unemployed university graduates (author's information from S. Davis, Jan. 2001). It is no wonder that many young people doubt education's value for their future, as unemployment and inflation grow. In Egypt, even if a young graduate is so fortunate as to obtain, for example, a secure government post, the salary may not cover even the costs of transportation from home to work!

As the percentage of girls in school rises, female participation in the labor force remains low although, like education, variable across the region. Working females were 23.8 percent of the total labor force in Egypt in 1990 but a mere 4 percent in Oman, Algeria, and Saudi Arabia (Moghadam 1993; Makhlouf & Abdelkader 1997). Conservatives call for women to stay at home; yet, as economic hardship worsens for many, more young women enter the labor force, often delaying marriage. Young women are heavily represented in the female labor force; "in general," says Moghadam, "female labor force participation [in the Middle East] tends to be concentrated in the age group fifteen to twenty-nine years old" (1993, 43). And men's labor migration has also tended to push female wage labor participation upward, although much of this is in informal sectors that are not always statistically counted and where wages are, characteristically, lower (Moghadam 1993; Hoodfar 1997).

But family decisions about resource distribution can mean more adolescent girls are prepared for participation in the formal sector. Among lower-middle-class families in Cairo, Hoodfar (1996) found that because boys were being sent out earlier to work in the private sector, family resources were released to keep girls in school: "Ironically, the withdrawal of sons from school has made more resources available for investment in the education of daughters, facilitating their acquisition of white-collar public sector jobs" (7). Rugh (1985) notes that civil service positions, with their stability, short hours, and status, are seen by Egyptian parents as respectable work for their daughters. But often, for young women, work outside the home is seen as a temporary status preceding marriage. More girls are growing up with older sisters who work outside the home; new role models may result in contradictory messages about future expectations for female adolescents.

Physical Health

With the exception of the wealthy Gulf states, most Arab countries fall below acceptable standards of health care for adolescents. And in prevailing social and economic conditions, many adolescents face circumstances that make it difficult to lead healthy lives. For instance, a recent study revealed that nearly half of adolescent Egyptians suffered from anemia and parasitic infections, more among the poor and rural populations but also among the wealthier (El Tawila et al. 1999).

Most Arab governments provide for school health insurance, while state-run primary care is available for mothers, children, and adolescents, especially in urban areas. Recent health trends emphasize incorporation of health and environmental topics into school curricula, and several governments are now working to implement the World Health Organization (WHO) school health program that emphasizes preventive care. Meanwhile, health care is one area in which Islamist groups have been active, providing clinics in areas where state care is inadequate and thereby garnering more popular support for their agendas.

Some health issues require more than simply adequate health care, entailing public debate and activism to change popular attitudes. Much attention has been given in the West to the practice of female genital mutilation (FGM, often euphemized as "female circumcision") in parts of the Middle East and Africa, as a practice physically and psychologically harmful, indeed sometimes fatal, to female children. While many in the region resent Western condemnation of FGM, there is also considerable opposition to it and debate over how to eradicate it. Many Arab activists and non-government organizations (NGOs) work to educate populations in the region about the practice, in order eventually to end it. In much of the region it was never practiced or has already largely ended. The degree to which it is practiced remains a subject of debate; it is thought to persist in parts of Egypt, Sudan, Somalia, Djibouti, and Yemen. A recent study claimed that 98.5 percent of married women aged 15–19 in Northern Sudan were at risk of reproductive health problems because of FGM (Mohamed 1999). The practice is condemned by the U.N. conventions on the "Human Rights of Women and Children" to which all Arab countries are signatories. There is no doctrinal basis in Islam for the practice. Yet, there remain voices who claim that it is a justifiable practice that guarantees the "cleanliness" and spiritual purification of females.

In addition to continuing challenges, newer dilemmas face health care authorities. In 1992, a WHO report noted that until recently it was believed by many that "the Arab-Islamic parts of WHO's Eastern Mediterranean Region were safe from the spread of AIDS and from the devastating effects of other sexually transmitted diseases." But, the report said, research and statistical data contradicted this notion, indicating that AIDS was spreading in most Middle Eastern countries, especially among young people, as population movements, urbanization, and tourism grew. Yet it held out optimism that AIDS might not constitute as large a problem as it does in other regions of the world, on grounds I have emphasized here as salient to adolescents' ability to cope with difficult conditions – the continued hold of "moral and religious values" in the region (WHO 1992, 5). The publication itself is interesting as a document that confronts AIDS in terms of religious precepts drawn from the Qur'an and Bible, put together by a group of religious authorities from the region. As this publication suggests, AIDS is now an acknowledged if highly sensitive problem. The fight against it is now carried out in the mass media as well as by health authorities. But without further studies, it is impossible to evaluate the extent of the problem among adolescents or their levels of awareness and thus to assess implications for adolescent experience in the near future.

On another front, the number of Arab adolescents taking narcotic drugs is a matter of concern – although rates of drug use in Arab nations are below those of Western countries. The use of heroin in the Gulf states, "bango" in Egypt and Sudan, hashish in Lebanon, Syria, and Jordan, qat in Yemen, and "poly-drugs" in Morocco and Tunisia are all reported to be on the increase. A study of 14,656 male secondary students in Egypt, aged 15–21, found that 5 percent had tried psychotropics at least once; 5.9 percent admitted to using "narcotics, mostly cannabis," and some used opium. Twenty-two percent of the teens admitted drinking alcohol, with the peak age of onset at about 12 years, and approximately 10 percent said they smoked tobacco. Students from urban areas significantly exceeded rural students in use of tobacco, alcohol, and "natural narcotics." Students were most likely to be introduced to substance use by schoolmates (Soueif et al. 1990). Heavy drug users in Jordan who began during adolescence tended to have friends who were heavy users, were introduced to drugs by friends, and bought from friends (Weiss et al. 1999). A 1987 study on drug use in Kuwait found that young users of alcohol and other drugs were motivated by "a monotonous lifestyle," friends' influence, curiosity, and a desire for excitement; drug users were "less religious and more indifferent to many issues than the nonusers who in turn tended to endorse family values" (Sabry 1998, 479, 480). While awareness of the health effects of heavy tobacco use has increased throughout the region, teen smoking remains a problem.

Governments and NGOs are combatting drug use through measures aimed at reducing both supply and demand. A new "Arab Strategy for Drug Control" sponsored by the region's Council of Arab Ministers of the Interior is ambitious in scope, and it remains to be seen how effective it will be, but it suggests a high level of awareness of the problem in official circles. Mass media campaigns have been initiated to increase public awareness that narcotic drugs pose a major threat to Arab male adolescents' mental and physical well-being. In Egypt, drug abuse and cigarette smoking measured among secondary schoolboys in Greater Cairo was on the decline as of 1990 (Soueif 1998). Saudi Arabia and the UAE have established specialized hospitals for treatment of drug addicts. In less fortunate countries such as Sudan and Somalia, war and other miseries may be turning more young individuals into addicts.

Mental Health and Problem Behavior

There are no national surveys of adolescent mental health in the Arab world, but a few studies bear on the mental health of college and secondary school students. Al-Saraf's (1994) study of 500 Kuwaiti students, aged 16–20, noted that the younger boys and girls reported conflict between school and personal needs as their most frequent problem; girls also named fear of obesity as a major concern. Among the oldest respondents, anxiety headed the list of concerns; girls also worried about family and marriage. An extensive epidemiological study of 3,278 students (aged 6–15) in the UAE found mental health disorders prevalent at a rate consistent with studies of Western youth: almost 24 percent were reported (by parents or school physicians) to have mental health problems. Risk factors included being male, having many siblings, experiencing polygyny in the family, and having low socioeconomic status (Eapen et al. 1998). A study of families in Algeria concluded that last-born children often experience rejection and are at risk for mental illness, but so are oldest sons who must replace migrant fathers by becoming responsible for the family (Al-Issa 1990).

Strong family relationships may temper potential risk factors for mental health problems. A study of Palestinian citizens of Israel (sometimes called "Israeli Arabs") that involved over 1,500 11th- and

12th-graders found moderately high self-esteem. Highest among urban residents and lowest among Beduoin youth, self-esteem correlated significantly with perceptions of academic achievement and also with positive evaluations of family and peer relationships, which mitigated the impact of "discriminatory aspects of the larger Israeli society on their global self-esteem" (Abu-Saad 1999, 484).

On the other hand, tension and conflict in the larger society can certainly contribute to mental health problems, as studies of Palestinian junior and senior high school students in the West Bank and Gaza have found (Elbedour, ten Bensel, & Maruyama 1993; Elbedour 1998). Even youth not directly involved in the conflict were paying a high price, especially in Gaza, where "the trauma of war overwhelms any developmental challenges and disrupts any available age-related coping mechanisms" (Elbedour et. al. 1993, 48). The authors found that religion provided one mechanism for stress management, a point to which I shall return.

Juvenile delinquency is often an indicator of adolescents' mental health. Relatively harsh treatment of overt misconduct in some Arab-Islamic cultures, coupled with the fact that certain Arab nations are blessed with an enviably high per capita income while remaining underpopulated, and the often rapid social transformations in these societies may give psychologically motivated types of delinquency predominance over socially motivated ones. That is, in some Arab countries, delinquent acts based on excitement-seeking and experimentalist tendencies outnumber antisocial conduct fueled by poverty, overcrowded cities, and perceptions of social marginality. In delinquency studies carried out in the highly specific conditions of Saudi Arabia, Malik (1990a) observed that psychologically driven antisocial acts are characteristically nonviolent, and those who carry them out tend to be low on the scale of psychological and social maturity. In Egypt, though, studies carried out in the 1980s suggested that unemployment, low salaries, and the high costs of getting married "contributed to an increase in individual and organized crime by [male] youth" (Sabry 1998, 476). These economic difficulties have intensified since then.

Among 14–18-year-old delinquent boys in the Arab Gulf states, the majority of youthful crimes consist of petty theft, homosexual acts (a punishable offense regardless of age), and sniffing solvents. Younger adolescent delinquents are referred to correctional institutions called "surveillance homes," while older ones are sent to semiprison type institutions known as "correctional homes"; in both, delinquents are occasionally subjected to severe corporal punishment (Malik 1987, 1990a). In most other Arab countries, juvenile delinquents are treated as adult criminals unless they are 16 years or under. They are treated often more severely than in the Gulf states, as their crimes can be more serious and more deliberate. Such crimes, in general, are socially motivated as are juvenile crimes in the rest of the world. But organized attention to juvenile delinquency is relatively recent in the region. In Bahrain, it was not until the increases in delinquent crime in the 1980s and 1990s that a residential juvenile home was established (Sabry 1998). Kuwait's first juvenile court was established in 1982.

We have seen the impact of political conflict on adolescent mental health among Palestinians. Unfortunately, they are not the only Arab adolescents who have faced such situations. A study of 224 Arab youth (aged 10–16) from Beirut shows the extent of war trauma impact among adolescents. Over 90 percent had been exposed to shelling or combat, although only 2.7 percent said they had been directly involved in hostilities. Seventy percent had known bereavement, and nearly 68 percent, displacement. Almost half had witnessed violent acts, 16 percent were separated from parents, and smaller numbers experienced "extreme deprivation" and physical injury. Older children and those with high-status fathers were more likely to adapt. Girls were more likely to report mental health symptoms, including those of post-traumatic stress disorder, depression, and adaptational difficulties (Macksoud & Aber 1996). Similarly, research on young Palestinian adolescents in Gaza found that they were "affected not only by acute, dramatic stressors, but also by chronic, cumulative forms of political tensions." These Palestinian youngsters eventually resorted to "active coping modes," involving reliance on "community structure and cultural and religious norms [that] promote the formation of cohesive groups" (Slone, Adiri, & Arian 1998, 1066–1067). Barber (1999) discovered that Palestinian youth who had been involved in the (first) Intifada were relatively well-adjusted; he attributed this to the power of cultural values that assign meaning and ideology to the conflict and support resilience in children. However, negative impacts of the Intifada surfaced in the research, too. Antisocial behavior and depression were positively correlated with involvement, possibly because children prematurely left home to assume autonomous roles in the conflict. Intifada involvement was strongly predictive of adolescents' tobacco use and running away from home.

Adolescents in Iraq, Kuwait, Sudan, and Algeria have also experienced disruption due to sustained political strife; the impact of war trauma on these young populations can only be guessed. Fictional literature may provide important clues; Hanan al-Shaykh's acclaimed novel *Hikayat Zahra* (*The Story of Zahra*, 1980; English trans., 1986) chronicled the tragic impact of civil war in Lebanon on an adolescent girl, whose desperate search for meaning and self-esteem resulted in her death from her sniper/lover's rifle.

Youth Services and Youth Programs

Arab governments show good intentions toward their adolescent populations through youth affairs programs, sports programs, and skill-learning centers. But such programs may also be geared toward securing youths' political allegiance, even if indirectly. Critics of governmental youth programs and services in the Arab world usually do not question intentions, but they do raise issues of utility, quality, and implementation. In the Gulf states, authorities established dozens of expensive cultural and sports clubs for adolescents. Yet these clubs failed to attract substantial numbers; adolescents appeared to prefer picnicking in the desert or strolling through markets. In Egypt's major cities, cultural and sports clubs – often extensive and well-equipped – are inaccessible to limited-income families, in other words to the vast majority of the Egyptian population. Youth with no access to these facilities must find other outlets, usually ones provided by small-scale private enterprise. Traditional and newer-style cafes are meeting places where low-income youngsters see their friends, play board games, smoke water pipes, and watch satellite television. Electronic-game shops, cyber cafés, and the Internet are becoming increasingly popular among well-to-do adolescents in urban areas. It is in such venues rather than in community-provided programs that adolescents are forming their senses of self and community, if they are fortunate enough to have the time, energy, and material resources for even modest entertainment.

The General Arab Scouts Union does provide opportunities for Arab youth, as do local branches of some international NGOs: KARITAS, PRIDE, Young Men's Christian Association (YMCA), Young Women's Christian Association (YWCA), and the World Federation for Mental Health. Perhaps the largest and best-funded Arab nongovernmental youth organization is the "World Assembly of Muslim Youth." With its headquarters in Riyadh, Saudi Arabia, and branches across the globe, this NGO organizes youth summer camps and conferences.

Most Arab NGOs focus on development and health areas. Often very new and small, they may lack both resources and expertise, while stringent government control can also hamper their effectiveness. But a few do attempt to deliver services to youth. Among these are the Islamic Relief Agency, the World Assembly for Islamic Youth, the Arab Council for Childhood and Development (Egypt), the Yemen Family Care Association, the Nur al-Hussein Foundation (Jordan), the National Association for AIDS and Youth Information (Algeria), and the Regroupment Mère de Lumière (Lebanon).

Political Engagement

Since the late 1970s, and due to complex international and internal pressures, several Arab nations have seen a measure of political liberalization (Egypt, Jordan, Yemen, Tunisia, Algeria for a time, Morocco), while those and others (Kuwait, Bahrain) have experienced public agitation for more liberalization. Even if allowing political parties and lifting press restrictions did not signal regimes' willingness to truly share power, these moves did create space for public discussion, and also for alternative notions of governance – such as political Islam, the idea that a government should base its legitimacy and its structure of rule on Islam, interpreted according to those in power or seeking it. And some governments encouraged Islamic activism as a way to counter leftist opposition groups (Anderson 1997).

Young people in the Arab world have provided Islam-oriented activism with an eager constituency, for Islamic groups offer both services and hope that youth sorely need. Often, it is university populations that provide the most able and active recruits, as in the past they often fueled leftist movements (Anderson 1997; Woodward 1997; Abdalla 1985). People have myriad reasons, from the spiritual to the ideological to the economic, to join such groups. A young person in Algeria put choices open to young people there bluntly, explaining the popularity of the Islamist opposition party (Front Islamique du Salut, FIS): "You have only four choices: you can remain unemployed and celibate because there are no jobs and no apartments to live in; you can work in the black market and risk being arrested; you can try to emigrate to France to sweep the streets of Paris or Marseilles; or you can join the FIS and vote for Islam" (Tessler 1991, 17; Anderson 1997, 24–25).

Whether part of a political opposition or of an established religion, organized religious activism takes many forms, as it does elsewhere in the world. It may be motivated by personal desire to be a better Muslim; on the other hand, it can offer a channel for oppositional activity within the political system that might not otherwise be allowed. The global

attention that violent activism in the region has drawn has overshad-
owed the many peaceful manifestations of religiously based group activity that exist throughout the region. Youths are active in Muslim and
Christian charity organizations, and youth clubs are often sponsored by
religious organizations. In many ways, religion has a positive influence
in giving order and direction to Arab adolescents' lives.

At the same time, and for myriad reasons, authority that is labeled
as "Islamic" can have a troubling impact on young people's lives; it can
also signal the dissatisfactions and frustrations that young people feel.
Muslim youth in Egypt, Sudan, Algeria, and elsewhere are persuaded
to take up the cause of political action in the name of jihad. (The term
means "striving" and can mean internal striving to be a good Muslim,
but in this context it implies voluntary acceptance of possible death in
defense of political Islam.) These youths are led to believe that not only
are they serving their societies and their religion but also that promises
of eternal reward await them; given the conditions in which many of
them live, these promises hold appeal. It is not surprising that many
despondent young males turn to the slogan "Islam is the Solution."
Yet, despite the special appeal of religion to the poor and deprived, the
efforts of adult activists to recruit more youths to their Islamist training
camps are not totally successful. The overwhelming majority of Arab
youths remain moderate, whether pressures to become otherwise come
from their governments or from oppositional movements.

Toward the Future

In the politically and economically stable countries (e.g., the Gulf states,
Egypt, Jordan, Tunisia, Morocco, and to some extent Syria and Lebanon),
the situation of adolescents seems promising on some accounts, as governments demonstrate concern about human development and particularly about the conditions of children and adolescents. The future of
adolescents in these countries seems likely to improve as measures are
taken to improve health and education and to create jobs. At the same
time, these countries face daunting problems. Will they be able to cope
with the large populations of young people that the near future appears
to promise?

In other Arab countries (e.g., Sudan, Iraq, Algeria, Libya, Somalia), it
is exceedingly difficult to find grounds for optimism, given the state's
preoccupations with maintaining power and the dire conditions of life
that young citizens face. Just to give one example, the Sudan Human

Rights Organization (SHRO) in Cairo receives on a weekly basis an average of 30 male adolescents fleeing compulsory military service. As prospects for work or continuing their education in Egypt are nil, they are sent to the U.N. Refugees' Office in Cairo with eligibility certificates issued by SHRO. After a year or more of waiting, usually in miserable conditions, only a few find their way to resettlement in faraway places such as the United States, Canada, Australia, or New Zealand, while the rest wait, and dream. None of the Sudanese youngsters with whom psychologist Sharafuddin Malik conversed in Cairo knew what future awaited them (S. Malik, personal communication June 5, 2000).

A recent report from Algeria describes the situation of adolescents in that country pessimistically, another harbinger of Arab adolescent futures. Having lost their young singing idols – Alshab Housni, Layla Amara, Shab Aziz, and others – to the bullets of Islamist activists, who regard singing as a capital sin, they are sunk in a mood of gloom. Their favorite songs are about death and distrust in life, politicians, and the military. One knowledgeable journalist commented that if foreign embassies in the country would grant the youth visas, 99 percent of them would leave. Another observer remarked that if the Mediterranean were to dry up for 24 hours, not a single youngster would be found in Algeria (*Al-Sharq al-awsat*, June 25, 1999). As anecdotal as this evidence is, and recognizing that conditions in Algeria at the moment are especially difficult, it does signal a profound sense of hopelessness and malaise.

Social changes throughout the region will continue to shape adolescent lives, while the gap between prescribed and actual behavior may cause stress for some, especially since, as Davis and Davis (1993) found in Morocco, "sexual values are rigidly defined despite real change in behavior" (5). Although disapproval of sexual activity before marriage and fear of teenage sexuality are likely to remain strong, some social practices aimed at controlling teenage behavior will continue to change. There will still be those who see in every change a danger to Islam, but their opponents, interpreting Islam differently and variously, will remain as well. And young individuals of both sexes who now intermingle freely in the cities, exchanging concerns and views, will provide role models to tomorrow's adolescents. Education and the communication opportunities provided by modern information technologies are likely to encourage the generally progressive trend that has characterized Arab societies over the past decades, despite the emergence of conservative backlash and countertrends. Many Arab intellectuals and social scientists subscribe to this view, although perhaps less surely than was the case two decades ago. Females of all ages, and young people of both genders, stand to gain most from this process of increasing democratization. If it is unrealistic to envisage the complete abolition of patriarchy in the Arab world within the foreseeable future, perhaps it is not unrealistic to hope that it will become more diffuse and flexible, while the positive aspects of strong family support and connection will help adolescents to emerge into productive adulthood. Without peace in the region it is difficult to predict improved lives, but gains in education, access to the wider world, and improving socioeconomic conditions may enhance the control that Arab adolescents have over their lives.

References

Abdalla, A. 1985. *The student movement and national politics in Egypt 1923–1973*. London: Al Saqi Books.

Abu-Lughod, L. 1993. *Writing women's worlds: Bedouin stories.* Los Angeles: University of California Press.

Abu-Saad, I. 1999. Self-esteem among Arab adolescents in Israel. *The Journal of Social Psychology.* 139(4):479–486.

Al-Husayni, S. 2000. *Muyul al-murahiqin: Al-Mazahir wa-al-asbab, al-wiqaya wa-al-'ilaj.* Beirut: Dar al-Hadi.

Al-Issa, I. 1990. Culture and mental illness in Algeria. *The International Journal of Social Psychiatry.* 36(3):230–240.

Alnajjar, A. 1996. Adolescents' perceptions of family functioning in the United Arab Emirates. *Adolescence.* 31(122):433–442.

Al-Saraf, G. 1994. *Shabab al-Kuwait wa-mushkilatuhum.* Kuwait: Al-Faisal Press.

Al-Shaykh, H. 1980. *Hikayat Zahra.* Beirut: N.p. Trans. as *The story of Zahra* (1986). Trans. Peter Ford. London: Quartet Books.

Al-Siheibani, A., A. Al-Hamed, G. Al-Mana'i, & A. Al-Turki. 1998. *Al-Taghrir al-iqtisadi al-'arabi al-muwahhad.* Abu Dhabi: Dar Al-Fajr.

Altorki, S. 1986. *Women in Saudi Arabia: Ideology and behavior among the elite.* New York: Columbia University Press.

Al-Zayyat, L. 1960. *Al-Bab al-maftuh.* Cairo: Maktabat al-Anglo-al-Misriyya. Trans. as *The open door* (2000). Trans. M. Booth. Cairo: American University in Cairo Press.

Ammar, H. 1998. *Dirasat fi al-tarbiya wa-al-thaqafa.* Cairo: Maktabat al-Dar al-'Arabiyya lil-kitab.

Anderson, A. 1997. Fulfilling prophecies: State policy and Islamist radicalism. In *Political Islam: Revolution, radicalism or reform?* ed. J. L. Esposito, 17–31. London: Lynne Rienner Publishers.

Baradei, M. 2000. Taking stock of education. *Ru'ya.* 14:8–10.

Barber, B. 1998. Youth experience in the Palestinian Intifada: A case study in intensity, complexity, paradox, and competence. In *Roots of civic identity*, ed. M. Yates & J. Youniss, 178–205. Cambridge: Cambridge University Press.

Barber, B. K. 1999. Political violence, family relations, and Palestinian youth functioning. *Journal of Adolescent Research.* 14(2):206–230.

Bluhm, H. 1983. The place of guidance in Egypt. *International Journal for the Advancement of Counselling.* 6:31–37.

Conger, J. & A. Petersen. 1984. *Adolescence and youth: Psychological development in a changing world.* New York: Harper & Row.

Courbage, Y. 1995. Fertility transition in the Mashriq and the Maghrib: Education, emigration, and the diffusion of ideas. In *Family, gender, and population in the Middle East: Policies in context,* ed. C. M. Obermeyer, 80–104. Cairo: American University in Cairo Press.

Davis, S. S. 1993. Changing gender relations in a Moroccan town. In *Arab women: Old boundaries, new frontiers,* ed. J. E. Tucker, 208–223. Bloomington and Indianapolis: Indiana University Press.

Davis, S. S. & D. Davis. 1989. *Adolescence in a Moroccan town: Making social sense.* New Brunswick and London: Rutgers University Press.

Davis, S. S. & D. Davis. 1995. "The mosque and the satellite": Media and adolescence in a Moroccan town. *Journal of Youth and Adolescence.* 24(5): 577–93.

Eapen, V., L. Al-Gazali, S. Bin-Othman, & M. Abou-Saleh. 1998. Mental health problems among schoolchildren in United Arab Emirates: Prevalence and risk factors. *Journal of the American Academy of Child and Adolescent Psychiatry.* 37(8):880–886.

Elbedour, S. 1998. Youth in crisis: The well-being of Middle Eastern youth and adolescents during war and peace. *Journal of Youth and Adolescence.* 27(5):539–556.

Elbedour, S., R. ten Bensel, & G. M. Maruyama. 1993. Children at risk: Psychological coping with war and conflict in the Middle East. *International Journal of Mental Health.* 22(3):33–52.

Elbedour, S., S. Shulman, & P. Kedem. 1997. Adolescent intimacy: A cross-cultural study. *Journal of Cross-Cultural Psychology.* 28(1):5–22.

El-Islam, M. 1983. Cultural change and intergenerational relationships in Arabian families. *International Journal of Family Psychiatry.* 4(4):321–329.

El Tawila, S., O. El Gibaly, B. Ibrahim, F. el-Sahn, S. Sallam, S. Lee, B. Mensch, H. Wassef, S. Bukhari, & O. Galal. 1999. *Transitions to adulthood: A national survey of Egyptian adolescents.* Cairo, Egypt: Population Council.

El-Zahhar, N. & D. Hocevar. 1991. Cultural and sexual differences in test anxiety, trait anxiety and arousability. Egypt, Brazil and the United States. *Journal of Cross-Cultural Psychology.* 22(2):238–249.

General Secretariat, Arab League. 1997. *Statistical abstract for Arab countries.* Cairo (Maadi): Arab League Press.

Ghaloum, A. 1983. *Junuh al-ahdath fi duwal Majlis al-Ta'awun al-Khaliji.* Manama, Bahrain: Cooperation Council of the Gulf States.

Hassan, K. 1998. Socio-economic determinants of age at first marriage in urban Upper Egypt. In *Cairo Demographic Center 27th Annual Seminar on Population Issues in the Middle East, Africa, and Asia,* 318–35. Cairo: CDC.

Hattab, Z. & A. Mekki. 1980. *Al-Sulta al-abawiyya wa-al-shabab.* Beirut: Arab Development Institute.

Hoodfar, H. 1996. Survival strategies and the political economy of low-income households in Cairo. In *Development, change, and gender in Cairo: A view from the household*, eds. D. Singerman & H. Hoodfar, 1–26. Bloomington and Indianapolis: University of Indiana Press.

Hoodfar, H. 1997. *Between marriage and the market: Intimate politics and survival in Cairo*. Berkeley: University of California Press.

Kamphoefner, K. R. 1996. What's the use? The household, low-income women, and literacy. In *Development, change, and gender in Cairo: A view from the household*, eds. D. Singerman & H. Hoodfar, 80–107. Bloomington and Indianapolis: University of Indiana Press.

Joseph, S. 1996. Gender and family in the Arab world. In *Arab Women Between Defiance and Restraint*, ed. S. Sabbagh, 194–202. New York: Olive Branch Press.

Joseph, S. 1997. Brother/sister relationships: Connectivity, love and power in the reproduction of patriarchy in Lebanon. In *Arab society: Class, gender, power and development*, eds. S. Hopkins & S. Ibrahim, 227–261. Cairo: The American University in Cairo Press.

Joseph, S. 1999. Introduction: Theories and dynamics of gender, self, and identity in Arab families. In *Intimate selving in Arab families: Gender, self, and identity*, ed. S. Joseph, 1–17. Syracuse: Syracuse University Press.

Macksoud, M. S. & L. Aber, 1996. The war experiences and psychosocial development of children in Lebanon. *Child Development*. 67:70–88.

Macleod, A. E. 1991. *Accommodating protest: Working women, the new veiling, and change in Cairo*. New York: Columbia University Press.

Makhlouf, H. & M. Abdelkader, 1997. *The current status of research and training in population and health in the Arab region and the future needs: The case of Egypt*. Cairo: Cairo Demographic Center.

Malik, S. 1987. *Taqyim dawr al-ahdath fi al-Mamlakah al-'Arabiyya al-Sa'udiyya*. Riyadh: Research Center for Crime Prevention. The Ministry of Interior.

Malik, S. 1990a. *Junuh al-ahdath fi al-Mamlakah al-'Arabiyya al-Sa'udiyya*. Riyadh: Research Center for Crime Prevention. The Ministry of Interior.

Malik, S. 1990b. Time use and juvenile delinquency in the Kingdom of Saudi Arabia. Paper presented at the Biennial Meeting of the Society for Research on Adolescence. March: Atlanta, GA.

Malik, S. 1996. *Idman al-mukhaddirat fi Lubnan*. Riyadh: Research Center For Crime Prevention. The Ministry of Interior.

Malik, S., H. Al-Marzouki, A. Al-Ghamdi, & A. Al-Sayyad. 1995. *Idman Al-mukhaddirat fi al-Imarat al-'Arabiyya al-Muttahida*. Riyadh: Research Center for Crime Prevention. The Ministry of Interior.

Melikian, L. 1981. *Jassim: A study of psycho-social development of a young man in Qatar*. London: Longman.

Moghadam, V. M. 1993. *Modernizing women: Gender and social change in the Middle East*. Boulder and London: Lynne Reiner.

Mohamed, M. 1999. *Factors affecting reproductive health in selected areas in Sudan*. Cairo: Cairo Demographic Center.

Nagaty, M. 1974. *Al-Madaniyya al-haditha wa-tasamuh al-walidayn* (2nd ed.). Cairo: Maktabat al-Nahda al-'Arabiyya.

Nawar, L., C. B. Lloyd, & B. Ibrahim. 1995. Women's autonomy and gender roles in Egyptian families. In *Family, gender, and population in the Middle East: Policies in context*, ed. C. M. Obermeyer, 147–78. Cairo: American University in Cairo Press.

Obermeyer, C. M. 1995. Introduction: A region of diversity and change. In *Family, gender, and population in the Middle East: Policies in context*, ed. C. M. Obermeyer, 1–15. Cairo: American University in Cairo Press.

Okeny, A. 1999. Sudanese children more deprived than they were in 1989. Khartoum. Deutsch Presse Agentur. Posted on the World Wide Web. June 11, 1999. Web address: http://www.reliefweb.int/w/rwb.nsf/s/2Bo 7A39C16F7D586C125678Doo607600

Punamaki, R. & R. Suleiman. 1990. Predictors and effectiveness of coping with political violence among Palestinian children. *British Journal of Social Psychology*. 29:67–77.

Rugh, A. B. 1985. *Family in contemporary Egypt*. Cairo: AUC Press.

Rugh, A. B. 1986. *Reveal and conceal: Dress in contemporary Egypt*. Syracuse: Syracuse University Press.

Sabry, Y. 1998. Criminal psychology: Past and present. In *Psychology in the Arab countries*, eds. R. Ahmed & U. Gielen, 463–94. Menoufia, Egypt: Menoufia University Press.

Saeed, I. 1996. Gender discrimination in education in the Sudan. *Sudanese Human Rights Quarterly*. 4:11–21.

Sharabi, H. 1988. *Neopatriarchy: A theory of distorted change in Arab society*. New York and Oxford: Oxford University Press.

Simmons, C., C. Simmons, & M. Habib Allah. 1994. English, Israeli-Arab and Saudi Arabian adolescent values. *Educational Studies*. 20(1): 69–86.

Slone, M., M. Adiri, & A. Arian. 1998. Adverse political events and psychological adjustment: Two cross-cultural studies. *Journal of the American Academy of Child and Adolescent Psychiatry*. 37(10):1058–1069.

Soitman, A. 1986. The counselling needs of youth in the Arab countries. *International Journal for the Advancement of Counselling*. 9:61–72.

Soueif, M. 1998. Drug use, abuse, and dependence. In *Psychology in the Arab countries*, eds. R. Ahmed & U. Gielen, 495–516. Menoufia, Egypt: Menoufia University Press.

Soueif, M., S. El-Saadani, & H. Taha. 1998. *Prediction of the use of narcotics in a nation-wide sample of Egyptian secondary school male pupils*. Cairo: The National Center for Social and Criminological Research.

Soueif, M. I., G. S. Youssuf, H. S. Taha, H. A. Abdel-Monem, O. A. Abou-Sree, K. A. Badr, M. Salakawi, & F. A. Yunis. 1990. Use of psychoactive substances among male secondary school pupils in Egypt: A study on a nationwide representative sample. *Drug and Alcohol Dependence*. 26:63–79.

Tessler, M. 1991. Anger and governance in the Arab World: Lessons from the Maghrib and implications for the West. *Jerusalem Journal of International Relations*. 13(3):

United Nations Education, Scientific, and Cultural Organization (UNESCO). 1999. *Statistical Yearbook 1999*. Lanham, MD: Bernan Press.

Weiss, S., G. H. Sawa, Z. Abdeen, & J. Yanni. 1999. Substance abuse studies and prevention efforts among Arabs in the 1990s in Israel, Jordan and the Palestinian Authority: A literature review. *Addiction*. 94(2):177–198.

World Health Organization (WHO). 1992. *The role of religion and ethics in the prevention and control of AIDS*. WHO Publications.

Woodward, P. 1997. Sudan: Islamic radicals in power. In *Political Islam: Revolution, radicalism, or reform*, ed. J. Esposito, 95–114. Boulder and London: Lynne Reiner Publishers.

Zuhur, S. 1992. *Revealing reveiling: Islamist gender ideology in contemporary Egypt*. Albany: State University of New York Press.

8

Adolescents in Russia

Surviving the Turmoil and Creating a Brighter Future

Anna Stetsenko

Introduction

Adolescence is when young people, for the first time in their lives, must become truly social agents – free but also responsible to make choices and commitments that to a large extent define their "social destiny," that is, their places and roles in society often for the rest of their lives. Hence, in order to understand adolescents, it is critically important to understand the socioeconomic and cultural-historical dimensions of the society that the young people are entering as they prepare to become its full members. However, the reverse is also true. The society itself is perhaps well understood only when we have an idea of who the young people populating it are, how these people are adapting to and participating in society's transforming structures, and what the trends are that specify the life course of its younger generations.

This certainly holds true for the Russian society. The education and development of the younger generation is a key factor in this country's future. Today's adolescents in Russia grew up in an unusually turbulent and dynamic sociocultural and political context. It is today's adolescents who have suffered most because of the worsening conditions in schools due to lack of funds for education. But it is also they who grew up in freedom and can now appreciate an unprecedented access to information and diverse education, can plan more varied career paths due to the emerging, more dynamic job market, and can generally enjoy advantages brought about by democracy. It is also they for whom the right to elect a president is as self-evident and indisputable as it is for their Western counterparts. The outcomes of today's reforms will and already does shape the life course of Russia's young generation. However, as just alluded to, the very outcomes of social change in Russia depend on its young generation – on the ways it is integrated into rapidly changing societal structures and is adapting to these structures, and at the same time, adapting them to their world views, their values, and orientations. Who are these young people in Russia today? What are they like? Is this, as is often presumed nowadays, a lost and disillusioned generation, devoid of ideals and commitments and unable to plan for the future?

In this chapter I will attempt to give some tentative answers to these questions. In doing so, I will rely heavily on available statistical information and on Russian adolescents' own voices as they are reflected in self-reports and opinion polls. Due to unprecedented rapid changes in Russian society, many reporting agencies have difficulties devising appropriate instruments to track them down. Moreover, these agencies themselves are by no means stable; many of them have been and are being reorganized and new ones emerge to tackle problems that used to be nonexistent or simply ignored (e.g., drugs, AIDS, unemployment). That is why, perhaps as in no other context, it is incredibly difficult to discern reliable trends in how young people's lives are changing in Russia. All these limitations notwithstanding, it is important to look closely into the reality-based indications of what is going on in this country. Hence, many findings from empirical research and statistical information will be presented in this chapter. Perhaps these findings can tell "their own story" that will go beyond what are often overgeneralized and stereotyped perceptions of Russia and its young generation. Certainly, to the extent that attempts to draw conclusions from the often scattered data will be made in the present chapter, they will be inevitably colored by the author's own general "world view," which happens to be ineradicably optimistic with regard to the future of Russia.

Overview of General Societal, Political, and Economical Issues

Most young people in today's Russia were actually born or at least went to school in a country that can be defined as an open and, by a classical definition, democratic society. Indeed, Russia went through its most significant historical changes at the end of the 1980s, during Gorbachev's *perestroika* when it became a pluralistic parliamentary democracy. Specifically, the first free elections on a multiparty basis were held in 1989, and 1 year later Boris Yeltsin, the first president of Russia, was elected in a free and democratic procedure. Freedom of the press was introduced by removing all controls on reporting, as well as freedom of religion, opinion, and demonstration. Russia also began transforming its centrally planned economy into a market economy with elements of private property: The first private enterprises emerged in the mid-1980s and served as a springboard for the initial accumulation of capital in private hands.

Geographically speaking, Russian adolescents live in the largest country in the world, almost 17.1 million square km in area. It has a population of approximately 146.5 million people. Russians predominate, but there are over 100 different nationalities represented in the country. Among them 83 percent are Russian, 4 percent Tatars, 3 percent Ukrainian, and the rest are composed of numerous ethnic minorities of small sizes. The official language is Russian, and schools award diplomas only in three languages – Russian, Tatar, and Bashkir – a requirement that puts many of the country's ethnic groups at a disadvantage. It should be taken into account that ethnic groups have become fairly mixed up and assimilated during the many centuries of the Russian empire. As a result, many people who are officially Russian have in fact a diverse ethnic background (note also that differences in physical appearance among most ethnic groups, e.g., Russians, Tatars, and Ukrainians, are negligible). Even though ethnic issues have recently become more prominent, amounting to even drastic confrontations such as the war in Chechnya, there are almost no data available on specific ethnic trends in adolescents living in Russia, and they will not be reported in this chapter.

The density of population in Russia is quite low compared to other European countries and even the United States (only 8.5 persons per square km). The level of urbanization is high: 74 percent of the population live in urban areas, which is roughly equivalent to the urbanization in the United States (Grob & Flammer 1999). The population has actually decreased in recent years, with a loss of 1.7 million registered over the past 7 years, and it is projected to decline even more over the coming years. These unfavorable population changes are accounted for by the negative reproduction rate in recent years. Indeed, the total birth rate is low and continuing to fall: it was 17.2 per 1,000 population in 1986, 9.3 in 1995, and 8.8 in 1998 (in 1996 the world average was 25, and Europe's average was 11.3), with the total fertility rate per woman now at only 1.3. Because of the low birth rate, together with an increased number of people in the older age groups (currently 1 in 9 people in Russia is older than 64), the population in Russia, as in most other industrialized countries, continues to age. For example, the population under age 15 is now only 19 percent (i.e., 28.5 million people), and this number is expected to further decline over the next decades (Karelova 1997).

Economically speaking, Russia is now coming to the end of a difficult period of transition from state controlled to market economy. According to some analysts, during the reform period and up to 1996 the Russian gross domestic product (GDP) fell by at least half, capital investment by 90 percent, and meat and dairy livestock herds by 75 percent. During the same time period, the number of people living in poverty has sharply increased and living standards for many rank- and-file citizens dropped. These declines are not surprising given that the country is in transition to a completely new economic and sociopolitical system (although some analysts argue that these losses did not have to be so drastic and were at least partly caused by political mistakes and bad management at both the top and the local governmental levels). It is also not surprising that a typical consumer of media news in the West has a perception that things are extremely gloomy in all aspects of life in Russia. However, the realities of life are much more complex than one could infer based on a superficial scan of media reports. For example, although official wages are appallingly low, they often make up only a fraction of a person's total income (42 percent according to some estimates). Much of income comes from other sources (e.g., under-the-table payments, barter exchange, employer-provided benefits, rental or small private business incomes), where wages and profits are not reported to tax bodies. Because the government tax policy is very inconsistent and controversial, a whole culture of tax evasion has recently emerged. Not only individual wages but also much of production, trade, and output at the state level goes unaccounted for. Also, direct comparisons should be avoided. For example, low wages do not mean the same in the United States and in Russia, where rent is very low, education at all levels and health care remain essentially free, gas costs 50 cents a gallon, bread is 15 cents a loaf, and public transportation is cheap.

Gloomy pictures of Russia also do not always reflect the rapid pace of changes taking place there. For example, it is not commonly known that the country experienced the worst transitional difficulties in 1992–94, whereas by 1996–97 the industrial recession was halted and the economy as well as the society at large started to show signs of revival. This revival included (a) growth in real incomes (by 48 percent between 1995 and 1996 alone) and in consumption levels, (b) decrease in poverty (percentage of people living below officially established existential minimum dropped from 33 percent in 1992 to 21 percent in 1997), and (c) several favorable trends in general health indications (e.g., life expectancy, infant and maternal mortality). For example, there was a dramatic fall in life expectancy in 1992–94 (especially for men and mostly due to excessive alcohol consumption), but starting in 1995 an opposite favorable trend is being observed with this important indicator rebounding to the prereform levels. Similarly, the infant, young children, and maternal mortality rates have been falling since 1996 although they still remain higher than in Europe (e.g., infant mortality is 16.4 per 100,000 live births in Russia compared to 12.6 in Europe; see World Health Organization Report 2000; WHO).

Socioeconomic stratification is literally emerging right now in Russia. A vast disparity in incomes exists and continues to grow. However, because these trends are so new and still so dynamic, and also because so much of the population's income goes unreported, there is very little reliable information on even the very contours of specific socioeconomic groups. The reader should also bear in mind that for many decades under the Soviet system Russia was virtually a "classless" society with little difference in standards of living between various groups – with the exception of a highly privileged layer of top Communist party, military, and state bureaucracy (the so called "nomenklatura") along with a few privileged members of "intelligentsia" (e.g., top artists and scientists).

According to some estimates, a vast Russian middle class has emerged in recent years. In 1996, 63 percent of the population had average-level incomes. Today more people than ever before can afford trips abroad as well as many previously unavailable goods and services. Despite the economic crisis in July 1998, these favorable trends are continuing and in some cases are even accelerating. For example, per capita gross domestic product (GDP) and industrial output increased respectively by 7.2 percent and an astonishing 9 percent in 2000. Very recent estimates put Russia in 10th place in the world in terms of the GDP, which is much higher than just a few years ago. Sustained growth in personal cash income in 2000 led to the expansion of consumer goods production and, for example, growth in light industry in 2000 amounted to 28.6 percent compared to 1999. Over the same period, real disposable household income rose by 9.4 percent.

The polls conducted in Russia also suggest that recent years of reforms cannot be viewed only in black colors and that the peak of the crisis is over. Although most young people in Russia do not necessarily like the exact type of ongoing reforms, most would not like to go back to the communist times either. For example, a large study of youth in Bashkortostan (an autonomous republic in the east of Russia) showed that most young people have largely accepted market economy. An overwhelming majority (approximately 70 percent) see it as the only way for development, whereas only 10 percent reject capitalism (Saliev 1997). A majority of young people also do not see themselves as particularly poor. When asked about how they see their family economic status, 1 percent depict their families as rich, 35 percent as wealthy, 40 percent as rather well off, 19 percent as rather poor, and only 1 percent as poor. When asked how their family's socioeconomic circumstances had changed recently, 6 percent said it had improved significantly, 25 percent claimed it had improved somewhat, 36 percent indicated it remained unchanged, 21 percent said it had worsened somewhat, and only 8 percent thought it had worsened significantly (Rouchkin 1997).

The recent changes can be illustrated by one journalist's comment. "I have been struck this time by the repaired and cleaned buildings and orderly streets, with fewer beggars and homeless in the central city [of Moscow – A.S.] than in Washington.... at Moscow University, where I gave three talks to journalism students, the handsome old building is indeed dilapidated, and repairs and paint are needed, but the students are better dressed and better groomed than at the more politically correct American universities, and they are intellectually alive, articulate, interested, and interesting. On past visits I have left Moscow relieved to be getting out and depressed about the state of the country. I did not feel that this time" (Pfaff 1998, 8).

What then is life like in socioeconomic terms for an average citizen of Russia at the beginning of the new millennium? On the one hand, it is certainly true that in general people in Russia still enjoy much lower standards of living compared to other industrialized countries. For example, adults in a typical Russian family are more likely than a typical western European family to live in a cramped apartment, work several jobs, and struggle to put enough food on the table. About three-quarters of Russians own a plot of land where many grow their own food, an important addition to often meager wages. This family is generally more likely to be financially strapped; GDP per person in Russia is now roughly one-third of that in Europe. It is also true that a considerable part of the population (estimates vary but most converge on about 15–20 percent) has been impoverished to previously unknown levels. Young parents with little work experience and more than one child, as well as lonely pensioners, are especially likely to be very poor.

Paradoxically, there are many "working poor" among those who work in education, culture, science, and health, most of which are considered middle-class occupations in the West (Curtis 1996).

On the other hand, a typical family in Russia enjoys much higher standards than in truly impoverished countries. They are likely to live in (and often own) a dwelling with central heating, water supply, electricity, and a sewer system, as well as many modern appliances such as refrigerators and TV sets. They also have access to reasonably good public transportation and a health care system (although the latter is experiencing many difficulties; see below), as well as free and often excellent education for their children. Although putting enough nutritionally valuable food on the table is a concern for many families, simple food (e.g., bread and other wheat products, milk, potatoes, cabbage) is certainly affordable to everyone, and this situation is a far cry from not uncommon starvation in many other parts of the world. This typical Russian family is also likely to be well educated: According to the last census, three-fifths of Russia's people aged 15 and older had completed secondary school (i.e., had spent 10 to 11 years at school), and 8 percent had completed higher education (equivalent to college or university education in the West). Also, the literacy rate of the adult population continues to be one of the highest in the world – 98.4 percent.

Trends in Adolescents' Family Relationships

The most immediate context affecting adolescents is certainly the family in which they live and grow up. The family is likely to act as a system of filters with a high safety factor that mediates the impact of changes within the larger socioeconomic environment. That is why it is so important to look at the composition and mentality of the Russian family as well as at recent changes within this small but crucially important societal institution in order to understand young people in this country.

In Russia, people are likely to get married and have children at an early age. This trend, also referred to as an early childbearing schedule, became especially pronounced over the last three decades: The average age for marriage in Russia in 1994 was 24.2 years for men and 21.7 years for women compared with 29.3 for men and 27.2 for women in 1966 (Kon 1979; Podolskij 1994). Most women have children when they are 20 to 24 years old, and fertility at ages 15–19 is almost the same as at ages 25–29. The incidence of childlessness is low compared to most other industrialized countries. Such an early childbearing schedule is typical also for Eastern Europe. Contrary to that, a late childbearing schedule has been documented for most industrialized countries, where people now get married and have children at later ages than ever before (Expert Group Meeting 1998).

There are as yet no indications of a reversal in this Russian pattern of marriage and childbearing at an early age. Although factors affecting this behavior are not well understood, they likely include these 2: First, because of housing shortages, many young people in Russia live with their parents until a rather mature age (often into their 30s). Second, Russian society is characterized by a traditional mentality regarding sexuality (compared to a more liberalized West), so that sexual contacts outside marriage, especially for young girls, are not well tolerated. The combination of these two factors in practice means that young people rarely have an opportunity to live with their sexual partner and the only way to have a regular sexual life is to marry at an early age. Given that recent generations mature earlier and are more exposed to liberal models of sexual behavior from the media, they might be eager to have a sexual partner earlier in life – which often automatically means marriage – compared to previous generations. As to having children, the societal stereotypes are very clear and related pressures are very strong on women to bear children at an early age. This is considered to be a woman's destiny and duty. A childless woman even in her late 20s and especially into her 30s is regarded as a failure, with suspicion and pity. It is not easy to explain this rather peculiar attitude other than by Russia's overall traditional mentality. However, given the growing liberalization of Russian society in general, including liberalization of the job market where it gradually becomes easier for young people to gain independence from parents, it is reasonable to expect that patterns of marriage and childbearing will change in the near future in the direction of a Western model. One illustration of this liberalization is the growth of out-of-wedlock birth rates: The percentage of children born to single mothers increased from only 15 in 1990 to 23 in 1996 (WHO Report 2000). That is, nowadays every 5th child in Russia is born to a single woman (Sobkin & Kuznetsova 1998).

In the 1980s, the divorce rate in the Soviet Union was second in the world, after that of the United States. Further increases were registered in the early 1990s. However, the number of divorces fell by 1.4 percent in 1998 and is now at 3.4 per 1,000 (WHO Report 2000). Still, many of today's adolescents in Russia (approximately 15 percent) will spend at least part of their life living with only 1 parent. In Iasnaja and Magun's

(1999) study of 800 urban, upper-grade students, three-quarters of adolescents reported living with their natural father and mother; an additional 9 percent reported living with 2 parents, 1 of whom was not the natural parent. Seventy-three percent of the upper-grade students reported having brothers or sisters, which appears to be representative for the population in general (cf., Rouchkin 1997). Almost 95 percent reported living in a separate apartment or the family's own home; 4 percent live in a communal apartment or a dormitory, and only about 1 percent of families rent. Almost half of the students – 45 percent – have their own room, while around 37 percent share a room with a sibling (see Iasnaia & Magun 1999).

Thus, a typical family in Russia consists of 2 parents (although not necessarily both natural) and 1 or 2 children (only about 15 percent of families have more than 2 children; see Rouchkin 1997). Quite often, a family also includes grandparents; as already mentioned, the housing shortage prolonged the tradition for married couples to live together with one of the spouses' parents. Many parents continue regular financial help to their children even after the latter become adults and get married. However, in very recent years this trend seems to be reversing: Because younger people are more likely to be involved in the new market sector of the economy, such as banking or computer-related and international business, they often get higher wages than their parents and hence are able to support them.

In general, family ties, including economic interdependency, are traditionally very important in Russia. For example, Russian adolescents emphasize their social responsibilities (e.g., taking care of parents) relatively more than their peers in most Western European countries (Nurmi, Liiceanu, & Liberska 1999). Indeed, many families reunite with their elderly parents in need of care (Rotkirch 1998). This pattern is especially pronounced due to shortages in social care institutions for the elderly. Although the picture should not be perceived as a rosy one (see section on child abuse below), family relations are traditionally not only very close economically but also emotionally and are often child centered.

Some support for the described family characteristics comes from a comparative study of how adolescents in different countries view contacts with their parents (King et al. 1996). Compared to other countries, boys and girls in Russia find it easier to talk to their fathers about their concerns (e.g., up to 70 percent of boys and 78 percent of girls among 11-year-olds), although no difference was found on how easy they thought it was to talk to their mothers. In another study, Russian adolescents were shown to be more likely than American adolescents to use social support as a coping strategy (Jose, D'Anna, & Cafasso 1998). Whether or not any of the described patterns are changing due to the recent societal turmoil in Russia is hard to establish. Substantial shifts in these types of interpersonal relations, deeply rooted in cultural tradition and history, are likely to take a considerable amount of time.

As in many other countries, child abuse continues to be a serious but poorly examined issue in Russia. Few empirical studies regarding this problem are available. For example, a study based on self-reported data from 375 early and mid-adolescents in a Siberian city estimated a prevalence of child abuse at 29 percent. Of those reporting abuse, 4 percent suffered injuries that required medical attention; 46.3 percent had experienced or witnessed child abuse. Punishment was reported to be a pervasive method for control of childhood behavior (Berrien et al. 1995). Given that child abuse is often related to excessive levels of alcohol consumption and that this consumption went up in recent years, it is likely that its prevalence has also increased. However, the exact cross-national and time-related trends are difficult to identify because criteria for what constitutes child abuse differ widely from country to country and even from study to study in the same country.

Similarly to Soviet times, today's attitudes in Russia show that the family continues to be viewed as the most important institution in society. The roots of this phenomenon perhaps lie in the widespread mistrust of most other institutions (e.g., trade unions, political parties, community-based organizations) – an attitude inherited from the Soviet times when these organizations were imbued with compulsory communist ideology. In a 1994 poll, less than 3 percent of respondents named "living alone without a family" as the best choice for a young person. Nearly 80 percent of respondents named children as the essential element of a good marriage (Curtis 1996). Among the positive changes in recent years (in addition to some decrease in divorce rates) is that compared with 1989, about 3 percent fewer individuals characterized their marriages as in conflict. According to experts, social and economic crises have caused Russians to rely even more heavily than before on the family as a source of support and personal satisfaction (cf., Curtis 1996).

In general, it appears that despite seismic changes in Russia, the family in this country continues to play the role of an important and rather stable societal institution. There are reasons to believe that, in any society, the family has a high degree of resilience in that it is one of the last entities to bend under pressure of socioeconomic changes (although this resilience is certainly not limitless). It appears that this is especially true for Russia with its traditional mentality that places high value on family, parenting, and intergenerational contacts. However, as economic reforms are pushing more and more people to work several jobs and spend more time at work, it is likely that it will eventually become harder for families to sustain their most cherished attributes.

Girls' Family Roles and Other Gender Issues

Quite significant changes are taking place in Russia with regard to women's status and role in society. For example, the 1994 Human Rights Watch report showed that women in Russia face widespread employment discrimination and that the introduction of democratic processes has not improved respect for women's rights. Across Russia, 2 out of 3 unemployed persons are women. In many regions, over 85 percent of the unemployed are women. Women also confront sex discrimination when seeking new employment (Human Rights Watch 1994). This is partly explained by the fact that employers want to avoid the obligation to provide benefits for women with children (e.g., long maternity leaves, child benefits).

Compared to Western European countries, a more traditional gender ideology seems to be typical of Russian adolescents, and it has probably been further strengthened recently. Some authors even claim that "the move toward a market economy has been accompanied by a celebration of masculinity, both literally and metaphorically, and the denigration of the strong and capable woman worker glorified in the first decades of Soviet history" (e.g., Attwood 1996a, 255). Indeed, girls from Russia show greater interest in future family and consider family to be more important than do boys, whereas in Western cultures no such sex difference is found (see Nurmi, Liiceanu & Liberska 1999). Also, older women in Russia are more likely than younger females to describe an ideal woman as strong, self-reliant, and career-oriented. Younger women tend to describe an ideal woman in more traditional terms – as gentle, caring, a good mother, faithful wife, etc. (Köbberling 1997).

A study by Lynn Attwood (1996b) supports this pattern. She examined sex-role and sexuality expectations of Russian youth in a 1994 survey of students from Moscow and Piatigorsk. Participants of both sexes identified ideal female traits as kindness and beauty, whereas the most important male traits included strength and ability to provide for family. Child rearing was seen as a female duty, and financial support of the family as a male duty. The majority held the traditional Soviet view that men and women occupy different but mutually complementary roles (Attwood 1996b; for similar findings, see Baraulina & Khanzin 1996).

It appears that many of the gender-related values and beliefs of the Soviet era, including formal claims of equality coexisting with factual male domination, have been reproduced and reinforced in contemporary Russia, thereby limiting opportunities for egalitarian practice and lifestyles (cf., Pilkington 1996). This shift can even be described as a "gender polarization" in that Russian males and females indeed appear to inhabit 2 different worlds that are drifting farther apart in recent years. Perhaps these findings can be explained as a temporary overreaction to a recent breakdown of the socialist ideals that entailed proclaimed equality between sexes. In a society that has resolutely broken with its recent history and has set itself on a new historical path, such overreactions are neither surprising nor, hopefully, permanent.

Importantly, Russian girls do not seem to give up their interests in career and education. For example, a study of values and expectations regarding love, sex, and marriage among young girls in Moscow in 1992–1994 (Kotovskaia & Shalygina 1996) revealed a conflict between their endorsement of a traditional female sex-role identity and the desire for professional and creative success; more-democratic forms of marriage and family were also desired. In another study, young Russian girls expressed a strong desire for both a career and a family, although the prevailing gender ideology of male domination was rarely challenged (Murcott & Feltham 1996).

Overall, it appears that Russian young women are struggling to come to grips with several contradictory trends in their society. Attempts to push them back into the realm of domesticity and motherhood, which result from the rejection of the old socialist ideology, compete with some liberalizing general trends of the emerging market economy and Westernization. With time, Russian women are likely to follow the path of their Western sex peers in pursuing more rights, power, and respect for women. Some signs that women are becoming more outspoken and politically motivated can already be observed. This includes the rise in the number of women entrepreneurs, emergence of feminist grass-roots organizations including those combating violence against women, and the persistent desire of young girls for a professional life.

Peer Relations and Sexuality

There are very few data on Russian adolescents' peer relations, let alone on possible changes in these relations in recent years. Although great emphasis has always been placed (especially in Soviet times) on the value of peer relations and more generally on collectivism, these phenomena rarely have been examined empirically. Traditionally, most efforts have been focused on promoting collectivism and developing methods to instill it in young people. These efforts followed the tradition founded by the Russian educator Anton Makarenko, whose popularity and influence can be compared to those of Dr. Spock in the United States. Unlike Dr. Spock, Makarenko's primary concern was not with the child's physical health but with the collectivist upbringing. His theories and techniques became widely adopted throughout the USSR and for many years constituted the central core of Soviet educational practice in both families and schools (cf., Bronfenbrenner 1970a). A series of crosscultural studies conducted by Urie Bronfenbrenner in the 1960s and 1970s documented that efforts at collectivist education were bringing desired outcomes. For example, Soviet adolescents were shown to be substantially less willing to engage in antisocial behavior than American age mates. Moreover, when told that their misconduct would become known to their classmates, Russian and American children reacted in opposite ways, the former being less ready to engage in adult-disapproved behavior, the latter more so (Bronfenbrenner 1970b).

Much of Russian philosophy of upbringing today emphasizes the same values of collectivism, respect for labor, love of Motherland and family, but without the appeal to communist ideals and compulsory atheism (cf., Hauer 2000). The collectivist structure of schools did not change radically under reforms, and the relationships between students and their class teacher in many cases continue to be lifelong. This is not surprising given that, typically, classes of 20 to 30 students of the same age enter school together and progress through the entire 11 years as an intact social group. This structure promotes strong group consciousness and bonds of affiliation.

A large comparative study of 24 countries from all parts of Europe conducted in 1993–94 under the auspices of the World Health Organization sheds some light on what is specific about peer relations in today's Russian youth (King et al. 1996). This self-report study involved large samples of adolescents matched by age (groups of 11-, 13-, and 15-year-olds) and size. Although it is not easy to estimate how representative of the Russian youth in general the findings from this study are, it can be viewed as a good source of comparative information.

According to this study, and paradoxically in view of the collectivist structure of schools, Russian adolescents do not think that their classmates are kind and helpful. For example, only 43 percent of Russian girls and 41 percent of boys among 11-year-olds held this view (the 2nd lowest rank among 24 sampled countries, compared with as high as 80 percent in Denmark); trends are comparable in 13- and 15-years-olds.

Russian boys and girls also seem to be bullied more often than their peers from other European countries. That is, 68 percent of girls and 75 percent of boys among 11-year-olds in Russia reported being bullied at least once during the current school term (compared to as low as 17 percent for girls and 20 percent for boys in Sweden), with similar trends observed in 13- and 15-year-olds. However, when estimating whether they took part in bullying others, Russians scored in the middle range of the distribution for the sampled countries. For example, 39 percent of girls and 51 percent of boys among 11-year-olds said that they bullied others (compared to as high as 67 percent of girls and 78 percent of boys in Greenland and as low as 11 percent and 19 percent respectively in Wales). As in cases of child abuse, criteria for what bullying means in different cultural contexts are often not well defined and hence caution should be taken to not overgeneralize these findings. According to a study by Andriushina (2000), only 14 percent of Russian students report serious problems affecting relations with classmates.

In addition, relatively few Russian boys and girls (50 to 60 percent, almost the lowest percentage of all 24 countries) find it "easy" or "very easy" to make new friends (King et al. 1996). Quite remarkably, however, Russian boys and girls report spending more time with friends than youth from most other countries. About 15 to 20 percent of Russian girls and boys among 11-year-olds and almost one-quarter of 13- and 15-year-olds reported spending 5 to 7 evenings per week with friends away from home.

Furthermore, quite a high percentage of Russian adolescents (70 to 80 percent) said they had 2 or more close friends, a percentage not very different from other sampled countries. It should be noted that the definition of "a close friend" might differ from country to country. In Russia, friendship is traditionally considered to be a very significant relationship that is strongly valued. Perhaps Russian adolescents set higher standards for friendship than their peers from other countries. This would explain why they do not think it is easy to make and have friends. These findings are not surprising given the collectivist structure of schools in Russia today, as described above.

A growing individualist tendency in interpersonal relations has been documented by Ol'shanskii, Klimova, and Volzhskaia (2000). This study compared how school students in 1982 and 1997 completed the following statement: "In order to be liked by someone else it is necessary to...." The significance of being attractive has increased dramatically. At the same time, the percentage of answers emphasizing moral qualities ("be good, a faithful friend," "be a person who is honest," "love and respect people," and so forth) declined. There was a 1.5-fold increase in orientations toward oneself ("To be on my own") and more than a twofold decline in orientations toward a partner ("To love and respect him/her").

Romantic love has always been highly appreciated and regarded as a precondition to marriage and to sexual intimacy by a majority of Russian young people. Recent surveys reveal continuity in this attitude (Curtis 1996). However, there are differences among various population groups. Young male Russians, especially in larger cities, tend to take a more liberal outlook on premarital sex than any other part of the population. Attitudes toward commitment to a long-term relationship and toward premarital sex are becoming more liberal. For example, in a 1993 survey, the percentage of those disapproving of premarital sex was substantially lower than it had been in previous years (Curtis 1996).

As to dynamics of sexual behavior in Russian young people, one study reports that an increasing percentage have first sexual contacts at an earlier age now than just a few years ago (Sobkin & Kuznetsova 1998). For example, in a self-report anonymous study of 370 adolescents in Russia (17-year-olds) 20 percent of females and 31 percent of males reported having had sexual intercourse (Lunin et al. 1995). However, according to the 1997 Dovonex Sex Survey (see Akopyan, Kharchenko, & Mishiev 1999), the mean age when adolescents started sexual life in 1997 was older in Russia than in many other parts of the world – 18.2 in Russia compared to 15.8 in the United States and 16.2 in Canada and Germany. Given some contradictory trends in findings across studies, more research is warranted before broad conclusions can be reached.

In any case, some Russian youth no doubt are sexually active, as indicated by the birth and abortion rates in young girls. According to some estimates, in 1995 there were 3,100 births to women younger than 16 (i.e., approximately 7 per 10,000 population) and 53,600 births

to women younger than 18 (Akopyan et al. 1999). Furthermore, the rate
of abortions in women before the age of 19 constitutes 126–136 per 1000
births (Grigorenko 1997). One should bear in mind that women in Russia
get married very early and that the abortion policy is extremely liberal
in this country. High abortion rates in young women also reflect the fact
that until recently, birth control measures and "safe sex education" were
practiced much less in Russia compared to Western countries. One optimistic sign is that the abortion rate has been falling since 1993 in both
the general population and among adolescents (Akopyan et al. 1999).

As to homosexuality in adolescents, there is very little empirical research on this issue. Traditionally, Russian society was quite intolerant
of this form of sexual behavior, and in Soviet times it was regarded as
a crime punishable by years of incarceration (not the case anymore).
However, in recent years there has been more discussion of this issue in
the media, which might be a precursor of an attitude change toward
more tolerance. Hundreds of gay rights organizations already exist in
Russia, mostly in big cities such as Moscow and St. Petersburg.

Changes in the Experience of Schooling

At the beginning of the 1997–98 school year there were 21.7 million
school students in Russia (aged 6–17). The pre-reform schooling system
in Russia was an ideological monolith. Since then, control of schools and
their ideological function has changed dramatically, and there is much
more freedom in schools. Radical educational reform actually started
in 1988. From 1988 to 1990, there was a vast public discussion about
the direction of reform. Draft legislation appeared in 1990, emphasizing individuality and abandoning the goal of molding the individual to achieve a communist society, which had underpinned Soviet
education.

However, with many negative aspects of the Russian education system gone, some positive aspects and even advantages have also disappeared. It was free for everyone at all levels, provided good conditions
for students and teachers, and instilled incentives for high academic
achievement. Now, starved of government funding, Russia's education
system is experiencing uncommon difficulties. Schools and universities
sometimes charge student fees. First, a brief overview of how this system is organized and structured will be provided, and then the dynamic
in adolescents' schooling experiences will be addressed.

The system of general education and vocational training in Russia traditionally – and even today – embraces the whole young generation: it is compulsory and still, in most cases, free. However, whereas the 1977 Soviet Constitution declared mandatory school lasting 10 years, the 1993 Russian Constitution reduced mandatory schooling to 9 years, which resulted in decreasing education levels. General school education now includes 4 years of primary school (grades 1–4, ages 6–9), and 7 years of secondary school (up to age 16). Secondary school is further divided into incomplete secondary school (grades 5–9) and complete secondary school (grades 10 and 11). After completing the first 9 compulsory years at school, students receive a certificate of "incomplete secondary education" (now also called basic education). After that, about half of students stay at the same school for another 3 years and upon graduation receive a certificate of a "complete general secondary education" (Konstantinovskij & Khokhlushkina 1998). Upon completing the first 9 years at school, some students enter vocational schools. These are typically students who have not passed the exams at the end of the 9th grade.

There are 2 main types of vocational schools: technical schools (industrial, transport, building trades) and specialized schools (medical, pedagogical, cultural etc., see Podolskij 1994). Most of these schools provide students with an equivalent of complete secondary general education and are documented by a "certificate of a complete secondary specialized education." Both types of certificates allow the students to proceed with higher learning, that is, to enter so-called higher schools – universities or institutes (equivalent to colleges in the United States) – or to continue vocational training in specialized vocational colleges. However, the certificate of a complete specialized secondary education also allows students to begin working careers as middle-level employees (e.g., technical staff, nurses, day-care teachers). After secondary vocational schools, only one-fifth continue higher education (Rubina & Sleptsov 1990).

At the university level, along with approximately 570 state universities there exist now up to 400 commercial ones. These commercial institutions are typically very small; less than 10 percent of all university-level students are studying in them. Most of these institutes typically offer only a few specializations – mostly economics, law, and management. State universities are now also allowed to charge students who did not pass the entrance exams but want to get an education.

As in many other areas, a typical trend in education over the past decade has been a decline of standards, followed by a return to previous levels and often growth thereafter. For example, a smaller percentage of students stayed in general secondary schools to receive complete general secondary education in 1993–94 (41 percent) than in 1982–83 (57 percent). The percentage of students receiving basic education (i.e., a total of 8 years) also dropped in the early 1990s compared with the previous decade (only 85.5 percent in 1993–94 compared with almost 100 percent before reforms). According to some estimates, this trend resulted in some 1.5 million children and youth who did not either study at school or work in the mid-90s. Many of them belonged to families that had been displaced due to ethnic conflicts (e.g., in Chechnya) or who had to emigrate to Russia from the former Soviet republics where the Russian population often had become an unwelcome minority (Konstantinovskij & Khokhlushkina 1998). Over the same period, applications for university admission fell and enrollment decreased from 190 per 10,000 to 178 (Aleshyonok, Chuprov, & Zubok 1995).

However, after a remarkable decline in 1992–94, most of these indicators stabilized by 1995 and then began increasing (Konstantinovskij & Khokhlushkina 1998). In addition, the percentage of those entering higher education after general secondary schools increased from 15.5 in 1975 to 25 in 1985 and to 33 in 1997. The total percentage of those graduating from secondary schools who immediately began further education at higher schools or higher vocational colleges grew from 31 percent in 1975 to 50 percent in 1995 to more than 60 percent in 1996 and 65 percent in 1997 (see Konstantinovskij & Khokhlushkina 1998). The total share of students who continued education after secondary schools was 75 percent in early 1990s, but it increased thereafter and now stays at around 80 percent.

The study by King and colleagues (1996) showed that Russian adolescents seem to like their schools less than adolescents from other European countries. Russian teenagers also show the lowest scores when estimating how much their teachers encourage them to express their own views in class. According to the same study, Russian students' perception of their school achievement is very low, especially in 11- and 13-year-olds. Finally, Russian students think their parents expect too much of them in terms of academic achievement. Whether these are indications of real processes or a reflection of some response bias is difficult to discern. However, findings from other studies seem to contradict these patterns in that, for example, Russian students were shown to have higher levels of self-efficacy within the achievement domain than their peers from many other European countries (Stetsenko et al. 1995; Little et al. 1995).

As to the educational and employment expectations of Russian youth, a survey of secondary school students conducted in 1991–1994 (Dmitrieva 1996) revealed that the Soviet-inspired perceptions of education still persisted, including (i) high value of education in itself, (ii) the use of education as cultural capital, and (iii) the desire to postpone adult life through continued education. In the earlier period (i.e., in 1991–93) women tended to link education with employment opportunities less frequently than their male counterparts. However, by 1994, both women and men increasingly referred to the necessity of education for attaining a good job.

Thus, it appears that one of the trends characteristic of today's young people in Russia is the growing demand for higher education (see also Shuvalova 1997). This does not mean that these young people think that education automatically provides them with all the prerequisites for a successful life. For example, one poll conducted among Russian youth (aged 20–25) shows that about 60 percent feel that their education did not prepare them for good careers (Komozin 1990).

Trends in Adolescent Employment

Very few adolescents in Russia combine school with regular work. The conventional wisdom in Russian society is that working long hours undermines teenagers' education and overall development. A representative poll conducted in 1997, including respondents ($N = 3,839$) from 139 cities and villages of 56 regions in Russia, showed that adolescents seem to follow this conventional wisdom. When asked whether they work in order to earn money, two-thirds of Russian 17-year-olds said no, 10 percent said they worked seasonally (e.g., in summer when school is in recess), 14 percent indicated that they worked occasionally, and less than 6 percent said they worked several times a month or more frequently (Rouchkin 1997).

These numbers are in agreement with the fact that approximately 80 percent of all adolescents continue to study after they graduate from all types of secondary schools (which is now close to 100 percent in this age group) into their 20s. Among the 20 percent who do not continue studies, most of the boys at the age of 18 are recruited for a mandatory 2-year service in the army. Some adolescents spend a year at home waiting for another chance to enter the desired higher institution, and the remaining young people enter the job market to occupy typically unskilled positions. The latter are unlikely to face unemployment because the demand for such positions (e.g., in construction work) exceeds the supply. Paradoxically, the more educated young people are, the more likely they are to face unemployment (Chernysh 1994), especially in so-called humanitarian professions such as librarians, historians, or museum workers. At the same time, the demand for school teachers is very high.

Indeed, many adolescents seem to be concerned about their future employment. For example, the same poll (Rouchkin 1997) shows that 27 percent of 17-year-olds fear unemployment very much, 43 percent fear it somewhat, and only 23 percent are not concerned at all (see similar findings in Rutkevich 1994). These fears are certainly not unfounded, especially in some regions of the country such as parts of the Far East and certain rural areas that are more economically depressed and generally more impoverished than the rest of the country. However, the market is so dynamic, especially in the last couple of years, that many young people are able to find jobs. The heightened fear of unemployment among young people perhaps reflects, at least in part, the overall shock of a society that in several past generations did not know unemployment and is only now learning how to react to it.

Findings of a 1995 study of value orientations among 1,796 students in Novosibirsk, Kirov, Ivanov, and Stavropol (all large industrial cities in Russia) show that most prestigious and popular forms of employment among young people include business, commerce, and finance; related educational spheres are management, law, and accounting (see Tavokin 1996).

In general, the transition from school to work still appears to be rather smooth for the majority of young people in Russia. Given that unemployment in the general population is not very high (about 9 percent) and that young people often have skills much needed in today's emerging market economy (i.e., commerce, management, computers), younger people are typically less likely to face difficulties finding jobs than older generations (some even speak about age bias in today's hiring practices). Many adolescents are now more than ever before motivated to postpone their employment until after they finish rather prolonged education (Chernysh 1994), and most young people do not work while they are attending school. There is also an obvious shift in interests toward market-oriented careers.

Adolescents' Political, Community, and Civic Engagement

Until the Gorbachev era, the social activity in Russia was under strong governmental and ideological control from the Communist Party. Liberalization of the cultural and political spheres during *perestrojka* and in the post-Soviet period has not been followed by a comparable diversification of civic activities and institutions (Apresian & Guseinov 1996). Although the number of nongovernmental organizations has increased recently, no substitute has emerged to the former communist youth organizations such as Komsomol and Pioneers, and there are generally few incentives for young people to participate in political and civic structures. Not surprisingly, in a 1993 survey of 1,037 young people, only 15 percent said they were politically interested, while 27 percent said they were not interested at all (Ilyinsky 1994).

A nationwide survey examined political orientations of 1,897 young people, aged 16–29 (Aleshyonok 1997). Over 50 percent saw no opportunities to make an impact on the life of their communities; only 10 percent trusted political parties and movements; 16 percent trusted the Parliament, and 22 percent trusted the government. Similarly, a 1996 survey of 700 students (aged 15–17) in a typical small Russian town revealed a complete absence of youth organizations, with the school being the center of social activism. Less than 1 percent of youth participated in political parties. More than half of all participants of this poll were not members of any organization. However, 13 percent said they would like to participate in some ecological organization, and about one-half said they would like to take part in saving a local lake (Aleshyonok 1997). Young people's concerns seem to lie mostly in the areas of sports, health, culture, and local environmental issues. A study that compared environmental awareness in German and Russian adolescents found that the willingness to engage in environmental behavior was at similarly high levels in both groups (Szagun & Pavlov 1995).

Thus, it appears that the disintegration of Soviet-era political and social institutions (e.g., the Komsomol) led to a situation in which young Russians tend to become increasingly more nihilistic and apolitical, at least with regard to the old Soviet types of activities (Genin, Vishnevskiy, & Korableva 1997). In addition, the tradition of volunteer work is very weak in Russia because people used to believe that the government and state should take care of the needy. Such forms of social activism will likely appear in the near future given the growing gap between the rich and the poor as well as the lack of societal support for the latter.

Intergroup tolerance is a relatively new issue in Russia, and reliable trends are difficult to establish. In a large study by the Youth Institute conducted in 1997 (Rouchkin 1997), only 14 percent of Russian youth said their own nationality was very important to them; nearly half said it was of little or no importance at all. At the same time, in a survey conducted in 1992, 33 percent of adolescents expressed verbally some hostility toward individuals of a different nationality (Zavrazhin & Khartanovich 1993). According to yet another study, approximately 33 percent of young people (aged 14–18) identify themselves with humankind as a whole and not with a particular nationality (Chuprov & Zubok 1998). One study claims that today's youth show greater intolerance for relations between ethnic and religious groups than before, with a rise in anti-Muslim sentiment especially stemming from the war in Chechnya (Gajnutdin 1997).

One clearly discernible trend in Russia today is the rise of religious faith. Formerly, religious faith was uncommon among youth; now, about two-thirds of 16- and 17-year-olds describe themselves as believers. Those who are educated tend to be less religious, and nontraditional forms of religion are most popular among them. Only 3 percent describe themselves as absolute atheists. However, only a small percentage of believers report attending church regularly (Mchedlov et al. 1994).

Social Services for Youth

In 1992, the State Committee on Youth Policy was organized (Grigorenko 1997). This Committee is responsible for providing services to young people and for monitoring the situation in this population group. In 1996, the social services included 2,048 organizations for support of families, children, and adolescents (compared to 107 in 1994). The number of social-rehabilitation centers as well as shelters and refuges for children and adolescents has also increased. In total, slightly more than 2 million adolescents received some form of social support in 1996. Despite these increases, according to estimates, only 10 to 15 percent of families, women, and children who needed social support actually received services. However, the state has not withdrawn from providing services for adolescents, focusing mostly, as before, on sports and arts. There are also many summer programs for youth, for example, summer camps for which parents often pay from their own pockets (although some employers still provide benefits to their workers such as free summer facilities for children and adolescents). All the financial troubles notwithstanding, the motivated youth can still find some forms of state support for the development of their talents, especially in sports (during the last Olympics, Russian athletes performed extremely well, reaching 2nd place in terms of medals).

Trends in Mental and Physical Health

First we turn to tobacco smoking and alcohol drinking in adolescence, which are arguably the 2 most serious and widespread health risk behaviors in Russian youth. Most studies find that a large percentage of adolescents in Russia smoke. As much as 20 percent of boys and 10 percent of girls age 15 smoke at least once a week (WHO Report 2000). The average age when adolescents begin to smoke has decreased recently to 11.3 years for boys and 13.5 for girls (Akopyan et al. 1999). Cigarette smoking of the general population in Russia increased by 30 percent between 1995 and 1997. Much more effort should be made to tackle this problem.

Historically, alcohol has been a major problem in Russia, dating to the time of the czars. As bad as the situation is today, it was far worse just 5 years ago. The stress of economic reforms, combined with the end of the government monopoly on alcohol, triggered a huge increase in drinking. Reports indicate that over 60 percent of Russian young people have tried alcohol. However, the highest level of alcohol addiction among adolescents was recorded in 1988 – 25.5 per 100,000 compared to 10.5 in 1996 (Akopyan et al. 1999).

There are indications that drug consumption in adolescence has increased quite dramatically in recent years (the rise is especially pronounced compared to the virtual absence of this problem in Soviet times). For example, diagnosed as drug addicted and receiving treatment were 431 adolescents in 1992 and 5,000 in 1996 (Akopyan et al. 1999; Gabiani 1990). In a 1996 survey of 1,577 young people in 14 Russian cities, some 1.4 percent of respondents reported using drugs frequently and 10 percent occasionally (Lisovskiy 1997). The stereotypical perception is that the main drug abusers are middle-class and rich youths with time and money on their hands, but it has not been supported by reliable empirical evidence. Because parents of today's adolescents in Russia grew up under the restrictive Soviet regime, they have never experienced a youth revolution of the 1960s and '70s with its infamous tolerance of drugs (unlike baby-boomers in Western countries). Hence most parents never tried any drugs at all and are extremely opposed to even light experimentation with drugs. That is why there is a hope that after experiencing a debilitating shock from facing a completely new phenomenon of drug consumption in youth, Russian society will develop some protective measures against such practices.

There has been little research done on eating disorders in Russian adolescents. However, it is likely that their rates are not lower than in other industrialized countries. As their peers do in many other countries, Russian young women aspire to have a thin physique. This is not a new development: Being thin was associated with being beautiful already in the Soviet era. The perception that being beautiful guarantees success in life is perhaps even stronger in Russian young girls with their traditional gender role ideology than in their more emancipated Western peers. The significance of this problem appears to be underestimated by Russian society, and prevention efforts are clearly lacking. Support for this assumption comes from the study by King and coauthors (1996), according to which one-quarter of 11-year-old, one-third of 13-year-old and almost half of 15-year-old girls in Russia want to lose weight or are on a diet (well-known precursors of eating disorders). These levels are roughly comparable to those in other industrialized countries.

Russian officials say the first AIDS case appeared in Russia in 1987. Many infected men at that time reported contracting the infection from sex with other men, and only 2 cases were reported among injecting drug users. Although the absolute prevalence of HIV infection in Russia is still lower than in many Western countries, its growth has become alarming in recent years. The bulk of the spread has been in injecting drug users. Among 15–17-year-olds there have been 1 to 3 cases of HIV infection per year from 1990 to 1995, but in 1996, 131 cases were registered (Sobkin & Kuznetsova 1998).

There has been a dramatic increase in other sexually transmitted diseases such as syphilis (Akopyan et al. 1999). Tuberculosis is also becoming a problem, unlike previous decades. The incidence is growing, especially among the male imprisoned population, but also (although less rapidly) in other groups such as girls 15 to 19 years of age (from 21.9 per 100,000 in 1991 to 29.5 in 1996; see Akopyan et al. 1999).

Although free medical care is guaranteed by the Russian Constitution, this goal is not achieved in full due to low funding. In practice this means that patients often need to pay for expensive drugs, and access to treatment that includes sophisticated modern equipment is often limited to those living in big cities or those able to cover the costs of such treatment at least in part. However, the ratio of medical doctors to the population is still one of the highest in Europe and is on the rise. Also, screening for infections and other diseases as well as rates of vaccination (provided free) are still very high in Russia.

All the difficulties in the health care system in Russia notwithstanding, some indications are positive. For example, infant and maternity mortality rates are decreasing. The mortality rate in children aged 0–14 also shows a downward trend and, in addition, there has been a steady decline in the incidence of many infectious diseases (e.g., of the respiratory system) in both children and adolescents (Akopyan et al. 1999). Finally, as mentioned before, life expectancy grew in the late 1990s after some dramatic declines in early '90s. Generally, according to experts, most of the negative health trends in Russia are linked to unhealthy practices of drinking and smoking that are especially typical of the adult male population (WHO Report 2000). That is why it is critically important to raise awareness in young Russians about the risks that such practices entail.

Adolescent Culture

Already in the 1970s and especially since democratic reforms started in mid-80s, a new youth culture emerged in Russia that took up the non-conformist dress, music, and antiestablishment stance of young people in the West. The Beatles have been an icon for several generations of young people in Russia, and having American blue jeans was often the most cherished dream, at least since the 1970s. The social and economic stresses and disappointments of the 1990s have strengthened this trend, pushing many young Russians completely out of traditional societal institutions. Many young people are divided into *tusovki*, mutually exclusive social circles, for example, those of football fans or hippies and "hard-metal" rock fans, which provide a sense of identity to their members (cf. Curtis 1996).

There is a growing number of media outlets specifically targeting Russian youth – TV programs, newspapers, and magazines. Most of the new media are commercial and West-oriented, and they often copy existing European and American models (e.g., fashion magazines). Their impact is ever growing, especially given that more and more young people now travel abroad on various exchange programs. The Hollywood movie industry is also enjoying enormous success in Russia, although this success is sometimes undermined by piracy practices that are quite prolific in this country. A study by Arzhakova (1999) that examined changes in young people's aspirations and life strategies from 1985 to 1995 shows that upper-grade students in Russia and Ukraine, with rare exceptions, admire and self-identify with people from the domain of Western, mainly American, mass culture. At the same time, a lot of local rock bands and movie stars have emerged and some tendency to get back to their own culture perhaps can be also noticed in the last few years (cf. similar trends of growing nationalism and patriotism reported in China).

As to computers, in Moscow 33 percent of school students have a computer at home. The number is clearly smaller in other parts of the country because Moscow, as a capital, is often far ahead of the rest of the country in terms of standards of living and technical progress. In small provincial cities such as Orel and Mtsensk, about 20 percent of students have computers at home. Interestingly, families are more likely to buy a computer for their sons than daughters (37 percent versus 12 percent, respectively; see Iasnaia & Magun 1999). A similar tendency has been observed in other countries such as Switzerland. The rates of computer sales in Russia are now among the highest in the world, and this country is regarded as one of the biggest markets by big firms such as Intel and Microsoft.

Perceptions of the Future

Russian adolescents appear to be quite pragmatic and materialistic in their future orientations. For example, according to a study by Nurmi and colleagues (1999), Russian adolescents tend to emphasize earning a lot of money and becoming famous and important in their profession as part of their future relatively more than their western European peers do. One possible explanation is that the introduction of the market economy has created a new type of dream according to which being rich is a high priority. Paramonova (1997) found further evidence for this when she explored the dynamics of moral consciousness among 9,000 university and high school students, young workers, and engineers in Russia, drawing on 1980–1995 survey data. She concluded that in recent years the "communitarist" orientation (i.e., values of collectivism, societal good, and work) has decreased, whereas orientation toward material possessions has increased (for similar findings, see Sibirev 1997).

Adolescents in Russia report less well-being than their Western peers but do not differ from other eastern European countries (Grob et al. 1999). At the same time, Russians self-attribute a higher degree of control over their future, and fewer of them feel helpless compared to their peers from other countries (Grob & Flammer 1999; see similar findings in King et al. 1996).

Interesting data come from a large representative self-report survey of Russian 17-year-olds, conducted in 1997. Half of this sample said they viewed their future with hope and optimism; only 15 percent expressed anxiety and uncertainty about their future (Rouchkin 1997). According to another study, whereas in 1992, 20 percent of young people looked into the future with anxiety, fear, and despair, this percentage dropped to 15 in 1995, to 9 in 1996 and, finally, to just 3 in 1997 (see Kolesnikov 1997).

Kassinove and Sukhodolsky (1995) found that both Russian and American youth (aged 10–28) had generally optimistic views about the future: The Americans were more optimistic about their personal future, whereas the Russians were generally more optimistic about geopolitical questions. Russians reported less faith that their leaders would be working to solve their problems than did Americans. However, on some items, Russians showed more hope than their U.S. peers. For example, they scored higher on questions regarding whether the life of their children is likely to be better compared to their own and on the belief that their problems can be solved.

Conclusions

Young Russians do not appear to be either in a desperate socioeconomical situation or demoralized and disoriented. Most of them are quite self-confident, feel in control of their own lives, are full of optimism, have big plans for the future, and are, to a great extent, motivated to make the best out of their lives. They are also quite critical of the societal structures that they have inherited from previous generations as well as of their proximal environment (e.g., schools). They want higher material standards of life than their parents had, but at the same time, many seem to still strongly appreciate romantic love and traditional family values. They are quite apolitical and do not put much trust in government. This is hardly surprising given the painful self-scrutiny that Russia has been going through since the reforms began. Some statistical data indicate that there is an increase in drug consumption and tobacco smoking as well as in the rates of sexually transmitted diseases in the young people of Russia. However, these changes are by no means unexpected, given that the country went through a transition period when much of the old state controls and ideological presses have been dismantled, whereas new, more democratic "safety valves" of a civic society have not yet emerged. What is unexpected and surprising is that the changes taking place in Russian youth so far do not seem to be as seismic as one could have expected. For example, one of the trends is the growing value that Russian boys and girls ascribe to education. This is expressed both in direct assessments of how important they think education is and in the growing number of students who delay their employment and aspire instead for the best educational paths extending beyond general secondary education. Doing well at school academically and being well-educated overall was and remains a high priority for Russian young people. Young Russians also appear to be quite flexible in that many of them seem to have embraced an entirely new set of rules for economic success, while Russia's older generations seem to be much less able to adapt to the post-Soviet world.

Loathing the young generation and yearning for lost traditions is as Russian as *kvas*.[1] However, when avoiding traps of the existing stereotypes and looking at the empirical research and statistical data instead, it appears that things are not as gloomy as one might have guessed by extrapolating from the sheer magnitude of changes taking place in the Russian society. Those in Russia who are yearning for a uniform ideology to inspire the whole of society have to realize that Russia has already become diversified, pluralistic, and free enough not to agree upon or even need such ideology. The older generation perhaps can also learn from the younger ones how not to get trapped in feelings of doom and gloom (i.e., when any even inevitable problem of a transition period is perceived as the end of the world) and how to be generally optimistic. The findings of a 1996 comprehensive survey of 1,577 young people in 14 Russian cities are quite indicative in this respect as they show that 78 percent of young Russians see themselves as a "generation of hope" – the generation that can bring fulfillment of hopes and make dreams come true (see Lisovskiy 1997).

There are some alarming trends in that young people are becoming more and more materialistic, more focused on making money as a priority goal in life, and thus generally falling into the traps of a consumption society. It is equally alarming that girls in Russia seem to adhere more and more to a very traditional gender role ideology that is not beneficial to their own future or the future of their country. However, there are no data to suggest that this shift in gender ideology is as strong in actual behavior of Russian girls as it is in their verbal assessments. Young Russian women appear to strive, as they did during the last 80 years, for both careers and families. Whether and how well they succeed in that is a question that will define the outlook for the Russian society in general.

Of course, the real dangers for adolescents in Russia may well lie ahead in the near future, when and if big portions of the Russian society get stratified into very rich and very poor with an insurmountable gap between them and little hope for those from the lower strata to move ahead. The danger can also lie in that over-indulgent practices will become more and more a priority in youth's system of values, as this has already happened in some other societies. As William Damon wrote in his 1995 book *Greater Expectations*, the "cult of self-esteem" and over-indulgent practices are responsible for the lower educational and moral standards that children are confronted with in the United States. According to Damon (1995), in order to thrive, children and teens need more challenges and responsibilities. This is certainly the case with Russian adolescents today. They have plenty of challenges and still very little chance for over-indulgent practices (e.g., it is practically unheard of for adolescents in Russia to have expensive things – such as TV sets, let alone cars – at their own disposal) and, as it appears, it is also they who face the great responsibility of restoring and developing further the Russian society.

The overall conclusion is that, indeed, Russian adolescents appear to be different from their peers of just a decade or two ago, and much of this change can clearly be attributed to the profound changes taking place in the society that these adolescents are entering into and learning to deal with. On the other hand, perhaps the most recent positive changes taking place in Russia can be accounted for by the fact that more and more young people (born into and brought up in the newly democratic Russia) are now entering the job market and politics. This reminds us (as mentioned right at the beginning of this chapter) how profoundly social the very phenomenon of adolescence is and how strong the links are between adolescence and the society they help to create.

Notes

1. A refreshing drink without alcohol similar to Coca-Cola.

References

Akopyan, A. S., V. I. Kharchenko, & V. G. Mishiev. 1999. *Sostojanie zdorovja i smertnosti detej i vzroslih reproduktivnogo vozrasta v sovremennoj Rossii* [*Health and mortality of children and adults of the reproductive age in contemporary Russia*]. Moscow: Supplement to the Statistical Issues.

Aleshyonok, S. V. 1997. Uchastie molodezhi v protsessah prinjatija politicheskih reshenij [Youth's participation in the process of making political decisions]. In *Molodezh 1997: Nadezhdi i razocharovanija* [*Youth 1997: Hopes and disillusionments*], ed. B. Rouchkin, 91–96. Moscow: Research Center at the Institute of Youth Policy Press.

Aleshyonok, S. V., V. Chuprov., & J. Zubok. 1995. Integrationsprobleme Jugendlicher in Russland. [Problems of youth's integration in Russia]. *Diskurs* [Discourse]. 5:48–54.

Andriushina, E. V. 2000. The family and the adolescent's health. *Russian Education and Society.* 42 (4):61–87.

Apresian, R. G. & A. A. Guseinov. 1996. Demokratiya i grazhdanstvo [Democracy and citizenship]. *Voprosy Filosofii.* 50:3–16.

Arzhakova, Iu. S. 1999. The objects of upper-grade students' admiration and identification. *Russian Education and Society.* 41(11):87–92.

Attwood, L. 1996a. The post-Soviet woman in the move to the market. In *Women in Russia and Ukraine*, ed. R. Marsh, 255–269. Cambridge: Cambridge University Press.

Attwood, L. 1996b. Young people's attitudes towards sex roles and sexuality. In *Gender, generation and identity in contemporary Russia*, ed. H. Pilkington, 132–151. London: Routledge.

Baraulina, T. & A. Khanzin. 1996. Gender differences in the life strategies of Russian youth. In *Women's voices in Russia today*, eds. A. Rotkirch and E. Haavio-Mannila, 107–123. Aldershot, England: Dartmouth.

Berrien, F. B., G. Aprelkov, T. Ivanova, & V. Zhmurov. 1995. Child abuse prevalence in Russian urban populations: A preliminary report. *Child Abuse and Neglect.* 19:261–264.

Bronfenbrenner, U. 1970a. *Two worlds of childhood: U.S. and U.S.S.R.* New York: Russell Sage Foundation.

Bronfenbrenner, U. 1970b. Reaction to social pressure from adults versus peers among Soviet day school and boarding school pupils in the perspective of an American sample. *Journal of Personality and Social Psychology.* 15:179–189.

Chernysh, M. F. 1994. Changing values: Russian youth in transition. In *Values in post-Soviet youth: The problem of transition*, ed. L. Tomasi, 161–176. Milan, Italy: Franco Angeli.

Chuprov, V. I. & J. A. Zubok. 1998. Russian youth on its way to world integration: Trends and problems. International Sociological Association (ISA). Association paper.

Curtis, G. E., ed. 1996. Russia. A country study published by Federal Research Division, Library of Congress (online). Available: http://lcweb2.loc.gov/frd/cs/rutoc.html

Damon, W. 1995. *Greater expectations: Overcoming the culture of indulgence in our homes and schools.* New York: Free Press.

Dmitrieva, E. 1996. Orientations, re-orientations or disorientations? Expectations of the future among Russian school-leavers. In *Gender, generation and identity in contemporary Russia*, ed. H. Pilkington, 75–91. London: Routledge.

Expert Group Meeting on below-replacement fertility. 1998. Future expectations. Report published by the Population Division of the United Nations (online). Available: http://www.undp.org/popin/wdtrends/p98/fp98.htm

Gabiani, A. A. 1990. Narkotiki s srede uchashcheysya molodezhi [Drugs in students' milieu]. *Sotsiologicheskie Issledovaniya [Sociological Studies]*. 17:84–91.

Gajnutdin, R. 1997. Parita di diritti e dialogo tra le religioni. Le istanze del mondo musulmano [The Parity of rights and dialogue between religions. The case of the Muslim world]. *Religioni e Società* [Religion and Society]. 12:35–45.

Genin, L.V., V. Y. Vishnevskiy, & G. B. Korableva. 1997. Kadrovyi potentsial raboty s molodyozh'yu [Cadre's potential for work with youth]. *Sotsiologicheskie Issledovaniya [Sociological Studies]*. 24: 10:87–92.

Grigorenko, S. A. 1997. Polozhenije molodezhi i gosudarstvennaja molodezhnaja politika [Youth and the state youth policy]. In *Molodezh 1997: Nadezhdi i razocharovanija [Youth 1997: Hopes and disillusionments]*, ed. B. Rouchkin, 46–52. Moscow: Research Center at the Institute of Youth Policy Press.

Grob, A. & A. Flammer. 1999. Macrosocial context and adolescents' perceived control. In *The adolescent experience. European and American adolescents in the 1990s*, eds. F. Alsaker & A. Flammer, 99–113. Mahwah, NJ: Lawrence Erlbaum.

Grob, A., A. Stetsenko, C. Sabatier, L. Botcheva, & P. Macek. 1999. A crossnational model of subjective well-being in adolescence. In *The adolescent experience. European and American adolescents in the 1990s*, eds. F. Alsaker & A. Flammer, 115–130. Mahwah, NJ: Lawrence Erlbaum.

Hauer, J. 2000. Class teachers in Russia: Personalizing moral education. Paper presented for the Association for Moral Education 2000 Conference, July 2000. Glasgow, Scotland.

Human Rights Watch. 1994. Women's rights project. Discrimination against women in Russia, (online). Available: www.carnegie.org/reports/great_transitions/gr_exec.html#intro

Iasnaia, L. V. & V. S. Magun. 1999. The parental home and its influence on the aspirations and life strategies of young men and women. *Russian Education and Society*. 41:(11):43–64.

Ilyinsky, I. 1994. Jugend in Russland. [Youth in Russia]. *Berliner Journal für Soziologie*. 4:513–522.

Jose, P. E., C. D'Anna, & L. Cafasso. 1998. Stress and coping among Russian and American early adolescents. *Developmental Psychology*. 34:757–69.

Karelova, G. N., ed. 1997. *O polozhenii detej v Rossijskoj Federatsii. Gosudarstvennij doklad [To the situation of children in Russian Federation. The State Report]*. Moscow: Sinergija.

Kassinove, H. & D. G. Sukhodolsky. 1995. Optimism, pessimism and worry in Russian and American children and adolescents. *Journal of Social Behavior and Personality*. 10:157–168.

King, A., B. Wold, C. Tudor-Smith, & Y. Harel. 1996. The health of youth: A cross-national survey. *WHO Regional Publications*. European Series No. 69.

Köbberling, A. 1997. *Das Klischee der Sowjetfrau. Stereotyp and Selbstverständnis Moskauer Frauen zwischen Stalinära und Perestrojka* [*The cliché of the Soviet woman. Stereotype and self-representation of Moscovite women between the Stalin era and perestrojka*]. Frankfurt/New York: Campus Verlag.

Kolesnikov, Ju. S. 1997. Stanovlenije rinochnikh standartov povedenija studentov [Development of market-oriented forms of students' behavior]. In *Molodezh 1997: Nadezhdi i razocharovanija* [*Youth 1997: Hopes and disillusionments*], ed. B. Rouchkin, 176–183. Moscow: Research Center at the Institute of Youth Policy Press.

Komozin, A. N. 1990. Trudovaya kar'era s pozitsii zhiznennoga tsikla [Work career in terms of life cycle]. *Sotsiologicheskie Issledovaniya* [*Sociological Studies*]. 17:3–11.

Kon, I. S. 1979. *Psihologija junosheskogo vozrasta* [Psychology of adolescence]. Moscow: Prosveshenije.

Konstantinovskij, D. L., & F. A. Khokhlushkina. 1998. Formirovanije sotsialnogo povedenija molodezhi v sfere obrazovanija. [The formation of the youth's social patterns of behavior in the domain of education]. *Sotsiologicheskije Issledovanija* [*Sociological Studies*]. 3/4:17–28.

Kotovskaia, M. & N. Shalygina. 1996. Love, sex and marriage: The female mirror. Value orientations of young women in Russia. In *Gender, generation and identity in contemporary Russia*, ed. H. Pilkington, 121–131. London: Routledge.

Lisovskiy, V. T. 1997. Molodyozh Rossii: Dinamika sotsial'nykh izmeneniy (sotsiologicheskoe issledovanie) [Russia's youth: Dynamics of social changes (sociological study)]. *Vestnik Sankt Peterburgskogo Universiteta* [News from St. Petersburg University]. 1:57–62.

Little, T. D., G. Oettingen, A., Stetsenko & P. B. Baltes. 1995. Children's action-control beliefs and school performance: How do American children compare with German and Russian children? *Journal of Personality and Social Psychology*. 69:686–700.

Lunin, I., T. L. Hall, J. S. Mandel, & J. Kay. 1995. Adolescent sexuality in Saint Petersburg, Russia. *AIDS*. 9:(1):53–60.

Mchedlov, M. P., A. A. Nurullaev, E. G. Filimonov, & E. S. Albakian. 1994. Religya v zerkale obshcchestvennogo mneniya [Religion in the mirror of public opinion]. *Sotsiologicheskie Issledovaniya* [*Sociological Studies*]. 21:9–13.

Murcott, A. & A. Feltham. 1996. Beliefs about reproductive health: Young Russian women talking. In *Gender, generation and identity in contemporary Russia*, ed. H. Pilkington, 152–168. London: Routledge.

Nurmi, J. E., A. Liiceanu, & H. Liberska. 1999. Future-oriented interests. In *The adolescent experience. European and American adolescents in the 1990s*, eds. F. Alsaker & A. Flammer, 85–98. Mahwah, NJ: Lawrence Erlbaum.

Ol'shanskii, V. B., S. G. Klimova, & N. Iu. Volzhskaia. 2000. School students in a changing society (1982–1997). *Russian Education and Society*. 42:(4): 44–60.

Paramonova, S. 1997. Tipy moral'nogo soznaniya molodyozhi [Types of youth's moral consciousness]. *Sotsiologicheskie Issledovaniya* [*Sociological Studies*]. 24:69–78.

Pfaff, W. 1998. A plutocrats' lull in Moscow, but better times can come. *International Herald Tribune*. March 30.

Pilkington, H. 1996. 'Youth culture' in contemporary Russia: Gender, consumption and identity. In *Gender, generation and identity in contemporary Russia*, ed. H. Pilkington, 189–215. London: Routledge.

Podolskij, A. I. (1994). Russia. In *International handbook of adolescence*, ed. K. Hurrelmann, 332–346. Westport, CT: Greenwood Press.

Rouchkin, B. A. 1997. Molodezh in stanovlenije novoj Rossii [Youth and the emergence of a new Russia]. In *Molodezh 1997: Nadezhdi i razocharovanija [Youth 1997: Hopes and disillusionments]*, ed. B. A. Rouchkin, 16–30. Moscow: Research Center at the Institute of Youth Policy Press.

Rotkirch, A. 1998. Mothers, daughters and marriages. The influence of mothers and mothers-in-law on married and love life in Russian and Finnish autobiographies. International Sociological Association (ISA). Association paper.

Rubina L. & N. Sleptsov, eds. 1990. *Sotsialnij portret molodezhi [Social portrait of youth]*. Moscow: Politizdat.

Rutkevich, M. N. 1994. Sotsial'naya orientatsiya vypusknikov osnovnoy shkoly [Social orientation of high school graduates]. *Sotsiologicheskie Issledovaniya [Sociological Studies]*. 21:30–43.

Saliev, R. Z. 1997. Ideologiya i tsennostnye orientatsii molodyozhi [Ideology and value orientation of youth]. *Sotsiologicheskie Issledovaniya [Sociological Studies]*. 24:24–30.

Shuvalova, V. S. 1997. Tsennost obrazovanija i tsennosti v obrazovanii [Value of education and values in education]. In *Molodezh 1997: Nadezhdi i razocharovanija [Youth 1997: Hopes and disillusionments]*, ed. B. Rouchkin. Moscow: Research Center at the Institute of Youth Policy Press.

Sibirev, V. A. 1997. Izmenenie sotsialnykh tsennostey molodyozhi. Opyt sravnitel'nogo analiza [Change in social values of young people. Comparative analysis]. *Vestnik Sankt-Peterburgskogo Universiteta [News from St. Petersburg University]*. 2:51–57.

Sobkin, V. S. & N. I. Kuznetsova. 1998. *Russian adolescent in the 90-ties: Movement into a risk zone*. Moscow: Unesco.

Stetsenko, A., T. Little, G. Oettingen, & P. B. Baltes. 1995. Control, agency and means-ends beliefs about school performance in Moscow children: How similar are they to beliefs of Western children? *Developmental Psychology*. 31:285–299.

Szagun, G., V. Pavlov. 1995. Environmental awareness: A comparative study of German and Russian adolescents. *Youth and Society*. 27:93–112.

Tavokin, E. P. 1996. Vtorichnaya zanyatost' uchascheysya molodyozhi: Mnenie ekspertov. [Secondary occupation among students: Experts' opinions]. *Sotsiologicheskie Issledovaniya [Sociological Studies]*. 23:92–96.

World Health Organization Report. 2000. Highlights on health in the Russian Federation (online). Available: www.who.dk/country/ruso1.pdf

Zavrazhin, S. A. & K. V. Khartanovich. 1993. Novoe pokolenie na periferii: Konformisty ili devianty? [The new generation on the periphery: Conformists or deviants?]. *Sotsiologicheskie Issledovaniya [Sociological Studies]*. 20:55–57.

9

Adolescents in Latin America

Facing the Future with Skepticism

Carlos Welti

According to a recent survey (United Nations International Children's Emergency Fund 2000; UNICEF), children and adolescents of Latin America think that they will have a better future compared to that of their parents, but at the same time they think that their countries will be a worse place to live. An important proportion of them does not have confidence in government institutions. The most frequent source of concern is violence and insecurity. The daily experiences of these youths reflect some of the problems and situations affecting the whole society, especially the younger generations.

This chapter describes some of the most relevant characteristics of the adolescent population in Latin America, with the aim of anticipating certain issues that adolescents could face in the 21st century. I will try to give an overview of their living conditions and behavior related to various aspects of social life in a relatively short text. Contrary to what one would like to do, the present text is a pessimistic vision of the youth in this region of the world. It is difficult to be optimistic if one knows in detail what the living conditions of the children, adolescents, and young adults are and what they can expect of their future.

Given that there is a lack of recent information on adolescents for most of the countries of this region of the world, I have used information from census or survey data for some countries representing the whole range of situations one can find in Latin America. The chapter focuses on individuals between 15 and 19 years of age. Because one could say that adolescence in Latin America begins at an earlier age and continues after the age of 20, I will also frequently refer to the 10–14-year-old and 20–25-year-old age groups.

Although adolescence has been a research issue in the United States since the beginning of the 20th century (specifically with the publication of *Adolescence* by G. Stanley Hall in 1904), in Latin America this population has been a concern of social scientists only since the 1960s and only with regard to a limited set of issues: sexual behavior, the incidence of early pregnancy, drug addiction, and violence. Even now, especially among the poor in Latin America and in other parts of the developing world, the structure of individual opportunities seems to eliminate this stage of life. For example, it is difficult to think of adolescence as a meaningful concept among indigenous people, or that its meaning is equivalent in rural and urban areas. In some social groups, young people get married at a very young age or take on the role of head of household at puberty. In these groups, one moves directly from childhood into adulthood.

The motivation to study Latin American adolescence comes from 2 specific situations: its continued growth in demographic terms (both in absolute numbers and in its relative share of the population among different age groups), and in terms of increased unemployment among this age group. The growth of adolescence is the product of a decrease in fertility and an increase in life expectancy, making it evident as an intermediate phase between childhood and adulthood. The reduction in relative participation of youth in economic activity in the modern sector of the economy and the increase in unemployment makes adolescence stand out at the end of the 20th century in this region, which doesn't happen in societies in which youth become part of the labor force at a very young age.

Background

Social Changes in Latin America and Its Youth

Today's adolescents were born in the first half of the 1980s or later. Because of this, we can assume that their behavior in adulthood and their living conditions in the next century will be affected by events in the last 2 decades of the 20th century. At a worldwide level and in political terms, the most relevant events that have affected Latin American youth in the last 2 decades have been related to the end of the cold war, the fall of the Berlin Wall, and the dismantling of the Soviet Union, which for some authors has meant the end of ideologies (Fukuyama 1992). In Latin America, these events have resulted in the loss of a model for society.

This model had an impact on youth behavior in previous decades. For many youths, this model or paradigm was the socialist world, and the closest example was Cuba.

This was reflected, for example, in clothing styles, characterized by the use of clothes previously worn only by workers or indigenous people, or in political actions to transform social structures. The model for youth in the '60s was the Cuban revolution and Che Guevara. A clear example of a political movement led by youth in the recent past is the "1968 movement" in Mexico (but also in Europe). In the following years, this segment of the population has participated in very few political movements.

In the last 2 decades, as it is described below, the Latin American regional economy has had its most significant crisis in modern history. This economic crisis seems to be a permanent state for societies of the region, so much so that, unlike their parents, today's young people have lived through this crisis for their entire lives.

Latin America has become an urban society in which the population has practically universal access to information through the media, such as radio and TV, which connects small towns with the world. Adolescents living in the smallest towns of a country find out about the accidental death of Princess Diana the same day it occurs. They watch wars live on TV, and many of them copy the clothing styles of popular singers or learn songs in other languages, even if they don't understand them.

The most recent communication revolution, e-mail, is now a common means of communication among urban, middle- and upper-class adolescents. In previous generations (such as that of the parents of today's adolescents) the first question a boy asked a girl he was interested in was: "Do you study or do you work?" The required question for today's adolescents is: "Do you have e-mail?"

A central hypothesis to begin with is that understanding the attitudes of parents, the family, and adults in general is essential to understanding adolescents. The world of adolescents has been built by adults, and youth behavior is best understood by starting with the attitudes and practices of adults. Adolescents are influenced by the world through 4 different means: family, school, the media, and their peers. It is obvious that 3 of these means are dominated by adults.

Although the Latin American situation cannot be considered entirely homogenous, since certain countries of the region have quite different situations from others (in terms of language, proportion of indigenous population, level of economic development, and political regime), certain common characteristics exist that allow us to speak of Latin American youth as a whole. This youthful population has a common history consisting of a combination of an indigenous past and immigration from Europe. Up until the generation of their parents, Europe had a strong influence on Latin American culture; this has now been replaced by a North American influence.

A series of social processes that directly affects adolescents characterizes these last 2 decades in Latin America. Each of the following represents a paradox:

A) The "sex revolution" increases the risk of unwanted pregnancies and sexually transmitted diseases, while the generalized use of modern contraceptives reduces these risks to a large extent. Quantitative information shows that sexual intercourse now begins at earlier ages. However, the attitudes of younger women appear to be increasingly conservative regarding premarital sex.

B) Life expectancy has increased in recent years, but at the same time, accidents and violence among youth have increased to such a degree that they have become the more significant causes of death among this age group.

C) The incorporation of youth in higher levels of education, especially the female population, contrasts with increasing unemployment in this age group. This creates a paradox in Latin American societies because the universities are now producing unemployed youth with higher levels of education.

D) Regarding health, the last few decades have produced a reduction in infectious diseases and other health problems, particularly those affecting children. At the same time, diseases such as AIDS have emerged, which affect the youth population. In other words, although youth are better able to survive childhood, they now face new health risks in adolescence.

E) In politics, democratic forms of government have replaced authoritarian political regimes. At the same time, youth participation in political parties is little or none. Thus, apathy characterizes the political attitudes of today's adolescents.

The social change that has taken place in the region in the last decades is also reflected in the role that religion plays in the lives of adolescents. One needs to recognize that religion is the core of traditional culture in Latin America, but at the same time one needs to identify the political function of religious institutions in the region. Religion helps to account for the political stability of the national states for many years.

Even before the Conquest, the pre-Columbian empires used religion to support their authority and power. It is difficult to understand the long duration of regimes such as Somoza's in Nicaragua or Pinochet's in Chile without the support of the Catholic Church. Conservative Catholics and Evangelicals supported the dictatorial or military regimes because of their opposition to Marxism. Perhaps this explains why religious institutions and the Catholic Church hierarchy were seen as enemies by the young generations who participated in political movements against the status quo. Nevertheless, many students were attracted to liberation theology; they saw the central thesis of the *church of the poor* as an alternative to social change in the region.

It is possible to say that the political influence of religion has diminished among adolescents for 3 reasons: the process of secularization; the position of the church against some issues that adolescents accept because they see them as natural, such as sexual relations outside marriage; and the growth of religions different from Catholicism. There are deep divisions between Catholics and Evangelicals. Some of the most important conflicts between religious groups are located in the southeast of Mexico and in Central America. There is a lack of recent data on religious ascription for the population in Latin America, but it is clear that most of the population is Catholic. However, in the last few years, Protestantism, especially in the Evangelical or Pentecostal tradition, has made spectacular advances. According to census data for Mexico in the year 2000, 88 percent of 15–24-year-olds are Catholic; 5 percent are Protestant, and the rest declare other or no religion (Instituto Nacional de Estadistica Geografia e Informatica 2000b; INEGI).

Luengo (1993, 1996) considers that there is an abandonment of religious practices among adolescents. They reject religious institutions because they perceive them to be far from the problems of daily life; they believe that the religious hierarchy represents the old regimes and legitimizes a social order based in exploitation. All this does not necessarily mean that religious beliefs are devaluated, but one cannot say that religion has an important influence in the lives of adolescents. No religion accepts sexual relations outside marriage (a common practice among adolescents), and most of the religions are against the modern methods of contraception and abortion. This is the case in a region where, according to data from the most recent Demographic and Health Surveys (DHS), more than 50 percent of married women use these methods and a majority of women have had an abortion.

The major religious systems in the region are against the practice of concubinage, but there is a significant percentage of youth living together. The Roman Catholic Code of Canon Law regards marriage as indissoluble, but the proportion of marriages that end in divorce is increasing, and adolescents, with very few exceptions, accept divorce and separation (according to data from the World Values Survey, see for example, Diez and Inglehart 1994).

Perhaps the most important role that religion plays for youth has to do with peer socialization. Many adolescents identify with peers with whom they attend private, religiously sponsored schools; those who attend religious services interact with peers while they go to hear Mass on Sundays.

Demographics

At the beginning of this century, individuals between 10 and 24 years of age represent about 30 percent of the region's population, or about 152 million people. The proportion ranges from 21 percent in Cuba up to almost 34 percent in Guatemala (which has retained a large youth population despite losses during the civil war).

The 15–19-year-old group represents only 10 percent, or 51 million people. This population will increase every year until the year 2030. However, a reduction in the region's birth rate means that there will be fewer young people in the future. According to most recent population projections, the maximum number of youth between 15 and 24 years of age in Latin America will be 161 million in the year 2030 (Centro Latinoamericano y Caribeño de Demografía 1998; CELADE).[1] A reduction in the growth rate of the youth population and its lowering in absolute numbers will make for a "demographic bonus" that will be reflected in a decreasing demand for educational services and jobs, which should improve both educational levels and the employment rate of this population.

Another relevant demographic issue is increased life expectancy. In the year 2000 an individual lived, on average, 10 years more than 30 years ago. The Latin American population has increased its survival rate to such an extent that the region's average life expectancy is 73 years old for women and 67 years old for men, with differences between countries of up to 18 years if we compare Haiti (60.2) with Costa Rica (78.3) (CELADE 1998). This increase means that, independent of any other social situation, each stage of the life cycle is chronologically increased. When life expectancy was no more than 50 years (which was true in some Latin American countries in the second half of the 20th century), adolescence was not evident because adult roles had to be taken on at an early age.

A comparison of the average number of years a young person can expect to live at 15 or 20 years of age in each of the region's countries shows that, upon leaving adolescence, a Guatemalan or Haitian young person will live an average of 10 years less than a Costa Rican or Cuban young person. This shows the differential chances of survival due to health conditions originated in childhood, access to health services and, especially, violence.

There is also a significant sex difference in life expectancy, favoring females by almost 5 years. This relates to the higher level of mortality of males due to violence and accidents (Pan American Health Organization 1998; PAHO) and reflects the roles men should play in society. Men should be brave, fight against other men, and play risky games or, in other words, behave like "machos."

Economic Conditions
After a period of sustained economic growth in Latin America between 1950 and 1980, an economic crisis occurred of such magnitude that the decade of 1980 to 1990 has been called "the lost decade." In 1981, the rate of national product growth in the region declined, which hadn't occurred in the last 40 years. With the exception of the Brazilian economy, per capita income went down so much that in 1985 it was 9 percent less than in 1980. Exchange prices for regional products fell, and interest payments on the foreign debt increased. The evolutionary trends showed negative economic activity, accompanied by a significant increase in open unemployment rates and various kinds of subemployment, especially in what we call "the informal sector."[2] The negative social effects of this crisis were noticed most clearly in the drop in salary rates. In the 5-year period between 1980 and 1985, real salaries were reduced in Mexico by 27 percent and in Peru by 43 percent (Comisión Económica para América Latina y el Caribe 1986; CEPAL).[3]

The crisis not only affected living conditions of the population at the moment it began, but it has affected possibilities for improving future living conditions of new generations, especially the youth population at the beginning of the century. Economic adjustment measures have included trade liberalization, an attempt to balance the budget through fiscal discipline, price increases for public services and goods, privatization of government companies, and deregulation of the financial and labor sectors. These economic adjustment measures, taken on by national governments to reduce the fiscal deficit, have affected social spending in the areas of education and health, public job creation, and deregulation of the labor market, which has meant a change in labor laws to eliminate job stability and increase temporary employment. All of these economic policy measures affect the general population, but they have especially affected the lives of young people.

At the end of the 20th century, although Latin America had achieved success in extending school to large sectors of the population, the number of adolescents that did not have access to high school or higher education had grown. It is possible to say that up until the 1970s almost all secondary school students had a chance to be enrolled in high school and later in universities, most of them public universities, without paying tuition. In recent years, the proportion of students admitted to universities has decreased, and the majority of students cannot pay the tuition in private or even in public universities.

Family Relations

Changes in family life and family relations in Latin America have varied among social groups and social settings. There are common features, however, that can explain how these changes influence adolescence. As stated by Salles and Tuirán (1997), in Latin America the family no longer can be characterized as a productive unit. Even in rural areas, the process of economic modernization and globalization has eroded its economic function. Patriarchal power has diminished while individuation has grown, which means greater autonomy among family members. Also, sexual activity is not necessarily confined to married partners.

Perhaps one of the most relevant changes in the family, which is generated through a combination of demographic and economic factors, is that 3 successive generations (children, parents, and grandparents) live together in a significant proportion of households. It is clear that despite socioeconomic and political differences there are family conditions that are common to many young people in most of the countries in the region. Leaving home, living with a partner, and forming a family are some of the most important stages that mark the passing of adolescence into adulthood. Latin American youth today stay at home with their parents longer than before. This is due to more years spent studying and the difficulty of finding a paid job that meets their aspirations.

The family plays a decisive role in the development and personality of its members, especially the youngest ones. It is a source of affection – though at times also of tensions and conflicts – and of socialization. It is a setting wherein living conditions and opportunities for its members are established, and wherein role models, knowledge, and basic values for living are provided. In the family, attitudes, motivations, and expectations are formed to deal with various aspects of life. Material conditions for existence are also provided for its members. From infancy through adolescence, sociodemographic and economic characteristics of the family environment affect both available opportunities for young people as well as the likelihood that youth will take advantage of them.

Most adolescents of the region live at home with their families. Unlike what is common in developed countries, Latin American youth don't tend to become independent from their parents until they get married. Young people increasingly continue to live at home with their parents, and the reasons are mainly economic. Faced with the difficulty of finding permanent employment, and because of the acute shortage of houses for rent, the economically rational decision for an adolescent or young adult is to continue living with parents.

When young people from rural towns migrate to the cities to work or study, they tend to live alone or in households in which the members do not form a family. Generally, a group of young people from the same town who move to the city to work will rent an apartment together to share living costs. But unlike what happens in other countries, where young people live in student zones, young Latin American students or workers usually live on the outskirts of cities in neighborhoods without public services or in the most rundown parts of the city, where the rents are lowest.

Youth are present in 52.4 percent of Mexican households. One out of every 4 households in the country (25.5 percent) has just 1 young person among its members; 1 of every 6 (17.0 percent) has 2 young people, and 10 percent have 3 or more young people.

According to recent information (INEGI 1995), most young people in Mexico live at home with their families. Two of every 3 young people between 15 and 24 years of age live at home with their parents. But also, 1 of every 6 young people (16.7 percent) has already established his or her own household and is head of household or wife of the head of household. An additional 13 percent live in a household whose head is someone other than their parents (grandparents, aunts or uncles, parents-in-law). One of every 6 young people (16.2 percent) lives in a single-parent household. Research has shown that these households are usually in a position of socioeconomic disadvantage compared with those in which both parents are present, and most are headed by women. In 10 percent of all Mexican households, there is at least 1 young person, the head of household is the mother, and the father is not present. In only 2.1 percent of households does one find an adolescent living with just the father present. A very small percentage of young people (less than 1 percent) live alone or live in households as domestic employees.

As we can expect, younger adolescents are more likely to live at home with their parents; the large majority only leave home when they marry. Men stay at home with their parents longer than women. Men who live in rural areas, even though they marry younger than their urban counterparts, stay at their parents' homes after getting married and bring their wives to live with them there. Young women who live in the cities stay home with their parents longer than young women in rural areas, which is explained by the fact that young women from the cities get married later than in rural areas, and once they have married, they form a new household. The number of households made up exclusively of women or of groups of young women who are not related is practically zero. We can assume that the difficulty in finding jobs and housing, and the fact that married couples have fewer children, will mean that in this century, youth will stay home with their parents longer, even after 30 years of age. This has become an increasingly important phenomenon in Latin America.

The mean age for getting married in Latin America is around 20. No significant differences exist between the region's countries, although in countries with a large proportion of indigenous population, such as Guatemala, the mean age for first marriage is younger.

In each country, large differences can be observed in age at 1st marriage depending on educational level. According to fertility surveys, it is estimated that 30 percent of women with 6 years of education or more were married before the age of 20, but this percentage grows to more than 60 percent among women with less than 6 years of education (Singh & Samara 1996). The increasing levels of education and employment among women do not seem to have affected the median age at which women marry.

One of the most significant changes regarding adolescent marriage is in the type of marriage. Among youth who marry, common-law marriages (or couples "living together") are increasing. In the case of Mexico, of the total female population of married adolescents between 15 and 19 years of age in 1970, 74 percent were legally married and 26 percent were in a common-law marriage. In 1990, the percentages were 63 percent and 37 percent, respectively, and in 2000, 48.5 percent and 51.5 percent.

However, the percentage of adolescent women never married is larger (78 percent in 1970 and 88 percent in 2000) (data from the IX, XI, and XII Census of Population). Therefore, there is no way of knowing whether this trend of an increasing percentage of common-law marriages will continue because, contrary to what has been expected (at least in Mexico), the younger generation increasingly considers marriage to be the only acceptable way of living as a couple (Encuesta Nacional de Planificación Familiar 1995; ENPF, Consejo Nacional de Poblacion; 1995 CONAPO). At the moment, we can assume that for a large portion of the region's adolescent women, especially those who reside in urban areas, the role of wife and mother is no longer the only role that defines her future. This is not the case in rural areas, where the most important roles she must take on are that of wife and mother, beginning at adolescence. The ENPF reveals that for women under 20 years of age who reside in urban areas, "what is most important for a woman" is to study and work in order to be independent. For women in rural areas, it is important to get married. Having children is least important for 15–19-year-old women in urban areas.

In the past, when women turned 15 years of age it was an important social event, celebrated with a party in which the family presented the new adult to society to announce that she was prepared for marriage and motherhood. The tradition of celebrating a woman's 15th birthday continues among certain social groups, especially in rural areas and among lower-class city residents. In rural Latin America, a woman who is not married by the age of 20 is considered to have few possibilities of getting married. If she is still single at 25, it is considered that if her family does not have economic resources (making her a candidate for a convenience marriage) she will remain single indefinitely (the popular expression used in Mexico is that "she will stay back and dress the saints").

Urban/rural differences in marriage rates are not quite as dramatic as one might imagine, however. Almost 20 percent of women between 15 and 19 years of age in rural areas are or have been married, compared with 13.5 percent of women in this age range in urban areas. Among women aged 20–24, the figures are 58 percent and 46 percent. Whereas a large majority of men between 15 and 19 years of age are still single in similar percentages in rural and urban areas, important differences appear for 20–24-year-old men. In the case of Mexico, 2 of every 5 young people between the ages of 20 and 24 who reside in rural areas have been married, whereas for youth of this age in the cities, 1 of every 3 (32.7 percent) is or has been married.

The differences observed in age of 1st marriage for youth in rural and urban environments reflect the greater opportunities in life offered to youth of both sexes residing in urban areas. Urban youth also have different perspectives on life, as well as a wider range of possibilities for personal growth as alternatives to marriage and forming a family.

Peer Relations

Adolescence initiates a process in which individuals search for their own personality and a sense of identity. With this aim in mind, they look for independence. In this period of life, the most important role in the development of values and attitudes is played by peers. Friends, *cuates, carnales, chamos, manitos, patas* (all expressions without an exact English translation but equivalent to "brother" or "friend") influence the critical decisions made by youth in the region.

Interactions with Friends and Peer Groups
Youth in Latin America as in other parts of the world congregate in more or less recognized peer groups and engage in collective behavior. They provide referential parameters and behavioral codes. The neighborhood and the school are the major locations for meeting and making friends. Sometimes these 2 locations are practically the same, especially for youths from lower classes, because their schools are located in areas close to where they (and their friends) live. Youths of higher status attend private schools. Their network of friends is wider and includes more than their classmates, and it is likely that very few are from the same neighborhood. They make friends in social clubs, in resort areas, or in places where they spend the weekends.

Perhaps one characteristic of the peer groups in the region is that most of them are organized around recreational activities such as sports. It is difficult to find youth groups organized around civic or cultural activities. In the case of males, football (soccer) represents an element of identification among adolescents and young adults living in the cities. In rural areas, not only football but also baseball or basketball teams are the juvenile peer groups. But engaging in sports is not the only reason to organize a group. After or during the game, depending on whether one is a player or only a spectator, the consumption of alcohol constitutes

the main activity for many youths and one of the reasons to be part
of the group. Therefore, it is not difficult to understand the increase in
violence in massive spectacles in the region, especially in cases such as
the football matches in Argentina, where the *barras bravas* fight against
each other and solve their problems with guns and knives.

For some other male adolescents, *la banda* is a peer group in which
they are engaged in collective activities around music. Although one
finds these groups mainly in urban areas, music is also an important
recreational activity for rural adolescents and young adults who organize musical groups or dance parties. For girls the school is the main
location to make friends. Most of the time girls spend with friends is
in school. For those who are working, the only chance to make friends
is the workplace or the neighborhood. Almost all of them spend the
weekends doing domestic work and sometimes going to the movies or
to dance parties to see their girlfriends or boyfriends. All of the above
has to do with adolescents from lower social classes. Adolescents of
upper classes spend their time with friends in recreational clubs or in
shopping malls.

In the past, the places of socialization were the central *plazas* for youths
of all social classes. Today, the shopping malls are the places where
teenagers of middle or upper classes meet with friends, while the lower
classes do the same in public parks. As in other levels of social life this
reflects a new type of segmentation.

Another type of peer group is the gang. Whatever its name is –
pandilla, banda, mara, quadrilha, barra – these groups have an inherent
association with illegal and violent activities. Most gang members are
male, but in some cases it is possible to find that females are not only
members of a gang but also the leaders of the group. Although there are
gangs that originate in the wealthier neighborhoods of the cities, like
the *pitucos* in Lima (Rodgers 1999), the gangs proliferate in poor urban
areas. They replace institutions like the family or the school because
they give visibility to people who, outside the gang, would be invisible.

We have very limited data to know the ways adolescents spend their
time, but we know that they spend a significant part of their free time
with peers. According to the data of a recent survey carried out in Mexico
on adolescents and young adults (Instituto Mexicano de la Juventud
2000; IMJ), this population spent almost the same amount of time with
peers as watching TV or listening to music. However, if we take into
account the time dedicated to participating in team sports, adolescents
spend most of their time with friends.

Sexual and Reproductive Behavior

Until recent years, high rates of mortality in Latin America justified the fact that sexual intercourse was linked with procreation and marriage. Survival of the population had to be guaranteed through high fertility rates. The Catholic Church took charge of making this idea widespread. Although high fertility rates were maintained for centuries, the model of religious marriage encouraged by the church was not followed and, as mentioned earlier, common-law marriages in the region have always represented an important proportion of total marriages among adolescents and adults. However, what is important to Latin American society is not the type of marriage itself, but the fact that a person has a marriage partner. Traditionally, a young woman who was sexually active had to have a stable partner. Otherwise she faced societal criticism and dishonored her family if she became pregnant. This explains why, in fertility surveys, the age of the 1st sexual intercourse (about 18 years old, on average) has coincided with the age of the beginning of a formal marriage (Welti 2001).

The situation has now changed, and large numbers of adolescents today have had sexual intercourse at early ages without planning to marry. If we observe the percentage of women 20–24 and 25–29 who had 1st intercourse and 1st union before age 20, we find countries such as Brazil, El Salvador, and Guatemala where there have been no significant changes in initiation of sexual activity and age at 1st union; however, the younger generation in all countries has a lower percentage of married women before age 20. It is interesting to compare these figures with those from the United States because they show the different behavior of adolescents in this part of the world. For example in Mexico or Colombia less than 50 percent of women 20–24 had 1st intercourse before age 20, whereas in the United States this percentage is 75 percent (Wulf and Singh 1991).

Information on Mexico from the National Survey on Sexuality and Family shows that, at the end of the 1980s, slightly more than 50 percent of men and 23 percent of women had engaged in sexual relations by the age of 16, (Welti 1988). More-recent surveys carried out in the '90s showed increases in these percentages: At the age of 16, more than 35 percent of female Mexican adolescents said they had had sexual intercourse (CONAPO 1995). Various studies conducted in the region confirm that sexual experience begins earlier for male adolescents than for females.

People often presume that the age of 1st sexual relation is younger for each successive generation. However, in 1999 a national survey in

Mexico showed that at age 16 only 22 percent of men and 11 percent of women had experienced intercourse (Fundación Mexicana Para la Planeacion Familiar 2000; MEXFAM). Moreover, premarital sexual activity occurs within a context of conservative attitudes. In one survey (CONAPO 1995), when asked, "Do you think it is right for women to have sexual intercourse before marriage?" 3 out of 4 women aged 15–19 and two-thirds of the females aged 20–24 said "no."

This trend toward more conservative sexual attitudes and activity is important in the case of Latin America because a significant number of young women who have sexual intercourse become pregnant. Only 1 out of every 10 adolescents uses birth control, and it is estimated that only 30 percent used birth control the first time they had sex (Guzmán et al. 2001). Because of this, for women who are not protected by birth control, both sexual intercourse and procreation occur at early ages, as in past decades.

About 20 percent of women between 20 and 24 years of age became mothers during adolescence (CEPAL 1998). In most Latin American countries, this figure has changed little in recent years, but there was an increase during the 1990s in some nations. The most significant increase was in Colombia, where the difficult economic situation and increasing violence may have prompted youth to have children at young ages. Parenthood justified their existence in a world that offered very few opportunities. They felt that they were adults (they exist as persons) when they became parents, while facing the uncertainties of the future.[4]

The higher percentage of adolescent mothers in rural versus urban areas is explained by the fact that, as already mentioned, marriage and pregnancy are considered normal in rural towns. They are linked with a life plan in which motherhood is the most important role for a woman. In urban areas, pregnancy is seen as a transgression from the role expected of city youth, where they should be students or workers in modern sectors of the economy.

In census and survey data we see large differences in adolescent fertility by size of the town of residence or by educational level (CEPAL 1998). This shows the effect that social and economic conditions have on young people's reproductive behavior. In the case of Mexico, which can be generalized to most of the region's countries, 60 percent of women who did not attend school were mothers before the age of 20, 6 times more than women who attended high school (10 percent) (Welti 1995).

Age of 1st marriage is the variable that appears to be the most important in explaining the regional differences in fertility. Knowledge of birth control is practically universal, and its use, as mentioned, is limited. But its use is not likely to increase among the sexually active adolescent population because, as mentioned several times, motherhood is part of a life plan. Even among adolescents who claim that their pregnancy was "not planned," it really is a "wanted pregnancy." It is only when young people have life plans other than motherhood that we see the incidence of pregnancies reduced through birth control. Thus, it is clear that a change in adolescent fertility rates can be achieved by broadening young people's future expectations, and increasing their level of education can do this.

In recent years, research and knowledge about homosexual activity among adolescents is mostly related to the increase of HIV and AIDS. Therefore, it has been treated as a problem of public health and not as an issue of sexual preferences or sexual rights. This can be explained by a homophobic attitude in the society that makes it difficult to accept homosexual practices. The state and the church, historically, have viewed homosexuals with hostility and even more, under a criminal perspective if they have sex. In contrast to some other parts of the world, homosexual behavior is not expected to be publicly seen.

An adult homosexual (referred to as *joto, mariquita, mayate, marimacha,* or *tortillera*) faces discrimination within the family, neighborhood, and workplace, but homosexual adolescents are seen as individuals who need psychotherapy because of their deviant behavior. Still, they are rejected by their family and their friends. For the upper class, homosexuality is more socially accepted, but it is almost a tragedy for a family of the lower class if one of its members is homosexual. In many cases, the person has to leave the household, which may explain, in part, male prostitution among the poor. However, this does not mean that most of the male prostitutes come from poor families (Shifter 1998). Among male adolescents living in rural areas, or those who come to the city from a rural environment, the 1st sexual experience may be with a same-sex partner. However, they do not see it as a homosexual experience and therefore, as something that has to do with their sexual orientation. This is a matter of the availability of a sexual partner, especially in the case of young workers in the construction industry who live with other men in the same place where they are working.

Although things are changing, Latin America is a society of "macho men." Homophobia anywhere in the region is more or less the same.

Education

The school system is structurally divided into 2 separate networks – private and public – and comprises 3 levels: basic, which in some countries includes only the primary school (6 years) and in some others secondary school (3 years); post secondary (2 or 3 years); and university education. Basic education is mandatory and free to everyone for 6 or 9 years of study.

Latin America has made significant progress in the coverage of primary education. Access to this level of education is practically universal. In 1980, in Mexico, almost half (46.6 percent) of all young people had not finished primary school. Among today's youth, only around 13 percent have not completed their primary school education and 57 percent have a junior high school education. Adolescents and young adults in the region have completed an average of 2 years more of schooling than the generation of their parents, and each younger generation shows higher levels of education.

The increase in coverage of education contrasts with its quality, which has to do not only with the methods of teaching but also with the physical environment, the lack of equipment, and a poor school infrastructure. Classrooms are overcrowded in public schools located in urban areas. In many rural areas the teachers are absent from school for large periods of time during the school year because of the lack of supervision or the need for teachers to address administrative problems at the central offices of the Department or Ministry of Education. Many children and adolescents drop out the system prematurely because of the lack of attention in classrooms, the lack of teachers, or the lack of economic resources in the family.

Throughout Latin America there has been a sharp reduction in the gender gap in education. Although the percentage of illiteracy is greater among females in all countries, one of the main changes in Latin American society has been the significant increase in the proportion of women that have access to higher education. In some countries the number of women enrolled in universities is almost the same as the number of men (see Table 9.1). Curiously, the university dropout rate is greater among men. Because of falling incomes, greater pressure is placed on men, as heads of households, to bring home an income (Muñiz 1996).

TABLE 9.1. *Percentage Female Enrollment in Latin America and the Caribbean by Level of Education, 1980–1995*

Year	1st level	2nd level	3rd level
1980	49	50	43
1985	48	51	45
1990	49	52	47
1992	48	52	48
1993	48	52	49

Note: 1st level refers to primary school; 2nd level refers to secondary school, high school, teacher training, and schools of a vocational or technical nature; 3rd level refers to university training.
Source: UNESCO, *1995 Statistical Yearbook*.

In contrast to reductions in the gender gap, substantial differences in educational level still can be observed by social class, ethnic group, and place of residence. These underscore differential access not only to educational services but also to employment and health. Children and adolescents from lower-class families attend public schools, which are free or charge minimal tuition. But the quality of the education in many of these institutions is low. Children and adolescents from upper-class backgrounds attend private schools with bilingual classes and solid academic programs. Of course, in some countries very prestigious public universities are surrounded by many dubious private institutions, especially in Central America. Generally, however, the educational system in this part of the world is segmented by economic status.

Certain conditions characteristic of rural areas constrain young people's access to higher levels of education (CEPAL 2000). In addition, in urban areas almost half of students who enter secondary school fail to complete it, whereas in rural areas this proportion approaches 75 percent (CEPAL 2000). The proportion of youth who continue to attend school goes down rapidly with advancing age; this drop occurs earlier and more abruptly among rural area residents. By age 15, only half of men and 2 of every 5 women in rural areas continue to attend school, whereas in the cities more than 70 percent continue studying. At the age of 18, only 1 of every 6 rural men and women remains in school (Muñiz 1996. op. cit.). A disproportionate number of those who drop out are poor. Therefore, only a small proportion of rural, poor adolescents makes it all the way to the university.

One can assume that the dropout rate among adolescents will increase in the future for 2 reasons: young people's growing need to work and an increase in the cost of education. The economic difficulties in the region have led to a decline in government spending on social services, including education, and therefore to a reduction in the number of places for new students in public schools and universities. Furthermore, many young people need to work to supplement family income. Most of the youth work long hours, which interferes with their education. This is a more and more complex situation, because without completing secondary school a person who gets a job usually obtains a low salary. For economically disadvantaged families, this creates a vicious circle of poverty.

At the beginning of the chapter I mentioned that the educational system in Latin America is creating a new type of unemployed: youth with high levels of education but no job. This is due not only to the reduction in the demand of new workers but also to the lack of appropriate training. Although still limited in scope, a new model of both public and private technology institutes is growing. Perhaps this is the alternative for the population who demands higher education

Employment

To understand the employment situation for youth in Latin America, it is important to understand the distinction between the formal and informal economy. Most statistics are based on the formal economy, which includes enterprises with law regulated employer-employee relationships. However, a significant portion of youth and adults are involved in the informal economy, comprised of small businesses, unregulated industries, and illegal enterprises, many of which operate out of "the street." The International Labor Organization's (1998; ILO) most recent evaluation of employment in Latin America concluded that the labor force was growing faster than positions offered in the formal economy. Thus, most new jobs – about 8 out of every 9 – are located in the informal sector and feature low wages, no contracts, and no benefits (Tockman 1996). These jobs are in the service sector or in commerce, with many people working as street vendors. Youth participation in the informal sector is very significant.

Unemployment rates among youth are high throughout most of Latin America – generally, double the rate among adults. One recent survey (CEPAL 2000) indicated that approximately 20 percent of males and

TABLE 9.2. *Percentage of Adolescents and Young Adults (15–24) Who Do Not Have a Job and Do Not Attend School, by Area of Residence and Country*

Country	Year	Urban			Rural		
		Total	Men	Women	Total	Men	Women
Argentina (Buenos Aires)	1998	21.0	15.7	26.2	–	–	–
Bolivia	1997	10.8	4.2	16.9	9.4	1.8	17.2
Brazil	1997	20.2	12.3	27.7	17.5	5.9	30.5
Chile	1998	21.9	15.4	28.3	31.5	17.9	46.5
Colombia	1997	22.7	15.0	29.3	26.6	8.0	46.3
Costa Rica	1998	17.1	10.1	24.2	28.3	10.7	47.1
Dominican Republic	1997	20.5	12.4	27.3	25.7	10.8	42.1
Ecuador	1998	20.1	10.8	29.0	–	–	–
El Salvador	1998	22.0	13.9	29.4	33.3	12.7	53.9
Honduras	1998	22.6	11.4	32.3	33.9	6.3	64.3
Mexico	1996	24.0	13.2	34.9	31.4	8.1	52.8
Nicaragua	1997	24.5	17.3	31.2	–	–	–
Panama	1998	21.3	15.4	26.9	32.3	13.1	53.4
Paraguay (Asuncion)	1997	17.8	11.9	23.0	29.2	8.8	51.1
Uruguay	1998	20.7	15.7	25.8	–	–	–
Venezuela	1998	25.2	16.3	34.4	–	–	–

Source: CEPAL 2000.

over 30 percent of females aged 15–24 who resided in urban areas neither worked nor were attending school (i.e., were not involved in "productive activities"). The figures for rural females in this age group are even higher (over 40 percent in many countries), although there are significant variations from one nation to the next (see Table 9.2). Of course, a substantial portion of women who fit into this category are dedicated to domestic activities, which are not included as productive activities in the economic statistics (even though their activities are essential for the women's families and the society as a whole).

In urban areas of Latin America the majority of employed adolescents and young adults (aged 15–24) work in trades and services, but during the 1990s the manufacturing sector became a more important source of jobs for adolescents – at least for countries that have a substantial manufacturing sector. In Mexico, for example, the proportion of adolescent workers involved in manufacturing rose from 25 percent in 1992 to almost one-third in 1996. Honduras displayed a similar increase, from 23 percent of employed adolescents in 1990 to 34 percent in 1997 (ILO 1998).

Many positions in manufacturing, however, involve low wages and oppressive conditions. The *maquiladora* industry in Mexico and other nations in this region, for example, features some of the lowest salaries for export-oriented industries in the world (*La Jornada*, August 12, 1999). Traditionally, in this trade, a retailer contracts work with a jobber, who subcontracts to a small factory in which cutting and sewing are done. This industry, as well as computer and electronics firms, prefer to hire teenagers (especially young girls) because they tolerate the low wages and are less likely to complain about illegal or unjust working conditions.

It is very likely that many adolescents who have jobs began working well before adolescence. In the 1990s, official figures showed that an estimated 20 percent of children aged 6–14 were working (UNICEF 1992). However, this is probably an underestimate because it excludes a significant proportion of girls aged 10–14 from rural areas who work as domestic laborers in their own community or in large cities. There is a substantial negative correlation between educational attainment and employment during adolescence, although it is not clear that one of these variables necessarily causes the other. With few opportunities to accumulate human capital, young people in Latin America negotiate the transition from adolescence to adulthood in labor terms, getting involved in jobs with low wages that do not require high levels of formal education. Reaching adulthood with little human capital is a situation that is difficult to overcome in Latin America. There are no incentives for managers to promote training programs within their firms. The long hours required of many jobs leave workers with little time to seek training outside of their jobs. The educational system also shows little flexibility. All young people are expected to complete formal education by age 20; continuing one's education part-time or returning as an adult student is not encouraged. Young people who continue full time in school past age 20 find, upon graduation, that their odds of landing a good job are reduced; they are more likely to be offered a job featuring a short-term contract and low wages.

It is important to point out that most children and adolescents who begin their working career in the informal sector remain there. Several reasons help to account for this. First, as already mentioned, these workers have limited human capital (e.g., education and training). Second, at the societal level, wages in the formal sector are very low. Third, in some countries (such as Mexico), workers with the lowest wages still pay higher taxes than workers who earn the same wage in the United States. Thus, there is little incentive for workers in the informal sector to look for a low-wage job in the formal sector.

In the 1990s, the number of adolescents in Latin America who worked increased by a little more than one-third if we compare the figures with those from the 1980s (Diez de Medina 2001). This has an important impact on the future of this population because adolescents who work receive less income over the course of their entire working career than youths who delay working until young adulthood. To work during childhood or adolescence is not the ideal situation for anyone because of its later repercussions. It is part of a circle of poverty that traps young people and, later, their families, from one generation to the next.

There is an even more troublesome side to youth employment in the informal sector. In urban areas, each year there is a rise in the number of young women involved as sex workers. Many children and adolescents are victims of sexual exploitation, especially street children. According to recent estimates, there are more than 100,000 street children in Brazil, many of whom are dedicated to the sex business. In the Dominican Republic, more than 20,000 children under age 18 work in prostitution. There is considerable documentation of the sexual exploitation of children in most of the countries in this region (End Child Prostitution in Asian Tourism 1996; ECPAT).

This is not the only source of prostitution, however. In other cases, young migrants to the city find the level of salaries so low and the journey to work so long that many times the only way for them to survive is to accept jobs in small restaurants and coffee bars. Once there, they discover that the establishments are dedicated to the sex business.

In Latin America, unemployment and underemployment are major problems for youth. Although most countries have experienced a decline in fertility recently, there will still be a substantial number of young people looking for jobs in the near future because of the demographic inertia from the years of high population growth rates.

Health

Until recent decades the infant mortality rate in Latin America was so high that it was commonly said "death from disease is an issue for children and the elderly because the young don't get sick." The infant mortality rate in the region declined at an accelerated pace largely because of vaccination of children and the use of oral rehydration therapy in the treatment of gastroenteritis.

Adolescent health problems are related primarily to drug use and sexual activity. The region has a high prevalence rate of smoking among adolescents – over 50 percent in some countries. With the decrease of tobacco consumption among older people, adolescents have become bigger targets of tobacco companies.

Alcohol consumption is growing among adolescents of all social classes. In some countries in the region, more than 30 percent of children less than 12 years old have consumed alcohol. One of every 4 thinks that she or he has problems with alcohol or drug consumption (PAHO 2000). The biggest differential in alcohol consumption between adolescents from rural or urban areas, or between adolescents from low or upper social classes, is the quality of the alcohol they consume. Although it is possible to find alcoholic beverages produced nationally or even imported, much of the alcohol is produced locally. Many times it is the main product of the community and the political leader or *cacique* is the owner of the alcohol industry there. In some regions of Colombia, the alcohol producers are public enterprises whose profits are used to pay the teachers' salaries (this was the case of *Licorera del Cauca*). In the city, the alcohol industry promotes massive spectacles such as sporting events. Therefore, it is difficult to fight against alcohol consumption among adolescents when this is a very big business at the local and national level.

According to drug-use surveys conducted in the 1990s, cocaine use is increasing among adolescents (Jutkowits 1992; Consejo Nacional para el Control de los Estupefacientes 1996; CONACE, Secretaria de Salud 1998; SSA). Cocaine use is especially popular in the cities; in many dancing clubs it is relatively easy to find drug dealers. Actually, one of the main concerns is that drug trafficking and drug consumption are becoming common in both public and private secondary schools. The consequences of increasing addiction to expensive drugs are serious for adolescents. Many girls are forced into prostitution for survival. Boys become addicts through contact with drug dealers and then are forced to participate in the business or in some other illegal activities such as car theft. In the case of adolescents living in the streets, inhalant abuse, particularly glue-sniffing, is pandemic. Because of its low cost many adolescents who work on the streets washing car windows or shining shoes consume inhalants.

Actually, the main concern about adolescent health has to do with the increase of sexually transmitted diseases, especially HIV. Information on

HIV incidence among adolescents is difficult to obtain because official statistics are not organized by appropriate age groups. National studies carried out in some countries show that the high proportion of young people having unprotected sex is spreading the infection among this population. At least half of those infected with HIV are 24 years of age or younger (PAHO 1998). Perhaps more important is the feminization of the epidemic. An example of this situation is Colombia, where the sex ratio fell from 37:1 in 1987 to 3:1 in 1998 (PAHO 2001).

There has been a shift in causes of morbidity and mortality, caused not only by individual risk behaviors but also by social factors. Mortality among adolescents is mostly due to external causes. In recent years, external causes were responsible for more deaths among youth than infectious diseases, circulatory diseases, and cancer (Yunes 1993). Without diminishing the attention paid to sexually transmitted diseases it is important to pay special attention to violence and its consequences on the health of adolescents.

Finally, with regard to mental health, the economic crisis and the social pressure to find a place in school or to find a job, in addition to alcohol and drug consumption, have made adolescents very vulnerable to stressors that lead to mental instability. All this is reflected in the high incidence of depression and suicide. The suicide rates are increasing (PAHO 1998), and very few institutions are paying attention to this problem.

Violence

An increasingly important issue to consider in analyzing the region's adolescent population is violence. According to the Pan-American Health Organization (OPS 1996), North and South America (including the United States and Canada) constitute the most violent region in the world. However, the homicide rate in Latin America is more than double that of the United States. In Colombia, the homicide rate rose from 101 per 100,000 in 1985 to 267 per 100,000 in 1994 (PAHO 1998). Violence in the region has reached epidemic proportions; 29 percent of deaths due to homicides belong to adolescents. The highest mortality rates are among males aged 15–24 in Colombia, Puerto Rico, Venezuela, and Brazil.

Of course, not all violence is reflected in the statistics on homicides. Violent crimes such as those against property are growing, but the information about them is not reliable. An important proportion of the victims does not bother to report these crimes because they are rarely solved. In the worst cases, delinquents count on the complicity of police members.

The phenomenon of violence among adolescents is recognized as a critical social problem in the region. Thousands of adolescents have become victims or perpetrators of violence. It is now one of the main causes of death among Latin American adolescents, and it will be important to pay special attention to this situation in the future. However, the rise of violence among urban adolescents is seen almost as a natural phenomenon of a modern society and the media reflects and even glorifies this situation.

Recently, a new type of violence has made its debut in Latin America: violence in schools, where armed adolescents have killed classmates or teachers. It is possible that this violence has its roots in 2 interrelated situations: a) the availability of guns in the black market at affordable prices, and b) the glorification in the media of violent behaviors and the media coverage of school shootings in the United States. Of course, in the past, one could find young gangs dedicated to violent activities in public schools. Those known as *porras* were organized by principals of the schools to control the political activities of youths organized around Marxist ideologies. In the present, youth gangs in public schools are dedicated to criminal activities and deeply implicated in drug dealing.

Social conditions such as poverty, neighborhood environment, and family dysfunction have contributed to the growth of youth violence. In addition, violence is now recognized as a macroeconomic problem because it is originated and promoted by the drug business. Delinquent groups seek the participation of youth under the age of 18 because laws in practically all Latin American countries do not impose serious penalties on delinquent youth.

Also, the difficulty that youth have in finding work makes crime an attractive activity. According to information from adolescents themselves, criminal activity reportedly pays a monthly income that not even the best job will offer. When they are apprehended by the police, the maximum penalty youth receive is a few months in a reformatory, from which it is relatively easy to escape. For this reason, in countries where the legal age is 18, there are efforts to reduce it to 16.

Gangs dedicated to car theft find in youths the ideal workforce. This is a very lucrative activity for adolescents and young adults from all social classes, and youth gangs dedicated to this activity or to drug dealing are increasing.

It is important to add that in Latin America there is a type of violence that one does not find in the developed world: the violence of war, which not only affects but involves children and adolescents. This is the case in Colombia today and was true for Guatemala, El Salvador, and Nicaragua in past years. Currently, in Colombia, armed conflicts represent the main concern not only for adults but also for children and adolescents. The protagonists recruit children below the age of 15, often to serve as guides and informants (Human Rights Watch 1998; HRW). It has been estimated that more than 1,700 minors fill the ranks of the National Liberation Army (ELN) and the Revolutionary Armed Forces of Colombia (FARC) (International Press Service 1999; IPS).

Also, in Colombia, significant percentages of some paramilitary groups are composed of youths under 18. Organizations dedicated to the defense of civil rights have estimated that around 2,000 youth below 18 are recruited by paramilitary groups such as the United Self-Defense Forces of Colombia (Mandato Ciudadano por la Paz 1999). By 2001, it was estimated that more than 6,000 members of both the guerrillas and paramilitary groups were children (El País 2001). Child soldiers were also common in Guatamala and El Salvador. The general perception among Salvadorians was that during the civil war the armed forces recruited children. It has been estimated that almost 20 percent of the Farabundo Marti Liberation National Front (FMLN) combatants were adolescents (Horeman and Stolwijk 1998).

Political Participation

Latin American adolescents, as in other regions of the world, do not believe in political parties. This is not a new situation. Because of a formal situation related to the age at which they can vote (normally 18 years of age), adolescents do not participate in electoral politics, and young people who are over 18 participate in political processes only through their vote.

Large youth organizations, in which the individual only exists as part of the collective group, are no longer of interest to the young. Today's youth are not interested in being militants of an organization. Because of this, youth participation is expressed in small groups of activists from larger organizations, such as universities or neighborhoods. Even here, however, youth organizations are related to what is known in Mexico as *la banda* (the band of youth), which first came about to participate in social events, particularly massive events such as musical concerts. Formed by lower-class adolescents, these organizations have grown in big cities. Often, their activities are simply a reaction to governmental actions that prohibit massive events of adolescents, with the argument that large quantities of drugs are consumed at these events. Middle-class adolescents also participate politically in small groups organized around issues such as defending the environment.

However, what stands out most in terms of youths' political participation at the beginning of the 21st century is their interest in supporting indigenous movements and defending the public university. Public university students in capital cities of certain Latin American countries (Buenos Aires, Quito, Lima, Mexico City, Caracas, and Santiago) have led these actions. These movements have been organized against privatization of public services and against globalization. It is likely that, in the next few years, these 2 issues will define Latin American youths' political participation, which, until very recently, was characterized by apathy.

Conclusion

Adolescence is seen as a time to make a life plan, involving expectations for the future. In Latin America, however, difficulties in gaining access to higher education and a lack of employment opportunities for an ever-increasing proportion of adolescents make the creation of this life plan difficult and explain youth behavior associated with frustration. It is no exaggeration to state that the youth population in this region is a generation without hope for the future, and, for this reason, Latin American adolescents want to live intensely in the present without paying attention to the risks associated with their behavior. If they finish school, even if they graduate from university, most of them will not find a job. If they do find employment, it is likely to be in the informal sector, with a low salary and without social security.

In the past, Catholicism and religion in general had a significant influence on the lives of individuals on matters such as marriage and sexual behavior. This is no longer true, especially among adolescents and young adults.

Despite the huge generation gap within families, Latin American adolescents do not have much hope of leaving their parents' house, even when they finish university: The unavailability of housing and the lack of jobs explain why offspring stay with their parents even at age 30 or older.

Violence involving children and adolescents is a growing phenomenon in the region. The lives of young people are severely affected by violence in their communities and this increases their vulnerability and insecurity. In the last years, violence has reached epidemic proportions in the region, becoming one of the most serious public problems. There are structural causes behind this problem, such as poverty or unemployment, but it is difficult to argue that the crime problems would be solved if we solved the economic problems of Latin America. The lifestyle of adolescents, the perception of their future, and the emergence of drug use or drug trafficking are also root causes of the increase in violence.

To a large degree the future of Latin America depends on having increasing proportions of young adults well educated, healthy, and economically productive, which means paying special attention to children and adolescents in the present. Specifically, in the case of girls, the modernization of the region has meant new educational opportunities for them, but their social conditions have improved less than their level of education. It is necessary to give them opportunities to be something in life in addition to childbearers or domestic laborers. If this is possible, some other things in the society will change.

A society that does not pay attention to its youth has no future. We should invest in children and adolescents as the only way to protect our generation and the younger generations from problems associated with social instability.

Notes

1. CELADE is the Spanish acronym of Centro Latinoamericano de Demografía. This is the Population Division of the Economic Commission for Latin America and the Caribbean.
2. The informal economic activity (IEA) has been defined as economic activity that escaped state regulatory control. Therefore, noncompliance of the established rules means that most of the time the workers receives low salaries and no social benefits.
3. CEPAL: Economic Commission for Latin America and the Caribbean.
4. The author of this chapter had the opportunity to interview adolescent single mothers in the cities of Bogota, Cali, and Popayan in Colombia in 1997 and 1998. For the majority of them, having a child means their lives have been

successful, since "there is a lack of men because they are killed by violence, so having a child is a blessing from God, even if the father is not present."

References

Centro Latinoamericano de Demografía (CELADE). 1998. Tablas de mortalidad. Santiago de Chile.

Comisión económica para América Latina y el Caribe/Economic Commission for Latin America and the Caribbean (CEPAL). 1985. *La juventud en América Latina y el Caribe.* Estudios e informes de la comisión económica para América Latina 47. Santiago de Chile.

Comisión económica para América Latina y el Caribe (CEPAL). 1986. *Crisis económica y políticas de ajuste, estabilización y crecimiento.* Cuadernos de la CEPAL 54.

Comisión económica para América Latina y el Caribe (CEPAL). 1998. Panorama social de América Latina. Santiago de Chile.

Comisión económica para América Latina y el Caribe (CEPAL). 1999. Panorama social de América Latina. Santiago de Chile.

Comisión económica para América Latina y el Caribe (CEPAL). 2000. Panorama social de América Latina 1999–2000. Santiago de Chile.

Consejo Nacional de Población (CONAPO). 1995. Encuesta Nacional de Planificación Familiar. México.

Consejo Nacional para el Control de los Estupefacientes (CONACE). 1996. Estudio nacional de consumo de drogas. Santiago de Chile.

Cotterell, J. 1996. *Social networks and social influences in adolescence.* London: Routledge.

De Vos, S. 1998. Nuptiality in Latin America: The view of a sociologist and family demographer. CDE Working Paper No. 98–21. Madison, WI: Center for Demography and Ecology, University of Wisconsin-Madison.

End Child Prostitution in Asian Tourism (ECPAT). 1996. Second report to the World Congress against commercial sexual exploitation of children, child pornography and international perspectives. Stockholm, Sweden.

Diez De Medina, R. 2001. Jóvenes y empleo en los noventa. Centro Interamericano de investigación y documentación sobre formación profesional. (CINTERFORT/OIT).

Diez, N. & R. Inglehart, eds. 1994. *Tendencias mundiales de cambio en los valores sociales y políticos. Fundación para el desarrollo de la función social de las comunicaciones.* Madrid: FUNDESCO.

El País. 2001. La guerrilla de pantalón corto. Más de 6,000 adolescentes, todos pobres, combaten en las filas de la guerrilla de Colombia. February 15. México.

Fukuyama, F. 1992. *El fin de la historia y el último hombre.* Ed. Planeta. México.

Guzman, J. M., R. Hakkert. J. M. Contreras, & M. F. De Moyano. 2001. Diagnóstico sobre salud sexual y reproductiva de adolescentes en América Latina y el Caribe. Fondo de Población de las Naciones Unidas. México.

Hall, G. S. 1904. *Adolescence: Its psychology and its relations to anthropology, sociology, sex, crime, religion and education.* New York. Appleton.

Horeman, B. & M. Stolwijk. 1998. *Refusing to bear arms: A world survey of conscription and conscientious objection to military service:* London: War Resisters' International.

Human Rights Watch (HRW). 1998. *War without quarter in Colombia and humanitarian law.* New York.

International Labor Organization (ILO). 1998. World employment report, 1998–99.

Instituto Mexicano de la Juventud (IMJ). 2000. Encuesta nacional de juventud. Resultados preliminares. Secretaría de educación pública. México.

Instituto Nacional de Estadística Geografía e Informática (INEGI). 1995. Conteo de población y vivienda 1995. México.

Instituto Nacional de Estadística Geografía e Informática (INEGI). 2000b. XII Censo general de población y vivienda. México.

IPS. 1999. Colombia: Children of war. International Press Service. March 12.

Jutkowits, J. 1992. Survey on drug prevalence and attitudes in urban Panama. Arlington, VA: Development Associates.

La Jornada. 1999. Los salarios de las maquiladoras en México, los peores del mundo: Universidad Obrera de Mexico. August 12.

Luengo, G. E. 1993 La religión y los jóvenes de México:¿ El desgaste de una relación?, Universidad Iberoamericana, Cuadernos de cultura y religión 3. México.

Luengo, G. E. 1996. Valores y religión en los jóvenes. In: *Jovenes: Una evaluación del conocimiento,* eds. J. A. Pérez islas and E. P. Maldonado. Causa Joven. México.

Mandato Ciudadano por la Paz. 1999. Notas de actualidad. Colombia.

MEXFAM. 2000. *Encuesta gente joven.* Fundación Mexicana para la Planeación Familiar. México.

Muniz, P. 1996. Crisis, familia y género en las trayectorias educativas universitarias. In *Dinámica dempgráfica y cambio social,* ed, C. Welti, 111–126, Mexico: PROLAP.

Organización Panamericana de la Salud (OPS). 1996. *La salud en las Américas.* Edición 1996. Organización Mundial de la Salud. Washington, D.C.

Pan American Health Organization (PAHO). 2001. HIV and AIDS in the Americas: An epidemic with many faces. Washington, D.C. World Health Organization.

Pan American Health Organization (PAHO). 2000. A portrait of adolescent health in the Caribbean. Washington, D.C.: World Health Organization.

Pan American Health Organization (PAHO). 1998. Health in the Americas. 1998 ed. Washington, D.C.: World Health Organization.

Rodgers, D. 1999. Youth gangs and violence in Latin America and the Caribbean: A literature survey. LCR Sustainable Development Working Paper No. 4. Urban Peace Program Series. The World Bank.

Salles. V. & R. Tuiran. 1997. The family in Latin America: A gender approach. *Current Sociology,* 45:141–152.

Schifter J. 1998. *Lila's house: Male prostitution in Latin America.* New York: Haworth Press.

Singh, S. & R. Shamara. 1996. Early marriage in developing countries. *International Family Planning Perspectives,* 22(1):48–157 & 175.

SSA. 1998. *Encuesta nacional de adicciones*. Secretaria de Salud. México.

Tockman, V. 1996. El trabajo de los jóvenes en el post-ajuste Latinoamericano. Unpublished manuscript.

United Nations Children's Fund (UNICEF). 1992. Children of the Americas: Survival, protection and integral development. Childhood in the 1990s. Bogota, Colombia.

United Nations Children's Fund (UNICEF). 2000. La voz de los niños y adolescentes de América Latina y el Caribe. Encuesta Regional. Santafé de Bogotá, Colombia.

Welti, C. 1995. Fecundidad adolescente. Demos. No. 8.

Welti, C. 1988. Los bachilleres y el sexo, Revista momento, segunda época, año III, Núm. 151.

Welti, C. 2001. Análisis demográfico de la fecundidad adolescente en México. Papeles de Población, No 25, Enero-Marzo: 43–88.

Wulf, D. & S. Singh. 1991. Sexual activity, union and childbearing among adolescent women in the Americas. *International Family Planning Perspectives.* 17 (1):137–144

Yunes, J. 1993. Mortalidad por causas violentas en la región de las Américas. *Boletín de la OPS.* 114:302–316.

10

Adolescents in Western Countries in the 21st Century

Vast Opportunities – for All?

Jeffrey Jensen Arnett

Introduction: Who Are Today's Western Adolescents?

Which image best represents the adolescents of the West at the outset of the 21st century? Is it the 17-year-old boy sitting in a public place with a group of friends, smoking cigarettes and listening to loud music, interested mainly in the pursuit of pleasure? Is it the 18-year-old girl rushing from school to soccer practice, followed by several hours of homework or community service? Is it the minority adolescent, brutalized by poverty and discrimination, being led off to jail? Or is it the minority adolescent entering a college classroom as the first member of the family ever to obtain university education?

In truth, no single adolescent could serve as an adequate representative of all the adolescents of the West today, because one of their defining characteristics is their remarkable diversity. More than any generation of young people in history, this generation of Western young people has unprecedented freedom to choose from many different possible identities and many different possible life courses in love and work. Young women, especially, have opportunities for educational and occupational choices barely dreamed of by any previous generation of young women, not just in the West but anywhere in the world. Yet many young people face daunting problems; a wide range of problems, from substance use to criminal activity to experiencing parents divorcing, became more prevalent for the young people of the West in the second half of the 20th century (Rutter & Smith 1995). And the freedoms available to young people in the West are not as great for members of minority groups as they are for the majority. In this chapter I will address both the opportunities and the difficulties presented to Western adolescents as they enter the 21st century.

Overview: 20th Century Changes in Adolescence

Adolescence has existed for centuries in many societies as a distinct period of the life course between childhood and adulthood (Schlegel & Barry 1991). However, in its distinctive contemporary form, as a period of prolonged preparation for adulthood characterized by institutional segregation from the world of adults, adolescence is largely a phenomenon of the 20th century and of industrialized societies. In 1900, typical 15-year-olds in Europe and North America had long ago completed any schooling they would receive and spent most of their days working alongside adults on farms and in factories (Kett 1977). In 2000, typical 15-year-olds in these countries are in school among their peers for the better part of each day (Flammer & Alsaker 1999). After school as well, a substantial amount of their time is spent among peers and friends – playing sports, hanging around, and in part-time service jobs (Flammer, Alsaker, & Noack 1999; Steinberg & Cauffman 1995). Much of their leisure includes electronic media, on an average day about 2 hours of television and 3 or more hours of music (Flammer et al. 1999; Arnett 1995).

As adolescence has developed its distinctive characteristics in the course of the 20th century, so too has a distinctive cultural conception developed in the West of what adolescence is and what adolescents are like. One feature of this conception is the association between adolescence and leisure. Since the 1920s there has been a sizable youth culture in Western countries, characterized by "subterranean values" of hedonism and delayed responsibility (Matza & Sykes 1961), and by distinguishing styles of dress, adornment, language, and music. Not all adolescents have participated in this youth culture, perhaps not even most, but enough in each generation have taken part to make youth culture highly visible throughout society and to establish an association between young people and the values and styles of youth culture. The striking styles of youth culture contribute to a cultural view of youth as a time of experimental leisure and playful violation of norms before the standards of adult society are accepted and adult roles are entered.

The 20th-century cultural conception of adolescence in the West also includes an association between youth and trouble. Adolescence is widely viewed as a time of "storm and stress" (Arnett 1999), and young people are often portrayed as a disruptive force and as a source of potential harm to themselves and others. News stories on crime often note the youthfulness of the offenders. Public concern is expressed over youthful alienation and what it reflects about the state of society. Academics, too, sound the alarm over the "crisis" among contemporary adolescents (Lerner, Entwistle, & Hauser 1994). In European societies, it is observed that the skinheads and others who commit anti-immigrant acts are mostly young males (Kracke et al. 1998).

There is some basis to this view of adolescents, in that young people in their teens and early 20s tend to be over-represented in statistics for areas such as crime, automobile fatalities, and substance use (Arnett 1999). At the same time, it is a relatively small proportion of adolescents who are the source of the perceptions of young people as potentially dangerous. Nevertheless, the occasional extreme acts of some adolescents leads many adults to regard all adolescents with a wary eye. Thus the cultural view of adolescence at the beginning of the 21st century in the West is decidedly ambivalent. Adolescents are admired for their spontaneity, their vigor, and their iconoclastic pursuit of fun, but they also provoke concern and sometimes fear among adults.

What does the current state of adolescence portend for adolescence in the 21st century in Western countries? This is the central question I will address here. However, most of the chapter will not be devoted to speculations about what Western adolescents might be like a century from now. Instead, my goal is to provide a sketch of the current state of adolescence in Europe, Canada, and the United States. (I will refer to these as "Western" countries for abbreviation, although I will also include studies from countries in eastern Europe.) For the most part, I will leave it to the reader to prognosticate on the courses that adolescence may follow from now through the next century.

The Widening Scope of the "Adolescent" Years

One other issue that should be addressed before proceeding to describe specific areas of development concerns the length of adolescence. Adolescence has typically been defined as extending from the first notable changes of puberty to the attainment of adult status (usually signified by marriage). At the beginning of the 20th century, this would have meant that adolescence extended from the midteens to the early 20s. (G. S. Hall specified an age range of 14–24; Hall 1904, Vol. 1, xix). However, by the end of the 20th century, the boundaries of adolescence had been stretched in both directions. The changes of puberty occurred steadily earlier in most Western countries during the 20th century before leveling out in recent decades. Currently, most girls in the West reach menarche before their 13th birthday, and menarche occurs relatively late in the sequence of pubertal events. For most Western boys and girls, the earliest somatic evidence of puberty develops at age 10–12, at least 2 years earlier than a century ago.

Meanwhile, the median age of marriage has risen steeply and steadily since the mid-20th century and is currently in the late 20s in all Western countries for both men and women. Similar changes have taken place with respect to the other demographic transitions that have often been used to chart the transition to adulthood. Median age of first childbirth followed a rising path almost identical to marriage age through the late 20th century (Arnett 2000a). Median age of completing education rose throughout the 20th century and continues to rise, so that an increasing proportion of young people in the West continue their education into their 20s (Chisholm & Hurrelmann 1995).

Perhaps because traditional transitions to adulthood such as marriage and completing education have come later and later over recent decades, today's young people experience an extended period in which they have a sense of being partly adult but not entirely. When asked whether they consider themselves to have reached adulthood, young people from their teens to their mid-20s tend to choose neither yes nor no but the ambiguous "in some ways yes, in some ways no" (Arnett 1994; 1998; 2000a). It is not until age 30 that a definite majority of young people believe they have reached adulthood. Although studies on this topic have been so far conducted on young people in the United States, European scholars have suggested that the same ambiguous and lengthy transition to adulthood applies to young people in Europe as well (Chisholm & Hurrelmann 1995).

The widening scope of the "adolescent" years has profound implications for an understanding of adolescence in the 21st century. Using the traditional boundaries, adolescence would begin in the West at about age 10, when the first noticeable physical changes of puberty often occur, and end in the late 20s, when most people have married, had their first child, finished their educations, and obtained stable employment. Because this is such a long range of years – at least 15 – and because the typical 10-year-old is so different developmentally from the typical 25-year-old, I have argued that it would make sense to divide this age range into 2 periods, adolescence and emerging adulthood (Arnett 2000a). Adolescence would be considered to comprise most of "the second decade of life," from age 10 to the end of secondary school at

18 or (often in Europe) 19. Emerging adulthood would extend from the end of adolescence (in the late teens) to the mid-to-late 20s. Because adolescence has become younger and transitions to adult roles have become later, it may be that in the 21st century the focus of research and policy attention with respect to preparation for adulthood will be not so much on adolescence as on emerging adulthood. Thus in the course of this chapter, I will include information on both adolescence and emerging adulthood, referring to adolescents and emerging adults together as "young people."

Now let us proceed to a brief review of various aspects of young people's lives. The areas examined will include family relationships, peer relationships (including sexuality), school, employment, community and civic engagement, media, mental and physical health, provision of services, and young people's perceptions of their futures. The conclusion will offer some overall thoughts on prospects in the 21st century for young people in the West.

Family Relationships

Over the course of the 20th century, family life in the West continued a long-term shift from being the basis for a variety of aspects of life (education, work, recreation, etc.) to serving mainly an affective function, as a source of love and comfort. By the year 2000, most adolescents growing up in the West had become remarkably autonomous from their families, by historical standards. Adolescents spend most of their time most days in school and in leisure with friends, while their parents usually have work lives of their own away from home. Studies of time use in both North America and Europe have shown that adolescents spend little time in interactions with their parents on a typical day (Alsaker & Flammer 1999; Larson & Richards 1994). Adolescents' most common activity when they are home with their families is watching TV.

Nevertheless, parents remain an emotional touchstone in adolescents' lives. Even if adolescents spend little time with parents, they typically remain attached to their parents and rely on them for emotional comfort and support (Bo 1996). For example, a study of adolescents in 12 cities in Western and Eastern Europe found that the great majority of adolescents in all the cities evaluated their family emotional climate favorably, and that only 5 percent judged their family climate to be poor or very poor (Steiner 1995). In many Western families, relationships between parents and adolescents are much less hierarchical than in the past, with parents less likely to demand obedience and more accepting of adolescents' autonomy. The ideal for parent-adolescent relationships in Western families deemphasizes parental authority and has strong elements of friendship; it is seen as desirable for parents and adolescents to communicate openly about a wide range of issues and participate occasionally in shared leisure as near-equals.

However, the lack of a definite hierarchy of authority between parents and adolescents also means that the limits of adolescents' autonomy must be constantly negotiated. Conflict between parents and adolescents is higher in the West than in traditional cultures, largely because parents and adolescents in the West grapple on a daily basis with the ambiguity of parental authority and the borders of adolescent autonomy (Arnett 1999; Schlegel & Barry 1991). A substantial proportion of Western parents opt for a permissive-indifferent parenting style, allowing their adolescent children to have separate, unmonitored lives as the parents have theirs (Bois-Reymond & Ravesloot 1996; Lamborn et al. 1991).

One area where open communication remains especially problematic between adolescents and their parents is sexuality. Many American studies have found that parents and adolescents rarely discuss sexual issues. European countries are often held up in contrast to the United States as models of healthy, open sexuality. However, even in European countries communication between adolescents and parents on sexual issues is fraught with ambiguity and avoidance. For example, Bois-Reymond & Ravesloot (1996) interviewed adolescents and their parents in the Netherlands regarding their communication about sexuality. They noted that in most European countries, "parents are prepared to either permit or tolerate premarital sexual behavior in their children, under one main condition: sexual relationships must be monogamous and serious, based on feelings of true love" (183). Nevertheless, their research indicated that even in the Netherlands – long regarded as one of Europe's most liberal countries on sexual issues – this permission is usually tacit and implicit, rarely based on open communication and negotiation. The authors observed "a certain embarrassment about communicating about sexuality among the parents. Their children feel this embarrassment and therefore refrain from confidential communication about their sexual lives" (193). Thus one interesting question for the 21st century is whether openness between parents and adolescents on sexual issues will increase, or whether inherent barriers to this communication (perhaps rooted in incest issues) will continue to make such communication uneasy for most parents and adolescents.

It should be noted that the family experiences of minority adolescents appear to be considerably different than white adolescents. In Latino families in the United States, there is a strong emphasis on family closeness and on respect for the parents' (especially the father's) authority, and Latino adolescents' relationships with their parents are often characterized by warmth and respect (Suarez-Orozco & Suarez-Orozco 1996). A similar emphasis on closeness, mutual obligation, and a definite hierarchy of authority is characteristic of Asian American adolescents' relationships with their parents (Fuligni, Tseng, & Lam 1999; Phinney, Ong, & Madden 2000). It should also be noted that for adolescents in families from traditional societies who have immigrated to the West, the allure of Western adolescents' autonomy is a common source of conflict with parents (Phinney et al. 2000), for example among Vietnamese adolescents in Finland (Liebkind & Kosonen 1998).

Other family relationships also play a part in the lives of many Western adolescents. Although the average number of births per woman has declined from 8 in 1,800 to 2 or fewer now, most Western adolescents today have 1 or more siblings. Research on sibling relationships in adolescence is limited, but there is some evidence that adolescents tend to have more conflict with their siblings than in any other relationship (Buhrmester & Furman 1987). Nevertheless, adolescents with more than one sibling rate their closeness to their "favorite" sibling as similar to their relationship with their best friend (Greenberger et al. 1980).

With regard to relationships with extended family, adolescents in American ethnic minority groups tend to be closer to their extended family members than white adolescents are (Fuligni et al. 1999; Suarez-Orozco & Suarez-Orozco 1996; Taylor 1996). Grandparents play an especially important role in African American families, because nearly three-fourths of African American families are headed by a single mother, and grandparents' involvement and assistance has a variety of positive effects on the lives of African American adolescents (Taylor 1996). Research suggests that adolescents in European countries also tend to have more contact with extended family than white American adolescents (Alsaker & Flammer 1999), perhaps because lower rates of geographical mobility mean that European adolescents are more likely to live in close proximity to extended-family members.

Relationships with parents remain important through emerging adulthood in the West. In fact, in American studies emerging adults report greater closeness and fewer negative feelings toward their parents after moving out of the parents' home (Dubas & Petersen 1996). In European countries, emerging adults tend to live with their parents for longer than in the United States, especially in southern and eastern Europe (cf. Goldscheider & Goldscheider 1999; Chisholm & Hurrelmann 1995). There are a number of practical reasons for this. European university students are more likely than American students to continue to live at home while they attend university. European emerging adults who do not attend university may have difficulty finding or affording an apartment of their own.

However, also important are European cultural values that emphasize mutual support within the family while also allowing young people substantial autonomy. Young Europeans find that they can enjoy a higher standard of living by staying at home rather than living independently, and at the same time enjoy substantial autonomy. Italy provides a good case in point (Chisholm & Hurrelman 1995). Ninety-four percent of Italians aged 15–24 live with their parents, the highest percentage in the European Union (EU). However, only 8 percent of them view their living arrangements as a problem – the lowest percentage among EU countries. Thus many European emerging adults remain at home contentedly through their early 20s, by choice rather than necessity.

When they do leave home, it is notable that for many emerging adults in Western countries cohabitation precedes marriage. In the United States as well as in northern European countries, at least two-thirds of emerging adults cohabit before marriage (Hurrelmann & Settertobulte 1994; Nurmi & Siurala 1994), with percentages as high as 97 percent, in Sweden (Hoem 1992). In these countries, the normative sequence of family formation is now dating, cohabitation, marriage, and parenthood, with parenthood sometimes preceding marriage (Chisholm & Hurrelmann 1995; Nurmi & Siurala 1994). However, this is an area for which there are distinct divisions within Europe between north and south and between east and west. Emerging adults in southern Europe are considerably less likely than their counterparts in the north to cohabit (indeed, this is one of the factors that explains young Italians' high rates of living at home). Perhaps due to the Catholic religious tradition in the south, cohabitation carries more of a moral stigma in the south than in the north (Martinez, Miguel, & Fernandez 1994).

Cohabitation is also relatively rare in eastern Europe (Nurmi 1998). This is partly due to cultural values emphasizing family ties but also to the scarcity of decent housing in these countries; even after marriage, the majority of couples in some eastern European countries continue to live with the husband's or wife's parents because independent housing is either not available or not affordable (Nurmi 1998). In the 21st century,

TABLE 10.1. *Divorce Rates in Western Countries*

Country	% Marriages Ending in Divorce
Sweden	64
Great Britain	53
United States	49
Canada	45
France	43
Germany	41
Greece	18
Spain	17
Italy	12

Source: Time magazine, September 25, 2000.

it will be interesting to see the extent to which the prevalence of cohabitation will continue to vary widely across Europe. It may be most likely that the east and the south will move toward the northern pattern, because of improved economic conditions in the east and because of the declining force of Catholicism in the south.

If the growing tendency toward cohabitation reflects a certain wariness among young people of the likely long-term stability of marriage, this would not be surprising given that so many of them have grown up to see their parents' marriages dissolve. Rates of divorce and remarriage rose substantially in most Western countries in the decades following World War II before leveling out in recent years (Hess 1995). Currently, rates of divorce are highest in the United States, Canada, and northern Europe, where more than 40 percent of marriages end in divorce, but rates in southern Europe are considerably lower (Table 10.1).

Although many adolescents adapt well to family transitions, it is not uncommon for adolescents to experience them as a source of distress. With respect to divorce, American studies have indicated that even though adolescents tend to be affected less negatively by divorce than younger children are, divorce is nevertheless related to a variety of negative outcomes in the lives of adolescents and emerging adults, from substance use to problems in heterosexual relationships to lower educational and occupational attainment (Buchanan 2000). With respect to remarriage, outcomes for adolescents (especially girls) in stepfamilies tend to be even worse than for adolescents in divorced families, and worse for adolescents than for younger children. In European studies, adolescents living with both biological parents also tend to evaluate their family climate more favorably than other adolescents (Steiner 1995).

Peer Relationships

Relationships with peers and friends have taken on increasing importance for adolescents in the course of the 20th century. This is partly due to the fact that, as noted in the introduction, the adolescents of 2000 spend a much greater proportion of their day with peers (and away from their parents) than the adolescents of 1900 did, in school, leisure, and in the workplace. Another reason for the prominence of peers in adolescents' lives is that in times of rapid social change – including the entire 20th century – adolescents tend to look to their peers as much or more than to their parents for clues as to where the world is going and what they will need to know to thrive in it.

For Western adolescents in the early 21st century, it is clear that peers are a vital part of their emotional lives. Studies of American adolescents indicate that they depend more on friends than on their parents for companionship and emotional support, and that they learn more from friends and feel more at ease with friends than with parents (Youniss & Smollar 1985). Friends appear to have a similar prominence in the lives of many European adolescents. For example, a study of Dutch adolescents (aged 15–19) asked them with whom they "communicate about themselves, about their personal feelings, and about sorrows and secrets" (Bois-Reymond & Ravesloot 1996). Nearly half of the adolescents named their best friend or their relationship partner, whereas only 20 percent named one or both parents (only 3 percent their fathers). Studies in both the United States and Europe confirm that adolescents tend to be happiest when with their friends, and that they tend to turn to their friends for advice and information on social relationships and leisure, although they usually come to parents for advice about education and career plans (Hurrelmann 1996; Larson & Richards 1994; Youniss & Smollar 1985).

Typically in Western countries, a transition in the composition of friendship groups takes place sometime in the midteens, from same-sex groups to mixed-sex groups. In the United States, the early-to-midteens are also the time when dating typically begins (Furman, Brown, & Feiring 1999). However, dating – in the form of an explicit plan for a couple to meet at a certain place at a certain time for a particular event – is relatively rare among European adolescents, who tend instead to go out in groups rather than in pairs (Alsaker & Flammer 1999).

Even without dating, European adolescents as well as American adolescents tend to form their first intimate emotional and sexual relationships during their mid- to late teens. Although there is some variation among Western countries, there is a fairly consistent normative pattern across countries that adolescents have sexual intercourse for the first time at some point in their late teens (e.g., Csapo 1994; Galambos & Kolaric 1994; Goossens 1994), with intercourse usually preceded by several other steps in sexual intimacy. Sexual experiences in adolescence and emerging adulthood generally take place in the context of an intimate relationship rather than in casual, uncommitted contacts; serial monogamy is the norm. In Europe as well as in the United States, having multiple sexual partners is socially disapproved by peers, especially for girls (e.g., Bois-Reymond & Ravesloot 1996).

The typical age of initiating sexual intercourse has fallen in the West in recent decades as the typical marriage age has risen, and consequently many young people in the West have a period of 10 years or more when they must use contraception consistently if they wish to avoid a nonmarital pregnancy. American adolescents are considerably less likely than western European adolescents to use contraception consistently in their early sexual relationships, for complex reasons including lack of effective sex education and highly ambivalent American cultural attitudes about adolescent sexuality. Although condom use among American adolescents increased substantially during the 1990s due to "safe sex" public health campaigns and the fear of AIDS, in 1998 only half of sexually active American adolescents reported that they or their partner had used a condom at their last episode of sexual intercourse and nearly one-fourth did not use any type of contraception (Centers for Disease Control & Prevention 2001).

As a consequence of using contraception less consistently, young people in the United States have higher rates of teen pregnancy than young people in western Europe (Table 10.2) (Singh & Darroch 2000). Teen pregnancy rates in eastern European countries are also quite high compared to western Europe, as Table 10.2 shows. Like the United States, eastern European countries tend to have ambivalent views of adolescent sexuality and allow adolescents only limited access to contraception (Macek & Rabusic 1994; Wlodarek 1994).

Peer relationships figure prominently in a variety of types of risky and antisocial behavior. Many American studies have shown that

TABLE 10.2. *Rates of Adolescent Birth, Abortion, and Pregnancy in Western Countries*

Country	Rates per 1,000 Females Aged 15–19		
	Birth Rate	**Abortion Rate**	**Pregnancy Rate (Birth+Abortion)**
Belgium	9.1	5.0	14.1
Canada	24.2	21.2	45.4
Great Britain	28.4	18.6	46.9
Italy	6.9	5.1	12.0
Netherlands	8.2	4.0	12.2
Spain	7.8	4.5	12.3
Sweden	7.7	17.2	24.9
United States	54.4	29.2	83.6
Czech Republic	20.1	12.3	32.4
Hungary	29.5	29.6	59.1
Romania	42.0	32.0	74.0

Source: All figures are from Singh & Darroch 2000.

adolescents and emerging adults who participate in behaviors such as drug use and crime tend to have friends who report similar behaviors. This similarity is due in part to self-selection into friendship groups with like-minded peers (Berndt 1996), but it probably also reflects some degree of mutual peer influence. Leisure in adolescence and emerging adulthood tends to involve a substantial amount of "unstructured socializing" (Flammer et al. 1999; Osgood et al. 1996), and unstructured socializing sometimes lends itself to participation in risky behavior, as friends seek out novel and intense experiences together.

In Europe, the most notable peer-related form of antisocial behavior in recent years has been acts of violence and intimidation toward immigrants. Immigration to western European countries has boomed in recent decades, from eastern Europe and from a variety of developing countries (Fussell & Greene this volume). Most Europeans have been tolerant and accepting of immigration, and young people tend to be more favorable toward immigration than older people (Kracke et al. 1998; Westin 1998). However, when anti-immigrant acts do occur, they tend to be committed by peer groups of young working-class men in their late teens and early 20s (Westin 1998), especially young men who are members of the "skinhead" youth subculture. These acts include verbal harassment, attacks on refugee centers, and even random murders of immigrants. Immigration will be an important issue in Europe in the next century, as European countries make decisions about how much immigration to allow and how to address the problem of the small proportion of young people who are disposed to commit violent acts against immigrants.

Skinheads are only one of many youth subcultures found in Western countries. Although the styles of youth subcultures are constantly changing, several durable general types of adolescent crowds have been observed over the past several decades (Brake 1985; Brown, Mory, & Kinney 1994):

1. A high-status, socially adept, affluent group, often from higher social class families;
2. A nonconformist, drug-using group;
3. An alienated, angry, violent group (e.g., skinheads); and
4. Music-centered groups (e.g., punk, heavy metal, reggae).

American high schools have 2 other prominent types, the academically oriented "brains" (a.k.a. nerds, geeks, dweebs, etc.) and the sports-oriented "jocks" (Brown et al. 1994). However, these types do not appear in the European literature on youth subcultures. "Jocks" may be peculiar to the United States, because in European countries there are no school-sponsored sports teams; instead, young people join sports clubs (e.g., Martinez et al. 1994; Roe, Bjurnstrom, & Fornas 1994; Stafseng 1994). "Brains" may also be less likely to be found in European countries, because the early school tracking in those countries may result in less variability in academic orientations within secondary schools, as discussed in the next section.

School

In most Western countries, secondary education is divided into 2 levels, secondary school I (or "lower secondary education") and secondary school II (or "upper secondary education") (Flammer & Alsaker 2001). For the most part, secondary school I continues the mission of primary school by providing a broad general education to all students. Only a few countries (e.g., Germany, Austria, Netherlands, Switzerland) separate students into different schools in secondary school I based on their different abilities and interests.

At the secondary school II level, the norm reverses – most countries have more than one type of school at this level, and students attend different schools based on different abilities and interests. The

United States and Canada are unusual in having only one institution – the "comprehensive" high school – as the source of upper-secondary education. In most European countries, there are at least 2 types of secondary schools (e.g., Csapo 1994; Hurrelmann & Settertobulte 1994; Nurmi & Siurala 1994). One type is a college-preparatory school that is similar in some ways to the American high school in that it offers a variety of academic courses and the goal of it is general education and preparation for university rather than education for any specific profession. In most European countries about one-half of adolescents attend this type of school. A 2nd type of secondary school is the vocational school, where adolescents learn the skills involved in a specific blue-collar occupation such as plumbing or auto mechanics. About one-third of adolescents in European countries attend this type of school. Some European countries also have a 3rd type of secondary school, for example, professional schools devoted to teacher training, the arts, or some other specific purpose (Flammer & Alsaker 2001).

One consequence of having a system of different types of secondary schools is that adolescents must decide at a relatively early age what direction they want to pursue for their education and occupation. In deciding which type of secondary school they will enter, at the age of 15 or 16 European adolescents are making a decision that is likely to have a great impact on the rest of their lives. Usually the decision of which secondary school to attend is made by adolescents in conference with their parents and teachers, based on the adolescents' interests as well as on their school performance (e.g., Motola, Sinisalo, & Guichard 1998). Although adolescents sometimes change schools after a year or two, and adolescents who attend a vocational school sometimes attend university, these switches are rare. However, in recent years most countries have added professional college curricula that students can take after pursuing a vocational education in secondary school. In addition to providing professional training, graduation from professional colleges also allows entrance to university. This has added flexibility to the system, by providing young people with an alternative route to university even if they did not attend the college-preparatory high school.

Nevertheless, in general the European system tends to require earlier decision making about career directions. A study by Motola and colleagues (1998) demonstrated how the timing of tracking (or "streaming" in European terminology) influences the timing of adolescents' decisions about which occupational path to pursue. They compared 11th-grade adolescents in France and Finland. French adolescents are tracked beginning at age 13, and at age 16 they must choose a stream from 5 academic and 16 technical programs or enter a vocational high school or apprenticeship. In contrast, Finnish adolescents are in one comprehensive school until age 16, then tracked into either an upper-secondary school or a vocational school. However, they are not required to make a decision about a specific occupation until they enter university or leave vocational school. Thus in the study by Motola and colleagues (1998), French adolescents were 3 times as likely as Finnish adolescents (58 percent to 19 percent) to have a clear idea of their chosen occupation. Although no comparable data exist for North American adolescents, one might expect that they would be even later than Finns to make such choices, given that North Americans who attend college or university typically do not have to decide on a major until the end of their 2nd year (usually about age 20) whereas Finns must decide upon entering university.

Perhaps because American young people have few options in terms of vocational training, dropping out of high school puts them at high risk for low wages and unemployment. Dropouts typically have struggled academically for many years before they leave school, and they often have other burdens and stresses such as learning disabilities, family poverty, early childbearing, and (for adolescents in immigrant families) difficulty using English. Rates of dropping out vary widely among American ethnic groups, from 30 percent among Latinos to 12 percent among African Americans, 10 percent among Asian Americans, and 7 percent among whites (Pollard & O'Hare 1999). Overall, the dropout rate has declined steadily over the past half century.

In all Western countries, there is a trend in recent decades toward extending the years that young people spend in education. In the United States, the proportion of young people entering higher education after graduating from high school now exceeds 60 percent (National Center for Education Statistics 2000), and Canadian figures are similar (Galambos & Kolaric 1994). These figures are higher than for most European countries, but all across Europe the proportion of young people obtaining higher education is rising; generally the current proportions in European countries are between 20 and 40 percent (Lagree 1995). This trend is well-suited to an increasingly complex information-based economy for which the best-paying jobs require a high amount of education. It is also part of the overall trend described at the outset of the chapter, of the growth of emerging adulthood as the number of years devoted to preparation for adulthood has been extended and full entry into adult roles has been postponed until at least the mid-20s.

In addition to the expansion in the proportion of young people obtaining higher education, the other striking educational trend of the 2nd half of the 20th century has been the rise in the educational attainment of women. In 1900 and even at midcentury, young women were far less likely than young men to attend colleges and universities. For the young women of 2000, this picture has changed dramatically. Across Western countries, there is a remarkably consistent pattern: in adolescence and emerging adulthood young women now exceed young men in educational performance and in educational attainment (Chisholm & Hurrelmann 1995).

However, major gender differences continue to exist in the specific educational and occupational paths young people pursue. Again with remarkable consistency across Western countries, young women are more likely to enter traditionally female fields such as teaching, nursing, counseling, and secretarial work, whereas young men are more likely to enter traditionally male fields such as science, engineering, and auto mechanics (e.g., Galambos & Kolaric 1994; Goossens 1994; Hendry & Shucksmith 1994; Hoem 1992). "Traditionally female" professions tend to be lower paying and lower in status than "traditionally male" professions (Motola et al. 1998). The gender balance has changed in some fields – for example, classes entering American business, law, and medical schools used to be almost entirely male but are now almost evenly divided between males and females (Dey & Hurtado 1999) – but sharp differences remain in many fields and in many countries. Thus a provocative question for the century to come is whether or not the gender boundaries in various professions will continue to dissolve.

Employment

In the United States, there is little in the way of a structured transition from school to work. Although some federal job-training programs exist and various states and localities have specific programs for job training or apprenticeships (Hamilton 1990), only a tiny proportion of young Americans ever take part in such a program. Consequently, young Americans generally must find their own route to employment, assisted by family members, friends, mentors, and prospective employers.

In contrast, most European countries have a tradition of school-to-work programs in which the government assists in coordinating the needs of employers with the preparation provided by schools. This system is most developed in northern European countries, where there is a tradition of apprenticeships for young people who plan to enter the workplace after secondary school rather than attend university (e.g., Csapo 1994; Hamilton 1990). These apprenticeships train young people not just for trades or skilled labor, but for professional and managerial positions as well. Usually young people are in the program for 3 years, and during that time they spend 1 or 2 days a week in a vocational school and 3 or 4 days in their apprenticeship placement. It is common for apprentices to move into a job with the company that trained them after they complete the apprenticeship (Hamilton 1990).

The kind of part-time work done by American adolescents differs markedly from the kind of work done by European adolescents in their apprenticeships and vocational programs. The majority of jobs held by American adolescents in high school involve restaurant work or retail sales, and these jobs rarely provide any skills that will lay the groundwork for a future occupation (Steinberg & Cauffman 1995). The main purpose of part-time jobs for American adolescents is not occupational preparation, nor is it saving for college or contributing to the family income. On the contrary, adolescents work so that they can finance an active leisure life – concert tickets, CDs, car expenses, travel, movies, eating at restaurants, and so on.

With regard to the effects of work, the amount of time worked per week is a crucial consideration. Most studies find that up to 10 hours a week working at a part-time job has few negative effects on adolescents' development and may even have benefits (Mortimer, Harley, & Aronson 1999). It is beyond 10 hours a week that problems arise, and beyond 20 hours a week the problems become considerably worse. For the most part, American adolescents who work are within or close to the threshold where problems become more likely. On average, employed high school sophomores work 15 hours per week and employed high school seniors work 20 hours per week (Steinberg & Cauffman 1995). American adolescents are far more likely than adolescents in any country in Europe to hold a part-time job unrelated to school (Flammer et al. 1999).

The 2 problems most consistently related to working part-time among American adolescents are school performance and substance use. Beyond 10 hours a week, working more hours is related to lower grades, less time spent on homework, cutting class, cheating on school work, less commitment to school, and lower educational aspirations. Working more than 10 hours a week is also related to substance use, partly because the income from part-time work allows adolescents to buy alcohol, cigarettes, and other drugs, and partly because substance use can be a way of relieving work-induced stress (Steinberg & Cauffman 1995). However, it should be noted that adolescents also report that their part-time jobs have a variety of benefits, such as helping them develop skills in managing time and money (Mortimer et al. 1999).

Despite the impressive efforts that European countries make to pro-mote a smooth entry into the workplace for young people, unemploy-ment among the young is a serious problem in most European countries. This is especially true for the countries of southern Europe, where youth unemployment (ages 15–24) has remained stubbornly over 20 percent for many years (Lagree 1995). Unemployment among adults (age 25 and older) is also high in southern Europe relative to the north, but youth unemployment is especially high. Consistently across Europe, in the north as well as the south, and the east as well as the west, the youth unemployment rate is about twice as high as the unemployment rate for adults. For example, in Sweden, the unemployment rate is 18 percent for young people, 8 percent for adults (Westin 1998). European countries (especially in northern Europe) are more likely than the United States to provide government-sponsored jobs to young people who would otherwise face long-term unemployment. For example in Finland, all 17- to 19-year-olds are entitled to 6 months employment in a public or-ganization after they have been unemployed for 3 months (Nurmi & Siurala 1994).

In the United States, unemployment is also higher among young peo-ple than among adults, and it is especially high among young Latinos and African Americans living in urban areas (Pollard & O'Hare 1999). Because fewer Latinos and African Americans enter higher education following high school (compared with whites and Asian Americans), they especially suffer from the lack of an adequate national school-to-work system in the United States. Inuit youth in Canada also tend to have lower levels of educational attainment and higher rates of unemploy-ment than the white majority population (Galambos & Kolaric 1994). Similar disparities are reported in Europe between immigrant youth and the majority population (e.g., Bois-Reymond & Zande 1994; Sansone 1995). Throughout Western countries, young minorities are disadvan-taged in the workplace in part because of lower levels of education and training and in part because of prejudice and discrimination from the majority (Kracke et al. 1998; Liebkind & Kosonen 1998). It is an open question whether or not minorities in the West will reach true equality of opportunity with the majority populations in the course of the 21st century.

Media

Media are a pervasive part of everyday life for adolescents in the West. American studies indicate that adolescents use media for a total of about 8 hours a day (Roberts et al. 1999). Music is especially popular – the typical American teen listens to music for 4 to 6 hours a day. Television is next most popular – adolescents in both the United States and Europe watch television for about 2 hours a day (Flammer et al. 1999; Roberts et al. 1999). Other media used by adolescents include movies, magazines, computer games, and the Internet.

Adolescents make a variety of uses of media, many of them quite positive (Arnett 1995). They use media for entertainment – as background music for activities with friends, or as an enjoyable way of passing the time. They also use media as materials for identity formation. In media stars they find ideals to admire and emulate, and possible careers to follow (or at least dream of temporarily). The posters of media stars they put up on their bedroom walls reflect their admiration and their interest in using them as models for their own development (Steele & Brown 1995).

Coping is another important use of media for adolescents. Media can help them to ponder and subdue the strong emotions that are often part of adolescence. Several studies indicate that "Listen to music" and "Watch TV" are the coping strategies most commonly used by adolescents when they are angry, anxious, or unhappy (Arnett 1995). Music may be particularly important in this respect. Larson (1995) reports that adolescents often listen to music in the privacy of their bedrooms while pondering the themes of the songs in relation to their own lives, as part of the process of emotional self-regulation.

However, most of the focus of public discussion on adolescents and media is not on uses such as these but on the potential danger believed to be present in the media materials used by adolescents. Claims of negative effects have especially concerned the potential for aggressiveness and violence believed to be caused by television, rap music, and computer games.

With regard to television and aggressiveness, content analyses show that violence on television has become considerably more frequent and more graphic in recent decades (Cantor 2000), during a period when violent behavior by young people has also increased. Also, children who watch violent television tend to be more aggressive than children who do not (Strasburger 1995). Do such correlations suggest that violent television contributes to young people's violent behavior? A number of prominent scholars in this area would answer this question affirmatively (e.g., Cantor 2000; Strasburger 1995), whereas others argue that research provides only tepid support for the claim that watching violent television causes adolescents to behave aggressively (Freedman 1984).

It is probably true that, for some adolescents, watching television violence serves as a model for their own aggressiveness (Strasburger 1995). Television may also play an indirect role in promoting aggressiveness among adolescents by making aggression more acceptable (Rutter, Giller, & Hagell 1998). However, it is important to recognize that adolescents vary in how they respond to the same media stimulus, and that adolescents who are most attracted to violent television may already have a tendency for aggressiveness (Arnett 1995; Freedman 1984).

Rap music has also been accused of fomenting violence among young people, in particular the genre known as "gangsta rap," in which songs depict scenes such as drive-by shootings, gang violence, and violent confrontations with the police. Women are frequently depicted as objects of hatred and violence, as "hos" (whores) and "bitches" who deserve sexual exploitation and even sexual assault (Berry 1995). The performers of such songs, and their defenders, have argued that their lyrics simply reflect the grim realities of life for young Black people in America's inner cities, who face problems such as poverty, crime, and lack of educational and occupational opportunties (Decker 1994). However, critics have accused the performers of contributing to the stereotype of young Black men as dangerous criminals (e.g., Berry 1995).

What effects – if any – do rap lyrics with themes of violence have on adolescents? Unfortunately, although there have been many academic speculations about the uses of rap by adolescents, thus far not a single credible study has provided research evidence on the topic. It may be that with "gangsta rap," as with TV violence, its most important and definite contribution to promoting aggressiveness among adolescents is that it makes aggression more acceptable by glorifying it.

Computer games have also been targeted as a possible cause of aggressiveness among adolescents, because the games have become more violent in recent years and because many of the games most popular with adolescents are among the most violent (Funk et al. 1999). However, only a handful of studies thus far have examined the relation between video games and aggressiveness, and the results of these studies are mixed (Funk et al. 1999, Scott 1995). It seems likely that with computer games as with other violent media there is a wide range of individual differences in responses, with young people who are already at risk for violent behavior being most likely to be affected by the games, as well as most likely to be attracted to them (Funk et al. 1999).

A new medium that is growing rapidly in popularity among young people is the Internet. In a 1998 survey by *Consumers' Research* magazine, 79 percent of high school students in the United States reported having regular Internet access, compared to just 13 percent of persons over age 50. Similar or even higher percentages are reported for young people in other Western countries (Anderson 2000). Internet access for young people in Western countries is expected to become nearly universal in the next decade, in part because schools are increasingly becoming linked to the Internet and encouraging students to use it for finding information.

The Internet makes available literally millions of different information sources, so the potential uses that adolescents could make of it are almost limitless. Scholars have suggested that young people's uses of the Internet are likely to include both benefits and risks (Bremer & Rauch 1998). Benefits of Internet use for young people include access to educational information, access to health information (e.g., about sexual health), and the opportunity to practice social interactions in "chat rooms" and via e-mail. Risks include exposure to pornographic material, substituting computer play for social interactions, and being exposed to adults in chat rooms who may seek to exploit them. Because Internet use is relatively new, little research has yet explored how young people use it, but it is sure to be an important medium for the young people of the 21st century.

Community and Civic Engagement

All across Europe as well as in the United States, young people's political participation is strikingly low by conventional measures such as voting rates and involvement in political parties (e.g. Bois-Reymond & Zande 1994; Buzzi & Cavalli 1994; Carvalho & Dias 1994; Hendry & Shucksmith 1994; Nurmi & Siurala 1994). Young people in their teens and early 20s in 2000 tend to have lower conventional political participation not only in comparison to adults but in comparison to previous generations of young people. They tend to be skeptical of the motivations of politicians and to see the activities of political parties as irrelevant to their lives (Flanagan et al. 1999).

However, this rejection of conventional politics should not be construed as a lack of civic engagement or as a lack of interest in improving the state of their communities, their societies, and the world. On the contrary, young people in the West are more likely than their elders to be involved in organizations devoted to particular issues, such as environmental protection and efforts against war and racism (e.g., Bois-Reymond & Zande 1994; Buzzi & Cavalli 1994). Often frustrated by and alienated from conventional political processes, they choose instead to direct their energies toward specific areas of particular importance to them, where they believe they are more likely to see genuine progress.

The political involvement of young people in eastern Europe is of particular interest on the threshold of the 21st century, given the abrupt transition from communism to democracy in that region since 1989. Young people played a prominent role in the revolutions that led to the fall of communism (Flanagan et al. 1999; Macek & Rabusic 1994). In the former Czechoslovakia, the "Velvet Revolution" began with a massive student-led strike and demonstration. In Hungary, young people organized demonstrations agitating for independence, and the first new political party after the fall of communism was an explicitly youth-centered party with membership restricted to persons under age 35. In Bulgaria, young people were active in the strikes and demonstrations that led to the fall of the communist government, and representatives of student movements took a prominent role in the new parliament. However, in the years since the transition to democracy, young people in eastern Europe have become disillusioned and frustrated by the pace of change and by the substantial social costs that have accompanied democracy and the transition to a market economy. By now, they have largely turned away from conventional politics, like their counterparts in western Europe and North America (Flanagan et al. 1999).

Another important form of community involvement in Western countries is community service. Young people in many countries report high rates of volunteering in their communities. In the United States, consistently from the mid-1970s through the 1990s about 22 percent of high school seniors have reported taking part in volunteer work on a weekly or monthly basis, and an additional 45 percent have reported volunteering at least once in the past year (Yates 1999). Rates of volunteering are in the range of 50 percent in eastern European countries such as Hungary, Bulgaria, and the Czech Republic (Flanagan et al. 1999). Community service is relatively rare in western European countries, because the generous system of government-provided services in those countries minimizes the need for the kinds of services that young people might provide.

The high rates of community service in eastern European countries appear to be due in part to the tradition of youth volunteering promoted under communism. However, it is also inspired by the daunting problems facing eastern European countries. Volunteering in environmental cleanup and restoration is the most common form of community service among young people in eastern European countries (Flanagan et al. 1999), reflecting their awareness of the devastating environmental destruction their countries suffered under communist governments and the threat that this destruction presents to the future of their societies.

Another form of community and civic engagement worth noting is adolescents' involvement in religious organizations. Religious participation varies widely among young people in the West. For example, only 10 percent of Belgians aged 17–34 attend religious services weekly (Goossens 1994), and only 15 percent of Swedes aged 15–24 report attending religious services in the past month (Roe et al. 1994). In contrast 71 percent of secondary school students in Poland report attending religious services at least weekly (Wlodarek 1994), a remarkable figure for a country in which, for over a half century until 1989, religious participation was actively discouraged and suppressed by the communist government. In the United States, 32 percent of high school seniors report weekly attendance at religious services and 36 percent report being involved with a religious "youth group" (Wallace & Williams 1997). Many young people in the United States perform community service through religious organizations, for example in church-sponsored programs that provide food, shelter, and clothing for the homeless (Yates 1999).

Mental and Physical Health

In many ways, the adolescents of the early 21st century are the healthiest generation in Western history. Unlike the adolescents of 1900, very few of the adolescents of 2000 will die of infectious diseases before they reach maturity. Unlike the adolescents of 1900, very few of the adolescents of 2000 are subject to extremely unsafe and unhealthy working conditions in mines and factories (Kett 1977). Nevertheless, the adolescents of the 21st century face health problems and challenges of their own. For Western adolescents today, the primary threats to their health arise from their behavior. In most Western countries, the 2 leading causes of death among young people in their teens and early 20s are automobile accidents and suicide (e.g., Hurrelmann & Settertobulte 1994). Rates of automobile fatalities are especially high in the United States, because the legal driving age is 16 in most American states (vs. 18 in most European countries) and because young Americans are more likely than young Europeans to have ready access to an automobile.

Suicide among the young is a concern in the West because in many countries suicide rates have more than doubled since 1960 (Diekstra, Kienhorst, & de Wilde 1995). Although youth suicide rates in most countries remain below the rates for adults, the increase in rates among young people has provoked concern. The reasons for the increase are not well understood. Suicide attempts tend to be higher among girls, but boys are more likely actually to die from suicide (e.g., Csapo 1994), primarily because boys tend to choose deadlier methods (guns or knives rather than pills). Rates of suicide are highest in Finland (Nurmi & Siurala 1994) and Hungary (Csapo 1994), again for reasons that are not well understood.

In the United States, the 2nd leading cause of death among young persons aged 15–24 is homicide (Rockett 1998), not because the suicide rate is relatively low in the United States but because the homicide rate is so high. Among young men aged 15–24, the firearm homicide rate in the United States is 5 times as high as in Canada, 12 times as high as in Denmark, and more than 50 times as high as in Great Britain (Table 10.3; Rockett 1998). Young Americans in their teens and early 20s are more likely than persons in any other age group to commit violent crimes and to be victims of violent crimes. In the poor urban areas of the United

TABLE 10.3. *Rates of Gun Deaths, Young Men Aged 15–24 in Western Countries*

Country	Gun Deaths Per 100,000
Great Britain	0.8
Netherlands	1.5
Sweden	3.7
Denmark	4.6
France	7.9
Canada	11.1
United States	54.0

Source: Rockett 1998.

States, homicide rates among the young are appallingly high; homicide is the leading cause of death among young Blacks and Latinos (Singh & Yu 1996).

The most important reason for high homicide rates in the United States is easy access to deadly firearms. Because of the widespread availability of firearms in American society – an estimated 200 million – what might be a fist fight between young men in London or Paris easily becomes murder in Chicago or Washington, D.C. Given the fierce opposition to gun control among a small but vocal and well-organized portion of the American population, it may take a century or more before the United States adopts the kinds of gun control laws that have long been typical of other Western countries. One can only speculate how long it would take to achieve any kind of social control over 200 million firearms even after such laws were passed.

Sexually-transmitted diseases (STDs) are another health concern with regard to young people, because rates of STDs tend to be higher among 15–24-year-olds than in the general population. Chlamydia is the most prevalent STD among young people (Panchaud et al. 2000). Rates of gonorrhea and herpes simplex are also high enough to be a substantial health problem. Rates of HIV/AIDS in the West are lower, but have drawn great attention because HIV/AIDS is fatal and because it is often acquired in adolescence or emerging adulthood. One unexpected effect of the rise of HIV/AIDS is that it has promoted more intensive sex education, which is believed to have contributed to the decline in teen pregnancies and STDs recorded in most Western countries during the 1990s (Singh & Darroch 2000).

Illicit drug use among the young, which is a topic of widespread public concern in the United States, is less prevalent in Europe, although rates differ from country to country (Silbereisen, Robins, & Rutter 1995). For example, in a survey of Belgian adolescents (aged 14–19), only 4 percent had ever used illicit drugs, and of these, 3 of 4 had used only marijuana (Goossens 1994). In Switzerland, only 25 percent of young people aged 15–25 report ever smoking marijuana and only 3 percent report ever using opiates, despite the Swiss policy of decriminalizing drug use (Buchmann 1994). In contrast, among 12th-grade American adolescents in a 1999 national survey, 50 percent had smoked marijuana and 29 percent had used an illicit drug other than marijuana (Monitoring the Future 2000). Canadian adolescents also report higher rates of drug use than European adolescents. In a survey of 15- to 19-year-olds, 10 percent had smoked marijuana in the past year and 27 percent had used stimulants (Galambos & Kolaric 1994). Use of illicit drugs rose in all Western countries during the 2nd half of the 20th century (Silbereisen et al. 1995). The reasons for this include increased affluence as well as the expansion of the period of emerging adulthood, as marriage and parenthood were increasingly postponed into the late 20s. Rates of all types of substance use tend to be higher in emerging adulthood than in adolescence (Arnett 2000a).

In contrast to illicit drugs, use of alcohol and cigarettes tends to be at least as high in Europe as in North America. For example, 69 percent of 13- to 19-year-olds in Poland report regular alcohol use (Wlodarek 1994). Cigarette smoking among young people is of particular concern, because it is the source of more illness and mortality in the long run than all illegal drugs combined and because the majority of persons who smoke begin as adolescents, in their midteens. Substantial proportions of young people smoke in all Western countries, with rates generally in the 20–50 percent range (e.g., Galambos & Kolaric 1994; Hurrelmann & Settertobulte 1994). Rates of smoking are especially high among young people in eastern and southern Europe (Martinez et al. 1994; Wlodarek 1994). Smoking has decreased among young people in most Western countries since the 1960s (e.g., Buzzi & Cavalli 1994; Galambos & Kolaric 1994), due to growing public awareness of the health hazards of smoking and to increased government efforts to discourage smoking among young people and to restrict cigarette advertising. Nevertheless, rates of smoking among young people have changed little (or even increased) in recent years and remain strikingly high, so it is difficult to predict whether or not smoking will remain a common form of health risk behavior for young people through the 21st century.

With regard to mental health, rates of depressive symptoms among the young are strikingly high, especially among girls. In a review of research on adolescent depression, Petersen and colleagues (1993) described a "midadolescence peak" in depressed mood, with higher rates among adolescents than among either children or adults. According to their analysis of 14 studies of nonclinical samples of adolescents, depressed mood is characteristic of over one-third of American adolescents at any given time. Similar findings have been reported in other Western countries. In a study of Canadian adolescents, one-third of 13- to 19-year-olds were classified as mildly to clinically depressed, with rates higher among girls after age 15 (Galambos & Kolaric 1994). In Germany, "subjective feelings of distress" were found among

25 percent of 15- to 19-year-olds, with higher rates among girls than boys (Hurrrelmann & Settertobulte 1994). In general, feeling of overall well-being tend to be lower in eastern Europe than in western Europe and the United States (Grob et al. 1999) because of lower standards of living and the recent political and economic disruptions in eastern European societies.

Provision of Services

In most Western countries, services to young people are provided in a haphazard manner (e.g., Buchman 1994; Buzzi & Cavalli 1994; Goossens 1994). Typically there is a vast proliferation of programs, provided through federal, local, and private agencies, with little coordination among them and little attempt made to assess their effectiveness. Common topics of these programs include job training and placement, educational counseling, drug use prevention and treatment, sexual abuse prevention and treatment, crime prevention, and recreation. The fragmentation of services to young people is most pronounced in the United States, partly because of the sheer size of the country and partly because of the long American tradition of local and state resistance to federal authority. At the federal level as in most states, there is no single agency or department that coordinates youth policy (Schulenberg & Ebata 1994). Instead, overlapping programs are distributed across the numerous different agencies that provide some form of services to young people.

Two Western countries with an unusually centralized and coherent program of youth services are Spain and Sweden. Since 1983, youth services in Spain have been administered by the Spanish Youth Council, which strives to promote young people's participation in the political, social, economic, and cultural development of Spain (Martinez, Miguel, & Fernandez 1994). The Council oversees services to youth in the areas of education, jobs, and substance use prevention, among others, with specific programs to address the needs of females, immigrants, and rural youth. The Council also has programs to promote youth travel and exchanges with other countries, especially Latin American countries.

Sweden has a long tradition of formal, government-sponsored youth organizations, including sports clubs, libraries, meeting halls, and youth clubs. Together, these organizations constitute "a professional system of socialization which is so extensive that it embraces the lives of most adolescents" (Roe et al. 1994, 383). Ironically, in recent years concern has grown in Sweden that this system may be *too* extensive, in that it involves adult intervention into the lives of young people so much that it may limit their freedom to pursue unstructured leisure.

Nongovernmental youth organizations also provide services to young people in some Western countries. In the United States, there are literally hundreds of adult-supervised, nonprofit youth organizations, such as the Young Men's Christian Association (YMCA) and the Young Women's Christian Association (YWCA), Boy and Girl Scouts, Boys and Girls Clubs, 4-H Clubs, and Junior Achievement (Schulenberg & Ebata 1994). These organizations tend to focus on providing recreation such as sports, camping, and outdoor activities while at the same time promoting character qualities such as responsibility and cooperation. Switzerland also has a strong tradition of nongovernmental youth services, provided through church organizations and nonprofit groups (Buchmann 1994). However, in most other European countries youth services and organizations are sponsored mainly through the government.

Adolescents' Perceptions of Their Futures

Given the rapid and accelerating pace of social change as the 21st century begins, the course of their futures is inherently difficult for adolescents or emerging adults to predict. Young people find themselves growing up in a time of increasing global integration even as the emotional salience of their local contexts – family, friends, community – remains strong. As Chisholm (1995) observes: "Young people are inescapably caught across the widening chasm of the global versus the local. In an individualized and risk-laden world, they find themselves building crazy patchwork bridges between the two: crazy, because the patternbooks appear to have disappeared; patchwork, because pluralisation and fragmentation of the social construction of youth makes *bricolage* the rational option" (31).

In light of this unstable situation, it is perhaps surprising to find that most Western adolescents view their personal futures with great optimism (Arnett 2000a; 2000b). Crossnational surveys in Europe have shown extremely high levels of personal life satisfaction among young people, although they express anxiety about collective future problems such as unemployment, drug addiction, and AIDS (Cavalli 1995). Most young people also have a strong sense of control over the shape their future will take. In one study of the United States and 12 European countries, across countries 85 percent of adolescents believed they were in control of their personal development in the future, and 88 percent believed they were in control of their success in their future workplace (Grob & Flammer 1999). When asked to rate the importance of various areas in their futures, adolescents in this study especially emphasized career objectives (getting a good education, acquiring a good profession), family objectives (getting married, having children), and leisure objectives (enjoying friends and vacations) (cf. Nurmi, Liiceanu, & Liberska 1999). Eastern European and American adolescents were more likely than western European adolescents to emphasize the future importance of being useful to their country and taking care of their parents.

Currently, eastern European adolescents report lower well-being and less optimism than adolescents in western Europe and the United States (Grob et al. 1999; Botcheva 1998). This difference appears to be due primarily to the massive cultural disruption experienced by eastern Europeans in the aftermath of the fall of communism. Although the transition to democracy has brought young people new opportunities for education, travel, and leisure, it has also exacted a price in the form of declining living standards and a high degree of political and social instability. The transition to democracy has also resulted in complications in identity formation and value orientations for young people, given the sharp disparity between the culture they were born into and the culture they have grown up in over the past decade.

In one especially notable and revealing study, Botcheva (1998) surveyed young people in Bulgaria aged 16–30 in 1989, before the fall of communism, and then annually for the next 3 years in the aftermath of communism. In almost every respect, young people viewed their lives as changing for the worse over the course of the study period. In the postcommunist years they viewed themselves as becoming less economically satisfied and less protected by law, more dependent and more oppressed, even as less free and less independent. Declines in well-being were especially steep from 1991 to 1992, the period in which "the most radical changes in social institutions took place" in Bulgarian society (123). However, it seems likely that over the decades to come, as eastern Europeans adjust to the radical changes that have taken place there and their economies strengthen, the benefits to young people from growing up in an open democratic society rather than a communist dictatorship will be highly favorable, and young eastern Europeans' well-being and views of the future will improve accordingly.

Conclusion

Adolescents in Western countries enter the 21st century with a future that is in many ways astonishingly bright. As a group they are endowed with more independence, more leisure, more education, more employment opportunities, and better health than any adolescents in human history. Compared to either their counterparts historically or their counterparts today in developing countries, they are the beneficiaries of remarkable advantages in almost every aspect of life. They are free to have a series of intimate relationships in their teens and 20s, then choose freely when and whom (and whether) to marry. They are free to choose from a wide range of possible educational and occupational paths to find one or more that they most desire. Their leisure options, too, are almost infinite and expanding every day. The opportunities available to young women are especially notable, given that a century ago women in the West were rarely allowed to take any roles in their societies outside of the domestic sphere.

Not all adolescents in 2000 in Western countries have equal access to these advantages. To some extent, access to opportunities for young people in Western societies varies by ethnicity and family socioeconomic status. Young people who are members of ethnic minorities and who also grow up in poor families face an especially formidable future. Although advances have been made in civil rights for ethnic minorities over the past half-century, it is difficult to say if young people from all ethnic backgrounds and all income backgrounds will gain equal opportunities in the course of the 21st century. Similarly, for young people in eastern Europe, whose societies have only recently made the transition from communism to democracy, their prospects at the outset of the 21st century are uncertain.

Of course, even if during the 21st century Western countries will succeed in making opportunities available to all of their young people, opportunities alone are no guarantee of a successful and happy passage to adulthood. On the contrary, it may be that variability of outcomes is an intractable feature of any society that allows a substantial amount of individual freedom and choice to its young people. Even with all of their advantages, unhappiness is strikingly pervasive among the adolescents of the West, with one-fourth to one-third experiencing depressed moods at any given time. Freedoms and opportunities can be daunting, as each young person must make choices in love and work from among what can be a formidable range of possibilities. Furthermore, for all of them an array of perils lurk amidst their privileges – pervasive family dissolution, high rates of youth unemployment, violence against minorities, STDs, and growing disillusionment with political institutions.

Still, for the most part young people in the West are optimistic about their futures, and they have good reason to be. No society can guarantee success and happiness to its young people, however much caring adults may wish they could. Every society in every era has its own problems and challenges that young people must confront. But Western societies are generally stable, affluent, and democratic, and these features make the West of the 21st century an exceptionally promising time and place to be young.

References

Alsaker, F. D. & A. Flammer, 1999. *The Adolescent experience: European and American adolescents in the 1990s*, 1–14. Mahwah, NJ: Erlbaum.

Anderson, R. E. 2002. Youth and information technology. In *The future of adolescent experience*: Societal trends and the transition to adulthood. New York: Cambridge University Press.

Arnett, J. J. 1994. Are college students adults? Their conceptions of the transition to adulthood. *Journal of Adult Development*. 1:154–168.

Arnett, J. J. 1995. Adolescents' uses of media for self-socialization. *Journal of Youth & Adolescence*. 24:519–533.

Arnett, J. J. 1998. Learning to stand alone: The contemporary American transition to adulthood in cultural and historical context. *Human Development*. 6:295–315.

Arnett, J. J. 1999. Adolescent storm and stress, reconsidered. *American Psychologist*. 54:317–326.

Arnett, J. J. 2000a. Emerging adulthood: A conception of development from the late teens through the twenties. *American Psychologist*. 55:469–480.

Arnett, J. J. 2000b. High hopes in a grim world: Emerging adults' views of their futures and of "Generation X." *Youth & Society*. 31:267–286.

Berndt, T. J. 1996. Transitions in friendship and friends' influence. In *Transitions through adolescence: Interpersonal domains and context*, eds. J. A. Graber, J. Brooks-Gunn & A. C. Petersen, 57–84. Mahwah, NJ: Erlbaum.

Berry, V. 1995. Redeeming the rap music experience. In *Adolescents and their music*, ed. J. S. Epstein, 165–188. New York: Garland.

Bo, I. 1996. The significant people in the social networks of adolescents. In *Social problems and social contexts in adolescence: Perspectives across boundaries*, eds. K. Hurrelmann & S. Hamilton, 107–130. Hawthorne, NY: Aldine de Gruyter.

du Bois-Reymond, M. & J. Ravesloot. 1996. The roles of parents and peers in the sexual and relational socialization of adolescents. In *Social problems and social contexts in adolescence: Perspectives across boundaries*, eds. K. Hurrelmann & S. Hamilton, 175–197. Hawthorne, NY: Aldine de Gruyter.

du Bois-Reymond, M. & I. van der Zande. 1994. The Netherlands. In *International handbook of adolescence*, ed. K. Hurrelmann, 270–286. Westport, CT: Greenwood Press.

Botcheva, L. 1998. The gains and losses of Bulgarian youths during the transition from socialism to democracy. In *Adolescents, cultures, and conflicts*, ed. J. Nurmi, 109–128. New York: Garland.

Brake, M. 1985. *Comparative youth culture*. New York: Routledge.

Bremer, J. & P. K. Rauch. 1998. Children and computers: Risks and benefits. *Journal of the American Academy of Child and Adolescent Psychiatry*. 37:559–560.

Brown, B. B., M. Mory, & D. Kinney. 1994. Casting adolescent crowds in relational perspective: Caricature, channel, and context. In *Advances in adolescent development: Vol. 6: Personal relationships during adolescence*, eds. Montemayor, G. R. Adams, & T. P. Gulotta, 123–167. Newbury Park, CA: Sage.

Buchanan, C. M. 2000. The impact of divorce on adjustment during adolescence. In *Resilience across contexts: Family, work, culture, and community*, eds. R. D. Taylor & M. Weng, 179–216. Mahwah, NJ: Erlbaum.

Buchmann, M. 1994. *Switzerland*. In *International handbook of adolescence*, ed. K. Hurrelmann, 386–399. Westport, CT: Greenwood Press.

Buhrmester, D. & W. Furman. 1987. The development of companionship and intimacy. *Child Development*. 58:1101–1113.

Buzzi, C., & A. Cavalli. 1994. Italy. In *International handbook of adolescence*, ed. K. Hurrelmann, 224–233. Westport, CT: Greenwood Press.

Cantor, J. 2000. Violence in films and television. In *Encyclopedia of international media and communications*, ed. R. Lee. New York: Academic Press.

Carvalho, A. & M. Dias. 1994. Portugal. In *International handbook of adolescence*, ed. K. Hurrelmann, 322–331. Westport, CT: Greenwood Press.

Cavalli, A. 1995. The value orientations of young Europeans. In *Growing up in Europe: Contemporary horizons in childhood and youth studies*, eds. L. Chisholm, P. Buchner H. H. Kruger, & M. du Bois-Reymond, 35–41. New York: Walter de Gruyter.

Centers for Disease Control and Prevention 2001. Youth risk behavior surveillance system. (online): www.cdc.gov/nccdphp/dash/yrbs/suse.htm

Chisholm, L. 1995. European youth research: Tour de force or turmbau zu Babel? In *Growing up in Europe: Contemporary horizons in childhood and youth studies*, eds. L. Chisholm, P. Buchner, H. H. Kruger, & M. du Bois-Reymond, 21–32. New York: Walter de Gruyter.

Chisholm, L. & K. Hurrelmann. 1995. Adolescence in modern Europe: Pluralized transition patterns and their implications for personal and social risks. *Journal of Adolescence*. 18:129–158.

Csapo, B. 1994. Hungary. In *International handbook of adolescence*, ed. K. Hurrelmann, 177–190. Westport, CT: Greenwood Press.

Decker, J. L. 1994. The state of rap: Time and place in hip hop nationalism. In *Microphone fiends: Youth music & youth culture*, eds. A. Ross & T. Rose, 99–121. New York: Routledge.

Dey, E. L. & S. Hurtado. 1999. Students, colleges, and society: Considering the interconnections. In *American higher education in the twenty-first century:*

Social, political, and economic challenges, eds. P. G. Altbach, R. O. Berdahl, & P. J. Gumport, 298–322. Baltimore, MD: Johns Hopkins University Press.

Diekstra, R. F. W., C. W. M. Kienhorst, & E. J. de Wilde. 1995. Suicide and suicidal behaviors among adolescents. In *Psychosocial disorders in young people: Time trends and their causes*, ed. M. Rutter & D. J. Smith, (686–761). New York: Wiley.

Dubas, J. S & A. C. Petersen. 1996. Geographical distance from parents and adjustment during adolescence and young adulthood. *New Directions for Child Development*. 71:3–20.

Flammer, A. & F. D. Alsaker. 1999. Time use by adolescents in international perspective: The case of necessary activities. In *The Adolescent experience: European and American adolescents in the 1990s*, eds. F. D. Alsaker & A. Flammer, 61–84. Mahwah, NJ: Erlbaum.

Flammer, A. & F. D. Alsaker. 2001. Adolescents in school. In *Handbook of adolescent development: European perspectives*, eds. L. Goossens & S. Jackson, Hove, UK: Psychology Press.

Flammer, A. F. D. Alsaker. & P. Noack. 1999. Time use by adolescents in international perspective: The case of leisure activities. In *The adolescent experience: European and American adolescents in the 1990s*, eds. F. D. Alsaker & A. Flammer, 33–60. Mahwah, NJ: Erlbaum.

Flanagan, C., B. Jonsson, L. Botcheva, B. Csapo, J. Bowes, P. Macek, I. Averina, & E. Sheblanova. 1999. Adolescents and the 'social contract': Developmental roots of citizenship in seven countries. In *Roots of civic identity: International perspectives on community service and activism in youth*, eds. Yates, M., & Youniss, J., 135–155. New York: Cambridge University Press.

Freedman, J. L. 1984. Effects of television violence on aggressiveness. *Psychological Bulletin*. 96:227–246.

Fuligni, A. J., V. Tseng, & M. Lam. 1999. Attitudes toward family obligations among American adolescents from Asian, Latin American, and European backgrounds. *Child Development*. 70:1030–1044.

Funk, J. B., B. Flores, D. D. Buchman, & J. N. Germann. 1999. Rating electronic video games: Violence is in the eye of the beholder. *Youth & Society*. 30:283–312.

Furman, W., B. B. Brown, & C. Feiring. 1999. *The development of romantic relationships in adolescence*. New York: Cambridge University Press.

Galambos, N. & G. C. Kolaric. 1994. Canada. In *International handbook of adolescence*, ed. K. Hurrelmann, 92–107. Westport, CT: Greenwood Press.

Goldscheider, F. & C. Goldscheider. 1999. *The changing transition to adulthood: Leaving and returning home*. Thousand Oaks, CA: Sage.

Goossens, L. 1994. Belgium. In *International handbook of adolescence*, ed. K. Hurrelmann, 51–64. Westport, CT: Greenwood Press.

Greenberger, E., L. Steinberg, A. Vaux, & S. McAuliffe. 1980. Adolescents who work: Effects of part-time employment on family and peer relations. *Journal of Youth & Adolescence*. 9:364–381.

Grob, A. & A. Flammer. 1999. Macrosocial context and adolescents' perceived control. In *The Adolescent experience: European and American adolescents in the 1990s*, eds. F. D. Alsaker & A. Flammer, 99–114. Mahwah, NJ: Erlbaum.

Grob, A., A. Stetsenko, C. Sabatier, L. Botcheva, & P. Macek. 1999. A cross-national model of subjective well-being in adolescence. In *The Adolescent experience: European and American adolescents in the 1990s*, eds. F. D. Alsaker & A. Flammer, 115–130. Mahwah, NJ: Erlbaum.

Hall, G. S. 1904. *Adolescence: Its psychology and its relation to physiology, anthropology, sociology, sex, crime, religion, and education*, Vols. 1 & 2. Englewood Cliffs, NJ: Prentice-Hall.

Hamilton, S. F. 1990. *Apprenticeship for adulthood: Preparing youth for the future*. New York: Free Press.

Hendry, L. B. & J. Shucksmith. 1994. The United Kingdom. In *International handbook of adolescence*, ed. K. Hurrelmann, 400–413. Westport, CT: Greenwood Press.

Hess, L. E. 1995. Changing family patterns in western Europe: Opportunity and risk factors for adolescent development. In *Psychosocial disorders in young people: Time trends and their causes*, eds. M. Rutter & D. J. Smith, 104–187. New York: Wiley.

Hoem, B. 1992. Early phases of family formation in contemporary Sweden. In *Early parenthood and coming of age in the 1990s*, eds. M. K. Rosenheim & M. F. Testa, 183–199. New Brunswick, NJ: Rutgers University Press.

Hurrelmann, K. 1996. The social world of adolescents: A sociological perspective. In *Social problems and social contexts in adolescence: Perspectives across boundaries*, eds. K. Hurrelmann & S. Hamilton, 39–62. Hawthorne, NY: Aldine de Gruyter.

Hurrelmann, K. & W. Settertobulte. 1994. Germany. In *International handbook of adolescence*, ed. K. Hurrelmann, 160–176. Westport, CT: Greenwood Press.

Kett, J. F. 1977. *Rites of passage: Adolescence in America, 1790 to the present*. New York: Basic Books.

Kracke, B., M. Oepke, E. Wild, & P. Noack. 1998. Adolescents, families, and German unification: The impact of social change on antiforeigner and antidemocratic attitudes. In *Adolescents, cultures, and conflicts*, ed. J. Nurmi, 149–170. New York: Garland.

Lagree, J. C. 1995. Young people and employment in the European Community: Convergence or divergence? In *Growing up in Europe: Contemporary horizons in childhood and youth studies*, eds. Chisholm, L. P. Buchner, H. H. Kruger, & M. du Bois-Reymond, 61–72. New York: Walter de Gruyter.

Lamborn, S., N. Mounts, L. Steinberg, & S. Dornbusch. 1991. Patterns of competence and adjustment among adolescents from authoritative, authoritarian, indulgent, and neglectful families. *Child Development*. 62:1049–1065.

Larson, R. 1995. Secrets in the bedroom: Adolescents' private use of media. *Journal of Youth & Adolescence*. 24:535–550.

Larson, R. & M. H. Richards. 1994. *Divergent realities: The emotional lives of mothers, fathers, and adolescents*. New York: Basic Books.

Lerner, R. M., D. R. Entwistle, & S. T. Hauser. 1994. The crisis among contemporary American adolescents: A call for integration of research, policies, and programs. *Journal of Research on Adolescence*. 4:1–4.

Liebkind, K. & L. Kosonen. 1998. Acculturation and adaptation: A case of Vietnamese children and youths in Finland. In *Adolescents, cultures, and conflicts*, ed. J. Nurmi, 199–224. New York: Garland.

Macek, P. & L. Rabusic. 1994. Czechoslovakia. In *International handbook of adolescence*, ed. K. Hurrelmann, 117–130. Westport, CT: Greenwood Press.

Martinez, R., M. de Miguel, & S. Fernandez. 1994. Spain. In *International handbook of adolescence*, ed. K. Hurrelmann, 360–373. Westport, CT: Greenwood Press.

Matza, D. & G. Sykes. 1961. Juvenile delinquency and subterranean values. *American Sociological Review*. 26:712–719.

Monitoring the Future. 2000. Trends in lifetime prevalence of use of various drugs for eighth, tenth, and twelfth graders. (online): www.monitoringthefuture.org.

Mortimer, J. T., C. Harley, & P. J. Aronson. 1999. How do prior experiences in the workplace set the stage for transitions to adulthood? In *Transitions to adulthood in a changing economy: No work, no family, no future?*, eds. A. Booth, A. C. Crouter, & M. J. Shanahan, 131–159. Westport, CT: Praeger.

Motola, M., P. Sinisalo, & J. Guichard. 1998. Social habitus and future plans. In *Adolescents, cultures, and conflicts*, ed. J. Nurmi, 43–73. New York: Garland.

National Center for Education Statistics 2000. *The condition of education 2000*. Washington, D.C.: U.S. Department of Education.

Nurmi, J. 1998. Growing up in contemporary Europe. In *Adolescents, cultures, and conflicts*, ed. J. Nurmi, 3–17. New York: Garland.

Nurmi, J., A. Liiceanu, & H. Liberska. 1999. Future-oriented interests. In *The adolescent experience: European and American adolescents in the 1990s*, eds. F. D. Alsaker & A. Flammer, 85–98. Mahwah, NJ: Erlbaum.

Nurmi, J. & L. Siurala. 1994. Finland. In *International handbook of adolescence*, ed. K. Hurrelmann, 131–145. Westport, CT: Greenwood Press.

Osgood, D. W., J. K. Wilson, P. M. O'Malley, J. G. Bachman, & L. D. Johnston. 1996. Routine activities and individual deviant behavior. *American Sociological Review*. 61(4):635–655.

Panchaud, C., S. Singh, D. Feivelson, & J. E. Darroch. 2000. Sexually transmitted diseases among adolescents in developed countries. *Family Planning Perspectives*. 32:24–32.

Petersen, A. C., B. E. Compas, J. Brooks-Gunn. E. S. Stemmler, M., & K. E. Grant. 1993. Depression in adolescence. *American Psychologist*. 48:155–168.

Phinney, J. S., A. Ong, & T. Madden. 2000. Cultural values and intergenerational value discrepancies in immigrant and non-immigrant families. *Child Development*. 71:528–539.

Pollard, K. M. & W. P. O'Hare. 1999. America's racial and ethnic minorities. *Population Bulletin*. 54: September, 1–44.

Roberts, D. F., U. G. Foehr, V. J. Rideout, & M. Brodie. 1999. *Kids & media in the new millenium: A comprehensive national analysis of children's media use*. New York: Henry J. Kaiser Family Foundation.

Rockett, I. R. H. 1998. *Injury and violence: A public health perspective*, Vol. 53, no. 4. Washington, DC: Population Reference Bureau.

Roe, K., E. Bjurnstrom, & J. Fornas. 1994. Sweden. In *International handbook of adolescence*, ed. K. Hurrelmann, 374–385. Westport, CT: Greenwood Press.

Rutter, M., H. Giller, & A. Hagell. 1998. *Antisocial behavior by young people*. New York: Cambridge University Press.

Rutter, M. & D. J. Smith. eds. 1995. *Psychosocial disorders in young people: Time trends and their causes*, 104–187. New York: Wiley.

Sansone, L. 1995. The making of a black youth culture: Lower-class young men of Surinamese origin in Amsterdam. In *Youth cultures: A cross-cultural perspective*, eds. V. Amit-Talai & H. Wulff, 114–143. New York: Routledge.

Schlegel, A. & H. Barry III. 1991. *Adolescence: An anthropological inquiry*. New York: Free Press.

Schulenberg, J. & A. T. Ebata. 1994. The United States. In *International handbook of adolescence*, ed. K. Hurrelmann, 414–430. Westport, CT: Greenwood Press.

Scott, D. 1995. The effect of video games on feelings of aggression. *Journal of Psychology*. 129:121–132.

Silbereisen, R. K., L. Robins, & M. Rutter. 1995. Secular trends in substance use: Concepts and data on the impact of social change on alcohol and drug abuse. In *Psychosocial disorders in young people: Time trends and their causes*, eds. M. Rutter & D. J. Smith, 490–543. New York: Wiley.

Singh, G. & S. Yu. 1996. U.S. childhood mortality, 1950 through 1993: Trends and socioeconomic differentials. *American Journal of Public Health*. 86:505–512.

Singh, S. & J. E. Darroch. 2000. Adolescent pregnancy and childbearing: Levels and trends in developed countries. *Family Planning Perspectives*. 32:14–23.

Stafseng, O. 1994. Norway. In *International handbook of adolescence*, ed. K. Hurrelmann, 287–298. Westport, CT: Greenwood Press.

Steele, J. R. & J. D. Brown. 1995. Adolescent room culture: Studying media in the context of everyday life. *Journal of Youth & Adolescence*. 24:551–576.

Steinberg, L. & E. Cauffman. 1995. The impact of employment on adolescent development. In *Annals of child development, vol. 1*, ed. R. Vasta. London: Jessica Kingsley Publishers.

Steiner, I. 1995. Growing up in twelve cities: The families in which pupils live. In *Growing up in Europe: Contemporary horizons in childhood and youth studies*, eds. L. Chisholm, P. Buchner, H. H. Kruger, & M. du Bois-Reymond, 73–82. New York: Walter de Gruyter.

Strasburger, V. C. 1995. *Adolescents and the media: Medical and psychological impact*. Thousand Oaks, CA: Sage Publications.

Suarez-Orozco, C. & M. Suarez-Orozco. 1996. *Transformations: Migration, family life and achievement motivation among Latino adolescents*. Palo Alto, CA: Stanford University Press.

Taylor, R. D. 1996. Adolescents and perceptions of kinship support family management practices: Association with adolescent adjustment in African American families. *Developmental Psychology*. 32:687–695.

Wallace, J. M. & D. R. Williams. 1997. Religion and adolescent health-compromising behavior. In *Health risks and developmental transitions during adolescence*, eds. J. Schulenberg, J. L. Maggs, & K. Hurrelmann, 444–468. New York: Cambridge University Press.

Westin, C. 1998. Immigration, xenophobia, and youthful opinion. In *Adolescents, cultures, and conflicts*, ed. J. E. Nurmi, 225–241. New York: Garland.

Wlodarek, J. 1994. Poland. In *International handbook of adolescence*, ed. K. Hurrelmann, 309–321. Westport, CT: Greenwood Press.

Yates, M. 1999. Community service and political-moral discussions among adolescents: A study of a mandatory school-based program in the United States. In *Roots of civic identity: International perspectives on community service and activism in youth*, eds. M. Yates & J. Youniss, 16–31. New York: Cambridge University Press.

Youniss, J. & J. Smollar. 1985. *Adolescents' relations with mothers, fathers, and friends*. Chicago: University of Chicago Press.

11

Adolescence in Global Perspective

An Agenda for Social Policy

T. S. Saraswathi and Reed W. Larson

The chapters in this volume have presented a panoramic view of adolescents in a global perspective. They draw attention to the diversity of contexts in which young people are growing up today, preparing themselves to assume adult roles in the years to come. The contrasts between regions are striking and at times startling. The likelihood of an adolescent girl being enrolled in secondary school is as low as 5–10 percent in many African countries but is virtually 100 percent in Japan and some European countries (United Nations International Children's Emergency Fund 1997; UNICEF). Equally striking, however, can be the similarities across large geographic and cultural distances. In many ways, the lives of middle-class youth in India, Southeast Asia, and Europe have more in common with each other than they do with those of poor youth in their own countries.

The portraits of adolescence presented here are important both in their own right – as a reflection of the well-being of a substantial segment of the population – and as a portent of the future of society. The nation that neglects to provide for its youth will see the costs of that neglect in the years that follow. The nation that equips and energizes its youth is likely to reap compounded benefits as these youth enter adulthood and take over the reigns of society as parents, workers, and leaders.

How are the world's societies doing on these counts? The current state of the world's youth is a good news and bad news story. There is cause for hope but also urgent need for social action to better kindle the enormous potential that adolescents bring to society. We will start by pulling together the general picture suggested by the previous chapters, then we will discuss what this picture suggests for social policy.

Causes for Hope

When one views the larger picture there are good reasons for optimism. At the macrolevel, several aspects of social development have strengthened or generated supportive institutional arrangements for adolescent development over the recent decades. A large number of governments have recognized the significance of youth in their nations' progress, and many have clearly articulated youth policies. Education has been recognized as a basic right of children in most countries, and more and more young people are in school, acquiring the skills and competencies required for effective survival. Around the world there are increasingly thousands of nongovernment organizations (NGOs) that provide support services for adolescents, complementing those of the community and the government. In addition to providing services and advocating for the rights of youth, certain NGOs involve young people themselves and provide a training ground for civic participation (Larson 2000). Reduction in family size the world over has led to more quality care in terms of health, education, and leisure activities. There is better access to basic health care and nutrition, even while the ogre of HIV/AIDS looms large. Liberalization of the economy in most countries and rapid technological developments have increased opportunities for employment and career development.

Reflections of these macrolevel changes are seen in the individual lives of young people. More adolescents the world over now go to school and stay in school longer. Several chapters report that an increasing number of girls are opting to combine a career with marriage and family life. Young men and women migrate to cities or even to foreign lands seeking employment, sending money back home to support their natal families. Adolescents in many regions report optimism about the future and have higher levels of educational and career aspirations. Information technology has generated opportunities for entrepreneurship, and in both the developed and the developing world young people with computer skills are propelling themselves into successful, sometimes extraordinarily successful, careers. Youth's engagement with their communities finds mention in several chapters, be it in overthrowing communist rule in the former Soviet block or in supporting indigenous people and ecological movements in Latin America.

Improved life circumstances for youth – and for people in general – are particularly apparent in some parts of the developing world. A

United Nations Human Development Report states, "Development process has succeeded beyond any reasonable expectations. Developing countries have achieved in 30 years what it took industrial countries nearly a century to accomplish" (United Nations Development Program 1991, 14; UNDP). For example for the world as a whole, the prospect of an infant living to age 60 has jumped from 32 percent in 1955 to 86 percent in 1995, and is expected to be 96 percent by 2015 (World Health Organization 1998; WHO). The number of adolescents enrolled in secondary education in the developing world has leaped from 23 percent in 1970 to 52 percent in 1997 (United Nations Education, Scientific, and Cultural Organization 1999; UNESCO). The most dramatic improvement in the circumstances of youth in the last half century has been in Japan and in the other countries known as "Asian Tigers," where deliberate governmental infusions of money into education have greatly increased the capabilities of youth. As they reached adulthood this education permitted young people to make valuable contributions to society, which have lifted these nations from the ranks of "developing" to "developed" nations (Baker & Holsinger 1997; Cummings 1997). We also point to the much different examples of China and Kerala (a state in southern India), where despite extreme poverty, commitment to education and universal health care has raised life expectancy above that for some Western populations (Sen 1999).

The key criterion, we and others argue, is whether adolescents are afforded opportunities to develop to their full capabilities – to prepare for an adulthood that is beneficial to themselves, their families, and their societies. The Nobel Prize-winning economist Amartya Sen (1999) has written that the development of a nation should be evaluated, not by the GNP of its economy, but by the opportunities – the "freedoms" for self-development and responsible action – it gives to its populace. This standard is particularly suited to evaluating the situation of adolescents: they are at a critical juncture in life at which outside forces and institutions have a major influence in constraining or facilitating their future paths. In Sen's words, the "unfreedoms" of poverty, lack of access to education, restricted economic opportunities, and political tyranny inhibit opportunities for people to develop and exercise their capabilities. The question is whether pathways are open or are being opened for adolescents. By this criterion there have been improvements in the freedoms available to youth – at least for many.

Causes for Concern

The optimism evoked by this positive profile of adolescents' lives is tempered by the proverbial "on the other hand ..." Throughout the world there is an erosion in the traditional systems of support to young people leading to destabilization of values, excessive materialism (often creating desires that cannot be fulfilled), and, in some cases, moral or social bankruptcy (e.g., when parents send their daughter to prostitute in the Far East or seek political patronage when their son turns to crime). In both the industrialized and developing world there is a rapid rise in international crime rings in prostitution, pornography, and drugs – all of which directly involve and impact youth (UNDP 1999).

Large macroprocesses lie behind many of the threats to adolescents' well-being. Uncontrolled population growth in developing countries poses a threat to the ecological settings in which adolescents live, contributing to crowding, poor sanitation, infectious diseases, and competition for limited resources. For many adolescents this means hunger, inadequate nutrition, and struggle for survival. High rates of migration all over the world – from rural areas to cities and from developing to industrialized countries – overwhelm the capacities of destination localities to provide adequate services, intensify competition for education and jobs, and increase the possibility of inter-ethnic conflict among adolescents (Larson 2000). The increasing numbers of youth in the developing world threaten to overwhelm the capacities of schools, reduce the availability of health care, and outpace the creation of new jobs (Fussell & Greene this volume).

Meanwhile, the amount of money that national governments are investing in their youth (e.g., in education and other social services) is static and even declining in some countries (UNESCO 1999), while the larger amounts of money going to the military show astounding increases (UNDP 2000). To make matters worse, the assistance that poor countries are obtaining for social development from the most wealthy is declining. The amount of official development assistance allocated to education, health, nutrition, and family planning has been declining in both relative and absolute terms. Monies for social development fell from 33 percent of the total overseas development aid in 1987–88 to 24 percent in 1998 (UNDP 2000).

The obstacles to freedoms – to full development – for youth exist at many levels and layers, both global and local. Behind a number of these concerns lie the processes of globalization and the negative impacts of international monetary policies. The new competitive global market economy provides opportunities for many youth, but also erodes opportunities for others by reducing the value of traditional means of subsistence, such as crafts and small farming. Many people, including entire nations in Africa, are being further disadvantaged (Castells 1998; Fussell & Greene this volume; UNDP 2000). The competitive handicap for many developing countries has been exacerbated by international monetary policies. In the 1980s, the World Bank and the International Monetary Fund responded to the economic crisis of developing countries by negotiating a package of policy prescriptions known as structural adjustment programs in return for loan guarantees. This package demanded major economic reform – including opening their markets to international trade – which fed the competitive forces just described. It also demanded reductions in government expenditures – with the axe falling on health, education, and other welfare expenditures (UNICEF 1997). Among the most vulnerable to these cuts, besides women and children, were rural youth (Azam et al. 1989; UNICEF 1997). Since the 1980s, the debts from these loans have kept in place or worsened the severe negative consequences of these policies, particularly in Africa and Latin America (Speth 1999; Welti this volume). These staggering debts, among other factors (including some that affect the poor and working classes in the developing countries; Castells 1998), sustain life conditions for youth that are depleted of opportunities – of freedoms for self-development, choice, and contributing to society. To make matters worse, they destabilize governments, leading to chaotic political conditions that further undermine the provision of services and adolescents' ability to reliably foresee and plan for their futures (Larson 2000).

The sad reality is that adolescents live in a world of disturbing contrasts and glaring inequalities, both between and within nations. The north-south divide provides the most startling contrast. More than three-quarters of the world's people live in developing countries (the south), but they enjoy only 14 percent of the world's income and 18 percent of the goods and resources, whereas the richest 20 percent (the north) have 86 percent of the global income and an 82 percent share in consumption (UNDP 1999). Furthermore, the inequalities both between and within countries are increasing rapidly (UNDP 2000; UNICEF 1997). This is a great moral issue. To quote Bruton (1997), "A world in which some people have so much while millions of others spend most of their life starving is a world which few would defend" (ix). Over 1.2 billion people in these regions live on $1.00 per day or less (UNDP 2000), while teens in other parts of the world think nothing of spending many times more per day on clothing, snack food, and entertainment. In many cases, inadequacy of resources falls unequally on women and specific indigenous or ethnic groups.

The chapters reflect what these larger institutional and macro concerns mean in terms of the immediate experiences of adolescents' lives, in both poor and wealthy nations. To begin with, we see worldwide challenges to families' ability to nurture youth. Authors express concern regarding decreases in contact time between adolescents and their parents, especially with parents' increasing career aspirations, mothers' participation in the labor force, and job pressures. Erosion of traditional family systems is evident in higher rates of divorce and family dislocation in many countries (Burns & Scott 1994; Nsamenang this volume; Santa Maria this volume), while continued authoritarianism by fathers in traditional cultures also alienate youth (Booth this volume). Several chapters note trends toward greater individualism and autonomy among youth, which, although not necessarily bad, does increase the challenges for parents.

In most parts of the world, peers are gaining a stronger, sometimes adverse, influence. Several authors comment on the emergence of a global youth culture, though some argue that it is far from homogeneous. Some consequences of youth culture are benign (such as popular music, dress forms, use of slang) and some obviously malignant (e.g., increase in smoking, consumption of alcohol, unsafe sex, drug use, violence, and crime). The steady decline in age of initiation of premarital sexual activity along with the spread of HIV/AIDS threaten to undo the tremendous gains made on the health front. Concerns are expressed about a peer culture of increasing commercialism, materialism, and self-indulgence at the cost of family obligations and community involvement. Arnett (this volume) also reports tension and overt conflict between youth of different ethnic groups in Western nations, a phenomenon that occurs in other nations as well.

The chapters also indicate challenges in education and other spheres of youths' experience and development. Many youth remain uneducated, and school curricula in many places are not relevant to the skills youth need (Nsamenang this volume; Santa Maria this volume). Public funds that go to education are disproportionately invested in higher education rather than in primary and secondary schooling where they would have more impact (Fussell & Greene this volume; Verma &

Saraswathi this volume; UNDP 2000). Even in the industrial world and among middle-class youth elsewhere, boredom and stress undermine adolescents' schoolwork and prevent them from obtaining the most out of their many hours in the classroom (Larson & Richards 1991; Verma, Sharma, & Larson 1999). In the sphere of work, inadequate support systems for apprenticeship, particularly for skills needed in the increasingly competitive and technological job market, have left large numbers of unemployed or underemployed. In the sphere of civic engagement, political instability, corruption, and the cynicism of politicians have left youth disenchanted and apathetic in many parts of the world.

So, while the good news is that opportunities have opened up for more youth, many continue to experience hindered pathways to a full adulthood. Many of the world's youth are simply being left behind: poor youth in many parts of the world do not have an "adolescence," they do not have a period of moratorium from labor to develop the capabilities that are necessary for adequate employment in the new economy (Saraswathi 1999; Welti this volume). They are subject to Sen's "unfreedoms" of poverty and restricted opportunities. But pathways are also hindered for other youth as well, including those in industrialized countries where family instability, negative peer influences, alienation, and apathy prevent young people from developing to their full potential.

From an economist's perspective, the failure to use adolescence for development of skills is an enormous squandering of human capital. From a deeper, more humanistic perspective young people are not being given the opportunity to fulfill their capabilities and make a full contribution to their communities and society. The issue is, how do we make it possible for more youth to activate these capabilities?

A Framework for Social Policy

Many social and youth policy experts have adopted a framework similar to Sen's that focuses on human opportunities. Coles (1995) uses the metaphor of the snakes and ladders game ("chutes and ladders" in the United States) to articulate this frame: "In designing better social policies for young people, we must be concerned to ensure that the ladders of opportunity are more secure and the routes to them properly signposted ... to guarantee that wise and beneficial decisions are taken and that these are made at the right time" (197). By implication, too, policy must work to reduce the number of "snakes" or "chutes" that undo or reverse progress individuals make, that create unfreedoms.

A similar framework is suggested by the 1995 United Nations Human Development Report, which states that the basic objective of social policy should be viewed as one of enlarging people's choices. The report emphasizes 3 essential components: (a) providing equal opportunity in education and employment for all people in the society; (b) achieving sustainability of such opportunities from one generation to the next; and (c) empowering people such that they participate in and benefit from the development process. In other words, the task of social policy is not to do things *to* or *for* adolescents, but to ensure that they have the opportunity and support to do things *for themselves*.

In 1996, the United Nations (UN) formulated a set of goals for youth policy entitled "World Programme of Action for Youth the Year 2000 and Beyond." It articulates the objectives of permitting youth "self-sufficient lives" and "full participation in the life of society" including: (a) attaining education commensurate with aspirations; (b) experiencing 2 employment opportunities equal to abilities; (c) having adequate food and nutrition; (d) experiencing a physical and social environment that promotes good health and offers protection from addiction and violence; (e) enjoying basic human rights and fundamental freedom, without distinction by race, sex, or religion; and (f) having a voice in decisions made regarding their lives.

The UN's list of proposed interventions to achieve these objectives include:

- universalizing first basic and then secondary education, with efforts to improve the quality of education and strengthen links between education and employment;
- expanding vocational and technical training, especially in skills related to modern technology;
- creating opportunities for employment not only in the formal sector but also through self-employment and entrepreneurship;
- guaranteeing full human rights and freedoms to all young people;
- reducing hunger and poverty, for example, through involvement of youth in rural development;
- improving basic health facilities and sanitation, education for reproductive health and decision making, prevention of sexual abuse and HIV/AIDS;
- addressing issues of drug abuse and juvenile delinquency through prevention, rehabilitation, and social marketing messages via effective use of media;

- fostering mutual respect, tolerance, and understanding among young people with differing racial, cultural, and religious backgrounds;
- providing access to leisure activities;
- removing discrimination by gender for health care, access to education, and employment; eliminating sexual victimization.

Based on the 8 chapters here, we would add to this list:

- ensuring supports for families so that they may support youth; avoiding policies that undercut families; helping families adjust to the dramatic economic, social, and cultural changes that undermine their nurturing functions;
- promoting the development of rich and interesting media options that provide alternatives to violent and commercial fare;
- revising school curricula to ensure that they teach life skills and career skills that are both locally and globally relevant to youth;
- developing intervention programs that develop the specific issues of girls and boys.

The UN's program of action views young people, not just as victims of societal changes, but also as agents and beneficiaries. The goal needs to be creating, supporting, and modifying institutions in order to ensure opportunities – "ladders" for youth to meaningful adulthood. Of course, it is easy to set goals, harder to know how to achieve them.

Multilayered Responses

The challenge to implementing effective social policy around this agenda, as richly illustrated in these chapters, is that many diverse institutions and factors mold and constrain adolescents' opportunities. The "chutes and ladders" for youth are shaped by many layers of global and local processes. These include international monetary policies, the vested interests of local community leaders, family traditions and expectations, and the motivations and aspirations of youth themselves. They include the multiple microsystems that directly influence adolescents' lives: family, peer groups, schools, employment, and media. Obstacles and potential for improving opportunities for youth exist simultaneously at these and other levels of influence. Furthermore the interrelationships between levels are complex and consequences of change can be unexpected, as when the opening of free markets in Russia had a disastrous effect on young women's employment opportunities (Stetsenko this volume).

What this complexity means is that effective social policy for youth must address these multiple levels. As stated by a World Bank (2000) report, "Globalization and localization are transforming many aspects of the human experience – so many that only a comprehensive, multi-layered response of policy and institutional reform will be adequate" (174). Social policy must be attuned to the influence of large socioeconomic forces and unique local circumstances. For example, recognizing the absence of boundaries for the 4 interrelated problems of drug abuse, prostitution, migration, and sexually transmitted diseases – but also regional variations – the United Nations (1996) recommends the need for both international and regional networks of cooperation to address these issues.

This complexity also means that input must be received from multiple agents. Effective youth policies depend on a synthesis of political priorities, professional agendas, and young people's perspectives and responses (Williamson, 1997). Thus, for example, local efforts to improve education and health care will be handicapped without cooperation and infusion of resources from higher levels. A UNICEF (1997) analysis found that by redirecting just one-quarter of the developing world's military expenditure (i.e. $30 billion of $125 billion) and adding $10 billion from overseas aid, enough additional resources can be generated to reach most of the goals of basic social services for children, adolescents, and their families, such as health care, education, and safe water. Likewise, national laws on child and adolescent labor will have little effect if there is no local commitment to enforcing them (International Labor Organization 1996; ILO); and programs aimed at improving opportunities for girls, will be stymied if parents and village elders undercut them. Most importantly, adolescents themselves must be invested; programs are consistently found to be most effective when youth have been involved in their development and management (WHO 1999). Policies, programs, and initiatives are much more likely to be successful when there is consensus and commitment from the stakeholders and actors from all levels.

Of course, some of the macrolevel factors we have discussed are beyond the reach of local communities to directly change. The pernicious effects of globalization and international monetary policy need to be addressed at the national and international level. Local practitioners and policy makers may not be able to stop the large macroforces closing the mines or undercutting the viability of small farms or craft operations. Their actions are more limited to adapting – helping develop alternative employment opportunities (e.g., using the Internet to tie into the new

economy), supporting families, limiting adolescents' exposure to pernicious media. At all levels, initiatives are most likely to be effective when
they build on existing structures and available resources (WHO 1999).

Nonetheless, there are numerous examples that suggest diverse ways
in which social action can be effective. An example of a successful governmental program is the "Light a Candle" initiative in 35 districts in
India aimed at empowering girls aged 9–14 (Population Council 1999b).
Traditional systems in India inhibit the development of girls by limiting
opportunities for education, obligating them to major responsibilities
in the household, and communicating a message that their status and
worth are far below those ascribed to boys. This program targeted rural,
out-of-school girls in poor and lower-caste families whose mothers were
also participating in a parallel program.

The success of this program lay in its multilevel conceptualization. In
each community, awareness-raising sessions were organized to create
community support. Informal and formal education centers were developed for these girls, with curricula focused on creating social awareness, building positive self-esteem, learning life skills, and developing
academic skills. Hours of operation were determined by consensus in
each village, to ensure that it did not interfere with the girls' work in
the fields during the day. The organizers worked constantly with families and girls to sustain participation, otherwise girls would be withdrawn for care of younger siblings, early marriage, or household labor;
in fact a stipend was paid to families to compensate them for the cost
of the forfeited labor of their daughters. Local folklore and stories were
woven into the curriculum to reinforce connection to the community.
It was only through this multipronged effort that the program slowly
began making a real difference in the lives and life opportunities of these
girls.

The "Children's Movement for Peace" in Colombia provides a much
different example of an initiative, one that was primarily instigated by
adolescents themselves (UNICEF 1997). Following a visit to its high
school by a UN activist, the student council in the town of Uraba organized a campaign among students in the 12 surrounding townships to
protest the rampant violence that has gripped their country for years.
Their activities led first to an amassing of over 5,000 stories, poems, and
pieces of artwork by youth expressing their protest, the organization
of multiple "peace carnivals," and eventually to a national movement
of adolescents and children advocating peace that included a special
national referendum, in which 3 million youth voted for the "rights to

survival, peace, family, and freedom from abuse." The Children's Movement is credited with making peace a central issue in the 1998 Colombian presidential elections and doubling the turnout of adult voters. As expressed by one participant, "When children talk about pain and sorrow, we make adults feel the pain as if it was their own. Children are the seed of the new Colombia. We are the seeds that will stop the war."

This last example illustrates the critical role that adolescents themselves can make to social policy and social change. Initiatives that are able to include and build on young people's interests and energies are guaranteed to be more successful. This example also illustrates that adolescents provide a rich corpus of human resources, and they can make tremendous contributions, beyond their own lives, to the well-being of their societies.

Knowledge and Social Policy

Since many readers of this volume are likely to be scholars, researchers, students, or other members of the "knowledge trade," we want to give attention to the special role that they can play in this enterprise. The 1996 UN resolution on youth emphasizes that "Every state should endeavor to ensure that its policies relating to young people are informed by accurate data [we would have preferred "knowledge"] on their situation and needs, and that the public has access to such data to enable it to participate in meaningful fashion in the decision-making process" (6). Data or knowledge should be seen as a critical resource to youth development, a critical form of "capital," and its absence recognized as another "unfreedom" affecting youth. In the words of the UNDP (2000), "Information and statistics are a powerful tool for creating a culture of accountability" (10). They also explain that data enhance public understanding of tradeoffs and help create social consensus on national priorities.

As of now, it would be accurate to say that youth policy decisions, especially in most of the developing countries, are based on guesstimates rather than recent and reliable knowledge. The authors of the chapters here note many gaps in information, especially for the developing world. We know virtually nothing about adolescents' peer relationships in many countries, and very little about parent-adolescent relationships, mental health, religious attitudes, personal strengths, and, especially, how youth experience and view the world. Here and elsewhere these authors have also pointed out that the Eurocentrism of much scholarship on adolescents creates a bias that can obscure understanding of youth in their region (Nsamenang 1992; Saraswathi 1999; Santa Maria 2000). There is a strong need for knowledge generated from indigenous perspectives.

Following the recommendations of the UN resolution, we will stress several different activities that are essential to strengthening the knowledge base:

Monitoring Critical Indicators

There is need for collection of regular indicators of adolescent well-being and development. This should be done at local, national, and global levels. Collection of data from diverse sources increases the reliability of conclusions (UNDP 2000). We need constantly updated statistics on adolescents' problem behaviors and health: prevalence of morbidity; reproductive health problems; abortion (legal and illegal); incidence of smoking, alcohol and drug use; and participation in delinquency and crime. We need information on their schooling and employment, including information on out-of-school learning, apprenticeships, and part-, full-, and under-employment, with information on differential wages. We also need information on the assets that youth have available and use: access to and utilization of loans and stipends, availability and utilization of health services, indicators of family and community supports, and indicators of internal strengths and capabilities (Benson 1997). To be most useful, such data need to be differentiated by gender, age, and ethnic groups. This type of regular, repeated gathering of social indicators is vital to identifying problems, monitoring progress, and assessing the needs of youth.

Understanding and Analysis

Such statistics alone, however, are not enough. Data by itself, while extremely valuable, is not knowledge. The particularly important contribution of these chapters is that they take us beyond enumerating. They combine quantitative and qualitative information to examine holistically the total surround of family, peers, community, and cultural systems that shape adolescents' experience. They provide interdisciplinary analyses that illuminate the interrelationships of multiple spheres of adolescents' lives – family, peers, etc. – that shape opportunities and paths of development. Such knowledge is important in and of itself. It is also crucial to the design of effective policies and programs for youth. We stress the importance of creating "free markets" of critical analyses that examine adolescents' experience from multiple points of view.

We also think there is value in comparative studies across nations (and between groups within nations) on issues and trends concerning youth. Such studies need to go beyond quantitative comparisons to include qualitative analyses and descriptive case studies to ensure that these comparisons are contextualized. Cross-cultural studies such as the Whiting and Edwards (1988) project of the 1980s and the holographic study by Schlegel and Barry (1991) serve to sharpen understanding of similarities and differences. This fund of cross-cultural inquiry can help make policies culturally sensitive as well as help build theory, broaden conceptualization, and strengthen methodology in research.

Evaluation Research

The next link in the enterprise of knowledge is information on interventions, policies, and programs for youth. These need to include systematic multidisciplinary pre- and post evaluation studies, with random assignment, comparison samples, and long-term follow-ups. And they need to include qualitative case studies aimed at understanding the experience of participants and leaders. Good design must involve two-way communication between practitioners and researchers (Fisher & Lerner 1994). A recent handbook by Chibuos and Lerner (1999) provides numerous valuable examples from the United States of how university researchers and practitioners can work together. Similar case studies of successful policies (such as the European Commission's 1997 project) need to be made widely available. We also point to the detailed case studies of successful intervention projects implemented by governments and by non-government organizations (Population Council 1999a). With adequate accommodation, the marriage between research and policy can work.

Dissemination

All of the above is of no use unless the information obtained gets into the hands of people who can use it. Writing about the situation in the West, Hudson and Galaway (1996) observe: "It is simply not enough for a researcher to write a report with recommendations and expect that decision makers will read the report, choose a course of action, and implement it. It is naïve to expect that research findings are a normal part of policy makers' reading materials" (340). If this is true of developed countries, where documentation and its use are more routine, it is even more telling in the case of most developing countries, where the link between research and policy is very nebulous. Arguing for a stronger link, Hudson and Galaway, add: "Research findings must be persuasively and engagingly communicated to the policy community; dissemination should be an ongoing process rather than stopping with the production of a technical report or publication. Researchers must write their reports to influence policies by producing readable publications and taking seriously the responsibility to make the practical implications of their findings clear" (340). Of course, it needs to be borne in mind that just as many policies do not take into account available research, not all research is useful to policy, and researchers need to listen closely to policy makers to ensure that their work is designed from the outset to be relevant to the most pressing issues.

Information also needs to get to other parties – business leaders, teachers, reporters, parents – who in various ways influence adolescents' opportunities, as well as to youth themselves. At the least, such information helps illuminate the different pathways that adolescents navigate in choosing their futures. But it can also serve to mobilize action to change institutions. Such communication can be challenging because, to be effective, it requires that communicators have knowledge of what their target audiences' preconceptions about the topic are. Beginning efforts to develop a science of strategic communication about youth (e.g., Gilliam & Bales 2001) need to be followed by all in the field of adolescent studies. Academics also need to take seriously their role in training human development professionals who have mastery of both academic and applied knowledge (see Ralston et al. 2000).

Toward Freedoms and Choice?

So what promise does the future hold for adolescents today as they face the threshold of adulthood? Will it be chutes or ladders? Are we moving toward or away from Sen's vision of freedoms for all? There was a great deal of similar speculation on the future at the end of the 19th century. In Act II of Anton Chekhov's *Three Sisters*, Colonel Vershinin predicts: "In a century or two, or in a millennium, people will live in a new way, a happier way. We won't be there to see it – but it's why we live, why we work. It's why we suffer. We're creating it. That's the purpose of our existence" (cited in Weinberg 2000, 3). If Colonel Vershinin were to take a new avatar (incarnation) and descend on the earth today, would he find that his hopes are being actualized? Are youth progressively finding themselves in a better world?

One possible scenario is based on the critiques one hears about global trade, the World Trade Organization, and the development of multi-nationals: World prosperity will improve, but wealth will continue to accumulate only among rich nations and among the wealthy of poor nations. Universal education and employment opportunities for all will continue to remain a distant dream, leading to exploitation of labor by multinational corporations and migration of skilled employees to more fertile lands. Even if education becomes universalized, it will be tiered, with the poor attending inadequate government schools and only the well-to-do receiving education that equips them to thrive in the new global information economy. One set of adolescents have their lives enhanced by a wide range of new technologies, including genetic counseling, new computer-driven devices, and sophisticated prosthetic aids, while another, larger set falls further into poverty. The scenario for this latter group comes alive in UNICEF's (1994) depiction of the vicious cycle of poverty, population, and environmental degradation (PPE). This spiral, wherein each factor logically feeds into the other, is only compounded by the industrialized world's policies related to trade and aid. What role will youth have in such a world? That of revolutionaries angered by the inequitable distribution of wealth or disillusioned by excessive materialism?

A second scenario is based on hope and faith. After all, history has placed before us models of men and women – Gandhi, Mandela, Anne Frank, Aung San Soo Kyi, Martin Luther King, Jr. – who sustained their hope and courage amidst seemingly impossible situations and, in the first 2 cases at least, kept their tryst with destiny. In this scenario, the 2 cultures of humanity and sciences (Snow 1959) will work hand in hand, leading to a richer and more egalitarian world. In such a world, the resource-rich countries will meet their humanitarian obligations on more altruistic grounds, and the resource-poor will arrest their population growth, decrease military expenditures, spend far more on basic education and health, increase their agricultural and industrial productivity, and spend more on infrastructure development (and less on lining the pockets of their politicians) so as to improve the quality of life of their people. For adolescents and youth in this world, there will be appropriate education, physical and mental well-being, more leisure and access to recreation, adequate employment, gender equality, and more freedom of choices.

The difference in which path the world takes ultimately comes back to youth themselves. Collectively and as individuals, there is a tremendous amount for adults to do to eliminate barriers, counteract malignant forces, create opportunities, provide supports, and be good role models for adolescents. Societies need to invest money, time, and care in their youth. But in the end the future is in the laps of young people. We are handing the next generation of youth a world rife with serious problems – global warming, looming environmental catastrophes, poverty, numerous international conflicts – just as similarly daunting problems were handed to us. Nothing less than a full mobilization of all young people to higher goals and ideals is required for humankind to make it through the new century.

The reason for hope and optimism was highlighted dramatically, while we were writing this, in youth's response to the major earthquake that occurred in Gujarat, India, on January 26th, 2001. Young people from all walks of life – school-going adolescents, college youth, vendors, artists – organized themselves on their own to offer succor in cash, kind, and more important, service to the needy. It has been a moving experience for young people who *wanted* to contribute in some way and become actively involved in the relief work, many times amidst personal hardship. It is noteworthy that even on Valentine's day (a recent fad in India), youth, especially college students, decided to collect the money they would have otherwise spent on cards, chocolates, and flowers and donate it to the relief fund. It is amazing how the otherwise seemingly self-centered young could rise to the occasion and prove how responsible and resourceful they can be. We could cite numerous other examples from all parts the world of how young people, when given the opportunity, make extraordinary contributions to humankind. The challenge for the future is for families, schools, businesses, governments, and other strands of society to work together to provide that opportunity to youth in all corners of the globe.

References

Azam, J.-P., G. Chambas, P. Guillaumont, & S. Guillaumont. 1989. The impact of macro economic policies on the rural poor. UNDP Policy Discussion Paper. (Translated from French). New York: United Nations Development Program.

Baker, D. P. & D. B. Holsinger. 1997. Human capital formation and school expansion in Asia: Does a unique regional model exist? In *The challenge of Eastern Asian education: Implications for America*, eds. W. K. Cummings & P. G. Altbach, 115–131. Albany, NY: State University of New York Press.

Benson, P. 1997. *All kids are our kids: What communities must do to raise caring and responsible children and adolescents*. San Francisco: Jossey-Bass.

Bruton, H. J. 1997. *On the search for well-being.* Ann Arbor, MI: University of Michigan Press.

Burns, A. & C. Scott. 1994. *Mother-headed families and why they have increased.* Hillsdale, NJ: Lawrence Erlbaum.

Castells, M. 1998. *End of millennium.* Oxford: Blackwell.

Chibucos, T. R. & R. M. Lerner, eds. 2000. *Serving children and families through community-university partnerships: Success stories.* Norwell, MA: Kluwer Academic Pub.

Coles, B. 1995. *Youth and social policy. Youth citizenship and young careers.* London: UCL Press.

Cummings, W. K. 1997. Human resource development: The J-Model. In *The challenge of Eastern Asian education: Implications for America,* eds. W. K. Cummings & P. G. Altbach, 275–291. Albany, NY: State University of New York Press.

European Commission. 1997. Helping young people along the path from school to work. ESF project examples. Employment & European Social Fund.

Fisher, C. B. & R. M. Lerner, eds. 1994. *Applied developmental psychology.* New York: McGraw-Hill.

Gilliam, F. & S. Bales. 2001. Strategic frame analysis: Reframing America's youth. SRCD Social Policy Report, XV:(3).

Hudson, J. & B. Galaway. 1996. Directions for future research. In *Youth in transition: Perspectives on research and policy,* eds. B. Galaway & J. Hudson, 338–341. Toronto, Ontario: Thompson Educational Publishing.

International Labour Office. 1996. Child labour: Targeting the intolerable. Geneva: Author.

Larson, R. & M. Richards. 1991. Boredom in the middle school years: Blaming schools versus blaming students. *American Journal of Education.* 91: (August): 418–443.

Larson, R. 2002. Globalization, societal change, and new technologies: What they mean for the future of adolescence. *Journal of Research on Adolescence.* 12 (1), in press.

Nsamenang, A. B. 1992. *Human development in cultural context: A third world perspective.* Cross-cultural research and methodology series, vol. 16. Newbury Park, CA: Sage Publications.

Population Council. 1999a. The adolescents in transition series. (Seven case studies). New Delhi: Population Council Asia Regional Office.

Population Council. 1999b. To light a candle: Educational initiatives for girls. Mahila Samakhya & Andhra Pradesh. New Delhi: Population Council Asia Regional Office.

Ralston, P. A., R. M. Lerner, A. K. Mullis, C. B. Simerly, & J. B. Murray, eds. 2000. *Social change, public policy, and community collaborations: Training human development professionals for the twenty-first century.* Norwell, MA: Kluwer Academic Pub.

Santa Maria, M. 2000. On the nature of cultural research. *ISSBD Newsletter.* 37: (1):4–6.

Saraswathi, T. S. 1999. Adult-child continuity in India: Is adolescence a myth or an emerging reality? In *Culture, socialization & human development,* ed. T. S. Saraswathi, 213–232. New Delhi: Sage.

Schlegel, A. & H. Barry III. 1991. *Adolescence: An anthropological inquiry*. New York: Free Press.

Sen, A. 1999. *Development as freedom*. New York: Random House.

Snow, C. P. 1959. *The two cultures and the scientific revolution*. New York: Cambridge University Press.

Speth, J. G. 1999. The plight of the poor. *Foreign Affairs*. 78:(3):13–26.

United Nations. 1996. Resolution adopted by the General Assembly. 50/81. *World programme of action for youth to the year 2000 and beyond*, 1–32. Doc. Number A/RES/50/81.

United Nations Development Programme (UNDP). 1990. *Human Development Report*. New York: Oxford University Press.

United Nations Development Programme (UNDP). 1991. *Human Development Report*. New York: Oxford University Press.

United Nations Development Programme (UNDP). 1995. *Human Development Report*. New York: Oxford University Press.

United Nations Development Programme (UNDP). 1999. *Human Development Report*. New York: Oxford University Press.

United Nations Development Programme (UNDP). 2000. *Human Development Report*. New York: Oxford University Press.

UNESCO 1999. *UNESCO statistical yearbook*. Lanham, MD: UNESCO Publishing and Bernan Press.

UNICEF 1994. *The state of the world's children*. New York: Oxford University Press.

UNICEF 1997. *The state of the world's children*. New York: Oxford University Press.

Verma, S., D. Sharma, & R. Larson. 1999. School stress in India: Effects on time and Daily Emotions. Unpublished manuscript.

Weinberg, S. 2000. Five and a half Utopias. *Span*, (March–April): 3–7, 15.

Whiting, B. B. & C. P. Edwards. 1988. *Children of different worlds*. Cambridge, MA: Harvard University Press.

Williamson, H. 1997. *Youth and policy: Contexts and consequences*. Aldershot, England: Ashgate Publications.

World Bank. 2000. *Entering the 21st century: World Development Report*, 1999–2000. New York: Oxford University Press.

World Health Organization. 1998. *The world health report 1998: Life in the 21st Century*. Geneva: Author.

World Health Organization. 1999. *Programming for adolescent health and development*. Geneva: Author.

Index